"Kudos to Daryl Cornett for organ... ...stian America" debate usually yields mc ...ants have different goals, employ diff r key terms in different ways. In this v gage each other—directly, with honest) ation continue and expand to include ot. orical understanding."

Douglas A. Sweeney
Trinity Evangelical Divinity School

"*Christian America? Perspectives on Our Religious Heritage* should be required reading for anyone even casually interested in this subject. While none of the authors articulate a view analogous to mine, I found their perspectives well-argued and thought-provoking. Readers will find the back-and-forth exchange among the authors to be both enjoyable and instructive."

Richard Land
Ethics and Religious Liberty Commission of the SBC

"Too often, professional historians and popular history writers talk past one another, but this provocative volume on America's Christian roots helps to bridge the gap between them. It shows that even among believers, there are major differences of opinion on whether America was founded as a Christian nation. Anyone looking for a substantial, lively debate on religion and America's founding will want to read this book."

Thomas Kidd
Baylor University

"Daryl Cornett is to be commended for bringing together this thoughtful and engaging symposium on the important topic of Christianity and American Identity. This multi-authored work offers a significant step forward in this longstanding debate. Readers will recognize the complexities involved as the contributors wrestle with these multi-faceted and challenging issues. The differences in perspectives regarding the place of the Christian faith in American history will be obvious; the commonalities, however, create a window for readers to take a fresh look at the place of faith for our twenty-first-century world. *Christian American? Perspectives on Our Religious Heritage* is a vitally important and informative contribution to the field of American Christianity."

David S. Dockery
President, Union University

CHRISTIAN
AMERICA?

PERSPECTIVES ON OUR RELIGIOUS HERITAGE

EDITED BY DARYL C. CORNETT

FOREWORD BY GEORGE MARSDEN

ACADEMIC

Nashville, Tennessee

Christian America? Perspectives on Our Religious Heritage
Copyright © 2011 by Daryl C. Cornett

ISBN: 978-0-8054-4439-1

Published by B&H Publishing Group
Nashville, Tennessee

Dewey Decimal Classification: 261.1
Subject Heading: CHRISTIANITY AND POLITICS \
UNITED STATES—RELIGION \
CHURCH AND STATE—UNITED STATES

Printed in the United States of America

1 2 3 4 5 6 7 8 9 10 11 12 • 17 16 15 14 13 12 11
VP

To those who have
sacrificed, both past
and present, to provide
American liberty.

Contents

Contributors

David Barton is the president of WallBuilders and is the author of numerous books, including *Original Intent, American History in Black and White*, and *The Bulletproof George Washington*. The subjects for his writings are drawn especially from his massive personal library that houses 100,000 documents predating 1812. He serves as an historical expert both in courts of law and state legislatures and has been selected to help guide the writing of the standards for history school books in states such as Kentucky, Texas, and California. His writings appear in national publications and law reviews, his works are used as texts on many university campuses, and he has helped produce history textbooks now used in public schools across the nation. David has received numerous national and international awards, including Who's Who in Education, the Medal of Honor from the Daughters of the American Revolution, and the George Washington Honor Medal from the Freedoms Foundation at Valley Forge.

Daryl C. Cornett holds both a Master of Divinity and Doctor of Philosophy in church history from the Southern Baptist Theological Seminary. He is an ordained minister with more than 20 years of experience in the local church. In addition, he served as associate professor of Church History at Mid-America Baptist Theological Seminary in Memphis, Tennessee, before re-entering local church ministry full time. He has authored various articles for scholarly journals and church curriculums. *Christian America? Perspectives on Our Religious Heritage* is his first major published work. He resides in the heart of the Appalachian Mountains in Hazard, Kentucky, where he serves as pastor of First Baptist Church and lives with his wife, Cindy, and their two children, Justin and Elizabeth.

William D. Henard serves as assistant professor of evangelism and church growth at the Southern Baptist Theological Seminary and as senior pastor of Porter Memorial Baptist Church in Lexington, Kentucky. He is a former president of the Kentucky Baptist Convention and first vice-president of the Southern Baptist Convention, along with having served two years as chairman of the board of trustees for LifeWay Christian Resources. He holds the Master of Divinity and Doctor of Ministry degrees from Southwestern Baptist Theological Seminary and a Doctor of Philosophy from the Southern Baptist Theological Seminary. He is married to his college sweetheart, Judy, and they have three grown children and two grandchildren.

George Marsden (BA, Haverford College; BD, Westminster Theological Seminary; MA, Ph.D., Yale University) is Francis A. McAnaney Professor of History Emeritus, University of Notre Dame. His books include *Fundamentalism and American Culture, The Soul of the American University, The Outrageous Idea of Christian Scholarship*, and *Jonathan Edwards: A Life*. He is coauthor (with Mark Noll and Nathan Hatch) of *The Search for Christian America*. He taught history at Calvin College from 1965 to 1986; the history of Christianity in America at The Divinity School of Duke University from 1986 to 1992; and history at Notre Dame from 1992 to 2008. He and is wife Lucie live in Grand Rapids, Michigan, where he is scholar in residence at Calvin College. They are members of the Christian Reformed Church.

Jonathan D. Sassi is associate professor of history at the College of Staten Island of the City University of New York and a member of the faculty of the Ph.D. Program in History at the CUNY Graduate Center. He is the author of *A Republic of Righteousness: The Public Christianity of the Post-Revolutionary New England Clergy* (New York: Oxford University Press, 2001; trade paper, 2008). Articles of his on revolutionary-era antislavery have also been published in the *Proceedings of the American Antiquarian Society, Journal of Early Modern History*, and *Pennsylvania Magazine of History and Biography*. He is an active member of the Society for Historians of the Early American Republic. He resides with his wife and two children in New Jersey and is a member of the Presbyterian Church at New Providence, where he has served as an elder and clerk of session.

Foreword

George Marsden

The United States is simultaneously one of the most secular and one of the most religious places in the world. Its secularity is driven largely by its being the leading industrial nation, and hence many of its activities, particularly the economic sides of life, are shaped by technologies or technical modes of operation that are largely detached from religious reference. Much of leisure is also dominated by technologies, techniques, ideologies, and competitions that are essentially secular. Yet the United States ranks very high among industrialized societies in religious profession among its populace. Contrary to predictions that industrialization would lead to dramatic decline in traditional religious practice, and in sharp contrast with Western Europe and Great Britain where churches have declined precipitously, in the United States religious practice by and large has held its own. Even though organized religion in America is bewilderingly diverse, with every religion in the world represented, those who would identify themselves as some sort of Christian are easily in the majority. That is complicated by the fact that the self-identified Christians come in so many, sometimes sharply opposing varieties (liberal and moderate mainline Protestant, evangelical, fundamentalist, Roman Catholic, Eastern Orthodox, Mormon, and so forth). Furthermore, many people who profess some sort of Christianity are rarely found in church. Still, the United States includes a substantial minority of citizens who are active Christians, and it also includes considerable numbers of devout Jews, Muslims, and practitioners of many other faiths. All of these face the question of how to relate their faiths to a culture that seems in so many ways to be shaped overwhelmingly by secular concerns.

That challenge is especially perplexingly when it comes to politics. Much of politics has to do with technical issues of building and regulating the economy or protecting the nation's security, and the very nature of representative politics involves compromise for building diverse coalitions in an immensely pluralistic setting. Nonetheless, even the most extreme secularist ought to recognize (though not all do) that there is no way that religious beliefs can be systematically excluded from the public arena. People and their elected representatives inevitably bring their beliefs, whether these are religious or secularist, into the public arena. Particularly for those who hold public office, it is a complex question as to how they should express or act on those beliefs, taking into account the beliefs of others, concerns for equity, the law of the land, and so forth.

The present volume is especially welcome because it addresses the historical question of just how much influence various forms of Christianity had in the formation of the nation. That question has been prominent in the last several decades, especially because many citizens who hold to a set of traditional Christian moral values have been concerned that their values have been losing in the political arena. In reaction to changing mores that often have gained judicial and other governmental support, they have emphasized the "Christian" origins of the United States. The implication is that the turn from the traditional Christian practices is illegitimate in part because it represents a turn from values that were part of the essence of the nation founded in 1776. Meanwhile, especially since the mid-twentieth century, secularists have been influentially arguing that, while indeed Christianity had long retained residual influences in public life and education, such privilege went against the true spirit of the nation's founding. They argue that the U. S. Constitution was strikingly "godless" for its time.[1] The beliefs of the Founders of the nation, they argue, were shaped primarily by Enlightenment principles that were intentionally distanced from anything specifically Christian.

In considering such matters, one should take into account that there are two major *types* of historical approaches to issues of this sort. The first is what might be called the legal/partisan approach. Suppose that lawyers from the ACLU vs. those from a Christian legal firm are arguing a church/state issue before the Supreme Court of the United States. For such a purpose, both sides assemble all the evidence that supports their cases and they ignore or explain away any evidence that does not suit their agendas. That is what is expected in court cases and it is proper to that setting. A similar approach is common when using history for partisan purposes, such as to rally people to a cause. For that purpose partisans usually select only those historical facts that promote their causes and so they simplify the past, typically ignoring or glossing over troubling counterexamples or ambiguities. Such partisan uses of history can serve useful purposes (not only in law courts, but also in sermons, church schools, political gatherings, and the like), although they need to be kept within the bounds of honesty (not changing the facts or making fantastic claims, etc.). A notable feature of the legal/partisan approaches, however legitimate they may be for their own purposes, is that they start their historical research with their desired conclusions already in place and then look for evidences to support those conclusions.

A quite different approach to history is that taken by people who want to arrive at their own conclusions about such debates by trying to determine what the full historical record is that bears on these issues. In such historical investigation one does not start with the conclusions that one would *like* to find, but just the opposite. Much as a judge should do in a court case, one tries to set aside one's own partisanship as much as possible while one weighs all sides of the argument and the evidence. In such historical inquiries the observer is never entirely value free, since one's values help shape the questions that one is investigating; but the ideal is to be open-minded even if we do not like the results. After that, once one has judiciously reached a fair-minded assessment of the historical record, then one can go on to think about the significance of that evidence in the light of one's own commitments. One can realistically face the problems involved and see how to address current issues in that light. Inevitably the outcome of this process will be more nuanced than partisan approaches.

The present volume is particularly welcome because, by presenting multiple sides of the arguments, it is unusually valuable for people who prefer either of these two major approaches to this topic. Those who are interested in partisan uses of history for present purposes can find arguments to support their partisan views and also examples of some of the best arguments for the opposite views that they might want to rebut. Or readers who prefer to step back and to make up their minds can find examples here of partisan arguments as well as helpful suggestions as to how to balance considerations from several sides. A particularly attractive feature of this volume is that each author responds to each of the others, thus bringing to light the most important points on which the debate hinges.

As becomes apparent in some of the exchanges, one's evaluations of the arguments can be advanced by making clear distinctions among the various ways that a single term may be used. For instance, the term *secular* has a number of different meanings. Perhaps the clearest definition for our purposes is that something is secular when it is detached from explicitly religious reference or control. As I suggested in the opening paragraph, much in contemporary society is secular in this sense. But the questions of how much particular religious beliefs should shape or interact with such a society will be clarified if we keep in mind a basic distinction between two uses of *secular* or *secularization*. On the one hand, much of the contemporary world, particularly its technology and practical organization, is shaped by what may be called "methodological secularization." If we temporarily lose the information on our computer, it may be good to pray about it, but the actual method that we use to find the information is quite secular: we talk to a technician who tells us the exact practical steps to take. The fact that the technician may be from another culture and may or may not be religious is irrelevant to the transaction. On the other hand is what can be called "worldview secularism" or simply "secularism." "Worldview secularism" advocates that non-religious approaches are the best in all aspects of life and that religious factors should be, so far as possible, kept out of public life. There are further distinctions that might be made, but this one bears most directly on the debates in this volume. It is often the case that people who are not in any way worldview secularists may nonetheless advocate the removal of direct religious reference from some aspect of public life.

Even more pivotal to the whole discussion in this volume is the definition of "Christianity," "Christian" influences, or a "Christian" nation. This issue involves three interrelated questions. (1) Specifically what is meant by "Christian" influences that might constitute a "Christian" nation? (2) How large were those influences relative to other influences? (3) What is the normative significance today for that degree of Christian influence on the nation's origins? For answering these questions there need to be clear definitions of what one is talking about and of what counts as "Christian." There also has to be some consideration of what might count as normative.

Being a substantially Christian nation might mean any of a number of things. (1) It could mean that most of the citizens were broadly Christians in that they were of generically Christian heritage and likely to have been baptized. (2) It might mean that most of the citizens were practicing Christians, or were of a particular sort of practicing Christians.[2] (3) It could mean that most of its leaders were practicing Christians, or were practicing Christians of a certain sort. (4) It could mean that a nation's government was officially Christian in some specified ways, as was the case of Great Britain and throughout Europe in the eighteenth century. (5) It might be Christian in the descriptive sense that its ethos and laws were predominantly, or at least substantially, shaped by a broadly Christian heritage. (6) It might mean, as a corollary to the previous point, that those laws and practices that were considerably shaped by a Christian heritage were therefore "Christian" in the normative sense of being examples that Christians today ought to follow.

In the case of the United States at its founding, the fifth of these sorts of meanings is the most interesting as a debatable historical question for which one might want to establish the facts of the matter regarding the relative degree of Christian influences. Yet it is important to recognize that even if it is agreed that there were large Christian influences in shaping the ethos and laws of the United States, that does not settle the question of what among the ethos and laws is normatively Christian. We can appreciate the force of this issue if we consider that Great Britain under George III, from which the Americans rebelled, was just as much shaped by a Christian heritage as was the United States, and was furthermore officially Christian by law. Much the same can be said of Roman Catholic France under Louis XVI. Or we should consider that American loyalists who believed that it was against God's laws to rebel against constituted authority were just as shaped by a Christian ethos and laws as were American patriots. So were pacifists, such as Moravians, Mennonites, and Quakers, who suffered for not supporting the patriot cause. So with respect to politics it appears that all sorts of contradictory political arrangements and policies were equally shaped by a Christian ethos. If we are looking for Christian influences in the nation's founding that will serve as normative precedents for today, we will need some additional criteria for sorting out which broadly Christian precedents we approve and which we reject.

That question becomes more pointed if we recognize that in the early United States, among the laws that were shaped to some degree by Christian influences were some that most Christians today would consider contrary to true Christianity. The clearest cases are the laws that preserved slavery, which were often defended from the Bible. Some African-American Christians today have pointed out that the question of whether early America was "Christian" looks very different from an African-American perspective than it does from a white Protestant perspective.[3] Native Americans might agree. Even within the white Protestant community, early laws and practices restricting the role of women, such as banning them from political life or denying them higher education, had considerable Christian heritage but are seldom seen today as entailed by Christian commitment. Such examples illustrate that if we are looking for normative precedents applicable for today, it is insufficient to demonstrate that a law or practice had a substantial Christian heritage. Since all of Western civilization was strongly shaped by Christian influences, Christian precedents can be found on both sides of most contested issues. Christian influences were strong in eventually bringing an end to slavery and more equal treatment of women. But since Christian influences were on both sides, the matter of determining what practices should be followed and what should not seems to be settled not simply by discovering Christian historical precedents but rather by establishing some normative criteria for determining which precedents should be followed.

The conceptual problem that these examples point to is that "Christian" is often used in a sense that confusingly conflates its descriptive and its normative senses. One step toward avoiding that ambiguous double meaning of "Christian" is to drop unspecified uses of the term "Christian" and substitute the particular *sort* of Christianity we are talking about. For instance, if we say that there were strong *Protestant* influences in shaping the early United States, it sounds a little less as though we are making a normative statement. Or we might go further and specify the particular subgroup or type of Christianity we are talking about. So we could talk about Presbyterian, Congregational, or Baptist influences in shaping the early American republic, as in the Great Awakening or in promoting religious freedom (by the Baptists). Such specificity would help avoid the confusing conflation of all sorts of contradictory things (Unitarian/Trinitarian, orthodox/heterodox, conversionist/anti-conversionist, conservative/liberal) under the general rubric of "Christian." It would also help reduce the ambiguities between the normative and the descriptive, though it does not eliminate that problem. One needs also to recognize that descriptively speaking, nearly every white person in early America shared to some degree generically Christian assumptions about social relationships, some of which most Christians today would consider normative and some of which most Christians today would reject.

The case of the early American Puritans is one of the most interesting to reflect on in this regard. Viewed from an evangelical Christian perspective today, the New England Puritan colonies were undoubtedly Christian in all the strongest descriptive senses listed above (most of their populace were practicing Christians, leaders were practicing Christian, government was officially Christian, and laws and practices were shaped by a Christian ethos). They were in many ways a most admirable society relative to their times. But they were still very much people of their times, so that many of the practices that they regarded as normatively Christian would not be so regarded by most Christians today. For instance, most Christians today would not approve of their very close association of church and state or their efforts to base civil law directly on Old Testament precedents. They made many good-faith efforts to get along with and to convert the Indians, but they also believed they had a God-given right to take their lands. Their firm belief that the pope in Rome was the Antichrist shaped much of their foreign policy. They accepted enslavement of Africans. They were often harsh in their treatment of dissenters. None of these factors means that we cannot also learn a great deal from the early Puritans and from precedents they provide for us. They are greatly admirable in many respects. It just means that citing Christian credentials does not settle the question of what we should take as normative and what we should not.

That issue becomes particular striking if we contrast the precedents from the Puritans of the seventeenth century with those of the American Revolution and early republic approximately a century and a half later. In the meantime a good deal of secularization had taken place, particularly in distancing of the churches from the state and in thus making the state a considerably more secular institution. Yet paradoxically, most Christians today see that degree of secularization as an improvement. Strictly speaking, the public culture had become less "Christian" in many respects, but the process involved was, as suggested above, what may be called "methodological secularization" and did not entail worldview secularism. Many Christians favored such secularizing developments as disestablishment of churches or the distancing of the Old Testament from the civil law. In fact, most interpreters today see the secularizing of the civil sphere, particularly the disestablishment of the churches, as one of the sources for the subsequent vitality of the voluntary Christianity that has long been conspicuous in American life.

One also can find much else to admire in the early American republic, and many of those admirable things are connected to Christian dimensions of their origins. But, as in the case of the Puritans, we should expect that even the most exemplary of Christian efforts to shape a society will be mixed with some things not so admirable. Even the best Christians are limited in their vision and are sometimes sinful. We may learn much from the virtues of people in the past and we may legitimately lament that those virtues have become much rarer in public life today. We may also work to restore such virtues based on normative Christian principles. But in doing so we will in the long run be better served by acknowledging that even the best of human societies have been a mix of good and evil and that there is no reason to expect that the early United States, whether properly called "Christian" or not, would be an exception to that rule. Even Old Testament Israel, the nation closest to God in all of history, was a mix of the admirable and the deplorable.

Finally, so far as the normative questions are concerned, Christians today need to consider the issue of civil religion. Civil religion is the phenomenon of a nation-state being regarded as in some sense sacred or invested with religious qualities. For instance, states have creeds, pledges, and flags that should be kept pure, as well as ceremonies, holidays, saints, iconic statuary, sacred sites, and sacred sagas or stories. In the case of the United States, which was the first modern nation-state and in which popular Christian influences were undoubtedly present, loyalty to the nation-state and loyalty to Christianity have often been closely mixed. Christians ought to be thinking carefully about what is legitimate about such reverence for the nation and what is not. For instance, to regard the nation as "under God" is certainly a good thing if it means that one regards the nation as subordinate to God, and that its activities should be evaluated in the light of God's will and law. Patriotism, including due service to one's people for mutual protection, rendering taxes to Caesar, and subordination to powers that be all can be subsumed under a distinctly Christian ethic. Yet there can be another version of civil religion in which "under God" means that one views one's own nation as chosen by God above other nations, that its self-interest is virtually always in the right, and that the nation is so highly sacred that its policies, especially in relation to other nations, are seldom scrutinized in the

light of God's higher law. Loyalty to the nation in such civil religion can function as virtually a highest loyalty, so that churchgoers who lack unquestioning patriotism may be regarded as
therefore less than Christian.

Between these two types of civil religion may be many other
variations, but the point is that the question of the relationship
of God to modern nations is one that invites reflection as the
theological context for thinking about the Christian factors in
America's origins. One might do well to start with St. Augustine's *City of God*, in which he provides the classic Christian
reflection on the relation of being a citizen of God's city or the
church, to subordinate citizenship in the nations of the world.
In such a context of broader theological reflection we can then
ask in the present debates: What is at stake? Is the fact that
Protestant Christianity contributed to shaping some American
institutions part of an argument that those institutions are
therefore sacred? Or does it show that Christians have long had
a shaping influence in the United States and a responsibility
to be continually evaluating their responsibilities in the public
arena in the light of God's Word? Or is it some combination of
these? Historical questions at their best should force us to philosophical or theological reflection. Philosophical and theological reflection can in turn provide the framework for evaluating
what is at stake in historical debates.

In the former, love to neighbor is to reign supreme. In the
latter, protection of self-interest is essential to a nation and yet
nations deserve our loyalty, limited only by our higher loyalty
to God and God's will.

Endnotes

[1] For example, I. Kramnick and R. L. Moore, *The Godless Constitution: A
Moral Defense of the Secular State*, updated ed. (New York: W. W. Norton & Co.,
2005).

[2] For instance, strict Protestant confessionalists or strict evangelicals might
want to restrict this category to orthodox Trinitarian Protestants who gave
some evidence of being regenerate or "born again," thus excluding Unitarians,
liberal Christians, Quakers, and perhaps even Catholics.

[3] See, for instance, Race to Unity, Cincinnati, Ohio: http://www.racetounity.
com.

Preface

Throughout her history America has possessed a rich religious component, which has been constituted overwhelmingly by different Christian traditions. This tide of personal religious devotion, public activism, and connection to government observances and policies has ebbed and flowed throughout the years, but has always been a part of American identity. This volume opens up a hearty discussion about the nature of the relationship Christianity has had with American politics and culture throughout the country's history. Although the discussion is not limited to the founding period, the reader will find within these pages a particular emphasis on that era.

Every culture is both formed by and propagates certain ideologies, religious and nonreligious. At any given time these strong currents of culture-shaping ideas are a mixture of embedded assumptions passed on from previous generations and innovations that challenge those assumptions. Often the old and the new find themselves at odds with one another, and on occasion they may find some common ground. The United States of America was an innovation emerging from an Old World provincial setting. Her birth came at the dawn of significant change in politics, challenges to orthodox Protestantism, and, when the industrial revolution was about to begin, a radical reshaping of how people lived.

Throughout the four centuries of American history, the presence of the Christian faith has been both embodied in many people and reflected in cultural assumptions and traditions. The question that this book tackles is essentially this: In what ways and to what degree has the Christian faith informed and impacted the American people throughout our history? Or the question could be put more concisely: What is the relation-ship of Christianity to American identity?

As I and the other three contributors sought to answer this question it became apparent to me that we are a microcosm of the debate that goes on every day in America. Through such avenues as CNN, Fox News, MSNBC, conservative talk radio, and the local newspapers' opinion pages, it's clear that America is inundated with sociopolitical commentary. Confusion reigns supreme as people seek to understand the essence of American values and ideas as representatives of the so-called Right and Left pontificate relentlessly. What are the extents and limits of the relationship between religion and government? Where do private freedoms end and public responsibilities begin? What kinds of values inform our public policies and where do they come from?

The United States has always been a place of divided views concerning morality, government regulation, and economic poli-cies. We even fought a bloody Civil War over such issues. These divides always become more obvious during seasons of difficulty. Currently, America faces daunting challenges from within and without. Much of our population has been seriously affected by the worst economic recession of my generation. Unemploy-ment is high, consumer confidence is low, and the stock market has had its worst ten-year period ever. For a decade we have been mired in military conflict with radical Muslim terrorist groups. And like the Vietnam conflict, as this one has dragged on, public support has weakened, troops have become some-what demoralized, and the mission has become muddled. Moral flashpoints continue to stir up tumultuous debate on abortion-related issues and same-sex marriage. The fear over terrorism is evidenced by the existence of the Department of Homeland Security, and resides in the back of every American's mind. Fears over illegal immigration and economic policies continue to rise, evidenced by the increasingly impassioned debate.

In many ways, America is searching again to figure out who we *really* are. The cultural assumptions of previous generations have eroded and it still is not clear what is becoming the new normal. Therefore, we live in a time with great uncertainties. And because of these problems and uncertainties the debate of what constitutes the right laws, policies, and attitudes only intensifies. Many Christians add to this list the uneasy feeling that their beliefs and moral positions are increasingly under attack. The topic of this volume seems particularly timely as America truly finds herself at another significant crossroad with passionate factions all staking their claims, defending their causes, and attempting to articulate what it truly means to be American.

The contributors to this book are all Christians with an interest in how our faith relates to our identity as citizens of the United States of America. We all share common concern about the ungodliness of so much in our culture and the weak state of American evangelical churches. And we all believe that history has something valuable to tell us concerning who we have been as a country and who we are now. And each of us has hopes for a better future for America.

Each of us brings a different perspective to this discussion; however, our views are not mutually exclusive of one other. The reader will find points of divergence in our interpretations and areas of agreement and overlap. One of the most interesting parts of this discussion pertains to how each writer chooses to frame his chapter. It seems that selection, analysis, and interpretation of the available historical data is not the only issue, but how one understands the term *Christian nation* lies just under the surface of the whole debate. Like so much of historical writing, one's beginning place, definition of terms, and assumptions determine much of the course that a writer's work takes. The reader will have to evaluate critically the reasonableness of each contributor's approach to the subject as well as his overall argumentation.

For me, reading history and writing about history are the pursuit of telling a story that makes sense. Additionally, and most importantly, it is telling that story with objectivity, honesty, and clarity. A historian's worst enemy is usually himself. This is why this kind of format that presents different perspectives is helpful not only to the reader who has a thirst for historical truth, but for the historians who need each other. It is within our debates that we are forced to consider ideas and evidence that we may have not previously integrated into our story. At the end of the day we may still not see eye to eye on every issue, but through the process the biblical wisdom is affirmed, "Iron sharpens iron, and one man sharpens another" (Prov 27:17).

Daryl C. Cornett
Hazard, Kentucky

America Distinctively Christian

David Barton

John Adams was one of a select group of individuals who helped direct the birth of America as an independent nation. Four decades after the Revolution, reflecting back over what he personally had seen and experienced, Adams declared:

> The general principles on which the fathers achieved independence were . . . the general principles of Christianity. . . . Now I will avow that I then believed (and now believe) that those general principles of Christianity are as eternal and immutable as the existence and attributes of God. . . . I could therefore safely say, consistent with all my then and present information, that I believed they would never make discoveries in contradiction to these general principles.[1]

Subsequent generations regularly reaffirmed what had been obvious to Adams, including South Carolina Governor James Hammond, who in 1844 also publicly characterized America as a nation built on Christian principles. Following that pronouncement, a small group openly censured him and demanded an apology. Shocked by that reaction, Hammond responded:

> Unhappily for myself, I am *not* a professor of religion—nor am I attached by education or habit to any particular

1

denomination—nor do I feel myself to be a fit and proper defender of the Christian faith. But I must say that up to this time, I have always thought it a settled matter that I lived in a Christian land and that I was the temporary chief magistrate of a Christian people! That in such a country and among such a people I should be publicly called to an account, reprimanded, and required to make amends for acknowledging Jesus Christ as the Redeemer of the world, I would not have believed possible if it had not come to pass.[2] (emphasis added)

Across three centuries of American history, there have been literally thousands of similar authoritative declarations about America being a Christian nation.

Ironically, however, few offenses today will subject an individual to greater public derision than to repeat what was said by John Adams, James Hammond, and hundreds of other American leaders. If someone today makes the mistake of invoking those historical declarations, he will quickly become the target of attack from the postmodern Left. Generally, postmodernists believe there are no definite terms, boundaries, or objective moral truths—that humanity has evolved beyond all of these and that truth is relative—that there are no moral absolutes and that each individual must discover truth for himself. Postmodernists therefore reject traditional Western culture, traditions, and institutions, including Judeo-Christian-based morals, sense of nationalism, free-market economic systems, and republican forms of government. Post-modernists tend to be secularist progressives, cynical and disbelieving, who consider themselves intellectual successors of the seventeenth-century secular Enlightenment writers, thinking of themselves primarily as citizens of the world. The invectives publicly applied to "Christian nation" offenders include "bigots,"[3] "homegrown ayatollahs,"[4] American "Taliban,"[5] "segregationists,"[6] "febrile fringe,"[7] "theocrats,"[8] and similar pejoratives. The critics further claim that Christian nation offenders are:

- "Christian fascists"—part of "the new militant Christianity" that "advocate the death penalty for a host of

'moral crimes,' including apostasy, blasphemy, sodomy, and witchcraft."[9]
- Moving "us one step closer to theocracy on the Muslim Brotherhood model."[10]
- Students of Machiavelli, whose followers include "Mussolini, Hitler, Lenin and Stalin"[11]

While the hysterical and often malicious tone used by modern attackers is excessive, inaccurate, and unwarranted, it also accomplishes strategic purposes by transforming discussions of the subject from the level of rational and intellectual to that of emotive. Furthermore, the critics' pillorying of Christian nation offenders offers a public example that successfully intimidates others from offering any intelligent dialogue on the topic; after all, who wants to be accused of being the neighborhood equivalent of Osama Bin Laden, Adolf Hitler, or Jeffrey Dahmer simply for suggesting that America might be a Christian nation? If an individual today does believe that America was a Christian nation (and polling shows that two-thirds of the nation currently holds that view[12]), he has learned to remain silent for his own protection. Consequently, public discussions of the topic are usually one-sided, with virtually no rebuttal offered by supporters of the belief.

This widespread silence—this lack of willingness to engage in legitimate debate—is in part because of the viciousness of the attackers but it also stems from the fact that supporters frequently feel themselves unprepared to engage the attackers on an intellectual level. A lack of cogent information (and how to respond with it) in four areas exacerbates this sense of unpreparedness: (1) a poor definition of what constitutes a "Christian nation," (2) an association of "Christian nation" with religious coercion and atrocities such as the Inquisition and the Crusades, (3) an unawareness that many of America's most laudable civic characteristics are the direct result of Christianity, and (4) a lack of familiarity with the massive body of official documentary evidence unequivocally affirming America to be a Christian nation. My contribution will address these four deficiencies of information.

Defining a "Christian Nation"

A Christian nation is not one in which all citizens are Christians, or in which the laws require everyone to adhere to Christian theology, or which stipulates that all leaders must be Christians, or any other such superficial measurement. As Supreme Court Justice David Brewer (1837–1910) long ago explained:

> In what sense can it [America] be called a Christian nation? Not in the sense that Christianity is the established religion, or that the people are in any manner compelled to support it. On the contrary, the Constitution specifically provides that "Congress shall make no law respecting an establishment of religion, or prohibiting the free exercise thereof." Neither is it Christian in the sense that all its citizens are either in fact or name Christians. On the contrary, all religions have free scope within our borders. Numbers of our people profess other religions, and many reject all. Nor is it Christian in the sense that a profession of Christianity is a condition of holding office or otherwise engaging in public service, or essential to recognition either politically or socially. In fact, the government as a legal organization is independent of all religions. Nevertheless, we constantly speak of this republic as a Christian nation—in fact, as the leading Christian nation of the world.[13]

So by what definition is America a Christian nation? According to Justice Brewer, America was a Christian nation because Christianity "has so largely shaped and molded it"[14]— a traditional historical definition confirmed by numerous other legal authorities,[15] including Chief Justice John Marshall, who explained:

> [W]ith us, Christianity and religion are identified. It would be strange, indeed, if with such a people our institutions did not presuppose Christianity and did not often refer to it and exhibit relations with it.[16]

By definition, then, a Christian nation is a nation founded on Christian and biblical principles, whose society and institutions have been largely shaped, molded, and influenced by those principles.

Christianity impacted many other nations long before it did so in America. The long history of Christianity's impact on nations was divided into three distinct periods by John Wise (1652–1725) of Massachusetts, whom distinguished historian Clinton Rossiter of Cornell University identified as being one of the six greatest intellectual leaders in colonial America.[17] Wise described each of those three periods:

PERIOD I constitutes the three centuries of Christianity immediately following the life of Christ. Wise described this period as "the most refined and purest time, both as to faith and manners, that the Christian church has been honored with."[18] For identification purposes, we will denote Period I as the Period of Purity.

PERIOD II spans the next twelve centuries and was a time when the state and the church united together, becoming almost one single institution instead of two. According to Wise, this was a period that "openly proclaimed itself to the scandal of the Christian religion."[19] The leaders of both state and church tried to imitate and assume the other's role, and they also forbid from the common man access to the Scriptures and education. Period II will be termed the Period of Apostasy—an age characterized by autocracy in both state and church, with monarchies and theocracies (usually oppressive ones) as the primary forms of governance. Significantly, the negative incidents in world history commonly associated with Christianity (e.g., the Inquisition, the Crusades, etc.) occurred during Period II; and although the title "Christian" is liberally applied to many nations during this period, those nations definitely do not conform to the definition of a true Christian nation set forth by Justice Brewer and others.

PERIOD III, according to Wise, is that which "began a glorious reformation." Wise explains: "Many famous persons, memorable in ecclesiastical history, being moved by the Spirit of God and according to Holy Writ, led the way in the face of all danger . . . for the good of Christendom."[20] Early seeds of this change began with the efforts of John Wycliffe (1320–84), called the "Morning Star of the Reformation"; the movement grew steadily over the next two centuries, becoming relatively mature by the 1600s. This period was characterized by a widespread return to the Bible as the guidebook for all aspects of life and living, and the impact of Christianity on nations during this time was almost exclusively beneficial, resulting in extensive and far-reaching positive reforms in both church and state. Period III may be called the Period of Reformation.

Before leaving Period III, two important points should be made about the Reformation. First, contrary to modern misportrayals, the Reformation was not a distinctly Protestant event, nor was it strictly a conflict of Protestantism vs. Catholicism. The Protestant churches did emerge from the Reformation, and many of the Reformers became Protestant leaders, but the teachings of the Reformation were targeted at autocracy in general, whether Catholic or Anglican, both civil and religious. Furthermore, both Catholic and Anglican Reformers were active in the Reformation; in fact, the overwhelming majority of Reformers undertook their beneficial work as Catholic priests.

Second, the Reformation was not an event that occurred at a specific point on the time line of world history, nor was it centered around a single individual in one nation. Most modern works erroneously identify the Reformation as beginning in 1517 when Martin Luther nailed his *Ninety-five Theses* to the door of the church in Wittenberg, Germany. To the contrary, the Reformation was a slowly plodding transformational movement that spanned three centuries, beginning almost two centuries before Luther and continuing for nearly a century after him. As historian Ernest Bates correctly acknowledged, Luther "came late in its [the Reformation's] development, riding to triumph on the crest of a tide that had been rising for centuries."[21]

Luther was indeed a famous figure in the Reformation, but the Reformation was actually led by numerous individuals in many countries, usually working independently of each other in spreading Reformation teachings across their respective nations. Among these were Englishmen such as John Wycliffe, Thomas Cranmer, William Tyndale, John Rogers, and Miles Coverdale; Czechs such as John Huss and Jerome of Prague; Germans Martin Luther, Thomas Münzer, Andreas Carlstadt, and Kaspar von Schwenkfeld; Swiss Ulrich Zwingli; Frenchmen William Farel and John Calvin; Scotsmen John Knox and George Wishart; Dutchmen Jacobus Arminius, Desiderius Erasmus, and Menno Simons; and many others.

The Reformation rekindled many of Christianity's original teachings, including those on the role of the individual believer. Among these teachings were the priesthood of the believer (emphasizing that the individual had direct access to God without need of assistance from any official in church or state) and justification by faith (emphasizing the importance of *personal* faith and an individual's *personal* relationship with the Savior). This renewed biblical emphasis on the individual altered the way that both church and state were viewed, thus resulting in new demands and expectations being placed on each.

The elevation of the common man that resulted from Reformation teachings was a direct threat to elitist totalitarian leaders in both state and church. Consequently, bloody purges, utilizing the most brutal tortures and barbaric persecutions, were initiated across Europe by both Catholic and Protestant leaders in their attempts to suppress Reformation followers and teachings.

For example, Catholic leaders in France conducted the St. Bartholomew's Day Massacre of August 24, 1572, eventually resulting in 110,000 French Reformation followers (Huguenots) being killed. Some 400,000 others fled France to avoid death and persecution, with many coming to America, especially to South Carolina and New York.

Similarly, Protestant leaders in England such as King Henry VIII attempted to suppress Reformation teachings by public executions and burnings at the stake; Edward VI, Elizabeth I, and subsequent monarchs continued those efforts. King James I even concocted two revolutionary new church "doctrines" to help him to suppress the growing influence of Reformation teachings in England: the Divine Right of Kings, and Complete Submission and Non-Resistance to Authority. Not surprisingly, Reformation followers (often known as "Dissenters") openly opposed James's "irrational and unscriptural doctrines,"[22] thus prompting James to level additional brutal persecutions, including mutilation, hanging, and disemboweling. The Pilgrims came to America in 1620 in part to escape the hounding persecution of Protestant King James; and a decade later, another 20,000 Puritans fled England after many received life sentences (or had their noses slit, ears cut off, or a brand placed on their foreheads) for adhering to Reformation teachings.

Despite the ruthless persecutions by both Catholic and Protestant autocrats, the Reformation eventually prevailed, resulting in massive changes in the practices of both state and church, thus bringing to an end the corrupt practices of Period II Christianity. So, then, the Reformation was an extended movement across centuries, involving both Catholics and Protestants.

The overwhelming majority of the early colonists who arrived in America were dedicated followers of Reformation teachings. They deliberately infused those teachings into the operations of both state and church, resulting in numerous distinct characteristics of American government still enjoyed by citizens today, five of which are identified below.

Civic Trait #1: A Christian Nation Is Republican, not Theocratic

The recorded history of man for the past five millennia has established that whatever the predominant religion in a nation, it will exert some type of influence on that nation's government. This truth has been acknowledged by numerous historians and political philosophers across the centuries:

> Never was a state founded that did not have religion for its basis.[23] (JEAN-JACQUES ROUSSEAU *(1712–78)*, POLITICAL PHILOSOPHER)

> [T]he governments and civilizations of all people are typed and determined by the character of their religions.[24] (BISHOP CHARLES B. GALLOWAY *(1849–1909)*, ACADEMIC SCHOLAR AND TEACHER)

> The influence of religions on government has always been profound.[25] (CLINTON ROSSITER *(1917–70)*, HISTORIAN)

Recognizing this truth, in 1748 political philosopher Charles Montesquieu (a favorite of America's Founders)[26] analyzed the impact of Islam, Catholic Christianity, and Protestant

Christianity on governments. He concluded that Islam resulted in "a despotic government,"[27] and that "the Catholic religion [Period II] is most agreeable to a monarchy, and the Protestant [Period III] to a republic."[28] Because Catholic nations eventually adopted many of the Reformation teachings that came to characterize the Protestant nations, both Catholics and Protestants today agree on most broad philosophical issues of liberty and government. Nevertheless, substantial differences between the two in their views of government did exist at the time of American colonization.

The American colonies were primarily established by those Christians who had imbibed most deeply the Reformation teachings (i.e., Protestants), and those teachings directly impacted their view of government. As Sir Edmund Burke reminded the English Parliament during America's struggle for independence:

> The people [in America] are Protestants—and of that kind which is the most adverse to all implicit submission of mind and opinion. This is a persuasion not only favorable to liberty but built upon it.[29]

Burke's declaration of the pro-liberty nature of Protestantism was merely the summation of a long-demonstrated historical fact. The organization of free elective governments in America was consistently the result of Bible-believing Christian leaders immersed in Reformation teachings.

For example, the first settlers who arrived in Virginia, in 1607, were thorough Protestants and included ministers such as Robert Hunt. After declaring their purpose of "propagating [the] Christian religion,"[30] they then formed a representative government—America's first. By 1619, the Virginia House of Burgesses had been established with leaders being elected from among the people.[31] That legislature met in the Jamestown church and was opened with prayer by the Rev. Mr. Bucke; the elected legislators then sat in the church choir loft to conduct legislative business.[32]

Similarly, in 1620, the Reformation Pilgrims landed in Massachusetts and established their colony. Their pastor, John Robinson, directed them to elect civil leaders who would seek the "common good" and eliminate special privileges and status between governors and the governed[33]—a message they took to heart. First affirming that their endeavors were "for the glory of God and advancement of the Christian faith,"[34] they then organized a representative republican form of government and held annual elections.[35] By 1636, they had also enacted a citizens' bill of rights—America's first.[36]

Likewise, in 1630, the Reformation Puritans arrived and founded the Massachusetts Bay Colony. After announcing their goal of winning others to "the Christian faith,"[37] they then established a representative republican form of government with annual elections.[38] By 1641, they, too, had established a bill of rights (the "Body of Liberties")[39]—a document drafted by Nathaniel Ward to secure individual rights and liberties.[40]

In 1632, a charter was issued for Maryland to Sir George Calvert (i.e., Lord Baltimore), a Protestant leader who later converted to Catholicism. That charter affirmed the colonists' "pious zeal for extending the Christian religion";[41] by 1638, they had established a republican representative government;[42] in 1649, their Protestant legislature passed the Act of Toleration;[43] and by 1650, they had established a bicameral system—America's first.[44]

In 1636, Reformation minister Roger Williams established the Rhode Island Colony for "the holy Christian faith and worship,"[45] simultaneously establishing a republican (representative) form of government.[46]

The same year, Reformation minister Thomas Hooker (along with the Revs. Samuel Stone, John Davenport, and Theophilus Eaton) established Connecticut.[47] After declaring that evangelizing others to the Christian faith was the "principal end of this [colony],"[48] those ministers established a republican elective form of government.[49] In a 1638 sermon based on Deuteronomy 1:13 and Exodus 18:21, Hooker explained the three biblical doctrines that guided the formation of representative elective government in Connecticut:

I.   [T]he choice of public magistrates belongs unto the people by God's own allowance.

II. The privilege of election . . . belongs to the people.

III. They who have power to appoint officers and magistrates [i.e., the people], it is in their power also to set the bounds and limitations of the power and place.[50]

From Hooker's teachings and leadership sprang the "Fundamental Orders of Connecticut"—America's first written constitution (and the direct antecedent of the federal Constitution[51]), thus causing Connecticut to be titled "The Constitution State."

But although Connecticut produced America's first written constitution, it definitely had not produced America's first written plan of government; to the contrary, written documents of governance were the norm for every colony founded by Reformation-minded Christians. After all, this was the self-evident scriptural model: God had given Moses a *written* law to govern that nation—a pattern that recurred throughout the Scriptures (cf. Deut 17:18–20; 31:24; 2 Chron 34:15–21, etc.). Reformation-minded pastors and colonists adopted that biblical model and were so committed to the principle of written documents of governance that they provided them not just for their governments but also for their own churches.[52]

Notice the three recurring traits of the governments established by Christian leaders in America: (1) they contained declarations of their Christian motivations in founding their respecting colonies, (2) they established representative governments with frequent elections, and (3) they issued written documents of governance.

To impartial observers, the source of these unique but now universally accepted American governmental characteristics was self-evident. As Daniel Webster (the "great defender of the Constitution") readily acknowledged, "[T]o the free and universal reading of the Bible in that age men were much indebted for right views of civil liberty."[53]

As a result of following Bible teachings, Reformation-minded Christian ministers in America established rights and freedoms not available even in the mother country of Great Britain. Consequently, when autocratic British governors occasionally attempted to reduce American liberties to the level of those experienced in England, it is not surprising that Christian ministers were at the forefront of resisting encroachments on the rights they had helped establish.

For example, when crown-appointed Governor Edmund Andros tried to seize the charters of Rhode Island, Connecticut, and Massachusetts to revoke their representative governments and force the establishment of the British Anglican Church upon them, opposition to Andros's plan was led by the Revs. Samuel Willard, Increase Mather, and especially John Wise.[54] Wise, imprisoned by Andros for his resistance, nevertheless remained an unflinching voice for freedom, penning in 1710 and 1717 two works forcefully asserting that democracy was God's ordained government in both church and state,[55] thus causing historians to title him "The Founder of American Democracy."[56]

When Governor Berkley refused to recognize Virginia's self-government, Quaker minister William Edmundson and Thomas Harrison led the opposition;[57] and when Governor Thomas Hutchinson ignored the elected Massachusetts legislature, Samuel Cooper led the opposition.[58] A similar pattern was followed when Governor William Burnet dissolved the New Hampshire legislature, Governor Botetourt disbanded the Virginia House of Burgesses, Governor James Wright disbanded the Georgia Assembly, etc.

Additionally, when the British imposed on Americans the 1765 Stamp Act (an early harbinger of the rupture between the two nations soon to follow), at the vanguard of the opposition were the Revs. Andrew Eliot, Charles Chauncy, Samuel Cooper, Jonathan Mayhew, and George Whitefield;[59] in fact, Whitefield even accompanied Benjamin Franklin to Parliament to protest the act and assert colonial rights.[60]

In 1770, when the British opened fire on their own citizens in the Boston Massacre, ministers again stepped to the forefront, boldly denouncing that abuse of power. A number preached sermons on the subject, including the Revs. John Lathrop, Charles Chauncy, and Samuel Cooke; and the Massachusetts House of Representatives even ordered that Cooke's sermon be printed and distributed.[61]

As the separation with Great Britain drew near, John Adams gratefully acknowledged that "the pulpits have thundered"[62] and identified ministers such as the Revs. Samuel

Cooper and Jonathan Mayhew as being among the "characters . . . most conspicuous, the most ardent, and influential" in "an awakening and a revival of American principles and feelings" that led to American independence.[63] Christian ministers, however, did not just urge the "principles and feelings" that led to independence, they also entered the battlefield to secure those principles.

For example, on April 19, 1775, after "the shot heard 'round the world" had been fired, British troops began retreating from Concord to Boston, encountering increasing American resistance along the way. That resistance was often led by pastors who not only took up their own arms against the British but who also rallied their congregations to meet the retreating aggressors. Weeks later at the Battle of Bunker Hill, American ministers were again at the forefront, both in the fighting and in leading their congregations to battle.[64]

This pattern was common through the Revolution—as when Thomas Reed marched to the defense of Philadelphia against British General Howe;[65] John Steele led American forces in attacking the British;[66] Isaac Lewis helped lead the resistance to the British landing at Norwalk, Connecticut;[67] Joseph Willard raised two full companies and then marched with them to battle;[68] James Latta, when many of his parishioners were drafted, joined with them as a common soldier;[69] William Graham joined the military as a rifleman in order to encourage others in his parish to do the same.[70] Furthermore:

> Of Rev. John Craighead it is said that "he fought and preached alternately." Rev. Dr. Cooper was captain of a military company. Rev. John Blair Smith, president of Hampden-Sidney College, was captain of a company that rallied to support the retreating Americans after the battle of Cowpens. Rev. James Hall commanded a company that armed against Cornwallis. Rev. William Graham rallied his own neighbors to dispute the passage of Rockfish Gap with Tarleton and his British dragoons.[71]

Given their leadership, it is not surprising that ministers were often targeted by the British, with many being imprisoned, abused, or killed.[72] In fact, imprisoned clergymen often suffered harsher treatment at the hands of the British than did imprisoned soldiers,[73] and the British burned down and destroyed their churches across America.[74]

Christian clergy were also leaders in the national and state legislatures during the Revolution,[75] and after the Revolution, Christian ministers led in the movement for a federal constitution.[76] When the Constitution was completed, nearly four dozen clergymen were elected as delegates to ratify it,[77] and many played key roles in securing its adoption in their respective states.[78]

Then when the first federal Congress convened under the new Constitution, Frederick Augustus Muhlenberg was chosen by his peers to become the first Speaker of the House. He guided the process of creating the Bill of Rights, and his is one of only two signatures that appear at the bottom of that document. His brother, John Peter Gabriel Muhlenberg (a gospel minister who had risen to the rank of major general by the close of the Revolution), was also a member of that Congress and he, too, helped frame the Bill of Rights. Many other Christian ministers also served in the federal Congress.

In short, ministers were intimately involved in *every* aspect of securing America's *civil* and religious liberties; and in the long march across American history, the direct involvement of Christian ministers and activists did *not* produce theocracies (as critics today claim will occur if Christians engage in or lead the civil process) but instead produced republicanism and liberty in both state and church.

American Christian leaders were well aware of the theocratic-monarchal European so-called Christian nations of Period II and resoundingly denounced that model as not being representative of a true Christian nation. For example, Noah Webster (a soldier in the American Revolution and a legislator and judge afterward) emphatically declared, "The ecclesiastical establishments of Europe which serve to support tyrannical governments are *not* the Christian religion, but abuses and corruptions of it"[79] (emphasis added).

Numerous other Framers, statesmen, Christian leaders, and courts made similar pronouncements.[80] In fact, the differences between America and Europe were so great that Thomas

Jefferson pointedly avowed, "[T]he comparisons of our governments with those of Europe are like a comparison of heaven
and hell."[81]

America's government was indeed dramatically and distinctly different from those in Europe; and the Framers openly
acknowledged that it was Christianity that produced the unique
republican form of government that Americans now cherish:

> I have always considered Christianity as the strong ground
> of republicanism. . . . It is only necessary for republicanism
> to ally itself to the Christian religion to overturn all the
> corrupted political and religious institutions in the world.[82]
> (BENJAMIN RUSH, SIGNER OF THE DECLARATION, RATIFIER OF THE
> U. S. CONSTITUTION)
>
> The Bible. . . . [i]s the most republican book in the world.[83]
> (JOHN ADAMS, SIGNER OF THE DECLARATION, FRAMER OF THE BILL
> OF RIGHTS, U. S. PRESIDENT)
>
> [T]he genuine source of correct republican principles is
> the Bible, particularly the New Testament of the Christian
> religion.[84] (NOAH WEBSTER, REVOLUTIONARY SOLDIER, LEGISLA-
> TOR, JUDGE)

Scores of other Framers, statesmen, and courts made similarly succinct declarations about Christianity and republicanism, thus affirming what Montesquieu had earlier concluded.
Therefore, the first characteristic of a true Christian nation
is that it zealously guards an elective republican form of government and rejects a theocratic or autocratic one. Had it not
been for Bible-reading and Bible-believing ministers and civil
leaders, America likely would have adopted the unstable forms
of government used across the rest of the world at that time
rather than the republican form recommended in the Bible.

Civic Trait #2: A Christian Nation Guards the
Institutional Separation of Church and State

Although secularists today credit Thomas Jefferson with
the "wall of separation" metaphor, the principle was espoused
by the Reformers well before Jefferson. In fact, the specific
"separation" metaphor was originated by an English Reformation clergyman,[85] and then introduced into America in the early

1600s by numerous Christian clergymen—all occurring well over a century before Jefferson repeated that phrase.

Recall that in Period I, there had been no attempt to merge the two God-ordained institutions of state and church. In Period II, however, that changed when, Emperor Theodosius I made Christianity the official religion of the empire, declaring all other religions illegal.[86] With that decree, Christianity repudiated the voluntariness infused into it by Christ Himself. No longer was the church a collection of individuals joined in a voluntary association, but it became an ecclesiastical hierarchy overseeing a massive organization and numerous facilities. The individual follower of Christ was no longer of consequence but leaders were now the pinnacle of consideration; hence, education and the Bible were removed from the common man and reserved for the elite in state and church. Furthermore, a state official, simply by virtue of his position, was made a church official, and vice versa. In short, in Period II the emphasis shifted from the personal to the structural, from the individual to the institutional—an anti-biblical paradigm that prevailed for the next twelve centuries. Religious coercion and widespread atrocities marked this period of world history, and it is impossible to invoke enough forcefully negative adjectives to describe the abuses of this era.

In Period III, however, the Reformers, both Catholic and Protestant, reintroduced the teachings of individualism and republicanism; and because the Bible clearly taught that the two institutions of state and church each had distinct jurisdictions, the Reformers were also among the first to call for a separation of the two, and the Pilgrims, while still in Europe, also loudly advocated separation, asserting that government had no right to "compel religion, to plant churches by power, and to force a submission to ecclesiastical government by laws and penalties."[87]

Not surprisingly, the ministers and groups traveling from Europe to America (e.g., the Pilgrims, Roger Williams, John Wise, William Penn, etc.), having been thoroughly imbued with Reformation teachings, openly advocated the institutional separation of state and church—often in more articulate language than the original Reformers.[88] But, they also understood that the two separate institutions could and should cooperate with each other, just so long as there was no compromise or usurpation of the distinct roles of either.[89] As one early American clergyman explained: Christ and Caesar are at peace; their kingdoms are independent. They cooperate, but should never unite.[90]

Two centuries later, President Franklin D. Roosevelt reiterated the same traditional American message, declaring: "[T]he Churches and the Governments—while wholly separate in their functioning—can work hand in hand. . . . State and church [can be] rightly united in a common aim."[91]

The purpose of an institutional separation between state and church was generally to keep one institution from controlling the other; but more particularly, the Reformers' call for separation specifically arose in order to separate the *state* away from the church—that is, to prevent the *state* from meddling with, interfering against, or controlling religious expressions. (History had repeatedly demonstrated that it was the state that regularly attempted to usurp and regulate the church, not vice versa.)

This philosophy of keeping the state limited and at arm's length was planted deeply into American thinking, eventually being nationally enshrined in the Establishment and Free Exercise clauses of the First Amendment. In fact, notice that both clauses of that amendment were pointed at the state rather than at the church: the Establishment Clause prohibits the *state* from enforcing religious conformity, and the Free Exercise Clause ensures that the *state* will protect (rather than suppress, as it currently does) the citizens' rights of conscience and religious expression.

That the First Amendment was *not* pointed at citizens' religious beliefs or expressions (but rather at the impropriety of the state interfering with those beliefs or expressions) was affirmed by Jefferson not only in his "separation of Church and State" letter[92] but also on numerous other occasions.[93] In fact, the first occasion on which the U. S. Supreme Court invoked Jefferson's separation metaphor was in 1878, when it affirmed that the purpose of separation was to *protect* rather than limit public religious expressions.[94]

This was the American (and the Reformation) view of separation, and had been from the beginning. Therefore, notwithstanding revisionist claims to the contrary, the institutional separation of church and state so praised by today's civil libertarians—the separation responsible for ending atrocities in the name of religion—was *not* originated by secularism nor did it have societal secularization as its object; to the contrary, that separation was to ensure the protection of public religious expressions and was the product of the Bible and Christian ministers.

As early Quaker leader Will Wood (1797–1877) affirmed:

America owes the separation of Church and State—her safety and her pride—to the Bible. The ideas of democracy and republican liberty in America are due to the Bible.[95]

Distinguished German historian Philip Schaff (1819–93) likewise declared:

[A] peculiarity in the ecclesiastical condition of North America connected with the Protestant origin and character of the country is the separation of Church and State.[96]

Regrettably, the once clear purpose of the separation of church and state has now been subverted into something it never was: a phrase mandating the secularization of the public square. Such was *never* the intent. As Wood affirmed in 1877, "The separation of Church and State does *not* mean the exclusion of God, righteousness, morality, from the State"[97] (emphasis added).

Bishop Charles Galloway similarly acknowledged in 1898, "[T]he separation of the Church from the State did *not* mean the severance of the State from God, or of the nation from Christianity"[98] (emphasis added).

And in 1952 the U. S. Supreme Court also affirmed:

The First Amendment, however, does *not* say that in every and all respects there shall be a separation of Church and State. . . . Otherwise the State and religion would be aliens to each other—hostile, suspicious, and even unfriendly. . . . When the State encourages religious instruction or cooperates with religious authorities by adjusting the schedule of public events to sectarian needs, it follows the best of our traditions. For it then respects the religious nature of our people and accommodates the public service to their spiritual needs. To hold that it may not would be to find in the Constitution a requirement that the government show a callous indifference to religious groups. That would be preferring those who believe in no religion over those who do believe. . . . [W]e find no constitutional requirement which makes it necessary for government to be hostile to religion and to throw its weight against efforts to widen the effective scope of religious influence. . . . We cannot read into the Bill of Rights such a philosophy of hostility to religion.[99] (emphasis added)

But over recent decades the Court has repudiated the position that predominated in America for more than three centuries, thus depriving society of the positive benefits it once experienced from Christianity. As James Adams (an editor of the *Cincinnati Post*) correctly noted:

The Founding Fathers called only for separation—not divorce. Only in the latter half of [the twentieth] century has the United States Supreme Court held that Church and State should be legally divorced. . . . To require religion to stand mute in any public debate deprives the nation of a voice that needs to be heard. We dare not muzzle morality in the marketplace or permit the wall of separation to turn into an Iron Curtain of religious expression.[100]

Unfortunately, the postmodern Left, abetted by a willing judiciary, has now rendered the protection intended by the wall of separation impotent by reversing its purposes and protections.

Nevertheless, modern critics continue to clamor that Christians active in the civil arena are attempting to establish a theocracy and tear down the wall between state and church—a charge as ridiculous today as it was in 1853 when the U. S. House of Representatives observed:

[We] know of no denomination of Christians who wish for such union. . . . The sentiment of the whole body of American Christians is against a union with the State. . . . [T]he tendency of the times is not to a union of Church and State but is decidedly and strongly bearing in an opposite direction. Every tie is sundered and there is no wish on either side to have the bond renewed. It seems to us that the men who would raise the cry of danger in this state of things would cry fire on the thirty-ninth day of a general deluge.[101]

Therefore, the second characteristic of a Christian nation is that it jealously maintains an institutional separation of church and state, but not a societal sterilization that requires either the secularization of the state on the one hand or the purging of political speech from the church on the other.

Civic Trait #3: A Christian Nation Opposes Coercion and Secures Religious Toleration and the Rights of Conscience

Modern critics frequently accuse Christians and Christianity of being coercive.[102] In fact, when controversies arise over Christian religious expressions in public, such as a prayer at a school or city council, a symbol on a city seal or in a cemetery, a Scripture on a memorial or in a park, etc., opponents invariably allege Christian coercion.[103]

Significantly, in Period I, Christ and his apostles established religious noncoercion as the standard for Christianity. Jesus offered His message to all, without pressure or coercion; and the apostles and early Christian leaders preserved that same standard, thus establishing noncoercion as an inherent characteristic of Christianity.

They also made the conscience a subject of significant emphasis, with thirty references to that topic in the New Testament alone. For example, the Scriptures not only urge individuals to protect and maintain a "good conscience" and have "a conscience void of offence toward God and men" (Acts 24:16 ASV; cf. 1 Tim 1:5,19; 1 Pet 3:16,21; etc.), but they also teach that there will be differences of conscience (cf. 1 Cor 8). The warning is even issued that if an individual "sin[s] like this against the brothers and wound[s] their weak conscience, you are sinning against Christ" (v. 12). Christians were therefore instructed to respect the differing rights of conscience (v. 13). But Period II Christianity repudiated that biblical position. As explained by Founding Father John Jay:

> For a long course of years, many European nations were induced to regard toleration as pernicious and to believe that the people had no right to think and judge for themselves respecting religious tenets and modes of worship. Hence it was deemed advisable to prohibit their reading the Bible.[104]

But in Period III, the Reformers reverted to the biblical teachings of Period I, believing that it *was* advisable for people both to read the Bible and "to judge for themselves respecting religious tenets and modes of worship." Consequently, based on the many scriptural teachings, Reformers such as Menno Simons in Friesland (central Europe),[105] Jacobus Arminius in the Netherlands,[106] John Calvin in France,[107] and others advocated tolerance, noncoercion, and protection for the rights of conscience.

The teachings of the Reformation were eventually carried to America, where they took root and grew to maturity at a rapid rate, having been planted in virgin soil uncontaminated by the apostasy of the previous twelve centuries. Hence, Christianity—especially as imported to America—became the world's single greatest historical force in securing noncoercion, religious toleration, and the rights of religious conscience

Interestingly, while the Scriptures were sufficient authority for the Reformers to advocate these rights, two additional factors helped reinforce their beliefs in these areas. The first was that of persecution. Many Reformers had personally been called before religious tribunals and threatened with punishment (and some even lost their lives) simply for speaking about the religious ideas and beliefs they held. Such persecutions reinforced their view of the Bible's teachings in favor of religious toleration and the religious rights of conscience.

A second factor strengthening the need to protect these rights was the nature of Protestantism itself. The root word for "Protestant" is "protest," meaning to "object, disapprove, or dissent."[108] (The original target of the dissenters' protests had been the established Catholic and Anglican churches, but over time Protestants even targeted other Protestants with whom they disagreed. The followers of each Reformer rallied behind their leader's positions and beliefs, giving rise to numerous denominations. Because of the great diversity within Protestant Christianity, tolerance was required by all if any were to survive, for no single Protestant group was large enough to predominate on its own, and any could be eliminated if all the others united against it.

Protestant Christians in America therefore were the first to champion and enshrine into their governing documents the rights of religious toleration and protection for religious conscience that had been earlier reintroduced by the Reformers. See, for example, the 1640 government for Providence,[109] the colony founded by Roger Williams; Christian theologian John Locke's 1669 Constitutions of Carolina;[110] Quaker minister William Penn's 1676 governing document for West Jersey,[111] 1682 Frame of Government for Pennsylvania[112]; and 1701 Charter of Delaware.[113] Those protections were reiterated and re-secured when the American states wrote their first constitutions during the American Revolution. For example, the 1776 Virginia constitution declared:

> [R]eligion . . . can be directed only by reason and conviction and not by force and violence; and therefore all men are equally entitled to the free exercise of religion according to the dictates of conscience; and that it is the mutual duty of all to practice Christian forbearance, love, and charity towards each other.[114]

When the 1776 Constitution of New Jersey secured similar rights,[115] Governor William Livingston (a devout Christian and signer of the Constitution) joyfully effused over the protection specifically accorded the rights of religious conscience.[116] And when the 1777 New York constitution also secured those rights,[117] Governor John Jay (an author of the *Federalist Papers* and the original Chief Justice of the United States as well as a devout Christian) was similarly jubilant.[118] A century later, the Supreme Court of New York reaffirmed that the rights of religious conscience secured in that document were the direct result of Christianity.[119] Clauses securing religious toleration and the rights of religious conscience also appeared in many other early state constitutions.

At the federal level, the First Amendment also secured religious toleration and the rights of religious conscience,[120] a fact affirmed not only by Thomas Jefferson[121] but also by the original wording proposals for the First Amendment.[122] Today, the safeguards for the rights of conscience first secured by Christian leaders now appear in forty-seven state constitutions.[123]

Such protections caused early U. S. Senate Chaplain C. M. Butler (1810–90) to gratefully note:

> Provision is now made in the public service for all who wish to avail themselves of religious instruction and services and sacraments to do so; and those who do not wish to avail themselves of them are not forced to accept them. Here is a provision made to satisfy the conscience of all.[124]

Unfortunately, however, as the judiciary over recent years has compelled a more secular public square and ordered the removal of Christian principles and expressions, the religious rights of conscience—particularly for Christians—have significantly diminished.[125] In fact, the judiciary now extends protections for the *religious* rights of conscience to overtly anti-religious individuals,[126] thus emasculating those religious rights and empowering secularists with a heckler's veto over genuinely devout and pious individuals. This has produced the absurd results forewarned by Chaplain Butler in 1856:

> [If] this arrangement [protecting the *religious* rights of conscience] were destroyed . . . here would be a case of gross violation of the rights of conscience. Thus they who are themselves permitted just as they please to worship or deny their God, would not permit others to worship or not to worship as they might prefer but would force them not to worship.[127]

Additional judicial invasion into the formerly inviolable rights of conscience is now apparent over the content of prayers, with judges not only directing which words may and may not be used in public prayers[128] but even authorizing civil punishments if the wrong words (i.e., distinctly Christian words) are used in prayers.[129] Framers such as Constitution signer William Livingston would have vehemently objected to this current invasion of the rights of conscience and religious expression:

> For what business, in the name of common sense, has the magistrate . . . with our religion? . . . The State [does not] have any concern in the matter. For in what manner doth it affect society . . . in what outward form we think it best to pay our adoration to God?[130]

Strikingly, secularism does not provide religious toleration or protection for the traditional rights of conscience, but Christianity does. Therefore, Period III Christianity not only abolished theocracies and achieved an institutional separation of church and state but also enshrined religious noncoercion, religious toleration, and protection for the rights of religious conscience—the third characteristic of a Christian nation.

Civic Trait #4: A Christian Nation Distinguishes between Theology and Behavior

Remarkably, critics on the postmodern Left charge that:

- cutting taxes and decreasing welfare spending constitute "the theological right zealously setting up to establish their beliefs in all aspects of our society."[131]
- attempting to end judicial filibusters in the U. S. Senate is an "aggressive new strain of right-wing religious zealotry."[132]
- urging cities to become "Communities of Character," or to promote the values of honesty, loyalty, respect, and courtesy, is "another step in the Christian right's determined campaign to transform the U. S. into a theocracy."[133]

With such scathing charges arising over issues that arguably have no or little relation to Christianity, it is not surprising that the rhetorical intensity increases over those onerous "traditional values" so often associated with Christianity. For example:

- A "crackdown on indecency on television" is an act of a Christian Taliban.[134]
- To oppose abortion is to "seek fundamentalist theocracy."[135]
- Authorizing a *de novo* legal appeal to permit Terri Schiavo the same access to federal courts already enjoyed by convicted criminals represented "the tactics of Muslim fundamentalists and theocrats in places like Egypt and Pakistan."[136]

According to these national writers from the postmodern Left, seeking a ban on cloning, promoting traditional marriage, supporting the Boy Scouts, seeking to preserve "under God" in the Pledge of Allegiance, teaching abstinence from sex in schools, urging Internet filtering for computers accessible by children, and a plethora of other similarly "dangerous" positions are proof of an imminent Christian theocracy.

Yet *none* of these issues deal with theology, which is necessary if there is to be a theocracy. The issues of judicial activism, Internet filters, voting, marriage, cloning, etc., relate not to theology (the study of God, divine things, or divinity[137]) but rather to values (the beliefs of a person or group either for or against something[138]).

Those on the postmodern Left regularly demonstrate their failure to distinguish between values and theology. When they disagree with a particular value, they simply impute it to theology and then accuse its promoters of being theocratic. They seem oblivious to the fact that many who support the values they oppose are not even religious individuals, thereby making it farcical to assert they are attempting to establish a theocracy.

As an example, the Left disagrees with Christmas acknowledgements and celebrations (a fact demonstrated each year during the Christmas season), but 93 percent of Americans celebrate Christmas.[139] It cannot logically be argued that 93 percent of Americans are seeking a theocracy simply because they support a value opposed by the Left. The same is true with dozens of other values that the postmodern Left wrongly attributes to theology (and thus theocracy). Despite the Left's apparent inability to do so, differentiating between values and theology in the civil sphere is crucial to securing sound public policy.

For instance, as a matter of policy, it matters not whether my neighbor is an atheist or infidel, but if he will govern his behavior by basic traditional values such as those in the Ten Commandments—that is, if he will refrain from killing me, stealing my property, or taking my wife—he will make a good citizen, regardless of whether or not he holds any religious beliefs. Similarly, my neighbor may not agree that Jesus Christ is the Son of God and Savior of the world, but if he will observe Jesus' behavioral teachings on the Golden Rule and the Good Samaritan, he will make an exemplary citizen. The fact that certain values may be derived from Christianity does not make them theological.

As the Pennsylvania Supreme Court acknowledged in 1859:

> Law can never become entirely infidel, for it is essentially founded on the moral customs of men; and the very generating principle of these is most frequently religion.[140]

A century later in 1961, the U. S. Supreme Court similarly affirmed:

> [The Constitution] does not ban federal or state regulation of conduct whose reason or effect merely happens to coincide or harmonize with the tenets of some or all religions. In many instances, the Congress or state legislatures conclude that the general welfare of society, wholly apart from any religious considerations, demands such regulation. Thus, for temporal purposes, murder is illegal. And the fact that this agrees with the dictates of the Judeo-Christian religions while it may disagree with others does not invalidate the regulation. So too with the questions of adultery and polygamy. The same could be said of theft, fraud, etc., because those offenses were also proscribed in the Decalogue [Ten Commandments].[141]

The Framers were able to distinguish between values and theology; they recognized that Christianity had not just a theological but also a behavioral component. As Dewitt Clinton (U. S. Senator under President Thomas Jefferson and the driving force behind the Twelfth Amendment) acknowledged:

> Christianity may be contemplated in two important aspects. First, in reference to its influence *on this world*; and secondly, in reference to our destiny in the world to come.[142] (emphasis added)

Signer of the Constitution John Dickinson similarly affirmed that Christianity had a purely behavioral aspect:

> Christianity is an active, affectionate, and social religion, chiefly consisting in discharge of duties to our fellow creatures. It therefore requires no separation from them.[143]

The Founders understood that the societal benefits of Christianity were salient to the public sphere and were completely separate from theological issues. In fact, early American ministers spoke so frequently about the positive benefits of Christian principles on society that Alexis de Tocqueville drew special attention to that fact in *Democracy in America:*

> The Americans not only follow their religion from interest but they often place in this world the interest which makes them follow it. In the Middle Ages, the clergy spoke of nothing but a future state; they hardly cared to prove that a sincere Christian may be a happy man here below. But the American preachers are constantly referring to the earth, and it is only with great difficulty that they can divert their attention from it. To touch their congregations, they always show them how favorable religious opinions are to freedom and public tranquility, and it is often difficult to ascertain from their discourses whether the principal object of religion is to procure eternal felicity in the other world or prosperity in this.[144]

Consequently, Americans—both religious and nonreligious —long understood the positive societal benefits produced by embracing certain behaviors and values, even though they were derived from the Scriptures. In fact, the Founders identified several specific societal benefits that were produced by Christianity, three of which will be identified below.

Societal Benefit #1: Benevolence, Compassion, and Humanitarianism

America is arguably the most benevolent nation on the face of the earth. Whenever tragedy—whether earthquake, famine, tsunami, war, or any other disaster—strikes any country, Americans rush in to help; and they do so regardless of whether the nation is an enemy or even of a different faith. Where did Americans learn the benevolence lacking in so many other nations? The Founders asserted that Christianity was the source of this national trait:

> [C]hristian philosophy, in tenderness for human infirmities, strongly inculcates principles of . . . benevolence.[145] (Richard Henry Lee, signer of the Declaration, framer of the Bill of Rights)

> Christian benevolence makes it our indispensable duty to lay ourselves out to serve our fellow-creatures to the utmost of our power.[146] (John Adams)

> Christianity . . . taught the duty of benevolence to strangers.[147] (James Kent, "father of American jurisprudence")

> [T]he doctrines promulgated by Jesus and His apostles [include] lessons of peace, of benevolence, of meekness, of brotherly love, [and] charity.[148] (John Quincy Adams)

The Christian teaching of benevolence is found in Jesus' lesson on the Good Samaritan (Luke 10:25–37)—a lesson thoroughly inculcated throughout American culture. For example, Benjamin Franklin selected the Good Samaritan for the logo of the Pennsylvania Hospital (America's first); American classic textbooks (such as the McGuffey Readers) taught students the account of the Good Samaritan;[149] and even today, states continue to pass "Good Samaritan" statutes to protect good-faith rescue efforts, medical intervention, donations of food or goods, etc.

Incontrovertibly, the teaching of the Good Samaritan was delivered solely by Jesus Christ and is therefore undeniably an overtly and uniquely Christian teaching, yet it cannot be reasonably argued that the "Good Samaritan" is a theological tenet. So, too, with the teaching of the Golden Rule ("Do to others what you would have them do to you" Matt 7:12 NIV)— another Christian teaching that elevates society.

Referring to these two teachings, John Adams declared:

One great advantage of the Christian religion is, that it brings the great principle of the law of nature and nations (Love your neighbor as yourself [the Good Samaritan], and do to others as you would that others should do to you [the Golden Rule]) to the knowledge, belief, and veneration of the whole people.[150]

Significantly, nations primarily secular in their orientation, or those predominated by non-Christian religions, rarely become involved in the benevolent endeavors that consistently characterize America. When the massive tsunami devastated Muslim Indonesia in 2004, other Muslim nations did little to assist a nation of their own faith; yet Christian America led the way in providing relief in money, supplies, technology, etc.—all for a country predominated by a religion that considers America the "Great Satan."

Societal Benefit #2: A Civilized Society

The Founders understood that civilized behavior was the product of neither good constitutions nor good laws. As Samuel Adams acknowledged:

[N]either the wisest constitution nor the wisest laws will secure the liberty and happiness of a people whose manners are universally corrupt.[151]

"Manners" (defined in Webster's original 1828 dictionary as "civility; decent and respectful behavior"[152]) was a subject frequently emphasized by the Founders. Unfortunately, however, manners, after being diligently taught to youth for well over two centuries, have become a declining emphasis of instruction

in recent years. Yet, manners directly benefit society by training citizens to think about others rather than themselves, thus
preventing an egocentric society and preserving a civilized one.

Significantly, the Framers recognized Christianity to be the
source of many societal manners. For example, Dr. Benjamin
Rush (signer of the Declaration) declared:

[C]hristianity exerts the most friendly influence upon . . .
the morals and manners of mankind.[153]

Declaration signer Robert Treat Paine similarly attested:

I believe the Bible . . . to contain in it the whole rule of faith
and manners.[154]

John Dickinson agreed:

I am contented with the volume of nature: the Old Testament and the New Testament. I want no more. These last
contain adequate and unparalleled maxims for the conduct
of private and public life.[155]

Indeed, whether addressing relationships with friends
or family, parents or siblings, rivals or enemies, neighbors or
aliens, authorities or inferiors, the young or the elderly, men or
women, the Bible provides clear guidance and rules for manners (the key to civilized behavior). Some parts of the nation
continue to practice the cultural remnants of such manners,
still voicing phrases such as "thank you," "no sir," or "please
ma'am," and even opening the door, pulling out a chair, or stepping aside for another to pass—all indicators that a person is
thinking respectfully of others. This produces a civilized society,
which is the second societal effect of Christianity.

Societal Benefit #3: Self-Government and Healthy Citizenship

The key to any self-governing nation is self-governing citizens. If citizens cannot control themselves, their government
must become more externally regulatory in order to compen-
sate for the internal weaknesses of its citizens; therefore, a self-
governing nation is no stronger than the strength of its citizens'

character. The Founders believed that Christian principles produced character and thereby strengthened self-government. As Daniel Webster (the great "Defender of the Constitution") affirmed:

> [T]he cultivation of the religious sentiment represses licentiousness, incites to general benevolence . . . inspires respect for law and order, and gives strength to the whole social fabric.[156]

Christian principles and values strengthen individual self-government by helping regulate the heart, which is the seat of all human behavior. Thomas Jefferson affirmed that while other philosophies and religions "laid hold of actions only, He [Jesus] pushed His scrutinies into the heart of man; erected his tribunal in the region of his thoughts, and purified the waters at the fountain head."[157]

For example, although civil law prohibits murder, from a legal standpoint it can do nothing about a murder until *after* it occurs; Christianity, on the other hand, addresses murder *before* it occurs—while it is still only a thought in the heart, thus preventing the murder (see, for example, Matt 5:22–28). Similarly, covetousness is not illegal but it often results in crimes that are (theft, burglary, embezzlement, etc.); it is religion and not law that can prevent covetousness and thus the crimes it produces.

Understanding that religion can effectively prevent crimes that originate internally but manifest themselves externally, John Adams insightfully acknowledged:

> [W]e have no government armed with power capable of contending with human passions unbridled by morality and religion. Avarice, ambition, revenge, or gallantry [hypocrisy] would break the strongest cords of our Constitution as a whale goes through a net. Our Constitution was made only for a moral and religious people. It is wholly inadequate to the government of any other.[158]

As Robert Winthrop (an early Speaker of the U. S. House) similarly affirmed:

All societies of men must be governed in some way or another. The less they may have of stringiest state government, the more they must have of individual self-government. The less they rely on public law or physical force, the more they must rely on private moral restraint. Men, in a word, must necessarily be controlled either by a power within them or a power without them, either by the Word of God or by the strong arm of man, either by the Bible or the bayonet.[159]

When citizens lack internal restraint, government must resort to external coercion to preserve order; and history proves that no government can survive once it resorts to force to control its citizens. To help avoid such convolutions of government, the Founders were convinced that Christian principles were crucial, for they produced self-governing citizens—the third societal benefit of Christianity.

In short, the Founders and previous generations recognized the distinction between Judeo-Christian values and theology (one was permissible as an object of civil action, the other was not), and they took great pains to instill those principles in society because of the numerous positive benefits they produced. As Founder Noah Webster affirmed:

> Where will you find any code of laws among civilized men in which the commands and prohibitions are not founded on Christian *principles* [not theology]? I need not specify the prohibition of murder, robbery, theft, trespass; but commercial and social regulations are all derived from those *principles*, or intended to enforce them. The laws of contracts and bills of exchange are founded on the principles of justice, the basis of all security of rights in society. The laws of insurance are founded on the Christian *principle* of benevolence, and intended to protect men from want and distress. The provisions of law for the relief of the poor are in pursuance of Christian *principles*. Every wise code of laws must embrace the main *principles* of the religion of Christ.[160] (emphasis added)

America long experienced the societal benefits of Christianity that came from distinguishing between behavior and theology—the fourth trait of a Christian nation.

Civic Trait #5: A Christian Nation Takes a Free-Market Approach to Religion, thus Ensuring Religious Diversity

Critics often accuse Christians of being narrow and intolerant, attempting to eradicate all other religions and forcing everyone to become Christians, but such is not the case. To the contrary, a Christian nation embraces a free-market approach to religious faith—it provides an open marketplace to all religions, where the vendor of any faith may attempt to impress potential customers (i.e., citizens) with the superior benefits of his particular religion; the customer may then make his selection (if any), or reject all options. In a true Christian nation, a citizen is neither punished nor rewarded for his choice of religious faith (or lack thereof).

God Himself established this approach as His *modus operandi* from the very beginning. After forming Adam and Eve and placing them in the Garden of Eden, He allowed them to make a choice—a choice that meant the difference between continued fellowship with Him, or complete separation from Him. God applied neither force, nor pressure, nor coercion to Adam and Eve in making their decision; it was solely and completely their own voluntary choice. They chose poorly, then lived with the consequences. God could have prevented them from choosing wrongly, but He allowed them the choice.

Joshua also offered a choice to the people when they were preparing to enter the Promised Land:

> Choose for yourselves this day whom you will serve, whether the gods your ancestors served beyond the Euphrates, or the gods of the Amorites, in whose land you are living. But as for me and my household, we will serve the LORD. (Josh 24:15 NIV)

The same pattern was demonstrated by the prophet Elijah in his contest against the prophets of Baal atop Mount Carmel. He offered the people a choice of following the God of Israel or the god Baal:

Then Elijah approached all the people and said, "How long will you hesitate between two opinions? If Yahweh is God, follow Him. But if Baal, follow him." (1 Kgs 18:21)

In fact, Elijah not only permitted the followers of Baal the opportunity to demonstrate the strength of their religion but he even encouraged them to take additional time to make their argument to the people (vv. 25–29). When finished, Elijah would present his case for the God of Israel, and the people could then choose. Elijah—though outnumbered 450 to one (v. 22)—believed that when the truth was presented and a comparison made, the people would choose correctly.

The New Testament is filled with examples following the same model. In the Gospels, listeners were given an opportunity to believe in and follow Jesus; they made their choice and then lived with the consequence. The same pattern was also demonstrated throughout the various missionary endeavors of the apostles. Unfortunately, this biblical approach was abandoned during Period II, but thankfully reintroduced by the Reformers in Period III. The Reformation-minded Christian ministers and individuals who came to America carried this scriptural free-market approach with them and thus allowed rather than excluded other religions in their Christian colonies. This was evidenced by their early charters and governments, which as previously mentioned, allowed for religious liberty and freedom of conscience.

Generations later, Christian Founders preserved this philosophy and approach. As Noah Webster (an early judge and legislator responsible for specific language in the U. S. Constitution) reminded Americans:

Let us remember that force never makes a convert—that no amelioration [improvement] of society can be wrought by violence—and that an attempt to reform men by compulsion must produce more calamities than benefits. Let us reject the spirit of making proselytes to particular creeds by any other means than persuasion.[161]

James Madison agreed:

If the public homage of a people can ever be worthy of the favorable regard of the Holy and Omniscient Being to Whom it is addressed, it must be that in which those who join in it are guided only by their free choice—by the impulse of their hearts and the dictates of their consciences; and such a spectacle must be [exciting] to all Christian nations.[162]

Ezra Stiles (1727–95), Christian theologian and president of Yale, rejoiced in the free-market approach to religion produced by American Christianity:

Here [in America] will be no bloody tribunals—no cardinal's inquisitors-general to bend the human mind, forcibly to control the understanding, and put out the light of reason. . . . Religious liberty is peculiarly friendly to fair and generous disquisition. Here Deism will have its full chance; nor need Libertines [morally unrestrained individuals] more to complain of being overcome by any weapons but the gentle, the powerful ones of argument and truth. Revelation [the Bible] will be found to stand the test to the ten thousandth examination.[163]

This free-market approach adopted by Christians was not because they believed their own religion to be weak; to the contrary, they strongly believed (and still believe) that Christianity is superior to all other religions—that faith in Jesus Christ is the only means of securing eternal life and enjoying personal communion with Almighty God (John 14:6; Acts 4:12; Matt 7:13–14; Phil 2:9–11; etc.). Yet, Christians also believe with equal conviction that every individual must make his own voluntary choices about his religion and eternal future, and must then live with the consequences—even if that choice means (from a Christian's viewpoint) the difference between heaven and hell. A Christian, out of his personal concern for the spiritual welfare of others, will share his own Christian faith with others (perhaps even zealously so) and seek to convert them to Christianity, but he will not coerce others to that belief; in all cases, it must be a matter of voluntary choice.

Because of this free-market approach, American Christians openly received numerous religious groups to America, including Jews, Muslims, Buddhists, and many others. Consequently, by 1658, a Jewish synagogue had already been established at Newport, Rhode Island; another was founded in Savannah, Georgia, only a year after that colony was founded; and Jewish synagogues were also founded in Richmond, Virginia, in 1719, and Charleston, South Carolina, in 1750.[164] Additionally, the Christian Founders showed great attachment to and affection for Jews;[165] and many Jews were active and distinguished patriots in the American Revolution, fighting side-by-side with Christians for American independence.[166]

In fact, Jewish leaders, recognizing that the freedoms they experienced in America resulted from the fact that America was a Christian nation, properly viewed an attack on religion and Christianity as if it were an attack on their own faith. Jews therefore would side with Christians when Christianity came under fire. (Similarly, Christians at that time also defended Jews and the Jewish faith; and even today, Evangelical Christians remain among the Jews' strongest allies and supporters.) For example, when Thomas Paine penned his *Age of Reason* attacking religion in general and Christianity in particular, not only were Christians quick to rebut Paine's attack but also Jews.[167] Similarly, during the Barbary Powers War (1784–1816), when Muslim terrorists attacked American interests and enslaved American seamen because of their Christian faith, Jewish diplomat Mordecai Noah negotiated with the Muslims in an attempt to secure the release of captured Christians.[168]

Jewish leaders, although firmly committed to their own faith, understood that by defending Christianity, they were defending what had provided them their own religious liberty in America—a fact still openly acknowledged by many Jewish leaders today. For example, Jeff Jacoby, a Jewish columnist at the *Boston Globe*, explains:

> This is a Christian country—it was founded by Christians and built on broad Christian principles. Threatening? Far from it. It is in precisely this Christian country that Jews have known the most peaceful, prosperous, and successful existence in their long history.[169]

Rabbi Daniel Lapin of the Jewish Policy Center unequivocally agrees, declaring,

[I] understand that I live . . . in a Christian nation, albeit one where I can follow my faith as long as it doesn't conflict with the nation's principles. The same option is open to all Americans and will be available only as long as this nation's Christian roots are acknowledged and honored.[170]

In fact, with foreboding he warns, "God help Jews if America ever becomes a post-Christian society! Just think of Europe!"[171]

Just as Jews were present in the Christian colonies from the very beginning, so, too, were Muslims, first coming to America in the early 1600s. Of the numerous African slaves brought to America, about 10 percent were Muslim,[172] many of whom became free and then settled permanently in America, retaining their Islamic faith. As a result, there were early Muslim communities in South Carolina and Florida,[173] and by 1806 there were so many Muslims across the country that America's first Koran was published.[174]

Other religions present in America during its earliest years included Asian and eastern Oriental religions. By the early 1800s, Buddhists had become firmly planted in America; in 1853, they built America's first Buddhist temple.[175] Native-American religions have always been present in America, and Unitarian-Universalism (an amalgamation of all the world's major religions) organized its first American church in 1782.[176]

There are many similar examples of other religions present in America from its earliest years. In 1877, Quaker leader Will Wood affirmed:

Exotic faiths have appeared since the days of the fathers. Rare plants or weeds, whichever they be, they have right to equal place in our free soil and the primitive American religion, whose root is the open—the entire—Bible. Though these religionists are new-comers, they are not, legally and constitutionally, interlopers. And, at least when they come to have considerable numbers, their voice is equally potent with that of original Americans in forming the State and its institutions.[177]

Period III Christian nations protected religious diversity, and history (both modern and ancient) consistently affirms that nations not grounded in Bible-based Christianity—whether religious or secular nations—rarely allow pluralism.

The U. S. Commission on International Religious Freedom monitors nations for egregious violations of religious liberty, and the most religiously intolerant nations currently include Burma (a Buddhist nation), China (Buddhist and Taoist), Eritrea (Muslim), Iran (Muslim), Iraq (Muslim), Nigeria (Muslim), North Korea (Communist), Pakistan (Muslim), Saudi Arabia (Muslim), Sudan (Muslim), Turkmenistan (Sunni Muslim), Uzbekistan (Muslim), and Vietnam (Buddhist and Communist).[178] On the watchlist for serious but slightly less egregious violations are Afghanistan (Muslim), Belarus (Belarusian Orthodox and Catholic), Cuba (Communist and Catholic), Egypt (Muslim), India (Hindu), Indonesia (Muslim), Laos (Communist), Russia (secular), Somalia (Muslim), Tajikistan (Muslim), Turkey (secular), and Venezuela (secular dictator).[179] Significantly, none of these numerous religiously intolerant nations are grounded in Reformation Christianity, thus providing a modern demonstration of the historical lesson that Reformation Christianity protects pluralism, but other beliefs (including secularism) do not.

Previous generations recognized that Christianity provided religious liberty for other faiths. As an early court acknowledged:

> What gave to us this noble safeguard of religious toleration, which made the worship of our common Father as free and easy as the air we breathe, and His temple as wide, capacious, and lofty as the sky He has spread above our heads? . . . It was Christianity—robed in light, and descending as the dove upon our ancestors—which gave us this provision [for toleration].[180]

Yet the toleration that Christianity produced was never intended to become a tool to repudiate or exclude Christianity itself. As prominent legal writer Stephen Cowell explained in 1854:

The Christian nation which adopted this Constitution invited the people of every country to come and live under it, but in so doing they did not abdicate their Christian ascendancy nor proclaim that their institutions were purged of the Christian element. They avowed toleration—and not infidelity—as their great principle. They said to all the persecuted and suffering throughout the world, "Come and dwell with us and you may enjoy manifold advantages and immunities. We are a Christian people, our institutions are constructed with reference to Christianity and are intended to be administered under its light and influences; it teaches us to offer you the largest Christian liberty ever enjoyed by a civilized people."[181]

The fifth characteristic of a Christian nation is that it ensures religious diversity through a free-market approach to religion.

The Christian Character of America

The first section of this piece has identified five characteristics of a Christian nation. This final section will provide eight categories of irrefutable historical-documentation proving that America was deliberately formed and continued to operate as a Christian nation. (The evidence provided in each category is merely representative of what would require numerous volumes if fully presented.)

Evidentiary Source #1: The Colonial Charters

Much has already been presented from the colonial charters to demonstrate the Christian foundations and purposes of America, but there is further evidence. For example, the Virginia Charter of 1606 declared that the colony was started for the "propagating of Christian religion to such people as yet live in . . . ignorance of the true knowledge and worship of God."[182] The Mayflower Compact of 1620 declared that the work was "undertaken for the glory of God and the advancement of the Christian faith."[183] The 1629 charter for the Massachusetts Bay Colony declared that winning the country "to the knowledge and obedience of the only true God and Savior of mankind and the Christian faith is . . . the principal end of this plantation."[184] The 1639 Fundamental Orders of Connecticut declared its main purpose was "to maintain and preserve the liberty and purity of the Gospel of our Lord Jesus which we now profess."[185] The 1643 United Colonies of New England affirmed: "[W]e all came into these parts of America with one and the same end and aim: namely, to advance the Kingdom of our Lord Jesus Christ and to enjoy the liberties of the Gospel in purity with peace."[186]

Numerous other colonial charters and governing documents contained similarly forthright Christian declarations. The historical evidence was so clear that in 1833, U. S. Chief Justice John Marshall concluded, "One great object of the colonial charters was avowedly the propagation of the Christian faith."[187]

Evidentiary Source #2: The Founding Fathers

Numerous Framers asserted the Christian purposes of America—including George Washington, who did not separate Christian principles from his public policies. For example, during the American Revolution he reminded his soldiers, "To the distinguished character of Patriot, it should be our highest glory to add the more distinguished character of Christian."[188] He called on "every officer and man . . . to live and act as becomes a Christian soldier, defending the dearest rights and liberties of his country,"[189] and he told a group of Delaware Indians seeking to have their children educated in American schools, "You do well to wish to learn our arts and ways of life, and above all, the religion of Jesus Christ. . . . Congress will do everything they can to assist you in this wise intention."[190]

Such Christian references and rhetoric were common in Washington's official acts and writings. And, as noted earlier, John Adams also openly avowed the Christian foundations of America, declaring, "The general principles on which the fathers achieved independence were . . . the general principles of Christianity."[191]

Numerous other Founders made similarly strong Christian pronouncements, including signers of the Declaration such as Charles Carroll,[192] John Hancock,[193] Benjamin Rush,[194] John

Witherspoon,[195] and Samuel Adams;[196] Constitution signers such as Alexander Hamilton,[197] Benjamin Franklin,[198] John Dickinson,[199] Abraham Baldwin,[200] James McHenry,[201] and Roger Sherman;[202] and other Framers and early statesmen such as Samuel Chase,[203] a signer of the Declaration and a U. S. Supreme Court justice; original Chief Justice John Jay;[204] Elias Boudinot,[205] a president of Congress during the Revolution and a framer of the Bill of Rights; DeWitt Clinton,[206] who introduced the Twelfth Amendment; John Quincy Adams;[207] and many others.

Daniel Webster accurately summarized the Founders' beliefs when he declared, "[T]he Christian religion—its general principles—must ever be regarded among us as the foundation of civil society."[208]

Evidentiary Source #3: The Revolutionary Era

In September 1774, America assembled its first national Congress in Philadelphia. One of the first acts of that Congress was to ask a Christian minister to open with prayer;[209] he prayed and led Congress in reading four chapters from the Bible.[210]

During the Revolution, Congress called the nation to official days of prayer on fifteen occasions, and did so with explicitly Christian language—such as on March 16, 1776, when Congress asked the country to observe.

a day of humiliation, fasting, and prayer; that we may . . . appease His righteous displeasure and, through the merits in mediation of Jesus Christ, obtain His pardon in forgiveness.[211]

In addition to times of prayer, Congress attended church as part of its official activities.[212] It also instructed the Continental Army that "all officers and soldiers diligently attend Divine service,"[213] and similarly directed the Navy that "Divine service be performed twice a day on board, and a sermon preached on Sundays."[214]

Seeking to strengthen its relationship with various Indian tribes, Congress recognized that "the propagation of the Gospel . . . may produce many and inestimable advantages,"[215] and therefore made congressional provision to send gospel ministers among the tribes to "instruct them in the Christian religion"[216]—a measure repassed by Congress on several subsequent occasions.

Just as Congress called the nation to prayer during the Revolution, state leaders also called their respective states to prayer. The state calls to prayer were far more numerous than the frequent calls of the Continental Congress but no less expressive in Christian language. For example, in 1777, Massachusetts called on its citizens to thank God that "we yet enjoy the glorious Gospel of Jesus Christ in meridian brightness." Citizens were then asked to "humbly implor[e] forgiveness through the merits of Jesus Christ our Lord" so that America might become known for "the practice of the religion of Jesus."[217]

In 1779, Governor Thomas Jefferson called Virginians to a time of prayer and thanksgiving. His proclamation asked the people to give thanks "that He hath diffused the glorious light of the Gospel, whereby through the merits of our gracious Redeemer we may become the heirs of His eternal glory."[218] Jefferson's call further asked Virginians to pray that

> He would grant to His church the plentiful effusions of Divine grace and pour out his Holy Spirit on all ministers on the Gospel; that He would bless and prosper the means of education and spread the light of Christian knowledge through the remotest corners of the earth.[219]

Massachusetts Governor John Hancock issued nearly two dozen calls for prayer, each with explicit Christian language— such as when he asked citizens to pray "that all may bow to the Scepter of our Lord Jesus Christ, and the whole Earth be filled with His glory."[220]

Additionally, the original state constitutions penned during the Revolution contained explicitly Christian declarations. For example, the 1776 Delaware constitution—written with the help of Declaration signers George Read and Thomas McKean and Constitution signer John Dickinson[221]—declared:

> Every person who shall be chosen a member of either house, or appointed to any office or place of trust . . . shall . . . make

and subscribe the following declaration, to wit: "I, _____, do profess faith in God the Father, and in Jesus Christ His only Son, and the Holy Ghost, one God, blessed for evermore; and I do acknowledge the Holy Scriptures of the Old and New Testament to be given by divine inspiration."[222]

Similar pronouncements are found in the Massachusetts constitution,[223] the Pennsylvania constitution,[224] the Maryland constitution,[225] and the New Hampshire constitution.[226]

In 1777, as a result of the Revolution and the British blockade of American ports, America began experiencing a shortage of several important commodities, including Bibles. On July 7, a request was placed before Congress to print or import more, because "unless timely care be used to prevent it, we shall not have Bibles for our schools, and families, and for the public worship of God in our churches."[227] Congress concurred and ordered 20,000 Bibles imported.[228] In 1781 when the need for Bibles arose once again, Robert Aitken, publisher of *The Pennsylvania Magazine*, petitioned Congress for permission to print Bibles on his presses in Philadelphia, thus precluding the need to import them. Specifying that his Bible would be "a neat edition of the Holy Scriptures for the use of schools,"[229] Congress approved his request and appointed a congressional committee to oversee the project. On September 12, 1782, that Bible received the approval of the full Congress and soon began coming off the presses, containing a full congressional endorsement in the front.[230]

On September 8, 1783, the peace treaty concluding the American Revolution was approved. Signed by John Adams, John Jay, and Benjamin Franklin (and then approved by the full Congress,)[231] that document was explicitly Christian, with its opening line declaring,

"In the name of the most holy and undivided Trinity."[232] There are dozens of similar congressional acts, thus causing historian B. F. Morris to observe in 1864, "These official state papers are rich in Christian doctrines and confirm the great truth that the religion of the fathers of the Revolution and the founders of our civil governments was the religion of the Bible."[233]

Evidentiary Source #4: The Executive
Branch—Presidents and Governors

Once the Revolution ended and the Constitution was written and adopted, Christian declarations continued to abound in all three branches of the new federal government as well as the various state governments. Consider first representative examples from the federal Executive Branch.

Declarations from America's first two presidents (George Washington and John Adams) have already been noted, but numerous other presidents made similar declarations—including Thomas Jefferson. While presidents before and after him signed presidential documents invoking the Christian language of Article VII in the Constitution (i.e., "in the year of our Lord"), Jefferson even used the phrase "in the year of our *Lord Christ*" in his presidential signings.

Other eighteenth- and nineteenth-century presidents who avowed that America was built on or operated by Christian principles included Andrew Jackson,[234] John Tyler,[235] Zachary Taylor,[236] James A. Buchanan,[237] Abraham Lincoln,[238] Ulysses S. Grant,[239] Grover Cleveland,[240] William McKinley,[241] and Teddy Roosevelt.[242]

The same trend continued in the twentieth century, with President Woodrow Wilson succinctly declaring, "America was born a Christian nation. America was born to exemplify that devotion to the elements of righteousness which are derived from the revelations of Holy Scripture."[243] President Herbert Hoover similarly declared, "American life is builded and can alone survive upon . . . [the] fundamental philosophy announced by the Savior nineteen centuries ago."[244] President Franklin D. Roosevelt regularly described America as a nation built on Christianity and the Bible and even warned, "If the spirit of God is not in us, and if we will not prepare to give all that we have and all that we are to preserve Christian civilization in our land, we shall go to destruction."[245] Roosevelt publicly pledged to fight "the forces of anti-Christian aggression" that might come against America.[246] After witnessing the progress of the war in Europe shortly before the 1941 attack on Pearl Harbor, Roosevelt reminded Americans that the conflict was one between Christianity and its opponents, and that America must therefore maintain its dependence on the Bible and its teachings.[247] Then in a Fireside Chat following the Pearl Harbor attack, he reiterated that those who fought against Christianity were also fighting against America.[248] Throughout his four terms as president, Roosevelt repeatedly acknowledged that America was a product of Christianity and the Bible.[249]

President Harry Truman on numerous occasions also described America as a Christian nation:

> [T]his is a Christian Nation. More than a half century ago that declaration was written into the decrees of the highest court in this land.[250]

> In this great country of ours has been demonstrated the fundamental unity of Christianity and democracy.[251]

In 1946 following the close of World War II, Truman emphasized that the reconstruction of the defeated nations must be undertaken on the basis of Christianity.[252] Then as Truman prepared to deal with the onset of the Cold War, he repeatedly stated that Communism represented a conflict between Christianity and anti-Christianity, and that the only lasting way for America to defeat Communism was through Christianity.[253]

President Dwight D. Eisenhower—commander of the Allied Forces during World War II—was also candid about the fact that America was a Christian nation and that our faith was the basis of our liberties. As he told a select diplomatic gathering, "We are Christian nations, deeply conscious that the foundation of all liberty is religious faith."[254] Other twentieth-century presidents also affirmed the Christian and biblical basis of America.[255]

Just as federal chief executives were outspoken in declaring America to be a Christian nation, so, too, were states' chief executives. While there are multiple sources of evidence to demonstrate this, the content of the thousands of prayer proclamations from the governors is sufficient to prove the point:

> [L]et us offer . . . sincere and solemn prayers . . . that the Gospel of our Lord and Savior may be extended throughout

all the habitations of men.[256] (*1807,* GOVERNOR JONATHAN TRUMBULL, CONNECTICUT)

Let us also beseech God to . . . vouchsafe to all mankind the . . . blessed hopes of the Gospel of His Son, our Savior.[257] (*1839,* GOVERNOR WILLIAM SEWARD, NEW YORK)

[L]et us thank Him for the gift of the Gospel of His Son Christ Jesus and implore His grace that we all may conform to its precepts and live as becomes His disciples.[258] (*1850,* GOVERNOR CHARLES WILLIAMS, VERMONT)

[Let citizens offer] thanks to God for "the wide-spread manifestations and presence of the Holy Spirit" and the "means of grace and the hope of glory still offered us in the religion of Jesus Christ."[259] (*1858,* GOVERNOR ELISHA DYER, RHODE ISLAND)

[I] heartily invite the people . . . to praise God . . . for the redemption of the world by our Lord and Savior Jesus Christ [and] for His Holy Word.[260] (*1877,* GOVERNOR ALEXANDER RICE, MASSACHUSETTS)

May the people of this Christian state . . . keep the simple faith of this [Thanksgiving Day] appointment.[261] (*1922,* GOVERNOR ALBERT BROWN, NEW HAMPSHIRE)

There are thousands of similar declarations. The evidence is unequivocal that for well over two centuries, American executives at both the federal and state levels succinctly avowed their belief that America was a Christian nation and their states were Christian states.

Evidentiary Source #5: The Legislative Branch—Federal and State

On April 1, 1789, the first federal Congress convened in New York City, the temporary federal capital. Shortly thereafter, a congressional committee recommended, and Congress approved,[262] the appointment of Christian chaplains for the

House and Senate—a practice that has continued for well over two centuries.

On April 6, Congress set the first Inauguration Day and planned its activities. Accordingly, George Washington was sworn in as president on the balcony of Federal Hall, taking the oath of office upon a Bible on a crimson velvet cushion. The Bible was opened (at random) to Genesis 49;[263] Washington placed his left hand on the open Bible, raised his right, took the oath of office prescribed by the Constitution, reverently closed his eyes, and then bent over and kissed the Bible.[264]

Washington then went inside and delivered a strongly religious Inaugural Address to a joint session of Congress. After expressing his own heartfelt prayer to God, he called on his listeners to remember and acknowledge God.[265] Following that address, Washington and all the members of Congress walked in a public procession to St. Paul's Church for divine service, where Senate Chaplain Samuel Provoost (who was also the Episcopal bishop of New York) led the service according to *The Book of Common Prayer*, using a number of prayers taken from Psalms as well as Scripture readings and lessons from the book of Ruth, the Gospel of John, and the Third Epistle of John.[266]

That first inauguration, with its activities arranged by Congress, along with the president's own contributions, set the precedent for all subsequent ones, containing seven religious activities that have been repeated in whole or part in every subsequent inauguration: (1) using the Bible to administer the oath; (2) affirming the religious nature of the oath (either by kissing the Bible or declaring, "So help me God!"); (3) inaugural prayers by the president; (4) religious content in the inaugural address; (5) calling the people to prayer or acknowledgement of God; (6) inaugural worship services at a church; and (7) clergy-led inaugural prayers.

In 1790, Congress authorized President Washington to secure a location for a permanent federal capital, and in 1791, land was obtained for that purpose. Under the oversight of Secretary of State Thomas Jefferson, surveyors began laying out the city that would become known as Washington, DC In 1793, construction began on the new Capitol, and by late 1800 it was ready for occupancy.

On November 22, Congress moved into the building, and then two weeks later approved its use as a church, with divine services to be held each Sunday in the House chamber (selected because it was larger than the Senate chamber).[267] The church services, to be administered alternately by the House and Senate chaplains, were often crowded beyond comfortable capacity,[268] with worshippers crammed in wherever possible.[269]

Significantly, Thomas Jefferson regularly attended Sunday church at the Capitol and did so not only as vice president[270] but also throughout his presidency. As U. S. Congressman Manasseh Cutler affirmed, "He [Jefferson] and his family have *constantly* attended public worship in the Hall."[271] Mary Bayard Smith also confirmed that Jefferson "was a most *regular* attendant," even noting that he had a designated seat at the Capitol church.[272]

Jefferson was such a faithful attendant that he would not even allow inclement weather to deter his attendance.[273] He also contributed to the worship atmosphere of the Capitol church by having the Marine Band play at the services. Furthermore, under Jefferson, church services were also started at the War Department and the Treasury Department.[274] Therefore, on any given Sunday, worshippers could choose between attending church at the U. S. Capitol, the War Department, or the Treasury Department. Why was Jefferson such a faithful participant at the Capitol church? Jefferson once explained to a friend while they were walking to church together:

> No nation has ever existed or been governed without religion—nor can be. The Christian religion is the best religion that has been given to man and I, as Chief Magistrate of this nation, am bound to give it the sanction of my example.[275]

Divine services continued at the Capitol for almost a century, with presidents, senators, and representatives regularly attending church there.[276] In fact, church at the Capitol was so much a part of authorized congressional activity that preaching at those services was part of the official job description of chaplains. As reported by the U. S. Senate Judiciary Committee in 1853:

At every session [of Congress], two chaplains are elected—
one by each House—whose *duty* is . . . to conduct religious
services *weekly* in the Hall of the House of Representatives.[277] (emphasis added)

Chaplains preached at the Capitol, but they often invited
other ministers to preach. As attendee Margaret Bayard Smith
explained: "Not only the chaplains but the most distinguished
clergymen who visited the city preached in the Capitol. . . .
Preachers of every sect and denomination of Christians were
there admitted—Catholics, Unitarians, Quakers, with every
intervening diversity of sect. Even women were allowed to display their pulpit eloquence in this national Hall."[278]

Numerous other distinguished ministers preached at the
Capitol. And sermons were preached there not just on Sundays
but also on occasion during the week—as in 1850, when Senate
Chaplain C. M. Butler delivered a Tuesday sermon in the Senate in which he reminded senators, "Christ assures us that all
who repent and forsake their sins and believe in Him and live
to Him shall rise to a life glorious and eternal with Him and His
in Heaven."[279]

Between 1836 and 1847, Congress commissioned four
paintings to be hung in the Capitol Rotunda (each picture was
14 feet by 20 feet) to depict the Age of Exploration and Discovery. Those massive paintings still hang in the Rotunda and
portray two prayer services, a Bible study, and a baptism—
indisputable Christian acts and practices.

In 1853, a U. S. Senate report succinctly declared, "We are
Christians . . . and in a land thus universally Christian, what
is to be expected, what desired, but that we shall pay a due
regard to Christianity."[280] In 1854, the U. S. House similarly
pronounced:

In this age there can be no substitute for Christianity; that,
in its general principles, is the great conservative element
on which we must rely for the purity and permanence of
free institutions. That was the religion of the founders
of the republic, and they expected it to remain the religion
of their descendents.[281]

In 1856, and then again in 1857, the House passed a resolution declaring that "the great vital and conservative element in our system is the belief of our people in the pure doctrines and divine truths of the Gospel of Jesus Christ."[282]

There are scores of similar acts by the federal Congress. And just as Christianity was embraced at the federal level, so, too, was it embraced at the state level, where the available documentation is even more abundant. For example, in 1838, after a petition was presented to the New York State Legislature seeking to secularize the public arena and eliminate Christian expressions from the public square, in a near-unanimous vote the legislature rejected the request, reporting:

> [T]his is a Christian nation. . . . It is quite unnecessary to enter into a detailed review of all the evidences that Christianity is the common creed of this nation. We know it and we feel it, as we know and feel any other unquestioned and admitted truth; the evidence is all around us and before us and with us.[283]

There are hundreds (if not thousands) of additional examples at the state level. And even contemporary state documents preserve overt acknowledgments of Christianity. For example, the current constitution of North Carolina explains:

> Beneficent provision for the poor, the unfortunate, and the orphan is one of the first duties of a civilized and a *Christian state*. Therefore the General Assembly shall provide for and define the duties of a Board of Public Welfare.[284] (emphasis added)

Similarly, the current Massachusetts constitution, in the section addressing education and literature, notes:

> The encouragement of arts and sciences and all good literature tends to the honor of God, the advantage of the *Christian religion*, and the great benefit of this and the other United States of America.[285] (emphasis added)

Such Christian declarations have been consistent features of the Legislative Branch at both the federal and state levels for over two centuries.

Evidentiary Source #6: The Judicial Branch—Federal and State

Several Supreme Court justices asserted that America was a Christian nation, including John Jay,[286] appointed to the court by President George Washington as its original chief justice. Justice James Wilson, a signer of both the Declaration and the Constitution also appointed by President Washington, agreed that America was a Christian nation and that the Bible was never to be separated from America's civil governance.[287] Justice William Paterson—another signer of the Constitution appointed to the court by President Washington—similarly asserted that in America, "good government, good order, and good laws" must be based on religion.[288] Declarations by Chief Justice John Marshall (appointed by President John Adams) about the Christian character and nature of America have been presented.[289]

Likewise, Justice Joseph Story, considered one of the two "Fathers of American Jurisprudence" and appointed to the court by President James Madison, openly declared:

One of the beautiful boasts of our municipal jurisprudence is that Christianity is a part of the Common Law. . . . There never has been a period in which the Common Law did not recognize Christianity as lying at its foundations.[290]

I verily believe Christianity necessary to the support of civil society.[291]

Story further asserted:

[T]here would seem to be a peculiar propriety in viewing the Christian religion as the great basis on which it [law and republican liberty] must rest for its support and permanence.[292]

Justice John McLean, appointed to the court by President Andrew Jackson, similarly affirmed:

[T]he perpetuity of our institutions has rested upon Bible morality and the general dissemination of Christian principles.[293] For our unparalleled advance in civilization and physical prosperity, our country is mainly indebted to the Bible. . . . There is no other foundation for free institutions. . . . It is the ground—and the only ground—on which my hope of this government rests.[294]

Justice David Brewer, appointed by President Benjamin Harrison, voiced the same message as justices before him, declaring:

Christianity came to this country with the first colonists; has been powerfully identified with its rapid development, colonial and national; and today exists as a mighty factor in the life of the republic. This is a Christian nation. . . . [T]he calling of this republic a Christian nation is not a mere pretence, but a recognition of an historical, legal, and social truth.[295]

The declarations of these justices are representative of those from many others. Additionally, hundreds of federal judges below the Supreme Court level have called America a Christian nation.

Notable state jurists were equally outspoken in their affirmations—such as Justice Thomas McKean (1734–1817), a signer of the Declaration of Independence and Chief Justice of the Supreme Court of Pennsylvania. McKean did not hesitate to invoke Christian principles directly into official judicial proceedings. In fact, if a defendant was sentenced to death, McKean would deliver—in the courtroom—a Christian message of salvation to the convicted.[296]

Judge Zephaniah Swift (1759–1823), author of the first American legal text, also declared America was a Christian nation.[297] Justice James Kent (1763–1847), Chief Justice of the New York Supreme Court and one of the two "Fathers of American Jurisprudence," was outspoken that Christianity and the

Bible were essential foundations both of law and society, openly declaring:

> [T]he Christian religion was a part of the law of the land—
> it was so interwoven with our institutions, sentiments, and
> feelings that it was in effect recognized as a part of the law
> of the land.[298]

Justice Joseph Hornblower (1777–1864), Chief Justice of the New Jersey Supreme Court and a professor of law at Princeton Law School, openly affirmed the positive influence of Christianity and the Bible on America and its governments and institutions.[299]

Justice Thomas Cooley (1824–98) of the Supreme Court of Michigan was nationally known for his constitutional writings. He asserted not only that "Christianity is a part of the law of the land"[300] but also that the general principles of Christianity were the proper standard for measuring criminal offenses.[301]

Judge Theodore Dwight (1822–93), dean of two law schools and a professor at four, was unequivocal in declaring the nation (and the states) to be founded on and operated by the principles of Christianity:

> Our national development has in it the best and purest ele-
> ments of historic Christianity as related to the government
> of states. Should we tear our Christianity out of our law, we
> would rob our law of its fairest jewels; we would deprive
> it of its richest treasures; we would arrest its growth and
> bereave it of its capacity to adapt itself to the progress in
> culture, refinement, and morality of those for whose benefit
> it properly exists.[302]

Just as leading federal and state judges were unequivocal in their declarations, so, too, were the rulings of federal and state courts. Consider a few of the U. S. Supreme Court decisions—such as in 1844, when the court unanimously declared:

> Christianity . . . is not to be maliciously and openly reviled
> and blasphemed against to the annoyance of believers or
> the injury of the public. . . . Such a case is not to be pre-
> sumed to exist in a Christian country.[303]

In 1892, in another unanimous ruling, the Supreme Court declared that any legislative act that would hinder the spread or propagation of Christianity would be completely repugnant to the Constitution, "[N]o purpose of action against religion can be imputed to any legislation, state or national because this is a religious people. . . . [T]his is a Christian nation."[304] And in 1931, the Supreme Court declared, "We are a Christian people . . . according to one another the equal right of religious freedom and acknowledging with reverence the duty of obedience to the will of God."[305] Significantly, these "Christian country" (1844), "Christian nation" (1892), and "Christian people" (1931) declarations by the Supreme Court were subsequently cited with approval by numerous lower federal courts for decades.[306]

Additionally, the U. S. Supreme Court regularly invoked Christianity and Christian standards as the final word in its rulings in a number of areas—including that of marriage, when the court ruled against polygamy because not only was it a "crime by the laws of all civilized and Christian countries"[307] but because it was also "contrary to the spirit of Christianity and of the civilization which Christianity has produced in the Western world."[308] The Supreme Court also invoked Christian standards as the basis of its policy in the area of conscientious objectors and antiwar pacifists,[309] international diplomatic relations,[310] and federal treaties.[311] In each of these (and many other) categories of official policy, Christianity provided the federal standard and served as the final authority.

State courts were equally forthright in their declarations (the following cases are representative of scores of others):

1799, Maryland Supreme Court
By our form of government, the Christian religion is the established religion; and all sects and denominations of Christians are placed upon the same equal footing and are equally entitled to protection in their religious liberty.[312]

1824, Pennsylvania Supreme Court
[T]he laws and institutions of this state are built on the foundation of reverence for Christianity. . . . No free government now exists in the world unless where Christianity is acknowledged and is the religion of the country. . . . Its

foundations are broad and strong and deep . . . it is the purest system of morality, the firmest auxiliary, and only stable support of all human laws.[313]

1846, South Carolina Supreme Court

Christianity is a part of the common law of the land, with liberty of conscience to all. It has always been so recognized. . . . Christianity has reference to the principles of right and wrong . . . it is the foundation of those morals and manners upon which our society is formed; it is their basis. Remove this and they would fall. . . . In the Courts over which we preside, we daily acknowledge Christianity as the most solemn part of our administration. A Christian witness, having no religious scruples about placing his hand upon the book, is sworn upon the holy Evangelists—the books of the New Testament which testify of our Savior's birth, life, death, and resurrection; this is so common a matter that it is little thought of as an evidence of the part which Christianity has in the common law.[314]

1861, New York Supreme Court

The Christian religion . . . [is] a part of the common law. . . . All agreed that the Christian religion was engrafted upon the law and entitled to protection as the basis of our morals and the strength of our government.[315]

1883, Illinois Supreme Court

[O]ur laws and institutions must necessarily be based upon and embody the teachings of the Redeemer of mankind. It is impossible that it should be otherwise. And in this sense, and to this extent, our civilization and institutions are emphatically Christian.[316]

1941, Florida Supreme Court

The common law draws its subsistence from [Christianity, and] . . . the Christian concept of right and wrong, or right and justice, motivates every rule of equity. It is the guide by which we dissolve domestic frictions and the rule by which all legal controversies are settled.[317]

1950, Mississippi Supreme Court
Our great country is denominated a Christian nation. We imprint "In God we trust" on our currency. Our state has even sometimes been referred to by cynics as being in the "Bible Belt." It cannot be denied that much of the legislative philosophy of this state and nation has been inspired by the Golden Rule and the Sermon on the Mount and other portions of the Holy Scriptures.[318]

1959, Oklahoma Supreme Court
[I]t is well settled and understood that ours is a Christian Nation, holding the Almighty God in dutiful reverence. . . . [W]e are a Christian Nation and a Christian State.[319]

Evidentiary Source #7: Prominent American Educators

Those who taught American students about their own country affirmed that America was a Christian nation. One such prominent educator was Noah Webster, a soldier in the Revolution and afterwards a legislator and a judge. Titled "America's Schoolmaster" for his significant contributions to education, Webster affirmed:

> [T]he Christian religion, in its purity, is the basis, or rather the source of all genuine freedom in government. . . . [N]o civil government of a republican form can exist and be durable in which the principles of that religion have not a controlling influence.[320]

His textbooks therefore instructed students:

> The brief exposition of the Constitution of the United States will unfold to young persons the principles of republican government and . . . that the genuine source of correct republican principles is the Bible, particularly the New Testament or the Christian religion.[321]

Benjamin Rush, a signer of the Declaration, was also one of America's top educators. In fact, he was the first founder to advocate free public schools for all youth,[322] for which he may properly be titled "The Father of Public Schools Under the Constitution." Rush asserted:

[T]he only means of establishing and perpetuating our republican forms of government . . . is the universal education of our youth in the principles of Christianity by means of the Bible.[323]

Similar declarations can be found from other leading educators, including Dr. John Witherspoon (signer of the Declaration and president of Princeton),[324] Dr. Jedidiah Morse (the "Father of American Geography"),[325] Dr. William Samuel Johnson (signer of the Constitution and president of Columbia),[326] Benjamin Franklin (signer of the Declaration and Constitution and founder of the University of Pennsylvania),[327] Dr. Calvin Stowe (college professor and founder of the College of Teachers of Ohio),[328] Dr. William Holmes McGuffey (president of three universities and "The Schoolmaster of the Nation"),[329] Horace Mann ("The Father of the American Common School"),[330] Charles Finney (president of Oberlin College—one of the first schools to admit men and women, blacks and whites, as equals),[331] Booker T. Washington (head of Tuskegee Institute),[332] Emma Willard (pioneer of academic education for women),[333] and many other notable educators.

So thoroughly did Christian principles permeate American education that a perusal of the textbook library of the Department of Education (housing thousands of textbooks used in America's schools from 1775 through 1900)[334] demonstrates that it is difficult to find *any* area of curricular studies that did not incorporate the Bible and Christian principles.

Evidentiary Source #8: Foreign Observers

Those from foreign nations who studied America to describe it to their fellow citizens also affirmed that America was a Christian nation. For example, Alexis de Tocqueville (1805–59), a historian and political writer from France, candidly reported:

The greatest part of . . . America was peopled by men who . . . brought with them into the New World a form of Christianity which I cannot better describe than by styling it a democratic and republican religion. This sect contributed powerfully to the establishment of a democracy and a republic, and from the earliest settlement of the emigrants, politics and religion contracted an alliance which has never been dissolved.[335]

[T]here is no country in the whole world in which the Christian religion retains a greater influence over the souls of men than in America—and there can be no greater proof of its utility and of its conformity to human nature than that its influence is most powerfully felt over the most enlightened and free nation of the earth.[336]

Upon my arrival in the United States, the religious aspect of the country was the first thing that struck my attention; and the longer I stayed there, the more did I perceive the great political consequences resulting from this state of things, to which I was unaccustomed. In France I had almost always seen the spirit of religion and the spirit of freedom pursuing courses diametrically opposed to each other; but in America I found that they were intimately united, and that they reigned in common over the same country.[337]

Other foreign visitors who wrote with equal candor of America as a Christian nation included Swiss citizen and German educator Philip Schaff,[338] English writer Edward Augustus Kendall,[339] French nobleman Achille Murat,[340] English writer Harriet Martineau,[341] and others.

These eight categories of evidence all proclaim the same truth, causing the U. S. Supreme Court in 1892 to conclude in a unanimous decision:

These are not individual sayings, declarations of private persons: they are organic utterances; they speak the voice of the entire people.... These, and many other matters which might be noticed, add a volume of unofficial declarations to the mass of organic utterances that this is a Christian nation.[342]

In fact, no other conclusion is possible after an honest examination of America's history. If anyone claims otherwise, it is because he is determined not to see the truth. In the words of military chaplain William Biederwolf (1867–1939), he is just as likely to "look all over the sky at high noon on a cloudless day and not see the sun."[343]

Conclusions: Historical and Modern

History proves that America was founded as a Christian nation, that Christianity shaped our major institutions, and that Christianity still influences our modern society and culture. Yet, is America still a Christian nation today? Measuring by the historical definition set forth at the beginning (i.e., a nation founded upon Christian and biblical principles, whose society and institutions are shaped by those principles), the answer remains yes—albeit judicial activism has certainly weakened the certainty of that answer as courts have undertaken an apparent crusade to expunge Christian influences, past and present, from many societal institutions and arenas.

While few Americans today will publicly acknowledge America to be a Christian nation for fear of the vicious attacks and derision they may face, in private most will still make that acknowledgment. In fact, recent national polls report that some two-thirds of the nation *currently* believes that America *is* a "Christian nation,"[344] As a recent report affirms:

> Majorities of all of the typology groups consider the United States to be "a Christian nation," with 71 percent overall saying that it is. Liberals and Disadvantaged Democrats are least likely to agree, but even among these groups, 57 percent say the U. S. is a Christian nation.[345]

Americans not only overwhelmingly acknowledge America to be a Christian nation but they also overwhelmingly choose Christianity as their personal religion. Even though citizens under America's free-market religious system have been exposed to every conceivable type of religion, according to dozens of polls over recent decades, an average of over 75 percent profess Christianity to be their personal religion.[346] The next largest religious affiliation is Jewish (about 1 percent),[347] and other groups are even smaller, with Muslims ranking third (0.6 percent), then Buddhism (0.5 percent),[348] and then still smaller groups such as Native American, Scientologist, Baha'i,

Taoist, New Age, Eckankar, Rastafarian, Sikh, Wiccan, Deity, Druid, Santeria, Pagan, Spiritualist, Ethical Culture, etc.[349] The combined total of the nearly fifty non-Christian religions in America[350] is consistently under 4 percent (but has occasionally ranged as high as 6 percent). Those claiming no religion varies from 10 to 16 percent, with atheists at only 0.7 percent and agnostics at 0.9 percent;[351] and those claiming "humanist" or "secular" as their religion are too small to report any national percentage. Only 16 percent of Americans claim to be "secular" or "somewhat secular" in their viewpoint, while 75 percent are religiously orientated.

How do these numbers in America stack up against the rest of the world? According to a recent ARIS (American Religious Identification Survey), 76 percent of Americans claim Christianity as their religion whereas only 33 percent of the rest of the world does; and while non-Christian religions represent 4 percent of Americans, they represent 52 percent of the rest of the world.[352] Richard Parker of the Kennedy School of Government at Harvard University accurately concludes: "The United States is more Christian than Israel is Jewish, or India is Hindu."[353] Undeniably, by choice, Christianity remains (as it has from the beginning) the predominant religious faith of Americans, despite the overt hostility regularly manifested against it.

Another factor inhibiting the public acknowledgment of America as a Christian nation stems from the numerous hostile judicial rulings that actively suppress Christianity but elevate other religions. This current policy is based on the Supreme Court's new "classes of religion" approach—an approach critically described by Justice Kennedy:

> [T]he Supreme Court of the United States has concluded that the First Amendment creates classes of religions based on the relative numbers of their adherents. Those religions enjoying the largest following must be consigned to the status of least-favored faiths so as to avoid any possible risk of offending members of minority religions.[354]

Consequently:

- Jewish and Islamic holiday symbols may be publicly displayed but not Christian ones,[355] and schools may sing songs about Jewish but not Christian holidays.[356]
- Classrooms may include information on Eastern oriental and Native American religions but not Christianity.[357]
- The U. S. military may provide Islamic materials for enemy captives but American soldiers who are Christians and serving in harm's way may not receive Christian materials from their families for their own personal use. (One national columnist concluded: "Islamist Fifth Columnists are benefiting from the very guarantees of religious freedom being denied to devout Christian soldiers.")[358]
- Schools may accommodate the distinct religious dress and clothing preferences of Muslim students[359] but not Christian ones.[360]
- Schools may require all students to participate in a three-week intensive indoctrination to Islam but not Christianity.[361]

An attorney with the Thomas More Law Center (a public-interest law firm that litigates to defend Christian values and expressions) correctly concludes:

Islam and other religions—specifically those that are not the dominant religions in America—are constantly being allowed to do things that Christianity cannot. . . . [I]n federal court and schools around the country, Christianity is "out" while Islam is "in."[362]

In short, 0.6 percent of Americans (i.e., Muslims) are allowed to do what 73 percent of Americans (i.e., Christians) cannot, even though the rights of both are supposed to be equally protected under the Constitution. Earlier courts—such as the 1859 Supreme Court of Pennsylvania—certainly would have found such a policy untenable:

It would be strange that a people Christian in doctrine and worship, many of whom (or whose forefathers) had sought these shores for the privilege of worshipping God in simplicity and purity of faith, and who regarded religion as the basis of their civil liberty and the foundation of their rights, should, in their zeal to secure to all the freedom of conscience which they valued so highly, solemnly repudiate and put beyond the pale of the law the religion which was dear to them as life and dethrone the God who they openly and avowedly professed to believe had been their protector and guide as a people.[363]

The overwhelming majority of Americans profess Christianity as their personal faith, privately hold that America *is* a Christian nation, and believe that their Christian faith has been made a public target. A recent poll affirmed that 77 percent of the nation believes that "the courts have overreacted in driving religion out of public life," and 59 percent believe that judges have singled out Christianity for attack.[364] Yet, even though Americans still consider America to be a Christian nation, does it really matter whether or not it actually is? Yes—for at least three reasons.

Reason #1: The Continuation of the World's Most Successful System

If the integrity of a building's foundation is compromised, the structure dependent on that foundation is endangered. For example, if the foundation of the Empire State Building in New York City, or the Sears Tower in Chicago, were removed and replaced with a completely different one, the entire structure would be placed in extreme peril, with the greatest likelihood of permanent and irreversible damage. The same is true with American government and society.

American institutions were constructed on the foundation of Christian principles. As a result, those institutions benefit not just Christians but every individual and every faith in the nation; if that foundation is removed, then all (and not just Christians) will experience the adverse effects. As legal writer Stephen Cowell affirmed in 1854:

Ours are Christian political institutions; they are not merely intended as convenient safe-guards under which Christians may dwell in peace and quietness—they are not designed merely for the negative object of administering justice and protecting person and property—they are powers designed to be exercised for *human* [and not just Christian] advantage.[365] (emphasis added)

The continuation of America's unique government and society is dependent on preserving the foundation of Christianity from which those civil blessings originate.

Reason #2: The Preservation of Inalienable Rights and Limited Government

American government was established on the premise that certain rights are given by God rather than government, and that those rights have been placed beyond the reach of government.

The Framers openly acknowledged that "all men . . . are endowed by their Creator with certain inalienable rights" and then took care to define "inalienable rights." For example, John Dickinson defined an inalienable right as one "which God gave to you and which no inferior power has a right to take away";[366] and John Adams affirmed that inalienable rights were "rights antecedent to all earthly government—rights . . . [that] cannot be repealed or restrained by human laws—rights derived from the great Legislator of the universe."[367] In short, an inalienable right was a right that God bestowed on every individual, regardless of race, gender, or social station.

Having asserted that God Himself gave man specific rights, the Framers next declared that "to secure these rights, governments are instituted among men," thus establishing that the purpose of government is to protect every individual's God-given rights. James Wilson, signer of the Declaration and Constitution, asserted that "every government which has not this in view as its principal object is not a government of the legitimate kind,"[368] and Thomas Jefferson similarly affirmed that the purpose of government "is to declare and enforce only our natural [inalienable] rights and duties and to take none of them from us."[369]

Among the God-given rights that American government was to protect were the first three specifically listed in the Declaration of Independence, "life, liberty, and the pursuit of happiness." Significantly, the Framers defined the "pursuit of happiness" as being the God-given right of acquiring, possessing, and protecting private property.[370] As Declaration signer Samuel Adams explained, "Among the natural [inalienable] rights of the colonists are these: first, a right to life; secondly, to liberty; thirdly, to property."[371]

Further inalienable rights were subsequently listed in the Bill of Rights. According to Albert Gallatin (a ratifier of the Constitution, a framer of Bill of Rights proposals, and secretary of the Treasury for Presidents Jefferson and Madison):

> The whole of that Bill [of Rights] is a declaration of the rights of the people at large or considered as individuals. . . . [I]t establishes . . . rights of the individual as *inalienable*.[372] (emphasis added)

For example, the First Amendment in the Bill of Rights protects the inalienable, God-given rights of conscience and religious expression. As James Madison affirmed:

> The religion, then, of every man must be left to the conviction and conscience of every man; and it is the right of every man to exercise it as these may dictate. This right is in its nature an *unalienable* right.[373] (emphasis added)

The Second Amendment secures the inalienable right of individuals to defend their lives, their families, and their property from aggression, whether by an individual or a government. As Alexander Hamilton acknowledged:

> [T]he Supreme Being . . . invested him [man] with an *inviolable right* to personal liberty and personal safety.[374] (emphasis added)

The Third Amendment established the sanctity of the private home and set it beyond the intrusion of government. As

James Wilson confirmed, "[E]very man's house is deemed by the law to be his castle; and the law . . . invests him with the power . . . of the commanding officer."[375]

The Fourth through Eighth Amendments forbid the government from depriving an individual of his God-given rights of life and personal liberty except through rigorous and stringent due process.

The Fifth Amendment additionally secured the inalienable rights of property. As noted by Bill of Rights framer Fisher Ames: "The chief duty and care of all governments is to protect the rights of *property*."[376] John Adams similarly affirmed, "*Property* must be secured, or liberty cannot exist"[377] (emphasis added).

In short, the Framers established American government on the thesis that certain rights came from God, not men, and that government was to protect those rights inviolable. So long as the recognition exists that specific rights cannot be infringed because they are God-given, those rights will remain safe. However, if that conviction is lost, then government will begin to regulate, alter, or even repeal those rights. Understanding this, Thomas Jefferson succinctly warned:

[C]an the liberties of a nation be thought secure when we have removed their only firm basis: a conviction in the minds of the people that these liberties are of the gift of God?— that they are not to be violated but with His wrath?[378]

Significantly, the increased secularization of public policy has resulted in a noticeable decrease in protection for many rights that were once considered inalienable. Citizens are now punished for praying or exercising their faith, prosecuted for defending their homes against criminal intrusions, and have their properties and businesses seized by government and given to others whom the government believes might produce more tax income. Legal process has been so perverted that guilty criminals often have more rights and greater protections than innocent victims. In short, the more secular the government, the more intrusive and overreaching it becomes and the less protected are personal rights—the second reason that our Christian nation must be preserved.

Reason #3: Preservation of the Culture

A society's culture is manifested in its art, manners, and behavior, each of which stems from the country's morals—its customary sense of right and wrong. In America, Christianity formed the basis of our societal beliefs and morals—a fact regularly acknowledged by previous courts:

> [T]he morality of the country is deeply engrafted upon Christianity. . . . [We are] people whose manners . . . and whose morals have been elevated and inspired . . . by means of the Christian religion.[379] (NEW YORK SUPREME COURT, 1811)

> Christianity has reference to the principles of right and wrong . . . it is the foundation of those morals and manners upon which our society is formed; it is their basis. . . . What constitutes the standard of good morals? Is it not Christianity? There certainly is none other. Say that cannot be appealed to and . . . what would be good morals?[380] (SOUTH CAROLINA SUPREME COURT, 1846)

Christianity provided a system of morals, and from that system of morals sprang the common law that defined America's major societal offenses (e.g., arson, robbery, rape, murder, assault, theft, polygamy, incest, etc.).

Significantly, there has always been a direct relationship between a society's morals and its laws. As Benjamin Franklin insightfully queried, "[W]hat can laws do without morals?"[381] Some today assert that "you can't legislate morality," but such claims are ridiculous: every law that exists is the legislation of morality. As John Witherspoon, signer of the Declaration, affirmed: "[C]onsider all morality in general as conformity to a law."[382]

Therefore, a nation's culture (including America's culture) is shaped by its morals, produced by its religion. As affirmed by constitutional law professor Edward Mansfield in 1851:

> In every country, the morals of a people—whatever they may be—take their form and spirit from their religion. For example, the marriage of brothers and sisters was permitted among the Egyptians because such had been the prec-

edent set by their gods, Isis and Osiris. So, too, the classic nations celebrated the drunken rites of Bacchus. Thus, too, the Turk has become lazy and inert because dependent upon Fate, as taught by the Koran. And when in recent times there arose a nation whose philosophers discovered there was no God and no religion, the nation was thrown into that dismal case in which there was no law and no morals. . . . In the United States, Christianity is the original, spontaneous, and national religion.[383]

If America should change from being a Christian nation, its culture (i.e., its morals and therefore its laws) would dramatically change. Consider what such a change might mean in just one area—that of free speech and dissent.

In America today, Muslims may (and do) take to the streets to protest our government's role in the War on Terror, and its support of Israel. Yet, would a Muslim culture allow similar protests against its government? or a Communistic culture? or a secular one? or a Buddhist?—would France, North Korea, Russia, India, Pakistan, Saudi Arabia, Turkey, etc., allow what America does in the areas of free speech and dissent? Certainly not—and this is only one example of how Christianity in America has produced a culture distinctively different from that of other nations. The continuance of the unique and laudable aspects of our culture is dependent on America remaining a Christian nation.

Based on the historical definitions, America was (and still is) a true Christian nation. Strikingly, the Christian nation that the secular left tries so diligently to portray has not existed in five centuries and is a nation in which no one today (including Christians) would choose to live. Furthermore, no such nation is visible even on the farthest distant horizon; that hypothetical nation exists only in the fantasies of critics—fantasies not grounded in realities. The fact is that all Americans (whether Christian, Jewish, Muslim, secular, or whatever) benefit from America remaining a Christian nation and should therefore seek to preserve rather than overthrow those foundations.

[T]hey, therefore, who are decrying the Christian religion . . . are undermining . . . the best security for the

duration of free governments.[384] (CHARLES CARROLL, SIGNER
OF THE DECLARATION, FRAMER OF THE BILL OF RIGHTS)

Endnotes

[1] John Adams letter to Thomas Jefferson, June 28, 1813, in *The Works of John Adams*, vol. 10, ed. C. F. Adams (Boston: Little, Brown and Company, 1850), 45–46.

[2] "The Israelites of South Carolina," *The Occident and American Jewish Advocate* II, no. 10 (January, 1845), available online at http://216.247.171.108/ Occident/volume2/jan1845/churchstate.html. See also *Allegheny v. ACLU*, 492 U.S. 573 (1989).

[3] M. Seesholtz, "Theocracy Alert: Theocratizing FEMA and Pregnancy," *Online Journal* (October 17, 2005), available online at http://www.onlinejournal .com/TheocracyAlert/html/101705seesholtz.html.

[4] B. Moyers, "9/11 And the Sport of God," *TomPaine.com* (September 9, 2005), available online at http://www.tompaine.com/articles/2005/09/09/911 _and_the_sport_of_god.php.

[5] J. Ward, "Left aims to smite 'theocracy' movement," *Washington Times* (May 1, 2005), available online at http://www.washingtontimes.com/functions /print.php?StoryID=20050501–124025–3104r.

[6] F. Rick, "A High-Tech Lynching in Prime Time," *New York Times* (April 24, 2005), available online at http://www.nytimes.com/2005/04/24/opinion/24rich .html?ex=1271995200&en=a0fbd4145b6785e0&ei=5090&partner=rssuserland &emc=rss.

[7] M. Goldberg, "In Theocracy They Trust," *Salon.com* (April 11, 2005), available at http://dir.salon.com/story/news/feature/2005/04/11/judicial_conference/ print.html).

[8] See for example Seesholtz, "Theocracy Alert: Theocratizing FEMA and Pregnancy"; a *New York Times* ad available at http://worldcantwait.net/flier/ nyt.pdf; J. M. Phillips, "When Columnists Cry 'Jihad'," *Washington Post* (May 4, 2005), available online at http://www.washingtonpost.com/wp-dyn/content /article/2005/05/03/AR2005050301277.html.

[9] C. Hedges, "Soldiers of Christ: Feeling the Hate with the National Religious Broadcasters," *Harper's Magazine* (July, 2005), available online at http://www .harpers.org/archive/2005/05/0080541.

[10] J. Cole, "The Schiavo Case and the Islamization of the Republican Party," *JuanCole.com* (March 22, 2005), available online at http://www.juancole .com/2005/03/schiavo-case-and-islamization-of.html.

[11] K. Yurica, "The Despoiling of America: How George W. Bush Became the Head of the New American Dominionist Church/State," *Yurica Report* (February 11,2004), available at http://www.yuricareport.com/Dominionism/TheDespoiling OfAmerica.htm.

[12] 71% in 2005, 62% in 2009, etc. See for example "Beyond Red vs. Blue," *Pew Research Center* (May 10, 2005), available online at: http://people-press .org/reports/display.php3?PageID=948; J. Harper, "Political Poll Finds Shades Between Red, Blue," *Washington Times* (May 11, 2005), available online at http://www.washtimes.com/national/20050510–113813–9288r.htm; "One Nation Under God?" *Newsweek* (April 6, 2009), available online at http://www.newsweek .com/2009/04/06/one-nation-under-god.html.

[13] D. J. Brewer, *The United States: A Christian Nation* (Philadelphia: John D. Winston Co., 1905; reprinted Atlanta: American Vision, 1996), 13–14.

¹⁴ Ibid., 40.

¹⁵ See for example *The Reports of Committees of the Senate of the United States for the Second Session of the Thirty-Second Congress* (Washington: Robert Armstrong, 1853), 3; *The Reports of Committees of the House of Representatives First Session of the Thirty-Third Congress* (Washington: Robert Armstrong), 3, 6, 8–9; J. Story, *Commentaries on the Constitution of the United States*, vol. III (Boston: Hilliard, Gray & Co., 1833), 722–27.

¹⁶ John Marshall letter to Jasper Adams, May 9, 1833, in *The Papers of John Marshall*, vol. XII, ed. C. Hobson (Chapel Hill: University of North Carolina Press, 2006), 278.

¹⁷ C. Rossiter, *Seedtime of the Republic: Origin of the American Tradition of Political Liberty* (New York: Harcourt, Brace & Co., 1953), 2.

¹⁸ J. Wise, *A Vindication of the Government of New-England Churches* (Boston: John Boyles, 1772), 3.

¹⁹ Ibid., 5.

²⁰ Ibid., 6.

²¹ E. S. Bates, *American Faith* (New York: W. W. Norton & Company Inc., 1940), 34. See also J. L. Adams, *Yankee Doodle Went to Church* (Old Tappan, NJ: Revell, 1989), 42.

²² J. M. Mathews, *The Bible and Civil Government, in a Course of Lectures* (New York: Robert Carter & Brothers, 1851), 231.

²³ C. B. Galloway, *Christianity and the American Commonwealth* (Nashville: Publishing House Methodist Episcopal Church, 1898), 20.

²⁴ Ibid., 17.

²⁵ Rossiter, *Seedtime of the Republic*, 36.

²⁶ D. Lutz, *The Origins of American Constitutionalism* (Baton Rouge: Louisiana State University Press, 1988), 144–46.

²⁷ Baron De Montesquieu, *The Spirit of Laws*, vol. II (Worcester: Isaiah Thomas, 1802), 127.

²⁸ Ibid., 129.

²⁹ Rossiter, *Seedtime of the Republic*, 39, quoting E. Burke, *Works*, II:34–35.

³⁰ "The First Charter of Virginia, 1606," in *The Federal and State Constitutions, Colonial Charters, and Other Organic Laws*, ed. F. N. Thorpe (Washington: Government Printing Office, 1909), 3784.

³¹ "The First Legislative Assembly at Jamestown, Virginia," *National Park Service*, available online at http://www.nps.gov/jame/historyculture/the-first -legislative-assembly.htm (accessed on August 30, 2010).

³² C. B. Galloway, *Christianity and the American Commonwealth* (Nashville: Publishing House Methodist Episcopal Church, 1898), 1131–34; J. Fiske, *Civil Government in the United States Considered with some Reference to Its Origins* (Boston: Houghton, Mifflin & Co., 1890), 146.

³³ "Words of John Robinson (1620)," in *Old South Leaflets* (Boston: Directors of the Old South Work, n.d.), 372; "John Robinson's Farewell Letter to the Pilgrims, July 22, 1620," *Pilgrim Hall Museum*, available online at http://www .pilgrimhall.org/RobinsonLetter.htm.

³⁴ "Agreement Between the Settlers at New Plymouth: 1620/ The Mayflower Compact 1620," *The Avalon Project*, available online at http://www.yale.edu /lawweb/avalon/amerdoc/mayflower.htm.

³⁵ "Plymouth Colony Legal Structure," *Plymouth Colony Archive Project*, 1998, available online at http://etext.virginia.edu/users/deetz/Plymouth/ccflaw. html. See also R. Baird, *Religion in America* (New York: Harper & Brothers, 1845), 51.

³⁶ "Plymouth Colony Legal Structure."

[37] "The Charter of Massachusetts Bay—1691," *The Avalon Project*, available online at http://www.yale.edu/lawweb/avalon/states/mass07.htm.

[38] "Massachusetts Bay," *USAhistory.info*, available online at http://www.usa history.info/New-England/Massachusetts.html (accessed on August 30, 2010).

[39] "Plymouth Colony Legal Structure."

[40] G. Bancroft, *History of the United States from the Discovery of the American Continent*, vol. I (Boston: Little, Brown & Co., 1858), 416–17; Galloway, *Christianity and the American Commonwealth*, 124–25; "The Body of Liberties: The Liberties of the Massachusetts Colonie in New England, 1641," in *Old South Leaflets* (Boston: Directors of the Old South Work, n.d.), 261–80.

[41] "The Charter of Maryland," in *Historical Collections: Consisting of State Papers and other Authentic Documents: Intended as Materials for an History of the United States of America*, vol. I, ed. E. Hazard (Philadelphia: T. Dobson, 1792), 327–28,.

[42] "An Act What Persons Shall Be Called to Every General Assembly and an Act Concerning the Calling of General Assemblies, 1638," in *Colonial Origins of the American Constitution*, ed. D. S. Lutz, (Indianapolis: Liberty Fund, 1998), 305.

[43] W. MacDonald, *Select Charters and Other Documents Illustrative of American History 1606–1775* (New York: MacMillan Company, 1899), 104–6.

[44] "Maryland," *USAhistory.info*, available online at http://www.usahistory. info/southern/Maryland.html (accessed on August 30, 2010); "Senate: Origins and Functions," *Maryland State Archives* (January, 2001), available online at http://www.mdarchives.state.md.us/msa/mdmanual/05sen/html/senf.html.

[45] Charter of Rhode Island and Providence Plantations—1663," in *The Federal and State Constitutions, Colonial Charters and Other Organic Laws*, vol. VI, ed. F. N. Thorpe (Washington: Government Printing Office, 1909), 3211.

[46] Ibid., 3214.

[47] "Connecticut to 1763," *Connecticut's Heritage Gateway*, available online at http://www.ctheritage.org/encyclopedia/ctto1763/overviewctto1763.htm (accessed on August 30, 2010).

[48] "Charter of Connecticut—1662," in *The Federal and State Constitutions, Colonial Charters, and Other Organic Laws*, vol. 1, ed. F. N. Thorpe (Washington: Government Printing Office, 1909), 534.

[49] Ibid.

[50] C. Rossiter, *Seedtime of the Republic*, 171.

[51] J. Fiske, *The Beginnings of New England* (Boston: Houghton, Mifflin & Co., 1898), 127–28.

[52] C. Rossiter, *Seedtime of the Republic*, 33.

[53] D. Webster, *Address Delivered at Bunker Hill, June 17, 1843, on the Completion of the Monument* (Boston: T. R. Marvin, 1843), 31.

[54] Fiske, *The Beginnings of New England*, 267, 269, 270, 272.

[55] Wise, *A Vindication of the Government of New-England Churches* (Boston: John Boyles, 1772), 45.

[56] T. F. Waters and E. W. F. Felten, *Top Ipswich Patriots* (Printed for the Historical Society, 1927), available online at http://www.bwlord.com/Ipswich /Waters/TwoPatriots/JohnWise.htm.

[57] J. Fiske, *Old Virginia and Her Neighbors*, vol. II (Boston: Houghton, Mifflin, and Company, 1901), 57; J. Fiske, *Old Virginia and Her Neighbors*, vol. I (Boston: Houghton, Mifflin, and Company, 1901), 306, 311.

[58] *Dictionary of American Biography*, s.v. "Samuel Cooper."

[59] A. M. Baldwin, *The New England Clergy and the American Revolution* (New York: Frederick Ungar, 1958), 90; S. Mansfield, *Forgotten Founding Father: The Heroic Legacy of George Whitefield* (Cumberland House, 2001), 112.

[60] Mansfield, *Forgotten Founding Father*, 112.

[61] C. H. Van Tyne, *The Causes of the War of Independence* (Boston: Houghton and Mifflin, Company, 1922), 362.

[62] J. Adams, *Diary and Autobiography of John Adams*, vol. I, ed. L. H. Butterfield (Cambridge: Harvard University Press, 1962), 263.

[63] John Adams letter to Hezekiah Niles, February 13, 1818, in *The Works of John Adams*, X:284.

[64] F. Cole, *They Preached Liberty* (New York: 1941), 36.

[65] J. T. Headley, *The Chaplains and Clergy of the Revolution* (New York: Scribner, 1864), 68.

[66] Ibid., 69.

[67] Ibid., 71–72.

[68] Cole, *They Preached Liberty*, 36.

[69] Headley, *The Chaplains and Clergy of the Revolution*, 72.

[70] Ibid., 69.

[71] D. Dorchester, *Christianity in the United States from the First Settlement Down to the Present Time* (New York: Phillips & Hunt, 1888), 265.

[72] B. F. Morris, *Christian Life and Character of the Civil Institutions of the United States* (Philadelphia: George W. Childs, 1864), 350; Dorchester, *Christianity in the United States*, 265, 267, 269.

[73] Headley, *The Chaplains and Clergy of the Revolution*, 58.

[74] Morris, *Christian Life and Character*, 350; Dorchester, *Christianity in the United States*, 266–67.

[75] Morris, *Christian Life and Character*, 366; W. W. Sweet, *The Story of Religion in America* (New York: Harper & Brothers Publishers, 1950), 182; F. Moore, *Patriot Preachers of the American Revolution* (New York: L.A. Osborne, 1860), 258–61.

[76] George Washington letter to Benjamin Lincoln, February 28, 1788, in *The Writings of George Washington*, vol. IX (Boston: Russel, Odiorne and Metcalf, 1835), 330; Moore, *Patriot Preachers of the American Revolution*, 260; A. Baldwin, *The New England Clergy and the American Revolution*, 172; J. Eidsmoe, *Christianity and the Constitution* (Grand Rapids: Baker, 1987), 352; J. H. Smylie, "American Clergymen and the Constitution of the United States of America 1781–1796" (PhD diss., Princeton Theological Seminary, 1958), iii, 127, 139–43, 185–86.

[77] Eidsmoe, *Christianity and the Constitution*, 352n.15.

[78] See for example Smylie, "American Clergymen and the Constitution of the United States of America," 185–86; Baldwin, *The New England Clergy and the American Revolution*, 145, 172; Benjamin Rush letter to Elias Boudinot, July 9, 1788, in *Letters of Benjamin Rush*, vol. I, ed. L. H. Butterfield (Princeton: American Philosophical Society, 1951), 474; Moore, *Patriot Preachers of the American Revolution*, 260.

[79] N. Webster, *History of the United States* (New Haven, CT: Durrie & Peck, 1832), 339.

[80] John Jay, "Address to the Annual Meeting of the American Bible Society," in *Correspondence and Public Papers of John Jay*, vol. IV, ed. H. P. Johnston (New York: G. P. Putnam's Sons, 1893), 491; J. Q. Adams, *An Oration Delivered Before the Inhabitants of the Town of Newburyport at Their Request on the Sixty-First Anniversary of the Declaration of Independence* (Newburyport: Charles Whipple, 1837), 17; J. Adams, "Speech to Both Houses of Congress," in *The Works of John Adams*, vol. IX, ed. C. F. Adams (Boston: Little, Brown and Company, 1850), 121; D. Webster, "Discourse Delivered at Plymouth in Commemoration of the First Settlement of New England," in *Speeches and Forensic*

Arguments, vol. I (Boston: Tappan & Dennet, 1843), 56; *Updegraph v. The Commonwealth*, 11 S. & R. 394 (Sup. Ct. Pa. 1824).

[81] Thomas Jefferson letter to Joseph Jones, August 14, 1787, in *The Works of Thomas Jefferson*, vol. V, ed. P. L. Ford (New York: G. P. Putnam's Sons, 1904), 332.

[82] Benjamin Rush letter to Thomas Jefferson, August 22, 1800, in *Letters of Benjamin Rush,* vol. II, ed. L. H. Butterfield (Princeton: American Philosophical Society, 1951), 820–21.

[83] John Adams to Benjamin Rush, February 2, 1807, in *The Spur of Fame: Dialogues of John Adams and Benjamin Rush 1805–1813*, ed. J. A. Schutz (Indianapolis: Liberty Fund, Inc., 1966), 82.

[84] Webster, *History of the United States*, 6.

[85] M. Luther, "Temporal Authority: To What Extent It Should Be Obeyed," University of Oregon, available online at http://www.uoregon.edu/~sshoemak/323/texts/luther~1.htm; J. Arminius, "On Reconciling Religious Dissensions Among Christians," available online at http://www.godrules.net/library/arminius/arminius6.htm (accessed on August 31, 2010); "Founders Constitution: John Calvin, Institutes of the Christian Religion," University of Chicago, available online at http://press-pubs.uchicago.edu/founders/documents/amendI_religions1.html; R. Hooker, *The Works of the Learned and Judicious Divine Richard Hooker*, vol. II (Oxford: University Press, 1845), 485–90.

[86] "Theodosian Code, XVI.1.2," *Documents of the Christian Church*, ed. H. Bettenson (London: Oxford University Press, 1943), 31.

[87] Van Tyne, *The Causes of the War of Independence*, 3.

[88] See, for example, Wise, *A Vindication of the Government of New England Churches*, 47–48.

[89] Rossiter, *Seedtime of the Republic*, 198; P. Hamburger, *The Separation of Church and State* (Cambridge: Harvard University Press, 2002), 76.

[90] Galloway, *Christianity and the American Commonwealth*, 144.

[91] F. D. Roosevelt, "Address before the Federal Council of Churches of Christ in America," *The American Presidency Project*, available online at http://www.presidency.ucsb.edu/ws/?pid=14574.

[92] Thomas Jefferson letter to Nehemiah Dodge, Ephraim Robbins, and Stephen S. Nelson, a Committee of the Danbury Baptist Association, in the State of Connecticut, January 1, 1802, in *Writings of Thomas Jefferson*, vol. XVI (Washington DC: Thomas Jefferson Memorial Association, 1904), 281–82.

[93] "Kentucky Resolutions," in *The Jeffersonian Cyclopedia*, ed. J. P. Foley (New York: Funk & Wagnalls, 1900), 977; T. Jefferson, "Inaugural Speech," March 4, 1805, in *Debates and Proceedings of the Congress of the United States*, 8th Congress (Washington, DC: Gales and Seaton, 1852), 78; Thomas Jefferson letter to the Society of the Methodist Episcopal Church, December 9, 1808, in *Writings of Thomas Jefferson*, vol. XVI (Washington, DC: Thomas Jefferson Memorial Association, 1904), 325; Thomas Jefferson letter to Samuel Millar, January 23, 1808, in *Memoir, Correspondence, and Miscellanies, From the Papers of Thomas Jefferson*, vol. IV, ed. T. J. Randolph (Boston: Gray and Bowen, 1830), 103–4.

[94] *Reynolds v. U.S.*, 98 U.S. 145, 162164 (1878).

[95] W. C. Wood, *Five Problems of State and Religion* (Boston: Henry Hoyt, 1877), 168.

[96] P. Schaff, *America: A Sketch of Its Political, Social, and Religious Character,* ed. P. Miller (1855; reprint, Cambridge: Harvard University Press, 1961), 73.

[97] Wood, *Five Problems of State and Religion*, 92.

[98] Galloway, *Christianity and the American Commonwealth*, 143.

[99] *Zorach v. Clauson*, 343 U.S. 306, 312315 (1952).

[100] Adams, *Yankee Doodle Went to Church*, 11, 14.

[101] *Reports of Committees of the House of Representatives Made During the First Session of the Thirty-Third Congress* (Washington, DC: A. O. P. Nicholson, 1854), 6.

[102] *Americans United for Separation of Church and State v. Prison Fellowship Ministries, Inc.*, U.S. Court of Appeals for the Eighth Circuit, No. 062741, Nov. 22, 2006.

[103] *Harris v. City of Zion*, 927 F.2d 1401 (7th Cir. 1991); *Robinson v. City of Edmond*, 68 F.3d 1226 (10th Cir. 1995); Marjie Lundstrom, "At a Crossroads for Diversity, ACLU Helps Officials Take Right Path," *Sacramento Bee* (June 3, 2004), available online at http://dwb.sacbee.com/content/politics/story/9518766p10442623c.html; *Doe v. Santa Fe Independent School District*, Civil Action No. G–95–176 (S.D. Tex. 1995) (court transcription of verbal ruling by Federal Judge Samuel Kent, 3–4); *Hinrichs v. Bosma*, 400 F. Supp. 2d 1103, 1120 (S.D. Ind. Nov. 30, 2005); *Doe v. Tangipahoa Parish School Board*, No. 05–30294 (5th Cir. Dec. 15, 2006); *Coles v. Cleveland Board of Education*, 171 F.3d 369 (6th Cir. 1999); *Wynne v. Town of Great Falls*, 376 F.3d 292 (4th Cir. 2004); *Rubin v. City of Burbank*, 124 Cal. Rptr. 2d 867 (Cal. Ct. App. 2002); *Lee v. Weisman*, 505 U.S. 577 (1992).

[104] Jay, "Address at the Annual Meeting of the American Bible Society," 491–92.

[105] M. Simons, "A Brief Complaint or Apology of the Despised Christians and Exiled Strangers," in *The Complete Works of Menno Simon* (Ann Arbor: University of Michigan Library, 2005), 118, available online at http://www.hti.umich.edu/cgi/t/text/text-idx?c=moa;cc=moa;rgn=main;view=text;idno=AGV9043.0002.001.

[106] J. Arminius, "Disputation LVI on the Power of the Church in Enacting Laws," in *The Works of James Arminius*, vol. 2, ed. J. Nichols (Auburn: Derby and Miller, 1853), available online at http://www.archive.org/stream/worksofarminius02armiuoft#page/136/mode/2up.

[107] J. Calvin, *Institutes of the Christian Religion*, Book III, Chapter 19, §14, 140, Book IV, Chapter 10, § 5, 416–17, available online at http://www.ccel.org/ccel/calvin/institutes.txt.

[108] *Dictionary.com*, s.v. "protest," available online at http://dictionary.reference.com/search?q=protest (accessed on August 31, 2010).

[109] "Plantation Agreement at Providence August 27–September 6, 1640," *The Avalon Project*, available online at www.yale.edu/lawweb/avalon/states/ri01.htm.

[110] "The Fundamental Constitutions of Carolina: March 1, 1669," *The Avalon Project*, available online at http://www.yale.edu/lawweb/avalon/states/nc05.htm.

[111] "The Concession and Agreement of the Lords Proprietors of the Province of New Caesarea, or New Jersey, to and With All and Every the Adventurers and All Such as Settle or Plant There, 1664," *The Avalon Project*, available online at http://www.yale.edu/lawweb/avalon/states/nj02.htm.

[112] "Frame of Government of Pennsylvania May 5, 1682," *The Avalon Project*, available online at http://www.yale.edu/lawweb/avalon/states/pa04.htm.

[113] "Charter of Delaware, 1701," *The Avalon Project*, available online at http://www.yale.edu/lawweb/avalon/states/de01.htm.

[114] "The Constitution of Virginia, 1776," 180,

[115] "Constitution of New Jersey," in *The Constitutions of the Several Independent States of America* (Boston: Norman and Bowen, 1785), 73–74.

[116] W. Livingston, "Cato," in *The Papers of William Livingston*, vol. II (Trenton: New Jersey Historical Commission, 1980), 234.

[117] "Constitution of New York," in *The Constitutions of the Several Independent States of America*, 67.

[118] Morris, *Christian Life and Character of the Civil Institutions of the United States*, 152.

[119] *Lindenmuller v. The People*, 33 Barb 548 (Sup. Ct. NY 1861).

[120] See the entries from August 15, 1789, to August 21, 1789, in J. Gales, ed., *The Debates and Proceedings in the Congress of the United States*, vol. I (Washington, DC: Gales and Seaton, 1834), 757–96.

[121] Thomas Jefferson letter to Nehemiah Dodge, Ephraim Robbins, and Stephen S. Nelson, 281–82.

[122] In 1788, following the ratification of the federal Constitution, six states submitted proposals for a Bill of Rights, with several specifically recommending national language that "all men have an equal, natural, and unalienable right to the free exercise of religion, *according to the dictates of conscience*" (the six states initially were Massachusetts, South Carolina, New Hampshire, Virginia, New York, and North Carolina; two years later, Rhode Island submitted its proposals.) See J. Elliot, The *Debates in the Several State Conventions on the Adoption of the Federal Constitution*, vol. I (Washington, DC, 1836), 322–33.

[123] See Texas State Constitution, Article 1, Section 6; Washington State Constitution, Article 1, Section 11; North Carolina State Constitution, Article 1, Section 13; Massachusetts State Constitution, Part the First, Article 2; New York State Constitution, Article 1, Section 3; and other state constitutions.

[124] C. M. Butler, *Addresses and Lectures on Public Men and Public Affairs* (Cincinnati: H. W. Derby, 1856), 271–72.

[125] See for example "Courts Driving Religion Out of Public Life; Christianity Under Attack," *Foxnews.com* (December 1, 2005), available online at http://www.foxnews.com/story/0,2933,177355,00.html. See also "Pro-life shirt equated with swastika," *World Net Daily* (January 31, 2003), available online at http://www.worldnetdaily.com/news/article.asp?ARTICLE_ID=30781.

[126] *County of Allegheny v. American Civil Liberties Union*, 492 U.S. 573 (1989); *Malnak v. Yogi*, 440 F. Supp. 1284 (N.J., 1977); *Fellowship of Humanity v. County of Alameda*, 153 Cal. App. 2d 673 (Ca. App. 1957); *Grove v. Mead School District No. 354*, 753 F.2d 1528 (9th Cir. 1985); *Crockett v. Sorenson*, 568 F. Supp. 1422 (W. Va. 1983); *Strayhorn v. Ethical Society of Austin*, 110 S. W. 3d 458 (Tex. App. 2003).

[127] Butler, *Addresses and Lectures on Public Men and Public Affairs*, 271–72.

[128] *Doe v. Tangipahoa Parish School Board*, No. 05–30294 (5th Cir. Dec. 15, 2006); *Furley v. Aledo Independent School District*, No. 4:99–CV–0416–A (N.D. Tex. Oct. 21, 1999); *Hinrichs v. Bosma*, 400 F. Supp. 2d 1103, 1120 (S.D. Ind. Nov. 30, 2005); *Doe v. Santa Fe Independent School District*, Civil Action No. G–95–176 (S.D. Tex. 1995) (court transcription of verbal ruling by Federal Judge Samuel Kent, 3).

[129] *Jane Doe v. Santa Fe Independent School District*, Civil Action No. G–95–176 (U.S.D.C., S.D. Tx. 1995) (court transcription of verbal ruling by Federal Judge Samuel Kent, 3).

[130] Livingston, "Cato," 235–36.

[131] Ward, "Left Aims to Smite 'Theocracy' Movement."

[132] Ibid. See also Goldberg, "In Theocracy They Trust"; C. W. Veazey, "On the Brink of 'Theocracy,'" *Center for American Progress* (May 5, 2005), available online at http://www.americanprogress.org/issues/2005/05/b667491.html.

[133] M. Washington, "Theocracy Now: Bush Puts America Under God's Law," *The Village Voice* (August 8–14, 2001), available online at http://www.village-voice.com/2001–08–07/news/nation/#Bush.

[134] Ward, "Left Aims to Smite 'Theocracy' Movement."

135 "Dobson Seeks Fundamentalist Theocracy, Church-State Watchdog Group Charges," *Americans United For Separation of Church and State* (May 4, 1998), available online at http://www.au.org/media/pressreleases/archives/1998/05 /dobsonseeksfun.html.
136 Cole, "The Schiavo Case and the Islamization of the Republican Party."
137 *Dictionary.com*, s.v. "theology," available online at http://dictionary.reference.com/browse/theology.
138 *Dictionary.com*, s.v. "values," available online at http://dictionary.reference.com/browse/values.
139 "In the U. S., Christmas Not Just for Christians," *Gallup* (December 24, 2008), available online at http://www.gallup.com/poll/113566/uschristmasnotjustchristians.aspx. See also D. Blanton, "Majority OK with Public Nativity Scenes," *FoxNews.com* (June 18, 2004), available online at http://www.foxnews .com/story/0,2933,105272,00.html.
140 *Commonwealth v. Nesbit*, 34 PA. 398, 411 (Su.C. Pa 1859).
141 *McGowan v. Maryland*, 366 U.S. 420, 442 (1961).
142 "Address Delivered to the American Bible Society," in *The Life and Writings of De Witt Clinton*, ed. W. W. Campbell (New York: Baker and Scribner, 1849), 305.
143 M. E. Flower, *John Dickinson: Conservative Revolutionary* (Charlottesville: University Press of Virginia, 1983), 300.
144 A. de Tocqueville, *Democracy in America*, vol. 2, trans. Henry Reeves (New York: A. S. Barnes & Co., 1851), 134–35.
145 Richard Henry Lee letter to Samuel Adams, March 14, 1785, in *The Letters of Richard Henry Lee*, vol. 3, ed. J. C. Ballagh (New York: De Capo Press, 1930), 343.
146 John Adams letter to Abigail Adams, October 29, 1775, in *Familiar Letters of John Adams and His Wife Abigail Adams*, ed. C. F. Adams (Boston: Houghton, Mifflin & Co., 1875), 118.
147 J. Kent, *Commentaries on American Law*, vol. 1 (New York: O. Halsted, 1826), 10.
148 Adams, *An Oration Delivered Before the Inhabitants of the Town of Newburyport*, 61.
149 W. H. McGuffey, *First Reader* (Cincinnati: Truman and Smith, 1853), 47.
150 J. Adams, diary entry for August 14, 1796, in *The Works of John Adams, Second President of the United States*, vol. III, ed. C. F. Adams (Boston: Charles C. Little and James Brown, 1851), 423.
151 W. V. Wells, *The Life and Public Service of Samuel Adams*, vol. I (Boston: Little, Brown, & Co., 1865), 22.
152 N. Webster, *An American Dictionary of the English Language* (New York: S. Converse, 1828), s.v. "manners."
153 B. Rush, "Thoughts Upon Female Education," in *Essays: Literary, Moral & Philosophical* (Philadelphia: Thomas & Samuel F. Bradford, 1798), 83.
154 R. T. Paine, "Confession of Faith," in *The Papers of Robert Treat Paine*, vol. I, ed. S. T. Riley and E. W. Hanson (Boston: Massachusetts Historical Society, 1992), 49.
155 J. Dickinson, "The Letters of Fabius, in 1788, on the Federal Constitution; and in 1797, on the Present Situation of Public Affairs," in *The Political Writings of John Dickinson*, vol. II (Wilmington: Bonsal and Niles, 1801), 258.
156 D. Webster, "Address Delivered at the Laying of the Cornerstone of the Addition to the Capitol," in *The Works of Daniel Webster*, vol. II (Boston: Little, Brown and Company, 1853), 614–15.
157 T. Jefferson, "Syllabus of an Estimate of the Merits of the Doctrines of Jesus, Compared with Those of Others," in *Memoir, Correspondence, and*

Miscellanies, From the Papers of Thomas Jefferson, vol. III, ed. T. J. Randolph (Boston: Gray and Bowen, 1830), 509.

[158] John Adams letter to the Officers of the First Brigade of the Third Division of the Militia of Massachusetts, October 11, 1798, in *The Works of John Adams,* IX:229.

[159] D. Barton, *The Practical Benefits of Christianity* (WallBuilders Press: Aledo, Texas, 2001). See also R. Winthrop, "Address Delivered at the Annual Meeting of the Massachusetts Bible Society in Boston," in *Addresses and Speeches on Various Occasions* (Boston: Little, Brown and Co., 1852), 172.

[160] N. Webster, "Reply to a Letter of David McClure on the Subject of the Proper Course of Study in the Girard College," in *A Collection of Papers on Political, Literary, and Moral Subjects* (New York: Webster and Clark, 1843), 291–94.

[161] N. Webster, *An Oration Pronounced Before the Citizens of New Haven on the Anniversary of the Independence of the United States, July 4, 1798* (New Haven: T. & S. Green, 1798), 13.

[162] "James Madison Proclamation, July 23, 1813," in *The Weekly Register* IV, no. 22 (Baltimore, July 31, 1813): 1.

[163] E. Stiles, *The United States Elevated to Glory and Honor: A Sermon . . . at the Anniversary Election, May 8th, 1783* (New Haven, CT: Thomas & Samuel Green, 1783), 56.

[164] Dorchester, *Christianity in the United States,* 43.

[165] John Adams letter to F. A. Vanderkemp, February 16, 1809, in *The Works of John Adams, Second President of the United States,* IX:609–10; Benjamin Rush letter to Elias Boudinot, July 9, 1788, *Letters of Benjamin Rush,* I:474; J. Witherspoon, "Introduction," in *The Holy Bible* (Trenton: Isaac Collins, 1791); George Washington letter to the Hebrew Congregation of the City of Savannah, May 1790, in *The Writings of George Washington,* vol. XII, ed. J. Sparks (Boston: American Stationers' Company, 1838), 186; will of Elias Boudinot, available from the New Jersey State Archives, or see excerpts in G. A. Boyd, *Elias Boudinot: Patriot and Statesman* (Princeton: Princeton University Press, 1952), 261.

[166] For example: Colonels David and Isaac Franks (military leaders), Isaac Moses (a blockade runner who secured supplies for the Americans), Major Benjamin Nones, Mordecai Sheftall (one of the patriot leaders in Georgia), Hyam Salomon (who secured much of the funding that enabled Washington to continue fighting the British), and many others. See L. M. Friedman, *Jewish Pioneers and Patriots* (Philadelphia: The Jewish Publication Society of America, 1942), 17, 37, 345–52; S. Wolf, *The American Jew as a Patriot, Soldier and Citizen* (Philadelphia: The Levy Type Company, 1895), 40–44, 50.

[167] D. Levi, *A Defense of the Old Testament in a Series of Letters Addressed to Thomas Paine, Author of a Book Entitled, "The Age of Reason, Part the Second, being an Investigation of True and of Fabulous Theology"* (Philadelphia: Hogan & M'Elroy, 1798).

[168] F. C. Leiner, *The End of Barbary Terror* (Oxford: Oxford University Press: 2006), 29–30; M. M. Noah, *Travels in England, France, Spain, and the Barbary States, in the Years 1813–14 and 1815* (New York: Kirk and Mercein, 1819); "Judaic Treasures of the Library of Congress: Mordecai Manuel Noah," *Jewish Virtual Library,* available online at http://www.jewishvirtuallibrary.org/jsource/loc/noah.html (accessed on August 31, 2010).

[169] J. Jacoby, "The Freedom Not to Say 'Amen'," *Jewish World Review* (February 1, 2001), available online at http://www.jewishworldreview.com/jeff/jacoby020101.asp.

[170] D. Lapin, *America's Real War* (Oregon: Multnomah Publishers, 1999), 116.

171 D. Lapin, "Which Jews Does the ADL Really Represent?" *WorldNetDaily* (August 25, 2006), available online at http://worldnetdaily.com/news/article. asp?ARTICLE_ID=51671.

172 T. A. Tweed, "Islam in America: From African Slaves to Malcolm X," *National Humanities Center*, available online at http://www.nhc.rtp.nc.us/tserve/twenty/tkeyinfo/islam.htm (accessed on August 31, 2010).

173 "American Muslim History," *DawaNet.com*, available online at http://www.dawanet.com/history/amermuslimhist.asp (accessed on August 31, 2010).

174 S. De Ryer, *The Koran* (Springfield: Henry Brewer, October, 1806).

175 "Buddhism in the New World," *Wikipedia*, available online at http://en.wikipedia.org/wiki/Buddhism_in_the_United_States#Buddhism_in_the_New_World (accessed on August 31, 2010).

176 R. Baird, *Religion in America* (New York: Harper & Brothers ,1845), 275.

177 Wood, *Five Problems of State and Religion*, 181.

178 "Countries of Particular Concern," *United States Commission on International Religious Freedom*, available online at http://www.uscirf.gov/index. php?option=com_content&task=view&id=1456&Itemid=59 (accessed on August 31, 2010).

179 "Watch List," *United States Commission on International Religious Freedom*, available online at http://www.uscirf.gov/index.php?option=com_content&task=view&id=1457&Itemid=60 (accessed on August 31, 2010).

180 *City Council of Charleston v. S. A. Benjamin*, 2 Strob. 508, 522 (Sup. Ct. S.C. 1846).

181 S. Cowell, *The Position of Christianity in the United States in its Relations with our Political Institutions* (Philadelphia: Lippincott, Grambio & Co., 1854), 20.

182 "Charter of Virginia," in *The Federal and State Constitutions, Colonial Charters, and Other Organic Laws*, ed. F. N. Thorpe (Washington: Government Printing Office, 1909), 3784.

183 "Mayflower Compact," in ibid., 1841.

184 "Charter of Massachusetts Bay," in ibid., 1857.

185 "Fundamental Orders of Connecticut," in ibid., 519.

186 "Articles of Confederation of the United Colonies of New England," in ibid., 77.

187 John Marshall letter to Jasper Adams, May 9, 1833, in *The Papers of John Marshall*, ed. C. Hobson (Chapel Hill: University of North Carolina Press, 2006), 278.

188 G. Washington, "General Orders, May 2, 1778," in *The Writings of George Washington*, vol. XI, ed. J. C. Fitzpatrick (Washington: Government Printing Office, 1934), 343.

189 G. Washington, "General Orders, July 9, 1776," in *The Writings of George Washington*, vol. V, ed. J. C. Fitzpatrick (Washington: Government Printing Office, 1932), 245. This statement of George Washington was also used by Abraham Lincoln in his November 15, 1862, order to the troops to maintain regular Sabbath observances. See A. Lincoln, *Letters and Addresses of Abraham Lincoln* (New York: Unit Book Publishing Co., 1907), 261.

190 G. Washington, "Speech to the Delaware Indian Chiefs," in *The Writings of George Washington*, vol. XV, ed. J. C. Fitzpatrick (Washington: Government Printing Office, 1936), 55.

191 John Adams letter to Thomas Jefferson, June 28, 1813.

192 Letter from Charles Carroll to James McHenry, November 4, 1800, in *The Life and Correspondence of James McHenry*, ed. B. C. Steiner (Cleveland: Burrows Brothers, 1907), 475.

193 See Boston's *Independent Chronicle* (November 2, 1780), last page.

[194] B. Rush, "Of the Mode of Education Proper in a Republic," in *Essays, Literary, Moral and Philosophical*, 8; Benjamin Rush letter to Thomas Jefferson, August 22, 1800.

[195] J. Witherspoon, "The Dominion of Providence Over the Passions of Men," in *The Works of the Rev. John Witherspoon*, vol. III (Philadelphia: William W. Woodard, 1802), 41–42, 46.

[196] S. Adams, "Natural Rights of the Colonists as Men," in *The Life and Public Services of Samuel Adams*, vol. I, ed. W. V. Wells (Boston: Little, Brown, and Company, 1865), 504.

[197] Alexander Hamilton letter to James Bayard, April 16–21, 1802, in *The Papers of Alexander Hamilton*, vol. XXV, ed. H. C. Syrett (New York: Columbia University Press, 1977), 605–10.

[198] B. Franklin, *Proposals Relating to the Education of Youth in Pennsylvania* (Philadelphia, 1749), 22.

[199] J. Dickinson, *The Political Writings of John Dickinson*, vol. I (Wilmington: Bonsal and Niles, 1801), 111.

[200] Galloway, *Christianity and the American Commonwealth*, 207. See also "The University of Georgia Charter, 1785," available online at http://www.libs.uga.edu/hargrett/archives/chartertranscript.html.

[201] Steiner, *One Hundred and Ten Years of Bible Society Work in Maryland*, 14, quoting James McHenry.

[202] See the entry for September 25, 1789, in *The Debates and Proceedings in the Congress of the United States*, vol. I (Washington: Gales and Seaton, 1834), 949–50.

[203] *M'Creery's Lessee v. Allender*, 4 Harris & McHenry 258, 259 (Sup. Ct. Md. 1799), where Justice Samuel Chase applied a belief in Christianity as the basis of citizenship in this case. *See also* from an original document in the author's possession that says "I, Samuel Chase, Chief Justice of the State of Maryland, do hereby certify all whom it may concern, that on the first day of February in the year one thousand seven hundred and ninety-four, personally appeared before Mr. Barnard Lafon and did repeat and subscribe a Declaration of his belief in the Christian religion and the oath required by the Act of Assembly of this state, entitled "An Act for Naturalization." In Testimony of the truth hereof, I the said Samuel Chase, have hereunto put my hand, at Baltimore Town, in the said state of Maryland, the day and year aforementioned."

[204] John Jay letter to John Murray, Jr., October 12, 1816, in *The Life of John Jay*, vol. II, ed. Jay (New York: J. & J. Harper, 1833), 376.

[205] E. Boudinot, "Speech in the First Provincial Congress of New Jersey," in *The Life, Public Services, Addresses, and Letters of Elias Boudinot*, vol. I., ed. J. J. Boudinot (Boston: Houghton, Mifflin and Co., 1896), 19, 21.

[206] Campbell, *The Life and Writings of De Witt Clinton*, 307.

[207] Adams, *An Oration Delivered Before the Inhabitants of the Town of Newburyport . . . on the Sixty-First Anniversary of the Declaration of Independence*, 5–6.

[208] D. Webster, *Mr. Webster's Speech in Defense of the Christian Ministry and in Favor of the Religious Instruction of the Young. Delivered in the Supreme Court of the United States, February 10, 1844, in the Case of Stephen Girard's Will* (Washington: Gales and Seaton, 1844), 41.

[209] *Journals of the Continental Congress*, vol. I (Washington: Government Printing Office, 1904), 26–27.

[210] John Adams letter to Abigail Adams, September 16, 1774, in *Familiar Letters of John Adams and His Wife Abigail Adams During the Revolution*, 37–38; *Journals of the Continental Congress*, vol. I (Washington: Government Printing Office, 1904), 27; *The Book of Common Prayer, and Administration of*

the Sacraments and Other Rites and Ceremonies of the Church (Cambridge: John Archedeacon, 1771), 24.

211 See the entry from March 16, 1776, in *Journals of the Continental Congress*, vol. IV (Washington: Government Printing Office, 1906), 209.

212 See the entry from July 19. 1775, in *Journals of the Continental Congress*, vol. II (Washington: Government Printing Office, 1905), 192.

213 See the entry for June 30, 1775, in *Journals of the Continental Congress*, vol. I (Washington: Government Printing Office, 1905), 112. Furthermore, George Washington ordered that those Articles of War from Congress be read to the soldiers weekly. See G. Washington, "General Orders, April 28, 1776," in *The Writings of George Washington*, vol. IV, ed. J. C. Fitzpatrick (Washington: Government Printing Office, 1931), 527.

214 See the entry for November 28, 1775, in *Journals of the Continental Congress*, vol. III (Washington: Government Printing Office, 1905), 378.

215 See the entry for February 5, 1776, in *Journals of the Continental Congress*, IV:111.

216 Ibid.

217 *State of Massachusetts-Bay, A Proclamation for a Day of Public Thanksgiving and Prayer* (Boston: 1777).

218 T. Jefferson, "Proclamation Appointing a Day of Thanksgiving and Prayer," in *The Papers of Thomas Jefferson*, vol. 3, ed. J. P. Boyd (Princeton, NJ: Princeton University Press, 1951), 178.

219 Ibid.

220 John Hancock, "A Proclamation for a Day of Public Thanksgiving," *The Columbian Centinel* (October 5, 1791), 1.

221 "Writing It All Down: The Art of Constitution Making for the State & the Nation, 1776–1833," *Maryland State Archives*, available at http://www.mdarchives.state.md.us/msa/speccol/sc2200/sc2221/000004/000000/html/00000004.html (accessed on August 31, 2010).

222 See article 22 of "Delaware, 1776," in *The Constitutions of the Several Independent States of the America*, 99–100.

223 See chapter VI, article I of *A Constitution or Frame of Government Agreed Upon by the Delegates of the People of the State of Massachusetts—Bay* (Boston: Benjamin Edes & Sons, 1780), 44.

224 See article II, section 10 of "Pennsylvania, 1776," in *Constitutions of the Several Independent*, 81.

225 See section 35 of "Declaration of Rights," in ibid., 108.

226 See article I, section 6, "Bill of Rights," in ibid., 4.

227 *Letters of Delegates to Congress*, vol. 7, ed. P. H. Smith (Washington: Library of Congress, 1981), 311n1.

228 See the entry for September 11, 1777, in *Journals of the Continental Congress*, vol. VIII (Washington: Government Printing Office, 1907), 734–35.

229 Memorial of Robert Aitken to Congress, 21 January 1781, obtained from the National Archives, Washington, DC.

230 See the entry for September 12, 1782, in *Journals of the Continental Congress*, vol. XXIII (Washington: Government Printing Office, 1914), 572 –74.

231 See the entry for January 14, 1784, in *Journals of the Continental Congress*, vol. XXVI (Washington: Government Printing Office, 1928), 23.

232 *Annual Register for the Year 1783* (London: G. Robinson, 1784), 113.

233 Morris, *Christian Life and Character of the Civil Institutions of the United States*, 527–28.

234 R. Reagan, "Proclamation 5018—Year of the Bible, 1983," *The American Presidency Project* (February 3, 1983), available online at http://www.presidency.ucsb.edu/ws/?pid=40728. See the same quote in President G. H. W. Bush's

proclamation on February 22, 1990, "International Year of Bible Reading," in Code of Federal Regulations (Washington, DC: Government Printing Office, 1991), 21.

[235] J. Tyler, "Proclamation," *The American Presidency Project* (April 13, 1841), available online at: http://www.presidency.ucsb.edu/ws/?pid=67344.

[236] S. A. Northrop, *A Cloud of Witnesses* (Fort Wayne, IN: The Mason Long Publishing Co., 1894), 447–48.

[237] See the entry for December 27, 1859, in *Journal of the Senate of the United States of America*, vol. 51 (Washington: George W. Bowman, 1860), 30.

[238] A. Lincoln, "First Inaugural Address, March 4, 1861," in *The Collected Works of Abraham Lincoln,* vol. IV, ed. R. P. Basler (New Brunswick, NJ: Rutgers University Press, 1953), 271.

[239] See entry for January 13, 1875, in *Journal of the Senate of the United States of America*, vol. 70 (Washington: Government Printing Office, 1874), 105.

[240] Galloway, *Christianity and the American Commonwealth*, 177.

[241] W. McKinley Speech to the Congress of the United States, in *A Compilation of Messages and Papers of the Presidents*, ed. J. D. Richardson (New York: Bureau of National Literature, 1897), 6292.

[242] T. Roosevelt, *American Ideals, The Strenuous Life, Realizable Ideals* (New York: Charles Scribner's Sons, 1926), 498–99.

[243] W. Wilson, "An Address in Denver on the Bible, May 7, 1911," in *The Papers of Woodrow Wilson*, vol. 23, ed. A. S. Link (Princeton: Princeton University Press, 1977), 20.

[244] H. Hoover, "Radio Address to the Nation on Unemployment Relief," *The American Presidency Project* (October 18, 1931), available online at: http://www.presidency.ucsb.edu/ws/?pid=22855.

[245] F. D. Roosevelt, "Address at Dedication of Great Smoky Mountains National Park, *The American Presidency Project* (September 2, 1940), available online at http://www.presidency.ucsb.edu/ws/?pid=16002.

[246] F. D. Roosevelt, "Campaign Address at Madison Square Garden, New York City," *The American Presidency Project* (October 28, 1940), available online at http://www.presidency.ucsb.edu/ws/?pid=15885.

[247] F. D. Roosevelt, "Radio Address of the President Announcing Unlimited National Emergency," *The American Presidency Project* (May 27, 1941), available online at http://www.presidency.ucsb.edu/ws/?pid=16120.

[248] F. D. Roosevelt, "Fireside Chat," *The American Presidency Project* (April 28, 1942), available online at http://www.presidency.ucsb.edu/ws/?pid=16252.

[249] F. D. Roosevelt, "Statement on the Four Hundredth Anniversary of the Printing of the English Bible," *The American Presidency Project* (October 6, 1935), available online at http://www.presidency.ucsb.edu/ws/?pid=14960.

[250] H. S. Truman, "Exchange of Messages With Pope Pius XII," *The American Presidency Project* (August 28, 1947), available online at http://www.presidency.ucsb.edu/ws/?pid=12746.

[251] H. S. Truman, "Address at the Lighting of the National Community Christmas Tree on the White House Grounds," *The American Presidency Project* (December 24, 1946), available online at http://www.presidency.ucsb.edu/ws/?pid=12569.

[252] H. S. Truman, "Statement by the President Upon Reappointing Myron Taylor as His Personal Representative at the Vatican," *The American Presidency Project* (May 3, 1946), available online at http://www.presidency.ucsb.edu/ws/?pid=9881.

[253] See, for example, Harry S. Truman, "Address to the Washington Pilgrimage of American Churchmen," *The American Presidency Project* (September 28, 1951), available online at http://www.presidency.ucsb.edu/ws/?pid=13934.

[254] D. D. Eisenhower, "Address Before the Council of the Organization of American States," *The American Presidency Project* (April 12, 1953), available online at http://www.presidency.ucsb.edu/ws/?pid=9816.

[255] R. Nixon, "Remarks at the National Prayer Breakfast," *The American Presidency Project* (February 1, 1972), available online at http://www.presidency.ucsb.edu/ws/?pid=3597; R. Reagan, "Proclamation 5018—Year of the Bible, 1983."

[256] J. Trumbull, *A Proclamation for a Day of Fasting, Humiliation, and Prayer* (Connecticut: 1807), for March 27, 1807, from an original in the author's possession.

[257] Morris, *Christian Life and Character of the Civil Institutions of the United States*, 569.

[258] C. Williams, *A Proclamation for a Day of Public Thanksgiving* (Montpelier, VT: 1850), for December 5, 1850, from an original in the author's possession.

[259] Morris, *Christian Life and Character of the Civil Institutions of the United States*, 586.

[260] A. Rice, *A Proclamation for a Day of Public Thanksgiving and Praise* (Boston: 1877), for November 29, 1877, from an original in the author's possession.

[261] A. Brown, *A Proclamation for a Day of Fasting and Prayer* (New Hampshire: 1922), for April 27, 1922, from an original in the author's possession.

[262] See the entry for April 15, 1789, in *Journal of the Senate of the United States of America*, vol. I (Washington: Gales & Seaton, 1820), 12.

[263] C. W. Bowen, *The History of the Centennial Celebration of the Inauguration of George Washington* (New York: D. Appleton & Co., 1892), 72.

[264] B. J. Lossing, *Our Country*, vol. IV (New York: James A. Bailey, 1895), 1124; H. C. Lodge, *American Statesman: George Washington*, vol. II (Boston: Houghton, Mifflin Co., 1898), 46.

[265] See the entry for April 30, 1789, in *The Debates and Proceedings in the Congress of the United States*, vol. I (Washington: Gales & Seaton, 1834), 27–28.

[266] *The Book of Common Prayer and Administration of the Sacraments, and Other Rites and Ceremonies of the Church, according to the Protestant Episcopal Church in the United States of America: Together with the Psalter or Psalms of David* (Philadelphia: Hall & Sellers,1789), s.v. "April 30."

[267] *Debates and Proceedings in the Congress of the United States* (Washington: Gales and Seaton, 1853), 797, Sixth Congress, December 4, 1800.

[268] J. Q. Adams, diary entry for February 28, 1841, in *Memoirs of John Quincy Adams*, vol. X, ed. C. F. Adams (Philadelphia: J. B. Lippincott and Company, 1874), 434.

[269] G. Hunt, ed., *The First Forty Years of Washington Society* (New York: Charles Scribner's Sons, 1906), 14.

[270] Bishop Claggett (Episcopal bishop of Maryland) letter of February 18, 1801, reveals that, as vice president, Jefferson went to church services in the House. Available in the Maryland Diocesan Archives.

[271] Manasseh Cutler letter to Joseph Torrey, January 3, 1803, in *Life, Journal, and Correspondence of Rev. Manasseh Cutler*, vol. II, ed. W. P. Cutler and J. P. Cutler (Cincinnati: Colin Robert Clarke & Co., 1888), 119. See also M. Cutler, journal entry for December 12, 1802, in ibid., 113.

[272] Hunt, *The First Forty Years of Washington Society*, 13.

[273] Manasseh Cutler letter to Joseph Torrey, January 3, 1803, 114.

[274] J. Hutson, *Religion and the Founding of the American Republic* (Washington: Library of Congress, 1998), 89.

[275] Ibid., 96.

276 Ibid., 84–91, 96.

277 *The Reports of Committees of the Senate of the United States for the Second Session of the Thirty-Second Congress, 1852–1853* (Washington: Robert Armstrong, 1853), 1.

278 Hunt, *The First Forty Years of Washington Society*, 14–15.

279 C. M. Butler, "A Discourse, Delivered in the Senate Chamber, April 2, 1850, at the Funeral of Hon. John C. Calhoun, Senator of the United States from South Carolina," in *Addresses and Lectures on Public Men and Public Affairs, Delivered in Washington, DC* (Cincinnati: H. W. Derby, 1856), 50.

280 *The Reports of Committees of the Senate of the United States for the Second Session of the Thirty-Second Congress, 1852–1853*, 3.

281 *Reports of Committees of the House of Representatives Made During the First Session of the Thirty-Third Congress* (Washington: A. O. P. Nicholson, 1854), 8–9.

282 See entry for January 23, 1856, in *Journal of the House of Representatives of the United States* (Washington: Cornelius Wendell, 1855), 354.

283 Morris, *Christian Life and Character of the Civil Institutions of the United States*, 237–39.

284 "North Carolina State Constitution," Art. XI, Sec. 4, *North Carolina General Assembly*, available online at http://www.ncga.state.nc.us/Legislation/constitution/ncconstitution_whole.html (accessed on August 31, 2010).

285 "Constitution of the Commonwealth of Massachusetts," Chap. V, Art. I, *Commonwealth of Massachusetts*, available online at http://www.mass.gov/legis/const.htm (accessed on August 31, 2010).

286 John Jay letter to John Murray, Jr., October 12, 1816, 376.

287 J. Wilson, "Of the General Principles of Law and Obligation," in *The Works of James Wilson*, vol. I, ed. Bird Wilson (Philadelphia: Bronson and Chauncey, 1804), 104–6; J. Wilson, "Of the Law of Nature," in ibid., 120, 137–39.

288 *United States Oracle of the Day,* Portsmouth, NH, (May 24, 1800). See also M. Marcus, ed., *The Documentary History of the Supreme Court of the United States, 1789–1800*, vol. III (New York: Columbia University Press, 1988), 436.

289 D. L. Dreisbach, *Religion and Politics in the Early Republic* (Lexington: University Press of Kentucky, 1996), 113.

290 J. Story, *Life and Letters of Joseph Story*, vol. II, ed. W. W. Story (Boston: Charles C. Little and James Brown, 1851), 8.

291 J. Story, *Life and Letters of Joseph Story*, vol. I, ed. W. W. Story (Boston: Charles C. Little and James Brown, 1851), 92.

292 J. Story, *Commentaries on the Constitution of the United States*, vol. III (Boston: Hillard, Gray, and Company, 1833), 724, § 1867.

293 Morris, *Christian Life and Character of the Civil Institutions of the United States*, 639, 642.

294 *Testimony of Distinguished Laymen to the Value of the Sacred Scriptures* (New York: American Bible Society, 1889), 51–53.

295 D. J. Brewer, *The United States: A Christian Nation*, 29–30, 33.

296 W. B. Reed, *Life and Correspondence of Joseph Reed*, vol. IV (Philadelphia: Lindsay and Blakiston, 1847), 36–37; A. J. Dallas, *Reports of Cases Ruled and Adjudged in the Courts of Pennsylvania* (Philadelphia: P. Byrne, 1806), 39, *Respublica v. John Roberts* (Pa. Sup. Ct. 1778).

297 Z. Swift, *A System of Laws of the State of Connecticut*, vol. II (Windham, CT: John Byrne, 1796), 323; Z. Swift, *The Correspondent* (Windham, CT: John Byrne, 1793), 119.

298 *Reports of the Proceedings and Debates of the Convention of 1821, Assembled for the Purpose of Amending the Constitution of the State of New York*, ed. N. H. Carter and W. L. Stone (Albany: E. and E. Hosford, 1821), 576.

[299] *Testimony of Distinguished Laymen to the Value of the Sacred Scriptures,* 27; See also S. W. Bailey, *Homage of Eminent Persons to the Book* (New York: 1869), 54.

[300] T. M. Cooley, *A Treatise on the Constitutional Limitations* (Boston: Little, Brown, and Company, 1890), 581.

[301] Ibid., 579.

[302] P. Schaff, *Church and State in the United States* (New York: Charles Scribner's Sons, 1889), 61.

[303] *Vidal v. Girard's Executors,* 43 U.S. 127, 198 (1844).

[304] *Church of the Holy Trinity v. U.S.,* 143 U. S. 457, 465, 471 (1892).

[305] *United States v. Macintosh,* 283 U.S. 605, 625 (1931).

[306] See, for example: *Warren v. United States,* 177 F.2d 596 (1949); *United States v. Girouard,* 149 F.2d 760 (1945); *Steiner v. Darby, Parker v. Los Angeles County,* 199 P.2d 429 (Cal. App. 2d Dist 1948); *Vogel v. County of Los Angeles,* 68 Cal.2d 18, 22 (Cal. 1967).

[307] *Davis v. Beason,* 133 U. S. 333, 341 n. (1890).

[308] *The Church of Jesus Christ of Latter-Day Saints v. United States;* 136 U.S. 1, 49; (1890)

[309] *U.S. v. Macintosh,* 283 U.S. 605, 625 (1931).

[310] *Ross v. McIntyre,* 140 U.S. 453, 463 (1891); *Reid v. Covert,* 354 U.S. 1 (1957).

[311] *Beecher v. Wetherby,* 95 U.S. 517, 525 (1877); *Lone Wolf v. Hitchcock,* 187 U.S. 553, 565 (1903). See also the same language in *Sioux Tribe of Indians v. U. S.,* 272 U.S. 351 (1926); *U. S. v. Choctaw Nation,* 179 U.S. 494 (1900); *Atlantic & P R Co v. Mingus,* 165 U.S. 413 (1897); *Missouri, Kansas & Texas Railway Company v. Roberts,* 152 U.S. 114, 117 (1894); *Choctaw & Chickasaw Nations v. U.S.,* Not Reported in Ct.Cl., 34 Ct.Cl. 17, 1800 WL 2139, Ct.Cl., (January 9, 1899); *Buttz v. Northern Pac. R. Co.,* 119 U.S. 55 (1886); *Tee-Hit-Ton Indians v. United States,* 348 U.S. 272 (1955).

[312] *Runkel v. Winemiller,* 4 Harris & McHenry 276, 288 (Sup. Ct. Md. 1799).

[313] *Updegraph v. The Commonwealth,* 11 S. & R. 394, 399 (Sup. Ct. Pa. 1824).

[314] *City Council of Charleston v. S. A. Benjamin,* 2 Strob. 508, 518–521 (Sup. Ct. S.C. 1846).

[315] *Lindenmuller v. The People,* 33 Barb 548, 560–564, 567 (Sup. Ct. NY 1861).

[316] *Richmond v. Moore,* 107 Ill. 429, 1883 WL 10319, 47 Am.Rep. 445 (Ill. 1883).

[317] *Strauss v. Strauss,* 148 Fla. 23, 3 So.2d 727 (Sup. Ct. Fla. 1941).

[318] *Paramount-Richards Theaters, Inc. v. City of Hattiesburg,* 210 Miss. 271, 49 So. 2d 574 (1950).

[319] *Town of Pryor v. Williamson,* 347 P.2d 204 (Okla. 1959). (Also cited in *County of Los Angeles v. Hollinger,* 221 Cal.App.2d 154, 34 Cal.Rptr. 387 (1963).

[320] Letter from Noah Webster to James Madison, October 16, 1829, cited in K. A. Snyder, *Defining Noah Webster: Mind and Morals in the Early Republic* (New York: University Press of America, 1990), 253.

[321] N. Webster, *History of the United States* (New Haven: Durrie & Peck, 1832), 6.

[322] D. Ramsay, *An Eulogium upon Benjamin Rush, M.D.* (Philadelphia: Bradford and Inskeep, 1813), 107. See also B. Rush, "A Plan for Establishing Public Schools in Pennsylvania, and for Conducting Education Agreeable to a Republican Form of Government," in *Essays, Literary, Moral and Philosophical,* 1–6,

[323] B. Rush, "A Defense of the Use of the Bible as a School Book," in *Essays, Literary, Moral and Philosophical,* 112.

[324] *The Laws of the College of New-Jersey* (Trenton: Isaac Collins, 1794), 5, 13; B. Rush, *The Autobiography of Benjamin Rush*, ed. G. W. Corner (Princeton: Princeton University Press, 1948), 31–32; J. Witherspoon, "The Dominion of Providence over the Passions of Men," in *The Works of the Reverend John Witherspoon*, vol. III (Philadelphia: William W. Woodward, 1802), 42.

[325] J. Morse, *A Sermon, Exhibiting the Present Dangers and Consequent Duties of the Citizens of the United States of America. Delivered at Charlestown. April 25, 1799, The Day of the National Fast* (Hartford: Hudson and Goodwin, 1799), 9.

[326] *Statutes of Columbia College* (New York: Samuel Loudon, 1785), 5–8; E. Beardsley, *Life and Times of William Samuel Johnson* (Boston: Houghton, Mifflin and Company, 1886), 141–42.

[327] B. Franklin, *Proposals Relating to the Education of Youth in Pennsylvania* (1749; reprint, Philadelphia: University of Pennsylvania Press, 1931), 22.

[328] S. Colwell, *The Position of Christianity in the United States in its Relations with our Political Institutions*, 121–24.

[329] W. H. McGuffey, *Eclectic Third Reader* (Cincinnati: Winthrop B. Smith, 1853), preface; W. H. McGuffey, *Eclectic Fourth Reader* (Cincinnati: Winthrop B. Smith & Co., 1849), 9.

[330] H. Mann, ed., *The Common School Journal for the Year 1839* (Boston: Marsh, Capen, Lyon, and Webb, 1839), 14, 235–36.

[331] C. G. Finney, "Men Often Highly Esteem What God Abhors," in *Sermons on Gospel Themes* (New York: Revell, 1876), 358.

[332] B. T. Washington, *The Booker T. Washington Papers*, vol. 1, ed. L. R. Harlan (Chicago: University of Illinois Press, 1972), 382.

[333] E. Willard, *A System of Universal History in Perspective* (Hartford: F. J. Huntington, 1835).

[334] *Early American Textbooks, 1775–1900* (Washington, DC: U.S. Department of Education, 1985).

[335] De Tocqueville, *Democracy in America*, 328.

[336] Ibid., 332.

[337] A. de Tocqueville, *The Republic of the United States of America and Its Political Institutions, Reviewed and Examined*, vol. I, ed. H. Reeves (Garden City, NY: A. S. Barnes & Co., 1851), 337.

[338] Schaff, *America: A Sketch of Its Political, Social, and Religious Character*, 11.

[339] E. Kendall, *Travels Through the Northern Parts of the United States*, vol. I (New York: I. Riley, 1809), 3–5, 270–71.

[340] A. Murat, *Moral and Political Sketch of the United States* (London: Effingham Wilson, 1833), 113, 132.

[341] H. Martineau, *Society in America*, vol. II (New York: Saunders & Otley, 1837), 366.

[342] *Church of the Holy Trinity v. U.S.* 143 U.S. 457, 470, 471 (1892).

[343] Quoted in F. Mead, ed., *Encyclopedia of Religious Quotations* (New Jersey: Revell, 1965), 50.

[344] 71% in 2005, 62% in 2009, etc. See note 12 above.

[345] "Beyond Red vs. Blue," note 12.

[346] For a small sampling, see "The 2004 Political Landscape," *Pew Research Center for the People and the Press* (November 5, 2003), available online at http://people-press.org/reports/display.php3?PageID=757 (accessed on August 31, 2010); "The Diminishing Divide . . . American Churches, American Politics," *Pew Research Center for the People and the Press* (June 25, 1996), available online at http://people-press.org/reports/print.php3?PageID=451 (accessed on August 31, 2010); "Annual Study Reveals America Is Spiritually Stagnant," *The*

Barna Group (March 5, 2001), available online at http://www.barna.org/barna-update/article/5-barna-update/37-annual-study-reveals-america-is-spiritually-stagnant (accessed on August 31, 2010).

347 "Summary of Key Findings," *The Pew Forum on Religion & Public Life,* available online at http://religions.pewforum.org/reports (accessed on August 27, 2010).

348 B. A. Kosmin and A. Keysar, *American Religious Identification Survey* (Hartford: Trinity College, 2008), 5, "Self-Identification of the U.S. Adult Population by Religious Tradition 1990, 2001, 2008," available online at http://www.americanreligionsurvey-aris.org/reports/ARIS_Report_2008.pdf (accessed on August 31, 2010).

349 "American Religious Identification Survey," *Graduate Center of the City University of New York* (http://www.gc.cuny.edu/faculty/research_briefs/aris/key_findings.htm (accessed on August 31, 2010). Unless otherwise noted, the statistics in this paragraph are drawn from this source.

350 "Poll: Most Americans Say They're Christian; Varies Greatly from the World at Large," *ABCNews.com* (July 18, 2001), available online at http://abcnews.go.com/sections/us/DailyNews/beliefnet_poll_010718.html.

351 Kosmin and Keysar, *American Religious Identification Survey*, 5; "Self-Identification of the U.S. Adult Population by Religious Tradition 1990, 2001, 2008," available online at http://www.americanreligionsurvey-aris.org/reports/ARIS_Report_2008.pdf (accessed on August 31, 2010).

352 Ibid.

353 R. Parker, "The Politics of God," *Kennedy School Bulletin* (Autumn 2007), available at http://www.ksg.harvard.edu/ksgpress/bulletin/autumn2004/features/god.htm.

354 *Allegheny County v. Greater Pittsburgh ACLU*, 492 U.S. 573 (1989) (J. Kennedy, dissenting opinion).

355 *Skoros v. City of New York*, No. 04–1229 (2d Cir. Feb. 2, 2006).

356 "Wisconsin School Policy Bans Religious Themes in any Song During Christmas Holiday," *Liberty Counsel* (December 5, 2005), available online at http://www.lc.org/pressrelease/2005/nr120505.htm.

357 *Roberts v. Madigan,* 702 F Supp. 1505 (D. Colo. 1989).

358 M. Malkin, "Christian Soldier, Muslim Soldier," *Jewish World Review* (October 1, 2003), available online at http://townhall.com/columnists/MichelleMalkin/2003/10/01/christian_soldier,_muslim_soldier.

359 F. Jackson and E. Thomas, "At Issue: 'Religious Accommodation' in Public Schools," *AgapePress* (September 29, 2006), available online at http://headlines.agapepress.org/archive/9/afa/292006d.asp.

360 "Free-speech fashion," *Los Angeles Times* (April 26, 2006), available online at http://www.latimes.com/news/opinion/editorials/la-ed-tshirt26apr26,0,1795156.story; "Brave New Schools: Students suspended for 'anti-gay' shirts," *WorldNetDaily* (May 3, 2006), available online at http://wnd.com/news/article.asp?ARTICLE_ID=50016; "Pro-life shirt equated with swastika"; *The Washington Times*, "Pro-lifers suited to a T," available online at http://www.washingtontimes.com/culture/20040426–102738–6978r.htm (accessed on August 31, 2010).

361 "According to Some Federal Courts and Public Schools: Christianity Out, Islam In," *Thomas More Law Center* (October 10, 2006), available online at http://www.thomasmore.org/qry/page.taf?id=19&_function=detail&sbtblct_uid1=83&_nc=466ad84c54cf53ae6dbff5fe6d238f36.

362 C. Groening, "Favoritism Toward Non-Christian Religions in U.S. Improper, Says Attorney," *AgapePress* (October 25, 2006), available online at http://headlines.agapepress.org/archive/10/afa/252006f.asp.

[363] *Lindenmuller v. The People*, 33 Barb 548, 561–562 (Sup. Ct. NY 1861).

[364] D. Blanton, "Courts Driving Religion Out of Public Life; Christianity Under Attack," *Foxnews.com* (December 1, 2005), available online at http://www.foxnews.com/story/0,2933,177355,00.html. See also "Most Americans Feel Religion Is 'Under Attack,' Poll Shows," *CNSNews.com* (November 21, 2005), available online at http://www.csnews.com/ViewCulture.asp?Page=\Culture\archive\200511\CUL20051121a.html.

[365] Cowell, *The Position of Christianity in the United States in its Relations with our Political Institutions*, 73–75.

[366] John Dickinson letter to the Society of Fort St. David's, 1768, in *Letters from a Farmer in Pennsylvania*, ed. R. T. H. Halsey (New York: Outlook Company, 1903), xlii. *See also* J. Q. Adams, *An Oration Delivered Before the Cincinnati Astronomical Society on the Occasion of Laying the Cornerstone of an Astronomical Observatory on the 10th of November, 1843* (Cincinnati: Shepard & Co., 1843), 13–14.

[367] J. Adams, "Dissertation on the Canon and Feudal Law," in *The Works of John Adams*, vol. III, ed. C. F. Adams (Boston: Charles C. Little and James Brown, 1851), 449.

[368] Wilson, "On the Natural Rights of Individuals."

[369] Thomas Jefferson letter to Francis Gilmer, June 7, 1816, in *Memoir, Correspondence, and Miscellanies, From the Papers of Thomas Jefferson*, vol. IV, ed. T. J. Randolph (Boston: Gray and Bowen, 1830), 278.

[370] See, for example, J. Madison, "Declaration of Rights of Virginia," in *Letters and Other Writings of James Madison*, vol. 1 (New York: R. Worthington, 1884), 21; W. Paterson, *The Charge of Judge William Paterson to the Jury, in the Case of Vanhorne's Lessee against Dorrance* (Philadelphia: Samuel B. Smith, 1796), 15–16; Dickinson, *Letters from a Farmer in Pennsylvania*, 137.

[371] S. Adams, "The Natural Rights of the Colonists As Men," 502–4.

[372] Albert Gallatin letter to Alexander Addison, October 7, 1789, in *The Papers of Albert Gallatin, Feb. 7, 1761–July 1, 1880* (Philadelphia: Historic Publications, 1969).

[373] J. Madison, *A Memorial and Remonstrance* (Massachusetts: Isaiah Thomas, 1786).

[374] A. Hamilton, *The Farmer Refuted* (New York: James Rivington, 1775), 6.

[375] J. Wilson, *The Works of James Wilson*, vol. III, ed. B. Wilson (Philadelphia: Bronson and Chauncey, 1804), 84–85.

[376] F. Ames, "Eulogy on Washington," in *The Works of Fisher Ames* (Boston: T. B. Wait & Co., 1809), 125.

[377] J. Adams, "Discourses on Davila; A Series of Papers on Political History," in *The Works of John Adams*, VI:280.

[378] T. Jefferson, *Notes on the State of Virginia* (Philadelphia: Matthew Carey, 1794), 236–37.

[379] *People v. Ruggles*, 8 Johns 545–547 (Sup. Ct. NY. 1811).

[380] *City Council of Charleston v. S. A. Benjamin*, 2 Strob. 508, 518–520, 523 (Sup. Ct. S.C. 1846).

[381] B. Franklin, "The Ephemera," in *The Works of Benjamin Franklin*, vol. II, ed. J. Sparks (Boston: Tappan, Whittemore, and Mason, 1836), 178. See also N. Webster, *An American Dictionary of the English Language* (1828), s.v., "morals."

[382] J. Witherspoon, "Lectures on Moral Philosophy," in *The Works of John Witherspoon*, vol. VII (Edinburgh: J. Ogle, 1815), 70.

[383] E. Mansfield, *American Education, Its Principles and Elements* (New York: A. S. Barnes & Co., 1851), 43.

384 Letter from Charles Carroll to James McHenry, November 4, 1800, in *The Life and Correspondence of James McHenry*, 475.

Response to Barton

Jonathan D. Sassi

D avid Barton wants you to think that the United States is a "Christian nation" and was so at its founding. This is important to him not just as a matter of historical accuracy, but because he contends that it has momentous consequences for the present day. Indeed, his essay is to a large degree a tract for the times that takes aim at his critics on "the postmodern Left," as he labels them. More than any of the other essays in this volume, his engages contemporary battles. My comments, however, like my essay, will stick mainly to the Founding Era. That said, it must be pointed out that Barton mischaracterizes and besmirches contemporary Islam when he refers to it as "a religion that considers America the Great Satan."

One thing about which Barton and I agree is that name-calling is not productive of understanding. That is why I thank the editor and publisher of this volume for giving the participants a forum to discuss the religious origins of the United States in a substantive and scholarly way. Aside from that point of agreement, however, I find Barton's essay otherwise unpersuasive. His case for the United States' status as a "Christian nation" is based on faulty reasoning and selective use of evidence.

Barton's essay fundamentally rests on circular logic. He first defines what constitutes a "Christian nation" in terms of certain characteristics that supposedly prevailed at the time of the founding of the United States and then concludes, based on his definition, that the United States was established as a Christian nation. According to Barton, a Christian nation is defined by five key principles: republicanism, separation of church and state, religious toleration, an emphasis on personal conduct over theological uniformity, and a "free-market" competition for the winning of religious adherents. Obviously, history includes many examples of self-professed Christian states that do not fit this bill, such as the Eastern Orthodox empire of Byzantium or the Roman Catholic empire of the Spanish Habsburgs, to name just two examples of world-historical significance. Barton, however, conveniently dismisses such counterexamples by consigning them to "the Period of Apostasy" that in his view of church history stretched for over a millennium, roughly from the Emperor Constantine to John Wycliffe. While it may be convenient for his argument to read so many historical examples and traditions out of Christendom, it is also enormously tendentious of him to do so.

Barton quotes several people in the second half of his essay who stated at one time or another that the United States was a Christian nation. However, it is not at all clear to me that their usage adheres to his strict definition of that term, and he makes no effort to demonstrate that these various writers and spokesmen are using "Christian nation" in his way, preferring quantity of examples over quality of analysis. No matter how many nineteenth- or twentieth-century writers or politicians opined that the United States was a Christian country, it does not prove much about the situation that prevailed at the nation's birth in the eighteenth century. Put another way, the subsequent attempts to sacralize the nation's origins would make for a fascinating story in their own right, but they do not provide the "irrefutable proof" about the Founding Era that Barton thinks, no matter how many quotations he piles up.

Turning to historical rather than logical or definitional problems, Barton's essay contains a host of inaccuracies and misrepresentations. In the first place, England's American colonies were not pure republics, but contained, like the mother country, a mixture of monarchical, aristocratic, and democratic elements. Before independence, they all acknowledged the authority of the Crown. By the eighteenth century none elected their governors outside of Connecticut and Rhode Island, and colonists widely celebrated their allegiance to the Protestant succession, which was fundamental to their British identity.[1]

Thus, Barton's first "civic trait" about the colonial antecedents of the future United States misses the mark.

Barton skims over the history of the colonial period and lumps all of England's North American colonies together as having had "Reformation" origins that took root in the "virgin soil" of America and grew into commitments to the separation of church and state, religious toleration, and a "free market" in religion. Such an argument fails to recognize that Christianity was a much more important motivating factor in the establishment of some colonies (Massachusetts or Pennsylvania, for example) than others (such as New York or South Carolina). It also papers over the profound differences in terms of church-state arrangements among the several colonies, many of which boasted religious establishments. Barton's claim that seventeenth-century Protestants enshrined religious toleration ignores the case of New England outside of Rhode Island or any of the colonies south of Pennsylvania. It is simply an ahistorical argument that glosses over the long and contentious colonial-era struggles to achieve the pre-Revolutionary ascendance of toleration. Likewise, Barton's depiction of a religious free market overlooks the two most important colonies, Massachusetts and Virginia, where the persecution and harassment of dissenters during the Great Awakening, Baptists especially, proves that even as late as the middle third of the eighteenth century untrammeled religious freedom was not to be found there.[2]

Barton exaggerates the leadership of Christian clergymen in the Revolutionary era. While some like John Witherspoon undeniably played important roles, they hardly ran the show. More important, Barton fails to acknowledge that the Revolution divided the Christian clergy of colonial British America and that large numbers of ministers took loyalist or pacifist positions. Moreover, why did the Revolutionary-era constitutions of South Carolina, North Carolina, and Georgia prohibit ministers from being elected to their legislatures if clerical leadership was so important?[3]

Barton asserts that the "general principles" upon which the nation was built were Christian, but if that were the case, why did the Constitution not make such a statement? Rather, the Constitution's authority was grounded in the basis of "We, the

People." As historian John M. Murrin has provocatively written, "The Federal Constitution was, in short, the eighteenth-
century equivalent of a secular humanist text." Barton likewise
cites various religious tests in some of the first state constitutions, but he silently skips over the federal Constitution's
explicit rejection of such tests in Article VI. He also notes many
of the fasting and thanksgiving proclamations that were issued
by various officeholders. On this last point, however, I agree
with the assessment of historian Thomas J. Curry, who writes
of one such bill for fasting and thanksgiving days from James
Madison, that it "proceeded from the habits of mind and unchal-
lenged assumptions about society of a people overwhelmingly
Protestant Christian. They did not constitute deliberate contradictions of enunciated principles, but were rather a result of the
absence within the new state of dissenters who might challenge
Virginia's government to bring all its practices into harmony
with its precepts."[4]

Based on the above, I conclude that David Barton's case for
the United States as a "Christian nation" lacks merit. Rather,
the Framers of the United States Constitution created a deliberately secular document under which people of an eclectic mix
of faith traditions could live together. I will give the last word to
George Washington, who in his letter to the Jewish congregation of Newport, Rhode Island, in 1790, captured perfectly the
ecumenical religious freedom of the new nation:

> The Citizens of the United States of America have a right to
> applaud themselves for having given to mankind examples
> of an enlarged and liberal policy: a policy worthy of imita-
> tion. All possess alike liberty of conscience and immunities
> of citizenship. It is now no more that toleration is spoken
> of, as if it was by the indulgence of one class of people, that
> another enjoyed the exercise of their inherent natural
> rights. For happily the Government of the United States,
> which gives to bigotry no sanction, to persecution no assis-
> tance requires only that they who live under its protection
> should demean themselves as good citizens, in giving it on
> all occasions their effectual support.[5]

Endnotes

[1] B. McConville, *The King's Three Faces: The Rise and Fall of Royal America, 1688–1776* (Chapel Hill: University of North Carolina Press, 2006).

[2] C. Beneke, *Beyond Toleration: The Religious Origins of American Pluralism* (New York: Oxford University Press, 2006); R. Isaac, *The Transformation of Virginia, 1740–1790* (New York: Norton, 1988); W. G. McLoughlin, *New England Dissent, 1630–1833: The Baptists and the Separation of Church and State*, 2 vols. (Cambridge, Mass.: Harvard University Press, 1971), vol. 1.

[3] J. M. Murrin, "Religion and Politics in America from the First Settlements to the Civil War," in *Religion and American Politics: From the Colonial Period to the 1980s*, edited by M. A. Noll (New York: Oxford University Press, 1990), 31; Curry, *First Freedoms*, 148.

[4] T. J. Curry, *The First Freedoms: Church and State in America to the Passage of the First Amendment* (New York: Oxford University Press, 1986), 150–53.

[5] "Letter from George Washington to the Hebrew Congregation in Newport, Rhode Island," in D. L. Dreisbach and M. D. Hall, eds., *The Sacred Rights of Conscience: Selected Readings on Religious Liberty and Church-State Relations in the American Founding* (Indianapolis: Liberty Fund, 2009), 464.

Response to Barton

William D. Henard

David Barton provides a robust perspective regarding his view of America as a Christian nation. He fills his chapter with a plethora of quotes from leaders of antiquity in order to defend his position. I was expecting, however, that Barton would provide a more substantial defense of "America as a Christian nation" with regard to the belief that America was established as a Christian nation in opposition to all other religions. His position appears to be only slightly different from the one I provided in my chapter. I believe it would have been important that Barton discuss America as a uniquely defined Christian nation, since there are those in our country today who hold to that position.[1] I have heard Barton speak on several occasions and have read several of his books. He offers a very compelling opinion with regard to America and religious freedom.

Where I would comment on this chapter begins with his historical assessment. Barton is correct with regard to the

Reformation's influence on the founding of America and the American republic. A review of John Calvin's ideas regarding the Two Kingdoms demonstrates the formulation of the distinctions between church and state, but also provides the connectionalism of the two. Where I believe that Barton fails in his analysis comes in his conclusions regarding the role of the Reformation, and particularly Calvinism, during the American Revolution. By the time of the Revolution, a form of Arminianism had swept many of the pulpits of America. The prevailing notion of freedom was not necessarily a Calvinist notion as it was an Arminian one, at least with regard to personal freedom and personal interpretation. Several of the pastors mentioned by Barton as leaders of the Revolution were not followers of the Calvinistic adherents of the Reformation but were heavily influenced by Jacobus Arminius, including Jonathan Mayhew, Charles Chauncy, and John Leland. I do not want to discount the influence of the Reformation on the founding of America, but it was not solely responsible. In order to more effectively evaluate the role of Christianity in the founding of America, one must explore several philosophies of theology.

One area of confusion in reading Barton's chapter arises out of his explanation or defense of the morals of Christianity in influencing America's founding in distinction to the role of the theological tenets. Barton states, "Yet *none* of these issues deal with theology, which is necessary if there is to be a theocracy. The issues of judicial activism, internet filters, voting, marriage, cloning, etc., relate not to theology (the study of God, divine things, or divinity) but rather to values (the beliefs of a person or group either for or against something)." In reading this section, I believe that Barton is more accurately attempting to distinguish between forced theological belief or adherence and the influence of the moral law of Christianity. He attempts to make a distinction between "principle" and "dogma," explaining, "A Christian, out of his personal concern for the spiritual welfare of others, will share his own Christian faith with others (perhaps even zealously so) and seek to convert them to Christianity, but he will not coerce others to that belief; in all cases, it must be a matter of voluntary choice." In my opinion, this quote provides an accurate perspective of the Founders.

Where I believe he falters originates in his attempt to divorce theology from moral influence. While I do not believe that Barton intends on denying theology, it seems that his snafu arises more out of definition than in application. For example, Barton correctly uses the story of the Good Samaritan to demonstrate how Christianity has morally impacted the American value system. He makes several interesting applicational implications, disputing those who deny Christianity's role in the founding of America. Yet he contradicts himself, asserting, "The Teaching of the Good Samaritan was delivered solely by Jesus Christ and is therefore an overtly Christian teaching; yet it cannot be reasonably argued that the 'Good Samaritan' is a theological tenet." Barton tries to limit the term "theology" to "the study of God, divine things, or divinity," using a dictionary for his definition. The problem develops because one cannot separate the words of Christ from theology. The fact that Jesus (and Jesus alone as noted by Barton) told this story immerses the entire narrative into theology. Jesus was not just telling a story as tale or lesson, he was injecting theological application into the lives of his hearers. The characters were not just normal individuals; they represented the foundation of religious society for Israel. The Good Samaritan characterizes theology at its best.

Further proof of this opinion stems from Barton's conclusion. He contends:

> Although civil law prohibits murder, from a legal standpoint it can do nothing about a murder until *after* it occurs; Christianity, on the other hand, addresses murder *before* it occurs—while it is still only a thought in the heart, thus preventing the murder (see, for example, Matt 5:22–28). Similarly, covetousness is not illegal but it often results in crimes that are (theft, burglary, embezzlement, etc.); it is religion and not law that can prevent covetousness and thus the crimes it produces.

This very claim demonstrates the connection of theology with practice. If these statements were purely moralistic, then the role of Christianity would be unnecessary. America could be founded as a Muslim nation, a Jewish nation, or a secular humanist nation, as long as their particular moral principles were included. Barton, however, proves that the unique feature of Christianity originates from its theology, its belief in Yahweh God, his Word, and his life-changing salvation. If theology did not matter, then similar moral teachings found in other religions would be just as sufficient as Christianity. He contends, though, that other religions are not sufficient.

Similarly, Barton tries to use the account of the prophet Elijah's encounter with the prophets of Baal as an example of how Christianity offers religious toleration. While I do not disagree with his premise, I think he offers a mistaken hermeneutic in using this passage to defend his position. Barton explains, "He [God] offered the people a choice of following the God of Israel or the god Baal." While it is true that Elijah offered the Israelites the chance to choose, Barton fails to recognize the consequences of their choices. If the Israelites had chosen to follow Baal, they would have encountered the judgment of God. The prophets of Baal were killed by Elijah (1 Kgs 18:40). A biblical theology shows that judgment accompanies disobedience. When Adam and Eve chose to disobey God, they were cast out of the Garden of Eden. When Pharaoh decided not to listen to God, he and his nation came under the judgment of God.

This same sense of judgment awaited the Israelites, had they chosen to continue to follow Baal. In my opinion, the biblical account does not provide a demonstration of toleration, nor does it suggest that principle. I agree with Barton in his assessment that Christianity offers a far greater love and acceptance of other religions, but I cannot find this assertion in the Scriptures cited in this chapter. This conclusion proves, in my mind, why theology cannot be separated from practice. In theological study, one must break down ideas into their smallest parts in order to best understand them. For example, in theological study one separates evangelism and discipleship. In practice, however, problems arise when an individual or church fails to see the essential connection between the two, as evidenced by Jesus' challenge in the Great Commission of Matt 28:19–20.

The Christian teaching that faith cannot be forced on another demonstrates that this conclusion originates through theology, not morality. Barton, in explaining how Christianity provides the foundation for a free-market society, affirms:

This free-market approach adopted by Christians was not because they believed their own religion to be weak; to the contrary, they strongly believe that Christianity is superior to all other religions—that faith in Jesus Christ is the only means of securing eternal life and enjoying personal communion with Almighty God (cf., John 14:6, Acts 4:12, Matt 7:13–14, Phil 2:9–11, etc.). Yet, Christians also believe with equal conviction that every individual must make his own voluntary choices about his religion and eternal future, and must then live with the consequences—even if that choice means (from a Christian's viewpoint) the difference between heaven and hell.

Yet he contradicts himself when he states, "In addition to times of prayer, Congress attended church as part of its official activities. It also instructed the Continental Army that 'all officers and soldiers diligently attend divine service,' and the Navy that 'divine service be performed twice a day on board, and a sermon preached on Sundays.'" These statements imply a coercion of sorts. While I believe that Barton is correct in his assessment that the Founders did not believe in a forced faith, Barton stumbles at this point. The answer lies in seeing that the Founders believed that theology led to practice and morality.

Finally, Barton offers some interesting statistics about the strength of Christianity in America, concluding that America still reigns as a Christian nation. One can find other statistics that disagree with that conclusion. In Barton's defense, one can find varying statistics that disagree with each other. Statistical gathering and analysis is not a perfect science. For example, the American Religious Identification Survey, comparing their stats of 2009 with 1990, says that "seventy-six percent of Americans say they are Christian (in 2009), down from 86 percent in 1990. Thirty-four percent of adults say they are born-again Christians. Those who claim that they have no religion: 14.3 million (8.2%) in 1990; 29.4 million (14.1%) in 2001; 34.1 million (15%) in 2008. Adults who adhere to a non-Christian religion: 5.8 million (3.3%) in 1990; 7.7 million in (3.7%) in 2001;

8.7 million (3.9%) in 2008." These conclusions disagree with Barton's statistics. What ARIS says is that America is far less a Christian nation now than it has ever been, and it seems that this conclusion only worsens over time.

Apart from these inconsistencies, Barton proves his point well. Again, while I thought that he would present the case for a solely Christian America, Barton provides ample evidence that fortifies his belief in the direct impact of Christianity in America's founding and his definition of America as a Christian nation.

Endnote

[1] Some years ago in Lexington, Kentucky, a church sponsored a Fourth of July rally at Applebee's Park. One of the speakers chided the audience that those who come to America from other religions need to leave the Bibles of their faith home because America is a Christian nation. The implication was that, because America is a Christian nation, other faiths are not welcome here.

Response to Barton
Daryl C. Cornett

David Barton offers a more apologetic than strictly historical treatment of the relationship of Christianity to American history. He defines a Christian nation as one "founded on Christian and biblical principles, whose society and institutions [are] shaped . . . by those principles." His depth of research is truly impressive and he has done a superlative job at demonstrating that a significant number of Americans have exhibited Christian belief and character, forcing us to recognize the place of Christianity within American culture. There can be no doubt of the significant role Christianity has played throughout American history. However, Barton's interpretation is ultimately insufficient, resulting in historical tunnel vision, mostly from what is omitted rather than what is included.

Barton offers a sweeping interpretation of Christianity's history in its relationship to government. Although I agree with his overall bird's-eye view of the nature of pre- and post-Constantine and pre- and post-Reformation times, it oversimplifies and ignores variations of Christian expressions within those periods and mischaracterizes some aspects of the Reformation Period. His politicized bias causes him to argue that the kind of government envisioned and then implemented by the Founding Fathers was the product of biblical Christianity. Therefore, what is Christian is American, and vice versa.

Although I would concede that the United States has had many Christians in its past and today and that Christians have been salt and light in American culture, sometimes with lesser or greater effectiveness, I do not accept the notion that America *is* a Christian nation. Fundamentally, I find the terms curiously contradictory. A Christian is a citizen of heaven, of the kingdom of God, which is not of this world. The institution that God has established for the advancement of the gospel is the church. God has ordained government for specific purposes, primarily to restrain evil and protect the innocent. A culture will embody and reflect certain ideologies whether that be Christian, Islamic, Communism, socialism, Marxism, republicanism, anti-clericalism, liberalism, secularism, and so forth. A government may be republican, Communist, socialist, or totalitarian. But a government cannot *be* Christian. One may argue that a republic with a democratic egalitarianism is more congruent with Christian ideals, but that is not to say that it can be Christian. *Christian* is a proper noun describing a person. *Christian* is not an adjective that can describe a whole country.

Barton's interpretation of American history suffers not only from a faulty understanding of the application of the word *Christian*, but also from some mischaracterizations of history. As Barton retells the movement of the sixteenth-century Protestant Reformation one is led to believe that the seeds of American political ideas such as republicanism, the separation of church and state, religious toleration, and freedom of conscience came from these Reformers. These ideas are not the direct result of the Reformation and its earliest proponents. The evidence is just to the contrary. The Magisterial Reformers

primarily dissented against the bureaucratic corruption and
theology of the Roman Catholic Church; however, they were not
tolerant of *any* form of Christianity. Reformers such as Martin
Luther, John Calvin, Ulrich Zwingli, and others condoned the
execution of heretics and the suppression of dissenting groups
such as the Anabaptists or Jews. The kind of religious liberty
and freedom of conscience that Americans enjoy today resulted
from the more radical kinds of Christians that came behind the
original Reformers coupled with the social and political ideas
of the Enlightenment philosophers. The Age of Enlightenment
that followed the Reformation was largely a reaction to the
political and religious intolerance and persecution of the Reformation.

Barton also mischaracterizes the American colonial period
of history. He paints a historical picture of a religiously tolerant
time in which people brought from Europe a "scriptural free-
market approach," and a modern-like sensitivity to religious
freedom, especially in the case of Jews and Muslims. However,
this is misleading. Numerous early charters and especially
early state constitutions could easily be cited to give evidence
to the contrary. The oaths that colony/state legislators had to
take were often explicitly Christian and exclusive of any who
could not affirm Protestant orthodox views. For example the
Constitution of Vermont (1777) required its representatives to
solemnly swear to the following: "I _____ do believe in one God,
the Creator and Governor of the Diverse [sic], the rewarder [sic]
of the good and punisher of the wicked. And I do acknowledge
the scriptures of the old and new testament to be given by divine
inspiration, and own and profess the protestant religion."[1] The
colony of South Carolina declared in its 1778 constitution that
the "Christian Protestant religion shall be deemed . . . the established religion."[2] Religious tests favoring Protestant Christians
for public office continued from state to state into the 1830s.

He correctly informs us that Roger Williams founded the
colony of Rhode Island with the explicit intention of providing religious freedom for its residents. But Barton fails to tell
his reader that the reason Williams founded the community of
Providence was that the religiously intolerant Puritans of Boston officially condemned and banished him. Places like Rhode

Island in colonial America were the exception, not the rule. In the Puritan-dominated New England and the Anglican-established South, radical religious dissenters such as Baptists and Quakers were persecuted in the colonial period, and Jews could not hold public office. This is why Roger Williams is a key figure in the historical development of religious freedom in America— he (and others) fought against persecuting, established majorities.

It is misleading to use certain public figures to give the impression of "Christian America." He references Jefferson numerous times. He also pulled out a lesser-known clergyman, Charles Chauncy, as an example of a Christian leader. The manner with which Barton handles these men is irresponsible. Jefferson was clearly not a Christian, rather a deistic moralist. Chauncy was a Unitarian, meaning he rejected the traditional tenets of Christianity (i.e., he did not believe in the divinity of Jesus). These men could speak of God and use religious language, even talk about the "Christian" ideals, but they were not Christian. Failing to highlight these important doctrinal issues gives the wrong impression to Christians who lack information about such figures. Anytime a Jefferson, Franklin, or Chauncy is quoted favorably in regard to God or prayer without proper qualification, a Christian who is less informed will see such generic statements through their own faith lens and assume such men to have been Christian.

The most serious deficiency of Barton's interpretation and argumentation is its one-sidedness. There can be no doubt of the presence of professing Christians throughout all American history, and ample evidence exists that marks the influence of Christian teachings and commitments. No historian of any credibility would deny this. However, other forces have been at work as well in the formation of the United States and through her development to this day. Barton shows how easy it is to simply pile up quote after quote containing religious or moral content from American history. However, this gives a distorted picture of the history. The strong currents of the Enlightenment infused the Founding Fathers with political ideas about liberty, social contract, inalienable rights, resisting tyranny, and so forth. The fact that the orthodox Christian, Unitarian, and deist could all rally around these thoughts points to the fact that these political ideas primarily came from a nonbiblical source. Those who cared to back them with Christian rhetoric simply used Scripture as a proof text. Those who did not feel it was important to have the approbation of the Bible simply appealed to common sense, reason, self-evident truth, or Nature's God.

Barton is a sincerely motivated Christian activist who possesses deep convictions about his faith and an intense love of his country, but comes up short on doing good history. He is extremely knowledgeable of the Christian presence in the past; however, such knowledge alone does not make one a good historian. A good Christian historian strives for objectivity in research and interpretation and fairness in presentation, both of which Barton habitually lacks. Those from the secular and liberal left often commit the same scholarly sin by discounting, ignoring, or marginalizing unfairly the real Christian influences on American history. Doing history is investigation, research, analysis, and interpretation of the available evidence left behind. Doing history is not an apologetic endeavor. Barton is a much better apologist for an idea he wants to prove than a historian who desires to paint the most objectively accurate picture he can.

Endnotes

[1] Constitution of Vermont: July 8, 1777, The Avalon Project at Yale Law School, http://www.yale.edu/lawweb/avalon/states/vt01.htm (accessed June 26, 2008).

[2] Constitution of South Carolina: March 19, 1778, The Avalon Project at Yale Law School, http://www.yale.edu/lawweb/avalon/states/sc02.htm (accessed June 26, 2008).

America Religious Eclectic and Secular

Jonathan D. Sassi

W hen the French aristocrat Alexis de Tocqueville arrived for his tour of the United States in 1830, he noted that "it was the religious aspect of the country that first struck my eye." It surprised Tocqueville to find that the world's foremost republic should also be intensely religious, since on the Continent, Christianity was often aligned with the forces of political reaction. In France, Tocqueville "had seen the spirit of religion and the spirit of freedom almost always move in contrary directions," but in the United States he "found them united intimately with one another: they reigned together on the same soil." Intrigued, Tocqueville asked a number of Americans he met about their country's blend of democracy and religion. He especially sought explanations from clergymen of assorted denominations, including Roman Catholic priests, to whose church he belonged. All of his informants "attributed the peaceful dominion that religion exercises in their country principally to the complete separation of church and state."[1]

Tocqueville's observations neatly encapsulate the central task of this essay, which is to provide a historical account of the United States as founded on the principle of "the complete separation of church and state" and characterized by a robust and diverse religious culture. Tocqueville had located the roots of the American combination of freedom and religion in the Puritan settlement of the seventeenth century, his historical "point

of departure" for the United States.² This essay instead argues
for the era of the American Revolution and early republic as
the decisive years for explaining what Tocqueville observed in
1830. In arguing for the religiously eclectic and secular natures
of America's beginning, as opposed to the notion of America
founded as distinctly Christian, one needs to be clear about terminology, so as to avoid confusion or misunderstanding. Three
parameters of the following essay need to be delineated at the
outset.

First, the term "America's beginning" here denotes chrono-
logically and geographically the period during the last quarter
of the eighteenth century when thirteen of Britain's mainland
North American colonies declared independence and united in
establishing the United States of America. One could locate
"America's beginning" in some other time and place, such as
at Jamestown or Plymouth during the early seventeenth century. However, that would obscure the tremendous changes
that took place over the first century and a half of the colonial
period and impose a proleptic unity over the colonies' diverse
histories. One could also take a broader view of "America" so
as to include the other European colonies throughout North
and South America. This would add an important comparative
dimension to the story, especially given the explicitly Christian
goals of some of the French and Spanish colonies.³ However, to
do so would take us too far away from our primary concern with
the founding period within the limited confines of this volume.
This essay will therefore begin with an overview of the religious
and church-state landscapes of the mature colonial period of
British North America, circa 1760.

Second, the essay focuses thematically on government, particularly its religious character (or lack thereof) and the relationship between church and state. One definition of "secular"
is "belonging to the world and its affairs as distinguished from
the Church and religion."⁴ It would be hard to argue that the
American people or their culture were secular in the eighteenth
century. However, if we confine our analysis to constitutional
and political matters, then it is the contention of this essay
that the Framers of the United States Constitution chose a
deliberately secular path in the interest of national unity. They

designed a government to deal with practical, worldly affairs and not to interfere with the religious realm.

Third, the essay takes the position that America was "religiously eclectic" at the time of its founding in the eighteenth century, rather than distinctly Christian, because to label late colonial and early national America as "Christian" would falsely homogenize a situation of fascinating complexity among professed Christians, not to mention those Americans who would have rejected identifying themselves as such. We live today in an ecumenical time, when old divisions between Christian traditions are breaking down and new patterns of interdenominational affinity are emerging amid a broader liberal-evangelical realignment.[5] Nevertheless, present patterns of Christian harmony should not mislead us into seeing the same in the eighteenth century. Deep theological and social disagreements divided American Christians of the late eighteenth century between Calvinist and proto-Unitarian camps in New England, between Anglicans and Baptists in the South, and between Quakers and Presbyterians in the Mid-Atlantic, to name just three pairs of groups opposed to each other, among many others. Moreover, historians have brought to light many dimensions of colonial religious experience that were not Christian at all. These ranged from Enlightenment rationalism and deism to magic and occult practices.[6] The new nation's small Jewish population, to take another example, scattered in cities along the Atlantic seaboard, asserted its religious liberty during the Revolutionary era and had its rights affirmed by none less than George Washington. As he told the Jewish community of Newport, Rhode Island, in 1790, "happily the Government of the United States, which gives to bigotry no sanction, to persecution no assistance, requires only that they who live under its protection, should demean themselves as good citizens, in giving it on all occasions their effectual support."[7] Therefore, while there were a variety of Christian influences on American civic life before, during, and after the era of the Revolution, the overall picture was an eclectic and secular one.

The following essay divides into three chronological periods in the relationship between religion and public life amid an overarching trend toward increasing religious eclecticism.

By the middle of the eighteenth century, an atmosphere of religious toleration prevailed throughout British colonial America,
primarily the result of Americans' diversity of beliefs, among
other factors. Following the end of the Seven Years' War in 1763,
policy disputes between the British government and its American colonies over primarily secular matters raised the fundamentally irreconcilable issue of sovereignty within the empire,
which eventuated in the Declaration of Independence in 1776.
The American Revolution initiated a second period marked by
dislocations in the colonial order and further expansions of religious liberty. When it came time to fashion a national government in the late 1780s, it would be a secular one that foreswore
any interference in religious matters. Beneath the canopy of
that limited national government, a welter of religious expressions flourished in a competitive marketplace during the early
republic, the essay's third period. Although religion became
embroiled in the partisan politics of the Federalist and Jeffersonian eras, the outcome of these struggles confirmed the government's secular stance. During the 1820s, however, religiously
inspired Reformers reentered the civic arena, realizing that
government policy did not always confine itself to purely secular matters but sometimes encroached on such moral issues as
Sabbath observance, Indian removal, and chattel slavery. By
the Jacksonian era, therefore, the religiously eclectic and secular nature of the nation's founding had ironically yielded a society and culture in which religious values occupied a prominent
(albeit controversial) place, as Tocqueville had observed.

The Colonial Legacies of Religious
Eclecticism and Toleration to circa 1760

The religious eclecticism and toleration that characterized Britain's North American colonies by the mid-eighteenth
century had developed as a result of both the colonies' distinct
histories and their ongoing interactions with the wider Anglo-
Atlantic world. The three broad regions—New England, the
Middle Colonies, and the South—each had a different denominational mix and different church-state traditions. At the same
time, a common ethic of religious toleration transcended all

three. There was agreement that matters of conscience should be beyond the reach of the state, and Protestants were generally free to practice their faith in whatever denominational form they preferred as long as they comported themselves in an orderly manner. This eighteenth-century spirit of toleration had come about from both the home-grown resistance of determined minority groups as well as English influences. The latter included the direct force of law, especially following the 1689 Act of Toleration; the culture of the Enlightenment; and the political pressure applied by English dissenting groups on behalf of their American co-religionists. Both the centrifugal forces of colonization and the centripetal pull of empire yielded the same results, namely greater religious eclecticism and toleration. The religious revivals of mid-century, collectively known as the Great Awakening, only accelerated these trends. The controversies that erupted over the revivals' propriety and legitimacy further divided the denominational landscape. The resulting increase in religious pluralism confirmed the necessity that governments confine themselves to secular matters.

The New England colonies of Massachusetts and Connecticut had the strongest claim to having been founded as distinctly Christian, but even the Puritans could not contain the religious diversity of their age. "In Massachusetts," observes historian Jon Butler, "Christian commitments as often produced tension and disorder as peace and harmony." Governor John Winthrop in 1630 had famously characterized the Massachusetts Bay Colony as a "City upon a Hill," where all the world could witness whether or not the settlers obeyed their covenant with the Lord and received in return either divine blessings or wrath. Winthrop and other leaders of the first generation instituted a variety of mechanisms to maintain social order and uphold fidelity to the national covenant. These included making church attendance mandatory and strictly enforcing the Sabbath, requiring prospective church members to recount their conversion experiences publicly, and limiting voting rights to male church members. The Congregational churches received public tax support for construction, maintenance, and ministerial salaries. Try as they might to establish uniformity, however, numerous dissenters to the Puritan way cropped up within the first decade. Anne

Hutchinson emerged as a polarizing figure during the "free grace controversy" when she accused several leading Puritan divines of preaching a doctrine of works, rather than salvation by grace. Roger Williams objected that magistrates in Massachusetts Bay had too much authority over Christ's church, and he also charged the colony with having defrauded the Indians of their land. The Puritan authorities banished both.[8]

Williams in his banishment fled to the Narragansett Bay region and there founded the colony of Rhode Island as a haven of religious liberty. Unlike its neighbors, the colony had no established religion and granted a broad liberty of conscience, and as a result Rhode Island became home to a diverse array of religious groups. Puritans heaped scorn on the colony as wayward and anarchic, and it remained a regional anomaly. "The stigma of its early radicalism clung," concludes historian Thomas J. Curry, "with the result that what was an extraordinary experiment in religious freedom turned out to be, apart from Rhode Island itself, an idea too advanced to achieve general acceptance."[9] Nonetheless, Rhode Island broke up the Puritan grip over New England and it would serve in later years as an important base for dissenters from the Massachusetts and Connecticut religious establishments.

When the Quakers entered Massachusetts in the late 1650s, they highlighted the Puritans' intolerant practices and brought English pressure for change to bear on the colony. The Puritan authorities responded to the first Quaker missionaries as they had to Hutchinson and Williams, by ordering their banishment. The Quakers were, like the Puritans, radicals of the English Reformation, but to an even greater degree. They denounced the Reformed churches they found in Massachusetts, as well as the Puritans' social order, testifying to their doctrines of the "inner light," nonconformity, and pacifism. When expelled from the colony, however, some of the Quakers defiantly returned. The Massachusetts authorities executed four of them in punishment, which "forc[ed] Puritan leaders to confront the full implications of their refusal to grant religious toleration to an increasingly diverse population." Quakers in England complained to King Charles II about Massachusetts' treatment of their brethren and the English government ordered that there be no further executions.[10]

Further intervention from England would play a critically important role in establishing religious toleration in New England. The Restoration regimes of Charles II and James II not surprisingly took a dim view of Puritan rule in New England. The Puritans' foot-dragging and outright disobedience of imperial mandates led England to revoke the Massachusetts Bay charter in 1684 and conglomerate all of New England with the colony of New York into a new entity known as the Dominion of New England. The Dominion did not last long, falling victim to the upheavals of the Glorious Revolution that brought William and Mary to the throne in 1688. Massachusetts received a new charter in 1691, but it did not restore the status quo ante. Massachusetts became a royal colony and, among other changes, it had to conform its practices to England's 1689 Act of Toleration. As a result, Massachusetts could no longer exclude non-Puritans from voting or practicing their faith openly. There remained a generation of working out the full dimensions of religious toleration in New England, as the Puritans only reluctantly recognized the legitimacy of other denominations to exist in their midst. Nevertheless, by the late 1720s, Anglicans, Baptists, and Quakers had all achieved exemption from the taxes that supported the Puritan churches in both Massachusetts and Connecticut.[11]

In addition to this budding denominational diversity, seventeenth-century New Englanders also resisted the imposition of any kind of monolithic Puritan orthodoxy by either engaging in a variety of non-Christian religious practices or simply hanging back from the churches. The recurrent witchcraft episodes revealed widespread dabbling in magic. Numerous diarists also recorded apparitions, fortune-telling, or "wonders," only some of which could be explained through Puritan providentialism. Many New Englanders failed to attain the Founders' lofty expectations for either fervent piety or doctrinal uniformity. Church membership rates initially exceeded those in England, but declined after 1650, especially among men. The leadership responded with the Half-Way Covenant of 1662, which gave unconverted children of church members the right to have their own children baptized and thereby kept within the fold. There were always also what historian David D. Hall has termed the "horse-shed Christians," those for whom the main attraction of going to church was the opportunity it presented to visit with neighbors. In the early eighteenth century, furthermore, Puritan ministers began to divide over the theological implications of the Enlightenment, with a "catholick" wing forming in opposition to the Calvinist orthodoxy of Increase and Cotton Mather. Ministers such as Benjamin Colman of Boston's Brattle Street Church shifted their preaching toward "natural causes and moral virtues," a trend that would receive even fuller expression outside New England. In short, John Winthrop's stated desire that the colonists would be "knitt together in this worke as one man" remained unfulfilled.[12]

That said, one should not underestimate the Puritans' considerable success in building their Christian commonwealths in New England. Although dissenters achieved toleration, the Congregational churches predominated numerically and culturally outside Rhode Island. Towns levied taxes to fund their churches, and the founding of Harvard College in 1636 would ensure that they were well supplied with ministers from the first years of settlement. Puritanism left a deep and lasting imprint on the regional culture. One measure of its reach is the number of sermons that a typical New Englander would have heard. "The average weekly churchgoer in New England," estimates historian Harry S. Stout, "(and there were far more churchgoers than church members) listened to something like seven thousand sermons in a lifetime, totaling somewhere around fifteen thousand hours of concentrated listening."[13] In creating a relatively sturdy religious culture, Puritan New England was an anomaly in British colonial America. Other regions would experience much greater denominational diversity and institutional disorder.

Across the South by 1760, in the five colonies from Maryland to Georgia, governments had enacted laws to establish the Church of England. Beneath that surface uniformity, however, was a more variegated religious fabric. The institutional weakness of the Anglican Church and the settlers' diversity of denominational backgrounds combined with influences from

the British Enlightenment to create a second region characterized by toleration and eclecticism.

Anglicanism was most firmly rooted in Virginia, where
"the initial session of the House of Burgesses in 1619 made
provision for financial support of the Anglican clergy, and soon
thereafter erected a system of parish government under locally
elected vestries." However, with no college to train them and
no bishop to ordain them, clergymen were in chronically short
supply throughout the seventeenth century. Anglican ministers
in Virginia often found themselves serving more than one parish, which were also geographically sprawling by English standards. Organization improved during the eighteenth century
under the leadership of the Reverend James Blair, the Anglican commissary, or bishop's designee, in the colony, who also
served as president of the College of William and Mary, which
he established in 1693. Soon, "Church of England adherence
and involvement in parish life and governance became a sine
qua non for success in Virginian society and politics from the
1680s until the time of the Revolution." As in New England,
Virginia and the rest of the Southern colonies were obligated to
respect the 1689 Act of Toleration and accommodate Quakers
and other dissenters, although they were few in number before
the Great Awakening and were not exempt from the taxes that
went to the established church.[14]

The Anglican Church in Virginia preached a "reasonable,
moderate, and judicious" message that reflected powerful currents in contemporary British thought. English theologians
beginning in the second half of the seventeenth century had
developed in opposition to Calvinism a "latitudinarian" outlook
that sought "to rehabilitate both the notion of morality in religion and the rationality of faith." This was the theology introduced by Anglican missionaries sent to Virginia by the Society
for the Propagation of the Gospel. Anglicanism accordingly
lacked the doctrinal rigor of New England Calvinism, emphasizing instead upright living and the dignified worship of the
Book of Common Prayer. There developed a deep reservoir of
Anglican lay religiosity in eighteenth-century Virginia that
featured regular attendance at worship and a central place for
the church in life's transitional rituals of baptism, marriage,

and burial. Other influential laymen such as Thomas Jefferson followed Enlightenment thinking to conclusions that traveled beyond the pale of Anglican orthodoxy. Jefferson leaned toward deism, the rationalist faith that dispensed with Christian revelation in favor of a natural religion. During the Revolutionary era, many of the Founding Fathers from Virginia showed the influence of this type of moderate Anglicanism mixed with or in some cases superseded by Enlightenment rationalism.[15]

A tolerant Anglican Church was likewise established in eighteenth-century Maryland, but that concealed an alternative route toward religious toleration that had been explored during the previous century. The proprietors of Maryland, the Calverts, were Roman Catholics, and they had wanted their colony to serve as a refuge for their persecuted English brethren. The colony attracted a diverse group of settlers, however, and Catholics always numbered in the minority. In order to keep the peace in this potentially volatile environment, the colony passed an Act Concerning Religion in 1649. The Act granted toleration to all Christians, Protestant and Catholic alike, and prohibited colonists from hurling a range of religious slurs at one another such as "heretic," "puritan," and "Jesuited papist," to list just three of the banned epithets. Maryland's unusual arrangement lasted until a local uprising in the wake of the Glorious Revolution overthrew proprietary rule. The Church of England then became the colony's officially established religion by legislation of 1702. In accordance with English practice, Protestants enjoyed toleration, but Catholics were now explicitly excluded from public office and voting rights.[16]

To the south of the Chesapeake colonies, religious diversity and indifference were rampant and toleration never in doubt. As had been the case in seventeenth-century Virginia, the Anglican Church in North Carolina, South Carolina, and Georgia struggled to cover a large expanse of territory with too few ministers. The chronic undersupply of clergymen meant that many people lacked regular religious instruction and strayed from Christian orthodoxy; ministers complained that some folks in their isolation had altogether abandoned the faith. In all of these colonies, the overriding concern for proprietors and legislators had been to foster growth by increasing the population. One reliable way to attract settlers was by welcoming religious dissenters, so as a result there was a broad mix of Protestant denominations across the lower South, with Presbyterians, Quakers, Huguenots, and Moravians, among others, joining Anglicans, who never amounted to a majority of the inhabitants. Although Anglicanism was the established religion throughout the region, Protestants of every stripe enjoyed toleration and, unlike in England, full participation in public life.[17]

The Middle Colonies of New York, New Jersey, and Pennsylvania, the third region under consideration, boasted both the broadest religious freedom and the highest degree of religious diversity in colonial British America. The region had arrived at this point along two different paths. In New York, initial dreams of religious orthodoxy and uniformity gave way to commercial, social, and political pressures for greater liberty of conscience. In Pennsylvania and the Jerseys, a heterogeneous settler population joined with Quaker principles to create colonies of great religious eclecticism and freedom. In many ways, the region would serve as a prototype for the future United States.

The colony of New York received that name following the English conquest of 1664; prior to that it was the Dutch colony of New Netherland, founded in 1624 after Peter Minuit's real estate purchase from the Indians. The last Dutch governor, Peter Stuyvesant, did much to clean up New Amsterdam, the settlement at the southern tip of the island of Manhattan, during the years of his rule from 1647 to 1664. He oversaw reforms ranging from the standardization of building codes to the removal of refuse from the newly paved streets, all of which aimed to remake the frontier outpost along the lines of a tidy Dutch city. In the area of religion as well, Stuyvesant sought to build a solid Dutch town and firmly establish the Dutch Reformed Church. He refused to grant a group of Lutherans the right to build a church and tried to prevent Jewish refugees from Brazil from taking up residence there. In these efforts, however, the Dutch West India Company overruled him, reasoning that granting toleration and welcoming settlers were in the best long-term interest of the colony.[18]

The religious diversity of New Netherland only multiplied after the English conquest. The Dutch Reformed lost their place to the Anglicans as the religion of the ruling class, but many Dutch families remained in New York and formed a prominent segment of the population. Quakers and New England Congregationalists added to the colony's diversity in the seventeenth century, as did German Lutherans and Scotch-Irish Presbyterians, to name just two groups, in the eighteenth, when non-English immigration took off in colonial British America.

Inheriting a population of such religious heterogeneity, the English rulers of New York tolerated these many Protestant denominations, and New York City's small Jewish community continued to live and worship there in peace. Controversy ensued, however, over Anglican efforts to gain legal preferment. Modern scholars continue to debate whether or not New York's four lower counties had an Anglican establishment, although historian Patricia U. Bonomi concludes that "such was the case only in the most strained and nominal sense."[19] Likewise, Presbyterians and others complained of perceived Anglican attempts to control King's College, now Columbia. Nevertheless, by the mid-eighteenth century, religious toleration for Protestants was an established fact of life in New York, as it was elsewhere in the colonies.[20]

In Pennsylvania there were no political struggles or demographic accidents needed to establish religious toleration, since the colony's founder, William Penn, had embraced religious liberty as a charter principle. Penn was a convert to Quakerism, and he universalized that group's experience of persecution into a fundamental belief in liberty of conscience. Pennsylvania "incorporated into its laws two Quaker characteristics, an abhorrence of oaths and a refusal to provide public tax support for churches and clergy."[21] The Pennsylvania legislature voted to grant political rights to all Christians, but England refused to give the royal assent until revised legislation in 1705 specifically excluded Catholics. Penn also marketed his colony throughout the British Isles and on the Continent as a haven of religious freedom, and as a result attracted a diverse array of settlers. That religious freedom combined with the fertile lands of the Delaware Valley to make Pennsylvania the most attractive destination for immigrants to colonial British America during the eighteenth century.[22]

Pennsylvania's most famous eighteenth-century arrival—from Boston, not overseas—was Benjamin Franklin, whose eclectic religious beliefs epitomized the rationalism and toleration of his age. Franklin discarded the Calvinism of his youth when he came to the conclusion that some of its central tenets "appear'd to me unintelligible, others doubtful." Instead, he developed his own stripped-down, deistical creed: "I never doubted," he wrote in his *Autobiography*, "the Existance of the Deity, that he made the World, & govern'd it by his Providence; that the most acceptable Service of God was the doing Good to Man; that our Souls are immortal; and that all Crime will be punished & Virtue rewarded either here or hereafter." Like the Anglican clergy of Virginia and many others in the eighteenth century, Franklin valued morality over theology in his religion. He quit attending the Presbyterian church in Philadelphia, because the minister there spent too much time in "polemic Arguments, or Explications of the peculiar Doctrines of our Sect," rather than in teaching useful morality. Franklin took what he wanted from the Bible, then ranged further afield in search of enlightenment. He concluded one list of virtues in an eclectic manner with the admonition, "Imitate Jesus and Socrates."[23]

Three common themes emerge from this thumbnail sketch of the religious landscape of colonial British North America to the mid-eighteenth century. In the first place, the colonies were the site of a bumptious religious pluralism. Between different regions there were widely divergent denominational profiles—Puritan New England, the Anglican South, and the pluralistic Middle Colonies—and even within individual colonies no one church held a monopoly. "The most striking aspect of colonial religious culture, and its sharpest departure from Old World tradition," observes Patricia U. Bonomi, "was the diversity—and thus the fierce competitiveness—of its beliefs and practices." Second, and in part a function of that diversity, every colony respected toleration for Protestants, regardless of whether or not it had an established church. As Thomas J. Curry points out, "toleration of dissenters from the dominant

religion of a region or country, which in the seventeenth century some groups resisted or only grudgingly accepted, came in
the eighteenth century to be commonly embraced as a matter
of principle." Third, the colonies existed within the context of
the Atlantic world. Metropolitan power, for example, played an
important role in establishing the colonies' religious toleration.
Despite their different histories, the colonies shared a connection to Britain that went beyond matters of imperial administration and governance. The continued arrival of both people
and ideas from Europe powerfully influenced the colonial religious sphere.[24]

The Great Awakening advanced all three of these trends
toward religious diversity, toleration, and a transatlantic orientation. Historians today situate the mid-century religious
revivals within a much larger transatlantic movement that
stretched in an arc from Central Europe, across to the British
Isles, and on to Britain's North American colonies. For example,
a leading participant such as John Wesley was in contact with
like-minded supporters of the Awakening in places as far flung
as Georgia, Oxfordshire, and Saxony. Likewise, printed accounts
of revivals and theological treatises that debated their meaning
flowed back and forth across the ocean. The Awakening's big-
gest celebrity, George Whitefield, crisscrossed the Atlantic on
several preaching tours, and his *Journals*, which were printed
in America by Benjamin Franklin, became a standard text
of the event. Jonathan Edwards, according to historian W. R.
Ward, "understood that the context of his ministry was no nar-
rower than the whole Protestant world."[25]

The revivals added to the complexity of the colonies' religious makeup by cross-fertilizing theological influences, bringing new people into the churches, dividing churches already
in existence, and encouraging new denominations. Wesley, for
example, was a theological omnivore, synthesizing a wide array
of influences into a new amalgam that came to be known as
Methodism. The colonies' spiritual eclecticism also dramatically increased, especially in the South, as enslaved Africans
and their descendants responded to the Christian gospel in
large numbers for the first time and added African elements
to worship and belief. In New England, the clergy divided into

pro- and anti-Awakening factions, and some churches split along the same lines, which resulted in scores of Separate congregations. The Presbyterians experienced a similar divide in the Middle Colonies, while in Virginia evangelical Presbyterians and Baptists arose to challenge the predominance of the Anglican establishment.[26]

Attempts by civil or religious authorities to suppress the Awakenings' proliferating sectarians generally backfired. The disdain of the Virginia gentry for the Baptists led to insults and sometimes violent persecutions that seemed only to nurture the Baptists' identification with the early church and the successful recruitment of new converts into their fellowship. When authorities in New England harassed the Separates with legal restrictions, Baptists, who enjoyed previously won toleration, stood to gain.[27] Baptists in both areas would emerge as leaders in the fight for increased religious liberty when the American Revolution caused a fundamental reexamination of church-state arrangements.

Religion, the American Revolution, and the Secular Founding of the United States

The thirteen colonies declared their independence from Great Britain in 1776 when patriot leaders reached the conclusion that the reign of King George III was "a history of repeated injuries and usurpations, all having in direct object the establishment of an absolute Tyranny over these States." The Declaration of Independence that they drew up to support their claim detailed how the royal government had tried to suppress the colonial legislatures, rule by force, and take away the colonists' rights and liberties.[28] The disputes that precipitated the American Revolution were, in brief, primarily secular ones over political sovereignty and natural rights, although opposition to both a colonial Anglican bishop and the Quebec Act added a religious dimension to the patriots' overall fear of a conspiracy against their freedoms. Religious spokesmen also provided legitimation to patriots, loyalists, and those pleading for neutrality by arguing that their side aligned with divine justice.

Religious factors, therefore, played only a subsidiary role in the coming of the American Revolution, yet the Revolution would form a watershed event in American religious history. The long, bloody, and divisive War for Independence deranged the religious landscape, especially as its ties to the mother country discredited the Church of England in the eyes of many. As Americans set about the task of writing state constitutions, the question of religious liberty was one that had to be addressed. While Connecticut, Massachusetts, and New Hampshire retained their support of the Congregational churches into the nineteenth century, the Anglican establishment would fall in states across the South. At the Constitutional Convention in 1787, the Founders took steps to make sure that the new United States government would not interfere with religion. When the ratifying debates revealed continuing unease about the issue, the religion clause of the First Amendment sought to make even more explicit that the federal government would respect freedom of religion and eschew a nationwide establishment. In short, the federal government would be a secular one as befitted a religiously eclectic people.

In looking for connections between religion and the American Revolution, one does not need to reach back to the Great Awakening of the 1740s in order to locate them. For two decades after the publication in 1966 of Alan Hemiert's seminal book, *Religion and the American Mind*, historians investigated possible links between the Awakening and the Revolution.[29] The conventional understanding of the clergy's role in the coming of the Revolution had depicted ministers, especially theological liberals like the Boston Congregationalist Jonathan Mayhew, as disseminating Whig theories from the pulpit. Heimert argued instead that the theological liberals preached a fundamentally conservative politics, and that it was the evangelicals who offered an inspiring, egalitarian message that prepared the people to resist authorities in the state, as they had defied those in the church during the Awakening. As imaginative as Heimert's formulation was, and as productive of fresh scholarly inquiry into the place of religion in the Revolutionary era, the purported connection between the Awakening and the Revolution has never been convincingly demonstrated. Too many theological liberals ardently supported the patriot side for there to be any simple correlation between evangelicalism and the Revolution. More compelling is the conclusion of historian John M. Murrin, who writes, "Without the Awakening, colonial resistance would have taken very much the same forms it did and within the same chronology."[30] The relevant links between religion and the Revolution are to be found instead in issues that could unite both evangelicals and liberals.[31]

The fear that an Anglican bishop might be appointed over the colonies was one such religious issue and contributed to the growing suspicion of a British conspiracy against American liberties. The lack of a resident bishop had hampered the Church of England since the seventeenth century, especially since in the Anglican hierarchy a bishop is needed to ordain clergymen and because he provides administrative oversight. At various times over the years the idea of appointing one had been advanced but had always fallen victim to opposition or competing priorities. During the eighteenth century, the Church of England had been expanding in the American colonies, as a result of both institutional growth in its Southern base and the Society for the Propagation of the Gospel's missionary activity in the Middle Colonies and New England. In the 1760s, a group of colonial Anglican ministers, the Reverend Thomas Bradbury Chandler of Elizabeth Town, New Jersey, foremost among them, made a renewed push for the appointment of an American bishop. Chandler and his allies issued petitions and published pamphlets to lay out their case, and they received a sympathetic ear from some church leaders in England, although Southern Anglicans were cool to the idea. However, this agitation for an American bishop ignited a strenuous reaction on the part of other Americans, particularly New England Congregationalists and Mid-Atlantic Presbyterians, who feared that a bishop would undermine the religious freedom and toleration that had been achieved in eighteenth-century America. Ministers and laymen opposed to an Anglican bishop for the colonies began corresponding, thereby building an intercolonial coalition, and gathered for meetings to coordinate opposition starting in November 1766. They also went to print with their arguments, which ignited an extensive pamphlet and newspaper war. In the end, the proposal for an American bishop came to naught, drowned in the flood of Revolutionary events of the mid-1770s. Nevertheless, the image of an American bishop for the Church of England formed another element in the pattern of conspiracy that American patriots saw coalescing during the late 1760s and early 1770s. Ezra Stiles, for example, the Congregational minister of Newport, Rhode Island and future president of Yale, suspected that the Stamp Act was linked to plans for an Anglican bishop as part of a two-pronged drive to tame colonial autonomy. Here allegedly loomed the threat of ecclesiastical tyranny to match the Crown's other moves toward political usurpation.[32]

The Quebec Act of 1774 only added to Americans' fears about Britain's nefarious designs on their religious liberty. In this legislation, Parliament dealt with how to govern the erstwhile French territory, which Britain had acquired in 1763 as a result of the Seven Years' War. Noting that it was "at present inexpedient to call an Assembly," the Act placed governing authority in the hands of a royal governor and an appointed council. It also granted "free Exercise" of religion to Quebec's Roman Catholic population and extended the Catholic clergy's "accustomed Dues and Rights, with respect to such Persons only as shall profess the said religion." In other words, the Catholic Church could continue legally to collect monetary support from Quebec's Catholics.[33] American patriots discerned dangerous precedents in the Quebec Act. As they pointed out in the Declaration of Independence, Quebec had only "arbitrary government," not a representative legislature as in the thirteen colonies, and they feared that the province would serve "at once [as] an example and fit instrument for introducing the same absolute rule into these Colonies." Moreover, the Quebec Act's allowances to the Roman Catholic Church raised the specter of "popery." Ever since the Reformation, English Protestants had been alert to Catholic plots, both real and imagined, to regain power in the kingdom, and the Quebec Act seemed to be the latest example. Coming less than six months after the so-called Intolerable Acts, Parliament's crackdown that followed the Boston Tea Party, the Quebec Act raised fears of an American colonial future marked by appointed government and the promotion of Catholicism. To those inclined to see a conspiracy, the Quebec Act added a perceived threat to religious liberty to the patriots' other grievances.[34]

Religion also factored into the coming of the American Revolution as spokesmen from various denominations defended neutral, loyalist, or patriot positions. Most Quakers reaffirmed their fellowship's peace testimony and avowed their neutrality in the Revolutionary War. The Philadelphia Quaker activist Anthony Benezet labeled war a "teeming womb of mischief," which he contrasted with Jesus' teaching that his followers love one another. Employing evocative prose, Benezet wrote "that [during wartime] property is confounded, scattered, and destroyed; that laws are trampled under foot, government despised, and the ties of all civil and domestic order broken into pieces; that fruitful countries are made desarts [sic], and stately cities a heap of ruins, that matrons and virgins are violated; and neither the innocence of unoffending infancy, nor the impotence of decrepit age, afford protection from the rage and thirst for blood."[35] For their neutrality, however, Quakers earned the enmity of partisans on both sides. The minutes of the Philadelphia Yearly Meeting's "Meeting for Sufferings" document Quakers being fined and imprisoned for refusing to take loyalty oaths or pay taxes that would support the war effort.

Loyalist ministers concentrated among the Anglican clergy, since King George III was head of both state and the Church of England, but they could be found among other denominations too. They urged their flocks to adhere to the established royal government, preaching from such texts as 1 Pet 2:13–14 (KJV), "Submit yourselves to every ordinance of man for the Lord's sake: whether it be to the king, as supreme; or unto governors, as unto them that are sent by him for the punishment of evildoers, and for the praise of them that do well," or 1 Tim 2:1–2 (KJV), "I exhort therefore, that, first of all, supplications, prayers, intercessions, and giving of thanks, be made for all men; for kings, and for all that are in authority; that we may lead a quiet and peaceable life in all godliness and honesty." To cite just one example, John Wesley directed a pamphlet to American readers in 1775 that defended Parliament's authority to tax them. In *A Calm Address to Our American Colonies*, he also responded to fears about endangered liberty, asking his American brethren, "Can you hope for a more desirable form of government, either in England or America, than that which you now enjoy? After all the vehement cry for liberty, what more liberty can you have? What more religious liberty can you desire, than that which you enjoy already? May not every one among you worship God according to his own conscience? What civil liberty can you desire, which you are not already possessed of?" He concluded by urging Americans to "fear God and honour the king."[36]

Ministers who supported the patriot cause, by contrast, justified the colonists' standing up for their rights as consonant with religious values and understanding. As Abraham Keteltas, preaching in the First Presbyterian Church of Newburyport, Massachusetts, phrased matters, "the cause of this American continent, against the measures of a cruel, bloody, and vindictive ministry, is the cause of God. We are contending for the rights of mankind, for the welfare of millions now living, and for the happiness of millions yet unborn." Clearly in his view, Christianity did not mandate submission to despotic rulers, the loyalists' preaching notwithstanding. Like Keteltas, the most vocal patriot ministers came from among the New England Congregationalists and Mid-Atlantic Presbyterians, although like the loyalist clergy they could also be found in other regions and denominations, including Southern Anglicans, for example. They reasoned that Americans had embarked on a "just war" in defense of their natural rights, the most precious of which was freedom of conscience. Contrary to Wesley's assertion that American colonists already had all the religious liberty that they could possibly ask for, patriot ministers warned that it was being undermined. The president of the College of New Jersey (now Princeton University) and signer of the Declaration of Independence, John Witherspoon, offered a typical and solemn admonition. "There is not a single instance in history in which civil liberty was lost, and religious liberty preserved entire," he noted. "If therefore we yield up our temporal property, we at the same time deliver the conscience into bondage." The stakes in the conflict with Britain could not have been any higher.[37]

Patriot preaching braided together Scripture with secular texts. Ministers delivered sermons on such verses as Gal 5:1 (KJV), "Stand fast therefore in the liberty wherewith Christ hath made us free, and be not entangled again with the yoke of bondage," or Gal 5:13 (KJV), "For, brethren, ye have been called unto liberty; only use not liberty for an occasion to the flesh, but by love serve one another." They also borrowed insights from "prominent Whigs such as Algernon Sidney, John Locke, James Harrington, John Trenchard, or Thomas Gordon." As historian Melvin B. Endy, Jr., concludes, patriot ministers furnished "arguments harmonizing religion with the Real Whig legitimations of the Revolution and with warnings of the adverse consequences that a British victory would have for religious liberty."[38] At a subtler level, historians have also pointed out how many of the principal terms of the political debate, such as "liberty," "tyranny," "slavery," "virtue," and "vice," also carried profoundly religious meanings. These overlapping vocabularies sprang from a common source, the English struggles of the seventeenth and early eighteenth centuries to secure political and religious liberty against "the high-church doctrines of divine right and passive obedience." Thus, when patriot clergymen warned about the threat of "slavery" or lambasted the "vice" of the king's ministers, they tapped into deep-seated phrases that resonated with their congregations' religious values.[39]

Patriot ministers also situated the American Revolutionary struggle within their providential narratives of history and national destiny. They added surprising American military victories such as the capture of Fort Ticonderoga to the catalog of providential deliverances that marked colonial history.[40] In New England, ministers remodeled the image of the national covenant. Whereas seventeenth-century divines had emphasized the covenant's theocratic elements, it reappeared as the "Jewish Republic" for the Revolutionary era. Ministers reminded their auditors that in the biblical account found in 1 Samuel 8, it had been a mark of the Israelites' corruption that they had asked for a king in order to be like their pagan neighbors. In contrast, argued Samuel Langdon, the Harvard president, in a sermon in 1775, "the Jewish government, according to the original Constitution which was divinely established, if considered merely in a civil view, was a perfect republic."[41] Other ministers glimpsed millennial implications in the Revolutionary struggle. Protestants had for over two centuries identified the papacy with the Antichrist, so the Seven Years' War, which pitted Britain against Catholic France, stoked expectations for a dramatic showdown. The Quebec Act, which seemingly surrendered the province to Catholicism, therefore dealt a poignant blow to Protestant hopes. As events moved toward a decisive break in 1776, patriots instead came to identify the Antichrist with "tyrannical" Britain.[42] They also anticipated millennial consequences for the new nation. The Connecticut Congregationalist Samuel Sherwood announced in 1776 that "the time is coming and hastening on, when Babylon the great shall fall to rise no more."[43] According to historian Ruth H. Bloch, "the belief that sacred prophecy foreordained the defeat of their enemies, especially when joined to expansive visions of forthcoming glory and happiness, inspired passionate commitment to the American cause despite all the risks and hardships of war."[44]

In sum, patriots received from their ministerial supporters a religious justification for their defense of American rights, a deep resonance between political and religious vocabularies that made their arguments that much more compelling, and a framework for viewing the struggle that endowed it with cosmic significance. These were not insignificant contributions, as the loyalist Peter Oliver recognized when he fumed about the influence of "Mr. *Otis's* black Regiment, the *dissenting Clergy*, who took so active a Part in the Rebellion" in Massachusetts and "distinguished theirselves in encouraging Seditions & Riots." In turn, because patriot ministers had allied themselves with the American Revolution, it would unleash no anti-religious backlash, as would occur in the aftermath of the French.[45] At bottom, however, these contributions were just that: *contributions* to a fundamentally political controversy. Even Peter Oliver, for all his loathing of patriot clergymen, considered them merely the dupes "of a few abandoned Demagogues," who had manipulated preachers into stirring up the populace, so that "a Vacuum was left for *Adams*, & his *Posse* to crowd in what Rubbish would best serve their Turn." Moreover, Christianity provided no unitary influence on the Revolutionary movement, as patriots, loyalists, and pacifists all tapped its resources in support of their positions. "At its heart," summarizes Jon Butler, "the Revolution was a profoundly secular event. The causes that brought it into being and the ideologies that shaped it placed religious concerns more at its margins than at its center."[46]

Nevertheless, the Revolution had a profound impact on American religion and the relationships between church and state that had developed during the colonial era. In the first place, religion suffered from the sheer destructiveness of the war. Wherever fighting occurred or armies invaded the land, houses of worship were likely to be damaged or destroyed. The battle zone between British-occupied Staten Island, New York, and patriot-controlled Essex County, New Jersey, provides a microcosm of this larger phenomenon, as armies and irregular raiders from both sides repeatedly crossed the narrow channel of water separating them. On Staten Island, British troops destroyed the patriot-leaning Dutch Reformed church, and in their search for firewood cut down trees and pulled down fences even on the property of the Anglican church, which also suffered damage in patriot attacks. When a combined force of British, Hessian, and loyalist troops invaded New Jersey in June 1780 in a failed attack on Washington's encampment at Morristown, they burned all three Presbyterian churches in their path.[47] Throughout the colonies, churches faced similar destruction or were converted to military uses as hospitals or barracks. Ministers also complained that current events distracted people's minds from heavenly concerns, as war and politics took center stage. Most important, the break with Britain caused a crisis for the Anglican Church in America, which had direct links to the British monarchy, and as many as one-quarter of the Anglican clergymen present in the colonies in 1775 abandoned their parishes, with many returning to England.[48] Finally, Independence forced a fundamental reevaluation of colonial-era church-state arrangements, as every state but two discarded its colonial frame of government in favor of a new constitution.[49]

Nowhere were the changes as dramatic as in Virginia, where the legislature ultimately dismantled what had been the sturdiest of the colonial Anglican establishments in 1786.[50] The Revolution divided Virginia's Anglican clergy and undermined

its authority. Although only slightly more than 20 percent
were open loyalists, less than half can be clearly identified as
patriots; a sizeable number of them, just over one-third, tried
to remain neutral.[51] In 1776 the Virginia Declaration of Rights
pronounced that "all men are equally entitled to the free exercise of religion, according to the dictates of conscience."[52] Such
revolutionary principles of liberty and equality sat uncomfort-
ably alongside continued preferential treatment for the Church
of England, so later that year the legislature "suspended
the laws giving salaries to the clergy, which suspension was
made perpetual in October 1779."[53] For the remainder of the
war years, the legislature could not come to a final agreement
about the future of the establishment, behaving like "a master
of indecision."[54] In 1784, however, it appeared that the legislature was going to adopt a "general assessment," under which
the individual taxpayer could designate to which denomination
he wanted his money to go. (Money from those indicating no
preference would support schools.) The rationale behind the
bill was that "the general diffusion of Christian knowledge
hath a natural tendency to correct the morals of men, restrain
their vices, and preserve the peace of society, which cannot be
effected without a competent provision for learned teachers."[55]
Patrick Henry threw his considerable influence behind the bill,
and the Presbyterians, who came out of a Scottish state-church
tradition, initially supported it too. However, James Madison,
in a deft legislative maneuver, got the bill postponed until the
next legislative session, which gave the public time to voice its
opinion directly through petitioning.

The petitions that reached the legislature, signed by thousands of Virginians, were overwhelmingly against the proposal
for a general assessment and effectively killed it.[56] The petition
that garnered the most signatures came from an anonymous
evangelical, who criticized religious establishments as "contrary to the Spirit of the Gospel, and the Bill of Rights," and
productive not of morality, but mischief.[57] Moreover, it argued
that the general assessment proposal "would do nothing to
check 'that Deism with its banefull Influence [which] is spreading itself over the state.'"[58] James Madison authored a second
petition, although it too appeared anonymously, that offered a

wider array of reasons why the general assessment plan should be rejected. His *Memorial and Remonstrance* in the first place argued that government has no business meddling with religion, which is—and here Madison quoted the 1776 Declaration of Rights—a matter of private conscience. In addition, he denied the fundamental premise of the general assessment plan, which was that government needed the support of religiously inculcated morality, and countered in Lockean fashion that government was a limited, secular thing. Madison's petition also employed the evangelicals' argument that Christianity does not need government aid, and had, in fact, flourished best without it. The experience of centuries of established religion proved that it produced "pride and indolence in the Clergy, ignorance and servility in the laity, in both, superstition, bigotry and persecution." Any government support of religion would violate the principle of "equality" with which all religious opinions ought to be treated and retard Virginia's development by making the state a less appealing destination for settlement. Finally, the petition warned that although the general assessment plan may seem benign, it set a dangerous precedent. Here Madison recalled the language of Parliament's 1766 Declaratory Act, which claimed the right to legislate for the colonies "in all cases whatsoever." "Who does not see that the same authority which can establish Christianity, in exclusion of all other Religions, may establish with the same ease any particular sect of Christians, in exclusion of all other Sects? [sic] that the same authority which can force a citizen to contribute three pence only of his property for the support of any one establishment, may force him to conform to any other establishment in all cases whatsoever?"[59] With their constituents having made their voices heard so clearly, the legislature dropped the general assessment plan.

In a momentous development, evangelical Christians and Enlightenment rationalists in Virginia formed a winning alliance against established religion. (The Presbyterians turned against the assessment plan in 1785, joining the Baptists in opposition.) In 1786, therefore, the legislature passed "A Bill 'for Establishing Religious Freedom.'"[60] The bill took its stand on the Enlightenment principle "that truth is great and will prevail if left to herself; that she is the proper and sufficient antagonist to error, and has nothing to fear from the conflict unless by human interposition disarmed of her natural weapons, free argument and debate; errors ceasing to be dangerous when it is permitted freely to contradict them." Adding that "our civil rights have no dependence on our religious opinions, any more than our opinions in physics or geometry," the bill dispensed with religious tests for office or voting. It also declared that no one would be compelled by law to attend or support religious worship, thus totally ending the establishment of religion in Virginia. "The Old Dominion," concludes historian Thomas E. Buckley, "with however much hesitation, had chosen a genuinely revolutionary course of action."[61]

Governments in the rest of the Southern states also disestablished the Church of England, although none enacted changes as sweeping as in Virginia. The South Carolina constitution of 1778 limited officeholding to Protestants, but the second one adopted in 1790 was open to all except clergymen. Both North Carolina and Georgia similarly prohibited clergymen from serving in the legislature and made only Protestants eligible for office, but Georgia eliminated the religious test for office in a second constitution of 1789. The process of separating church and state was slowest and least consistent in Maryland, but the state nevertheless halted tax support for the Church of England in 1776. A general assessment plan similar to Virginia's went down to defeat in Maryland about the same time as the one in Virginia. Maryland restricted officeholding to Christians, which made Catholics eligible again.[62]

In the Mid-Atlantic states there were no colonial-era religious establishments to overturn, so state constitutions reaffirmed the region's historical commitment to religious liberty. However, Delaware, New Jersey, and Pennsylvania all retained in their first independent constitutions their colonial-era religious tests for office, which restricted service to Christians only. The Pennsylvania constitution of 1790 lowered the bar to a belief in God and judgment in the afterlife, which made Jews eligible too. New York clarified the disputed status of the Church of England, making it plain that there was no established religion in the state, although its test for office shut out Catholics.[63]

Only in the New England states of Connecticut, Massachusetts, and New Hampshire did public support for religion withstand the upheavals of the Revolutionary era. A comparison between the debates in Virginia and Massachusetts reveals a number of similar issues raised and positions taken, although the two states arrived at different results. Article III of the 1780 Massachusetts constitution adopted the equivalent of Virginia's rejected general assessment. It authorized tax support for "public Protestant teachers of piety, religion, and morality," on the grounds that "the happiness of a people, and the good order and preservation of civil government" depend on such teachers. Taxpayers could earmark their payments for a minister of their own denomination, and all sects would be treated equally.[64] Proponents of Article III stressed its impartiality and denied that Massachusetts thereby created any religious "establishment." Instead, they likened public support of religion to that provided for other societal goods, such as public education.[65] "Thus the makers of the constitution of 1780 stood their Puritan ancestors on their heads," concludes Thomas J. Curry. "Those founders had come to America to set up a government that would guard the true religion. Members of the Massachusetts Constitutional Convention hoped to use religion to protect and sustain good government."[66] As in Virginia, the Baptists spearheaded the opposition, claiming that Article III continued an unwarranted interference by the state in Christ's kingdom, which "is not of this world" (John 18:36). Their leading spokesman, Isaac Backus, argued that "the Civil magistrate's power is limitted to the affairs that lie between man and man and not betwixt man and God."[67] The Baptists' position of strict separation failed to carry the day, however, and Article III remained entrenched in the state constitution until repealed in 1833. Furthermore, Connecticut, Massachusetts, and New Hampshire all limited officeholding to Protestants; of the original thirteen states, only Rhode Island joined Virginia in completely abolishing religious tests for office.[68]

Several reasons account for the different results of the debate over public support for religion in Massachusetts and

Virginia.[69] Congregational ministers in Massachusetts had overwhelmingly allied with the patriot cause, unlike Virginia's divided Anglican clergy. They also represented a substantial majority of the state's population. In addition, "the congregational structure of the Puritan churches and the democratic control of the establishment by the majority vote of the parish (which in effect included all inhabitants of voting age) made it difficult for opponents of the establishment to argue that it constituted a threat to their liberty."[70] Most important is that whereas evangelical Christians and religious rationalists in Virginia came together against the general assessment proposal, in Massachusetts they did not. Religious liberals there, among both the clergy and the political leadership, were among the leading exponents of public support for the Congregational churches.

At the national level, the Continental Congress took a largely hands-off approach to religious matters, leaving them to the several states. The Continental Congress came into being in 1774 as an intercolonial gathering organized to protest the Intolerable Acts, and it transformed into the national government the next year as resistance turned into warfare and revolution. It continued as such under the Articles of Confederation, which Congress passed in 1777, until superseded by the ratification of the United States Constitution in 1788. Preoccupied as they were with momentous issues of war and diplomacy, delegates to the Continental Congress spent little time articulating coherent church-state principles. Instead, they responded to situations as they arose in an ad hoc manner and followed conventional practice in recommending various days of fasting or thanksgiving during the course of the war, appointing chaplains to serve with the army, and paying for other local clergymen to serve as congressional chaplains and to open Congress's sessions with prayer. These actions, however, should not be construed as intended to set up any type of national religious establishment. Congress's fasting and thanksgiving proclamations were non-binding "recommendations" of observance, and the appointment of military chaplains recognized that servicemen were frequently stationed where attendance at religious services would be inconvenient, if not impossible. The congressional chaplains came from different denominations, so as to avoid any appearance of preferential status. In the one instance when Congress did consider support for religion, it rejected the proposal. In 1785, a preliminary draft of the Northwest Ordinance would have set aside land in every township for the support of religious institutions, but the final version only designated land for education. It also guaranteed settlers' religious liberty, which "effectively prevented new states from having religious establishments." In short, while the Congress sometimes referenced God in its pronouncements or provided for the pastoral work of military and congressional chaplains, it largely steered clear of religion in recognition of the states' sovereignty and diverse traditions.[71]

These varying arrangements—with a few states providing public support for religion, and most deciding not to; with most states requiring some kind of religious test for office, and a couple rejecting one; and with the national government giving the states a free hand in religious matters—form the backdrop against which delegates gathered in Philadelphia in the summer of 1787 for the convention that hammered out the United States Constitution. The document that they produced said very little at all on the subject of religion. Only Article VI did so and that was for the purpose of explicitly stating that "no religious Test shall ever be required as a Qualification to any Office or public Trust under the United States." Elsewhere the text was silent about religion. The preamble, for instance, contained no invocation of God's name, instead grounding the Constitution's authority in "We, the People." "Unlike the Declaration of Independence," notes historian Henry F. May, "it does not invoke the laws of Nature and of Nature's God, or express a firm reliance on the protection of Divine Providence," much less affirm anything explicitly Christian.[72] It was "a perfectly secular text" for the founding of the new nation.[73]

Reasons both practical and principled explain the Constitution's secularity. It reflected, in the first place, the concept of federalism; that is, as under the Continental Congress, religious questions would be relegated to the states to work out to their own satisfaction. There was, as described above, simply too much diversity among the states in their church-state arrangements for any overarching national formulation to emerge. The members of the convention also had plenty of other contentious issues to deal with, so they preferred to leave religion undisturbed; the Constitution might not abrade the scruples of any denomination or sect if it maintained a stony silence. As John M. Murrin points out, "Although the Constitution was in no explicit way a religious text, it was also not antireligious. It provided no overt threat to anybody's doctrinal convictions." Some such as Madison also held to the belief that religion needed no governmental support. Finally, "a few delegates, highly suspicious of the power-seeking so characteristic (in their view) of institutional religion, envisioned a newly created central government emancipated from all priestly politicians or clerical lords."[74]

During the ratifying conventions, some critics took the Framers to task for having so thoroughly omitted religion from the Constitution, but they were rebuffed in the end. The prohibition of religious tests for office, which differed from most of the state constitutions, came under fire, because it left the national government open to anyone at all, regardless of his beliefs or even lack thereof. To take one example, the Maryland Antifederalist, Luther Martin, "sarcastically observed that in the Philadelphia Convention, some were '*so unfashionable* as to think . . . that in a Christian country it would be at *least decent* to hold out some distinction between the professors of Christianity and downright infidelity or paganism.'"[75] Others lamented the text's lack of an acknowledgement of the nation's allegiance to Christianity or of God's ultimate authority or providential oversight. One anonymous critic writing in the *Virginia Independent Chronicle* in October 1787 decried the Constitution's "cold indifference towards religion." These occasional objections, however, did not lead to the addition of any further religious language to the text. Defenders of the Constitution's secularity prevailed, making their case on either Enlightenment principles of free inquiry or evangelical concerns for maintaining the church's purity from state interference.[76]

Some of those concerned for the separation of church and state feared that the Constitution did not go far enough. Elder

John Leland wrote to President George Washington in 1789 on behalf of the General Committee of Virginia Baptist churches and remarked that they had "unusual strugglings of mind" over the Constitution, because they worried "that the liberty of conscience, dearer to us than property or life, was not sufficiently secured."[77] Antifederalists called for the inclusion of a declaration of rights, as was to be found in many of the state constitutions, and their proposal gained traction. Supporters of the Constitution, James Madison foremost among them, promised that they would introduce a list of amendments once the Constitution was ratified and the new Congress met. Accordingly, Congress proposed and the states ratified in 1791 the Bill of Rights, the first ten amendments to the Constitution. The first contained a sixteen-word religion clause—"Congress shall make no law respecting an establishment of religion, or prohibiting the free exercise thereof"—that further sought to guarantee religious freedom in the new nation. Ratification was made easier by the fact that everyone did not have to concur in the exact definition of religious freedom being protected, because Congress was merely being forbidden to meddle in religious matters.[78]

The American Revolution, therefore, resulted in the expansion of colonial-era toleration into a broader, more fundamental right to religious liberty. As the Founders drafted state constitutions, they scrutinized their church-state arrangements and disestablished the Church of England wherever it had been privileged by law. At the national level, they designed a secular Constitution, which they reinforced like prudent engineers with the redundancy of the First Amendment's religious protections.[79] Many Americans would have added that their new republican institutions needed the support of morality and virtue, but they would have offered differing opinions as to how to cultivate those qualities. Their differences of opinion on a variety of matters, including religion and morality, would lead to the political controversies of the early republic. At the same time, Americans' enhanced religious freedom paved the way for an even more raucous spiritual eclecticism in the years to come.

The Politics of Religion and the Religion of Politics in the Early Republic

Thomas Jefferson cut a large figure in many areas of endeavor during the early republic, including science, politics, and education, and religion is no exception to the list of fields that felt his influence.[80] As the author of Virginia's 1786 Bill for Establishing Religious Freedom, he played a major role in the movement for the disestablishment of the Church of England and thereby also inspired New England dissenters, who chafed under their states' Congregational establishments. Jefferson's religious beliefs became a lightning rod for controversy during his campaigns for the presidency, especially on account of comments he had published in *Notes on the State of Virginia*. Nevertheless, his electoral victories in 1800 and 1804 confirmed the secularity of the national government.

Jefferson hated that his personal religious beliefs were a matter of public discussion, both because he valued his privacy and because he thought such matters irrelevant to officeholding. (The Constitution had banned religious tests, after all.) In private, however, Jefferson gave serious thought to religious matters, critically evaluating Christianity in light of his Enlightenment convictions, and he shared some of these thoughts with a few close confidants. During the nineteenth century, he came to an idiosyncratic set of conclusions about religious matters that defies simple categorization, rejecting the miracles recorded in the Bible, for example, but holding that Jesus' ethical teachings were unsurpassed. "I am of a sect by myself, as far as I know," he wrote in 1819. Three years later, Jefferson predicted that the nation would soon concur with the major outlines of his religious beliefs, famously forecasting that "the present generation will see Unitarianism become the general religion of the United states."[81] Of course, Jefferson was grossly wrong on that one, but in a larger sense his thinking mirrored that of millions of his fellow Americans, who were likewise engaged in their own eclectic quests for salvation and who shared his concern for trying to reconcile religion with life in a secular democracy. In short, Jefferson's thoughts and actions in the religious realm epitomize many of the major preoccupations of his day. These issues in the history of the early American republic finally render fully explicable Alexis de Tocqueville's observations about the compatibility of "the spirit of religion and the spirit of freedom" that were noted at the outset of this essay.

By 1789 it may have appeared at first glance that contentious questions of religion and politics had been resolved and that public affairs were entering a new period of tranquility. The end of the War for Independence in 1783, the launching of the new federal government in 1789 with George Washington as the consensus choice to be the first president, and the outbreak that same year of the French Revolution all fed an initial burst of optimism about the new nation's prospects. For example, Ezra Stiles titled his 1783 Connecticut election sermon *The United States elevated to Glory and Honor* and detailed how the nation's enlightened Christian republicanism would set a worldwide model for emulation. The new Congress continued the conventional practices of appointing chaplains and calling for periodic days of thanksgiving, and "the public religiosity of the United States continued to consist primarily of verbal exhortation, as it had under the Continental Congress." Also in 1789 Anglicans emerged from their Revolutionary trials and reorganized as the Protestant Episcopal Church. With the Church of England having been disestablished throughout the states, the arrival of Samuel Seabury as the denomination's first American bishop gave no cause for the revival of that prewar controversy. All in all, national affairs were superficially placid and upbeat in 1789 and the years immediately following. It seemed as if the Revolutionary experiment was on the right track, and the French Revolution provided exciting confirmation that liberty was marching onward.[82]

Neither American religion nor politics, however, had settled into a period of peace and quiet. Two very different varieties of religious radicalism in the 1780s revealed that the Revolutionary era had initiated a profound ferment over questions of belief. In the frontier region of northern New England, a religious revival flared from 1778 to 1782 and fueled three new sects, the Shakers, Freewill Baptists, and Universalists. Each took inspiration from direct revelations announced by a

charismatic leader.[83] From the opposite end of the epistemo-
logical spectrum, deists simultaneously attacked any revelation that could not be squared with reason and nature. Deism
was not new, and its influence on theologians as well as learned
laymen such as Benjamin Franklin and Thomas Jefferson has
already been noted, but it gained a new prominence in the Revolutionary era from writers such as Ethan Allen, Elihu Palmer,
and Tom Paine. These men were "aggressive, populist, polemi-
cal, disdainful of a Bible riddled with contradiction and immorality, eager to debunk the gospel stories, and hopeful that a
religion of nature would altogether replace an effete Christianity." Paine's *The Age of Reason*, published in two parts in 1794
and 1795, displayed the same verve that had established him
as the most important pamphleteer of the Revolution and made
deist arguments widely known.[84] Both radical evangelicalism
and radical deism were harbingers of the kind of dynamic religious eclecticism that would characterize the early republic.

Deism's newfound boldness alarmed many Americans of a
more traditional outlook, especially the Northeast's Congregational and Presbyterian clergymen. Conservatives linked deistic "infidelity" with two other doleful developments of the 1790s,
the nation's growing political polarization and the French Revolution's radical turn against Christianity. Most Americans of
the time assumed that partisan divisions were a symptom of
some serious malady in the body politic, so the emergence of
competing Federalist and Republican parties by the second
half of the decade seemed to indicate that the new nation was
plunging toward either despotism or anarchy.[85] Even President
Washington, formerly a unifying figure, could not remain above
the partisan fray, especially after his 1796 *Farewell Address*
took a swipe at the Democratic-Republican societies as an illegitimate "faction" and warned of the danger of "attachments"
to foreign nations. For Federalists who positioned themselves
as the defenders of political order and religious orthodoxy,
Washington's words became an iconic statement that school-
children committed to memory, and clergymen quoted approvingly his admonition that "reason and experience both forbid
us to expect that national morality can prevail in exclusion of
religious principle."[86] In the thinking of some Federalists, politi-

cal discord, religious infidelity, and French Revolutionary sympathies intertwined in a nefarious conspiracy. Jedidiah Morse, the Congregational minister of Charlestown, Massachusetts, alleged in the late 1790s that a shadowy international cabal, the Bavarian Illuminati, had orchestrated a massive plot aimed at the destruction of governments and religion everywhere.[87] Federalists also descried domestic enemies. They observed that in Thomas Jefferson, deistic beliefs, support for France, and alienation from the Washington administration all converged.

Therefore, Jefferson's two bids for the presidency in 1796 and 1800 unleashed an aggressive campaign by Federalists and their clerical allies to portray him as unfit for office on account of his unorthodox religious views. For evidence they pointed to passages in *Notes on the State of Virginia* that expressed doubt about the biblical account of the flood or that advocated toleration for heterodox beliefs. "It does me no injury for my neighbour to say there are twenty gods, or no god," Jefferson had opined. "It neither picks my pocket nor breaks my leg."[88] From such statements, Federalists charged that Jefferson was an atheist or infidel, who should not be elected to the nation's highest office. To take just one example, a Federalist newspaper, the *Gazette of the United States*, editorialized "that a voter need ask himself one easy question: 'Shall I continue in allegiance to God—and a Religious President; Or impiously declare for Jefferson—and No God!!!'"[89] Historian Frank Lambert has astutely observed that the Federalist campaign against Jefferson's religion constituted an attempt to circumvent Article VI's ban on religious tests for office by creating what amounted to a "voter-imposed religious test."[90]

Nonetheless, Jefferson was narrowly elected president in 1800 and reelected by an even wider margin in 1804. The Federalists' attempt to tar him as an infidel failed to resonate beyond their Northeastern base. Put another way, many Americans embraced Jefferson's defense of religious freedom and a secular government whose "legitimate powers . . . extend to such acts only as are injurious to others." As one historian concludes, "While Federalists labored to reverse the secularization of public life, Republicans struggled for its advancement." The political controversies of the 1790s, culminating in the election of 1800, confirmed yet again the secular character of the federal government.[91]

Once in office, Jefferson sought to reinforce that character, and he seized two opportunities to do so on January 1, 1802. On that day Elder John Leland arrived with a 1,235-pound cheese that he and another man had transported from Cheshire, Massachusetts, as a congratulatory gift from the dairy farmers of that town. (Federalists mockingly referred to it as "the mammoth cheese," and the label stuck.) Speaking on behalf of his townsfolk, Leland told Jefferson that "we believe the supreme Ruler of the Universe, who raises up men to achieve great events, has raised up a Jefferson at this critical day, to defend *Republicanism*, and to baffle the arts of *Aristocracy*." That statement contradicted the calumnies that Jefferson's opponents had heaped on him in the recent presidential contest and then returned fire on the Federalists by accusing them of nursing aristocratic ambitions. Likewise, Leland remarked that the citizens of Cheshire had an "indissoluble" devotion to the United States Constitution, among the most "beautiful features" of which was Article VI's "prohibition of religious tests," and thereby denied Federalists' assertions that the absence of a religious test had been a grave mistake. Jefferson thanked the people of Cheshire and agreed with their high estimation of the Constitution. Newspapers picked up the story and publicized the incident nationwide.[92]

The Republican press also carried Jefferson's letter to the Baptist association of Danbury, Connecticut, which he wrote the same day. The Danbury Baptists had written to the president for a reason similar to that behind the mammoth cheese, namely "to express our great satisfaction, in your appointment to the chief Magistracy in the United States." Their letter went on to contrast Jefferson's commitment to religious liberty with their situation in Connecticut, where under the "ancient charter . . . what religious privileges we enjoy (as a minor part of the state) we enjoy as favors granted, and not as inalienable rights." "It is not to be wondered at therefore," they explained, "if those, who seek after *power* & *gain* under the pretence *of government* & *Religion* should reproach their fellow men—should reproach their chief Magistrate, as an enemy of religion Law & good order because he will not, dares not assume the prerogative of Jehovah and make Laws to govern the Kingdom of Christ." In other words, the Federalist clergy's hostility to Jefferson they attributed to their fellow New Englanders' erroneous notions of church and state. They concluded that although they were aware that Jefferson as head of the federal government could not change the Connecticut establishment, they still hoped that his disestablishmentarian principles would "shine & prevail through all these States."[93] In the final draft of his reply, Jefferson wrote the following famous sentence:

> Believing with you that religion is a matter which lies solely between Man & his God, that he owes account to none other for his faith or his worship, that the legitimate powers of government reach actions only, & not opinions, I contemplate with sovereign reverence that act of the whole American people which declared that *their* legislature should "make no law respecting an establishment of religion, or prohibiting the free exercise thereof," thus building a wall of separation between Church & State.[94]

The Danbury Baptists' letter and the mammoth cheese gave Jefferson the opportunity, in sum, to respond discreetly to his Federalist vilifiers by reasserting his beliefs in the private nature of religious views under a secular government and the wisdom of banning religious tests for office. His two letters also allowed Jefferson to curry favor with his constituents among religious dissenters in New England, to subtly criticize the church-state arrangements in those states, and to extol the First Amendment's guarantees of religious liberty.

Having driven the Federalists from power in what he considered "the revolution of 1800" and preserved constitutional guarantees of religious freedom thereby, Jefferson turned in his private moments to a closer examination of his own religious convictions. The Federalists' barbs must have stung, and although he could suffer them in silence, he wanted his family and closest friends to know that he was no contemnor of religion—perhaps he also needed to convince himself. In 1804 Jefferson compiled "The Philosophy of Jesus" by cutting out passages of Jesus' moral teaching from a copy of the New

Testament, and thus discarding the miracles and other portions of the text that he thought defied reason. Jefferson also
found in the writings of the English Unitarian Joseph Priestley
a religious rationalism close to his own. He urged Priestley to
publish a simplified Christian morality that would be suitable
for the education of the nation, because he had concluded "that
Christian morality could serve as one of the basic foundations
of the country's republican experiment by promoting the social
harmony among the citizenry that he considered essential for
the survival of the republic."[95] Jefferson's religious views were
ultimately his alone, but they epitomized broad themes in the
religious history of the early republic. Like Jefferson, many
Americans were theological simplifiers and idiosyncratic seekers, who cut through traditional creeds in order to recover a
pure essence of religion and added other elements, either rational or supernatural, to create innovative syntheses. Jefferson's
fellow Americans also hungered for a religious message that
was congruent with life in the new republic.

Several denominations, including Baptists, Christians (i.e.,
Disciples of Christ), and Methodists, promulgated a common-
sense Christianity that jibed with being a citizen of the new
nation. If Americans experienced the divisive politics of religion during the election of 1800, with the full-blown democratization of American Christianity they embraced the religion of
politics. These religious "populists," to borrow historian Nathan
O. Hatch's term, ridiculed the pretensions of learned theologians and proclaimed that the Bible spoke plainly to every
man. As one Methodist missionary to New England declared,
"larnin isn't religion, and eddication don't give a man the power
of the Spirit. . . . St. Peter was a fisherman—do you think he
ever went to Yale College?"[96] De Tocqueville was referring to
the same unpretentious quality of American Christianity when
he wrote, "I have not seen a country where Christianity wraps
itself less in forms, practices, and [representational] figures
than the United States, and presents ideas more clearly, simply, and generally to the human mind." Methodists especially
adapted to American society in the early nineteenth century by
employing ordinary young men with preaching gifts and send-
ing them westward, riding circuit to where the people lived.

Bishop Francis Asbury, one man who could rival Jefferson as a defining figure of the period, set the pace by itinerating nonstop and crisscrossing the Appalachians in search of souls to save. Neither the Methodists nor the Baptists required that their ministers have a college education, which removed a major bottleneck in ministerial supply. The end result of the period was a complete reordering of the denominational hierarchy, with Methodists and Baptists surging to the top in terms of membership numbers and leaving such prominent colonial-era groups as the Episcopalians or Quakers in the dust.[97]

Jefferson and many Americans went their separate ways, however, in their estimation of nineteenth-century religious enthusiasm. Jefferson's rationalist beliefs had no place for the outpouring of the Holy Spirit or the ecstatic experiences of camp meeting attendees. Historians sometimes date the Second Great Awakening, an umbrella term for the revivals of the first third of the nineteenth century, to the ones that took place in Kentucky in 1800 and 1801. Accounts of the Cane Ridge revival made famous both the camp meeting format of preaching that extended over several days and the image of scores of listeners literally struck down by the overwhelming sense of their own sinfulness. To take another example, early Methodism was an eclectic blend of Wesleyan theology, democratic populism, and supernatural dreams and revelations. The latter tend to be forgotten, given Methodism's reputation as a straightlaced, respectable denomination of the Victorian era. But before about 1820 many Methodist men and women, white as well as black, "believed in the efficacy of prophetic dreams, visions, and supernatural impressions and were not afraid to base day-to-day decisions on such phenomena."[98]

Nothing better exhibits America's spiritual eclecticism than the rise of the Mormons, who tapped such diverse legacies of the early modern world as alchemy, treasure hunting, and magic, and formulated a novel theological alloy. Like many other charismatic religious figures of the early republic, Joseph Smith declared his independence from squabbling denominational theologians and blazed his own path to spiritual fulfillment. Going far beyond most, however, Smith published his own scripture in 1830 as the *Book of Mormon*. Smith claimed that the book represented his translation of ancient golden plates, the upstate New York location of which an angel had revealed to him. He had been able to translate the tablets thanks to his use of a special "peep stone," a common treasure-seeking tool along the same lines as a divining rod.[99]

There is only space to briefly mention some of the other groups that gave the early republic its stunning religious diversity. Lest one think that revivalism overran the country, it must be noted that it had numerous critics. These ranged from Boston Unitarians who emphasized reason over revivalism's emotion, to immigrant theologians who defended their Old World confessions. Like Joseph Smith or the early Methodists, many others claimed to have special revelations in dreams or to communicate directly with angels. In short, the early American republic was nothing if not religiously eclectic. The Jeffersonian consensus that religious beliefs were an individual matter with which the state could not interfere created the conditions for all sorts of visionaries and prophets to enter the marketplace of ideas, proclaim their messages, and seek to attract followers.[100]

Amid all these changes, New England ministers entered the nineteenth century having been defeated in their attempt to thwart Jefferson's presidential bid. Their despair became more urgent as the War of 1812 loomed, for it threatened to ally the United States with the French Antichrist. "To ally America to France is to chain living health and beauty to a corpse dissolving with the plague," declared Timothy Dwight, the president of Yale, in the summer of 1812. After the war, however, Calvinist clergymen finally abandoned their reliance on the Federalist magistracy, which in Massachusetts seemed hopelessly in the Unitarian fold anyway. After almost two centuries, disestablishment occurred in the New England states. Connecticut abolished Congregationalism's privileged status in 1818, as Baptists, Episcopalians, and other religious dissenters voted with the Republicans to gain the legislative power needed to push through a new state constitution. New Hampshire disestablished Congregationalism the following year. In Massachusetts, final disestablishment occurred in 1833, after the old Congregational standing order divided between Unitarian and orthodox, or Trinitarian, Congregationalists.[101]

In conclusion, the religiously eclectic society that Tocqueville observed in 1830, with its separation of church and state, had developed over the course of the preceding six decades at least. Jefferson had died on the fiftieth anniversary of American independence, July 4, 1826, but bequeathed to the nation its secular government. That government, which protected the rights of conscience and privileged no sect above another, enabled religion to flourish during the early republic to an extraordinary degree. Hence, Tocqueville would conclude that in America "the spirit of religion and the spirit of freedom . . . reigned together on the same soil."[102]

Of course, Tocqueville had not arrived at the end of history in 1830, and controversies over religion and government would continue to erupt. Right around the time of his tour, for instance, reformers accused the federal government of violating its own secularity and trampling over matters of great moral import. In 1830, a second major campaign aimed at shutting down the federal post office on Sundays had just been defeated in Congress. Many evangelical Christians, Northeastern clergymen conspicuous among them, had argued that operating the post office on the Sabbath transgressed a sacred boundary line. Some of the same men and women denounced President Andrew Jackson's policy of Indian removal as another betrayal of moral obligations, made especially flagrant since the tribes in question had welcomed Protestant missionaries and taken great strides toward adapting to Euro-American culture. In many ways, the protest against Indian removal prepared the ground for the abolitionist movement that protested against the moral turpitude of chattel slavery. As the abolitionists would expose, the federal government was complicit in perpetuating slavery, even allowing the slave trade to operate in the District of Columbia.[103] Tocqueville explained the underlying motivation behind such movements when he declared that "the greatest advantage of religions is to inspire . . . instincts" contrary to materialistic individualism. "There is no religion that does not place man's desires beyond and above earthly goods and that does not naturally raise his soul toward regions much superior to those of the senses. Nor is there any that does not impose on each some duties toward the human species or in common with it, and that does not thus draw him, from time to time, away from contemplation of himself."[104] Nevertheless, all three protest movements failed to achieve their objectives in the short term: the post office continued to operate on Sundays until the early twentieth century, Jackson expelled the Indians from the Southeast, and slavery would not be abolished until the Union Army defeated the Confederacy in 1865. All three generated countermovements that sometimes turned violent, as in the anti-abolitionist mobs. In short, questions of morality and public policy, or religious belief and government action, continued to generate heated debate in the antebellum era, and in altered forms that debate continues to this day.

Endnotes

[1] Alexis de Tocqueville, *Democracy in America*, trans. and ed. H. C. Mansfield and D. Winthrop (Chicago: University of Chicago Press, 2000), 282–83.

[2] Ibid., 27–43.

[3] For an excellent example of what can be gained from such comparative analysis, see M. A. Noll, *A History of Christianity in the United States and Canada* (Grand Rapids: Eerdmans, 1992).

[4] *Shorter Oxford English Dictionary*, 5th ed., s.v. "secular."

[5] R. Wuthnow, *The Struggle for America's Soul: Evangelicals, Liberals, and Secularism* (Grand Rapids: Eerdmans, 1989); M. A. Noll and C. Nystrom, *Is the Reformation Over? An Evangelical Assessment of Contemporary Roman Catholicism* (Grand Rapids: Baker Academic, 2005).

[6] J. Butler, *Awash in a Sea of Faith: Christianizing the American People* (Cambridge, MA: Harvard University Press, 1990).

[7] Quoted in P. F. Boller, "George Washington and Religious Liberty," *William and Mary Quarterly*, 3d ser., 17, no. 4 (1960): 504.

[8] Butler, *Awash in a Sea of Faith*, 37; J. Winthrop, "A Modell of Christian Charity," in P. Miller and T. H. Johnson, eds., *The Puritans*, rev. ed., 2 vols. (New York: Harper & Row, 1963), 1:198–99; D. H. Fischer, *Albion's Seed: Four British Folkways in America* (New York: Oxford University Press, 1989), 189–205; E. S. Morgan, *The Puritan Dilemma: The Story of John Winthrop* (Boston: Little, Brown, 1958), 115–54; M. P. Winship, *Making Heretics: Militant Protestantism and Free Grace in Massachusetts, 1636–1641* (Princeton, NJ: Princeton University Press, 2002).

[9] T. J. Curry, *The First Freedoms: Church and State in America to the Passage of the First Amendment* (New York: Oxford University Press, 1986), 21.

[10] Ibid., 21–24; P. U. Bonomi, *Under the Cope of Heaven: Religion, Society, and Politics in Colonial America* (New York: Oxford University Press, 1986), 26–29, quote on 26.

[11] Bonomi, *Under the Cope of Heaven*, 65–66; Curry, *First Freedoms*, 89. For the full account of the struggle for toleration in New England, see W. G. McLoughlin, *New England Dissent, 1630–1833: The Baptists and the Separation of Church and State*, 2 vols. (Cambridge, MA: Harvard University Press, 1971), 1:91–277.

[12] Butler, *Awash in a Sea of Faith*, 55–67, 70–73; D. D. Hall, *Worlds of Wonder, Days of Judgment: Popular Religious Belief in Early New England* (New York: Knopf, 1989), 15–17, 71–104; E. B. Holifield, *Theology in America: Christian Thought from the Age of the Puritans to the Civil War* (New Haven, CT: Yale University Press, 2003), 79–83, quote on 83; Winthrop, "A Modell of Christian Charity," 1:198.

[13] H. S. Stout, *The New England Soul: Preaching and Religious Culture in Colonial New England* (New York: Oxford University Press, 1986), 4.

[14] Bonomi, *Under the Cope of Heaven*, 16–17, 42–44, 97–102, quote on 16; Butler, *Awash in a Sea of Faith*, 99–101, quote on 100.

[15] Holifield, *Theology in America*, 59–60, 84–86, quotes on 85 and 59; C. L. Heyrman, *Southern Cross: The Beginnings of the Bible Belt* (New York: Knopf, 1997), 11–15; E. S. Gaustad, *Sworn on the Altar of God: A Religious Biography of Thomas Jefferson* (Grand Rapids: Eerdmans, 1996), 1–41.

[16] Bonomi, *Under the Cope of Heaven*, 21–24; Curry, *First Freedoms*, 31–53.

[17] Bonomi, *Under the Cope of Heaven*, 30–33; Curry, *First Freedoms*, 54–62; Butler, *Awash in a Sea of Faith*, 64.

[18] E. G. Burrows and Mike Wallace, *Gotham: A History of New York City to 1898* (New York: Oxford University Press, 1999), 41–61; Bonomi, *Under the Cope of Heaven*, 24–26.

[19] "Only to the extent," writes Bonomi, "that the salary of the senior minister of Trinity Parish was paid from a public rate was the Church of England established in New York County" (*Under the Cope of Heaven*, 52).

[20] For an overview of religious liberty in colonial New York, on which this account is based, see Curry, *First Freedoms*, 62–72.

[21] Ibid., 75.

[22] Bonomi, *Under the Cope of Heaven*, 36; S. Schwartz, *"A Mixed Multitude": The Struggle for Toleration in Colonial Pennsylvania* (New York: New York University Press, 1987), 12–35.

[23] *The Autobiography of Benjamin Franklin*, ed. L. P. Masur (Boston: Bedford Books, 1993), 88–91.

[24] Bonomi, *Under the Cope of Heaven*, 39; Curry, *First Freedoms*, 78; C. G. Pestana, "Religion," in *The British Atlantic World, 1500–1800*, ed. D. Armitage and M. J. Braddick (New York: Palgrave Macmillan, 2002), 69–89.

[25] W. R. Ward, *The Protestant Evangelical Awakening* (New York: Cambridge University Press, 1992), quote on 275; F. Lambert, "Subscribing for Profits and Piety: The Friendship of Benjamin Franklin and George Whitefield," *William and Mary Quarterly*, 3d ser., 50, no. 3 (1993): 529–54.

[26] Ward, *Protestant Evangelical Awakening*, 311–13; S. R. Frey and B. Wood, *Come Shouting to Zion: African American Protestantism in the American South and British Caribbean to 1830* (Chapel Hill: University of North Carolina Press, 1998), 80–117; Bonomi, *Under the Cope of Heaven*, 123–52.

[27] R. Isaac, "Evangelical Revolt: The Nature of the Baptists' Challenge to the Traditional Order in Virginia, 1765–1775," *William and Mary Quarterly*, 3d ser., 31, no. 3 (1974): 345–68; idem, *The Transformation of Virginia, 1740–1790* (Chapel Hill: University of North Carolina Press, 1982); McLoughlin, *New England Dissent*, 1:360–85, 421–39.

[28] The Declaration of Independence, http://www.archives.gov/national-archives-experience/charters/declaration_transcript.html.

[29] A. Heimert, *Religion and the American Mind: From the Great Awakening to the Revolution* (Cambridge, MA: Harvard University Press, 1966). This paragraph draws on the insights of two outstanding historiographical essays that examine the scholarly literature on the Awakening and the Revolution that grew up in Heimert's wake: P. Goff, "Revivals and Revolution: Historiographic

Turns since Alan Heimert's *Religion and the American Mind," Church History* 67, no. 4 (1998): 695–721; and P. F. Gura, "The Role of the 'Black Regiment': Religion and the American Revolution," *New England Quarterly* 61, no. 3 (1988): 439–54.

³⁰ J. M. Murrin, "No Awakening, No Revolution? More Counterfactual Speculations," *Reviews in American History* 11, no. 2 (1983): 164.

³¹ Both Harry S. Stout and Patricia U. Bonomi make this point. "Following war with France," the former writes, "rationalist and evangelical ministers discovered anew the need to come together against common enemies in pursuit of a common cause. This time the common enemy was 'tyranny,' embodied in corrupt English officials, and the common cause was 'liberty'" (*New England Soul*, 259). Similarly, Bonomi argues that "an ideology of dissent that linked religious with civil tyranny created a common ground upon which rationalists and evangelical alike could join to justify their opposition to England" (*Under the Cope of Heaven*, 208).

³² E. S. Morgan, *The Gentle Puritan: A Life of Ezra Stiles, 1727–1795* (Chapel Hill: University of North Carolina Press, 1962), 215–19, 237–56; Bonomi, *Under the Cope of Heaven*, 199–208; Butler, *Awash in a Sea of Faith*, 100–5, 195–98. For the fullest recounting of the Anglican bishop controversy, see C. Bridenbaugh, *Mitre and Sceptre: Transatlantic Faiths, Ideas, Personalities, and Politics, 1689–1775* (New York: Oxford University Press, 1962), although I do not share his contention that "religion was a fundamental cause of the American Revolution" (xiv). See also N. L. Rhoden, *Revolutionary Anglicanism: The Colonial Church of England Clergy during the American Revolution* (Houndmills, Basingstoke, Hampshire: Macmillan, 1999), 37–63.

³³ An Act for making more effectual Provision for the Government of the Province of Quebec in North America (1774), http://www.yale.edu/lawweb/avalon/amerrev/parliament/quebec_act_1774.htm.

³⁴ Butler, *Awash in a Sea of Faith*, 198–99; R. H. Bloch, *Visionary Republic: Millennial Themes in American Thought, 1756–1800* (New York: Cambridge University Press, 1985), 58–59.

³⁵ [Anthony Benezet], *Serious Considerations on several Important Subjects; viz. On War and its Inconsistency with the Gospel. Observations on Slavery. And Remarks on the Nature and bad Effects of Spirituous Liquors* (Philadelphia, 1778), 8.

³⁶ Noll, *A History of Christianity in the United States and Canada*, 115–32; J. Wesley, *A Calm Address to Our American Colonies* (London, 1775), in *Political Sermons of the American Founding Era, 1730–1805*, ed. E. Sandoz (Indianapolis: Liberty Press, 1991), 417–18.

³⁷ A. Keteltas, *God Arising and Pleading His People's Cause* (Newbury-Port, MA, 1777), in Sandoz, *Political Sermons*, 595; M. B. Endy, Jr., "Just War, Holy War, and Millennialism in Revolutionary America," *William and Mary Quarterly*, 3d ser., 42, no. 1 (1985): 3–25; J. Witherspoon, *The Dominion of Providence over the Passions of Men* (Princeton, NJ, 1776), in Sandoz, *Political Sermons*, 549.

³⁸ Stout, *New England Soul*, 260, 299; Endy, "Just War, Holy War, and Millennialism," 4.

³⁹ Bloch, *Visionary Republic*, 4, 45, 63; Bonomi, *Under the Cope of Heaven*, 189–99, quote on 190; Butler, *Awash in a Sea of Faith*, 201.

⁴⁰ Stout, *New England Soul*, 302–3.

⁴¹ Quoted in ibid., 294.

⁴² Bloch, *Visionary Republic*, 43–44, 57–61.

⁴³ Quoted in ibid., 80.

⁴⁴ Ibid., 87.

[45] D. Adair and J. A. Schutz, eds., *Peter Oliver's Origin & Progress of the American Rebellion: A Tory View* (San Marino, CA: Huntington Library, 1961), 41, 43; Bonomi, *Under the Cope of Heaven*, 222.

[46] Adair and Schutz, *Peter Oliver's Origin & Progress of the American Rebellion*, 145–46; Butler, *Awash in a Sea of Faith*, 195.

[47] P. Papas, *That Ever Loyal Island: Staten Island and the American Revolution* (New York: New York University Press, 2007), 102–3; T. Fleming, *The Forgotten Victory: The Battle for New Jersey, 1780* (New York: Reader's Digest Press, 1973).

[48] Rhoden, *Revolutionary Anglicanism*, 102. The statistic of one-quarter of Anglican ministers opting to flee is an aggregate figure for all thirteen colonies, and the numbers look different on the level of individual colonies. As Rhoden elaborates, "In the middle colonies and New England, the vast majority of Anglican ministers were loyalists, but in the southern colonies most were patriots. The proportion of Anglicans who were loyalists in each colony was in inverse ratio to their numbers, as conscious religious minorities tended to be loyalist" (ibid., 88–89).

[49] Connecticut and Rhode Island continued to operate under their colonial charters into the nineteenth century.

[50] The following discussion of disestablishment in Virginia is based on T. E. Buckley, *Church and State in Revolutionary Virginia, 1776–1787* (Charlottesville: University Press of Virginia, 1977).

[51] These figures come from Rhoden, *Revolutionary Anglicanism*, 89, table 5.1, "Political orientation of Anglican clergy, 1775–83." Among a total of 130 Anglican priests, Rhoden counts 28 loyalists, 58 patriots, and 44 neutrals.

[52] Quoted in Buckley, *Church and State in Revolutionary Virginia*, 19.

[53] T. Jefferson, *Notes on the State of Virginia*, ed. W. Peden (Chapel Hill: University of North Carolina Press, 1954), 158.

[54] Buckley, *Church and State in Revolutionary Virginia*, 62.

[55] "A Bill 'Establishing a Provision for Teachers of the Christian Religion,' 1784," reprinted in ibid., 188–89.

[56] Of the 101 petitions, only 11 favored the general assessment plan and 90 opposed it (ibid., 145).

[57] Quoted in ibid., 148.

[58] Quoted in R. A. Rutland and W. M. E. Rachal, eds., *The Papers of James Madison* (Chicago: University of Chicago Press, 1973), 8:298.

[59] "Memorial and Remonstrance against Religious Assessments," in ibid., 8:295–306. See also the extended discussion of it in Buckley, *Church and State in Revolutionary Virginia*, 131–35.

[60] Reprinted in Buckley, *Church and State in Revolutionary Virginia*, 190–91.

[61] Ibid., 173.

[62] Curry, *First Freedoms*, 148–58.

[63] Ibid., 159–62.

[64] Article III is reprinted in full in McLoughlin, *New England Dissent*, 1:603–04.

[65] Ibid., 1:610–12; Curry, *First Freedoms*, 172–75.

[66] Curry, *First Freedoms*, 165.

[67] Quoted in McLoughlin, *New England Dissent*, 1:605.

[68] Curry, *First Freedoms*, 162–64, 180, 188.

[69] William G. McLoughlin provided a concise summary of reasons for the different outcomes of the church-state debates in the two states in *New England Dissent*, 1:591–94.

[70] Ibid., 1:593.

[71] D. H. Davis, *Religion and the Continental Congress, 1774–1789: Contributions to Original Intent* (New York: Oxford University Press, 2000), 172.

[72] The Constitution of the United States, http://www.archives.gov/national-archives-experience/charters/constitution_transcript.html; H. F. May, "The Constitution and the Enlightened Consensus," in *The Divided Heart: Essays on Protestantism and the Enlightenment in America* (New York: Oxford University Press, 1991), 150.

[73] "Whatever else may be said about American political culture in that period," wrote historian Stephen Botein, "it cannot be denied that the Constitution was a perfectly secular text—if, by that term, nothing more or less is signified than the absence of manifest religious content" (S. Botein, "Religious Dimensions of the Early American State," in *Beyond Confederation: Origins of the Constitution and American National Identity*, ed. R. Beeman, S. Botein, and E. C. Carter II [Chapel Hill: University of North Carolina Press, 1987], 317).

[74] J. M. Murrin, "Religion and Politics in America from the First Settlements to the Civil War," in *Religion and American Politics: From the Colonial Period to the 1980s*, ed. M. A. Noll (New York: Oxford University Press, 1990), 34; E. S. Gaustad, "Religious Tests, Constitutions, and 'Christian Nation,'" in *Religion in a Revolutionary Age*, ed. R. Hoffman and P. J. Albert (Charlottesville: University Press of Virginia, 1994), 225.

[75] Gaustad, "Religious Tests, Constitutions, and 'Christian Nation,'" 227.

[76] I. Kramnick and R. L. Moore, *The Godless Constitution: The Case against Religious Correctness* (New York: Norton, 1996), 27–43, quote on 33.

[77] Quoted in L. H. Butterfield, "Elder John Leland, Jeffersonian Itinerant," *Proceedings of the American Antiquarian Society* 62, no. 2 (1952): 195. For his part, Washington replied that he would never have signed the Constitution had he thought that it "might possibly endanger the religious rights of any ecclesiastical society," and that now if "the general government might ever be so administered as to render the liberty of conscience insecure, . . . no one would be more zealous than myself to establish effectual barriers against the horrors of spiritual tyranny, and every species of religious persecution" (ibid.).

[78] Curry, *First Freedoms*, 193–94. He elaborated, "The passage of the First Amendment constituted a symbolic act, a declaration for the future, an assurance to those nervous about the federal government that it was not going to reverse any of the guarantees for religious liberty won by the revolutionary states" (ibid., 216).

[79] As Stephen Botein pointed out, "whatever may or may not have been intended between the lines, the text of the First Amendment merely added two more prohibitions in confirmation of the new government's secularity" (Botein, "Religious Dimensions of the Early American State," 317).

[80] Much has been written about Jefferson and religion; the following draws on two of the best studies: Gaustad, *Sworn on the Altar of God*, and E. R. Sheridan, "Introduction," in *Jefferson's Extracts from the Gospels: "The Philosophy of Jesus" and "The Life and Morals of Jesus,"* ed. D. W. Adams, *The Papers of Thomas Jefferson*, 2d ser., ed. C. T. Cullen (Princeton, NJ: Princeton University Press, 1983), 3–42.

[81] Quoted in Sheridan, "Introduction," 42, 36.

[82] E. Stiles, "The United States elevated to Glory and Honor. A Sermon, Preached before His Excellency Jonathan Trumbull, Esq. L.L.D. Governor and Commander in Chief, And the Honorable The General Assembly of The State of Connecticut, Convened at Hartford, at the Anniversary Election, May 8th, 1783," in *The Pulpit of the American Revolution: or, the Political Sermons of the Period of 1776*, ed. J. W. Thornton (Boston, 1860), 397–520; Botein, "Religious Dimensions of the Early American State," 322–23, quote on 322; Curry,

First Freedoms, 217–18; M. L. Bradbury, "Structures of Nationalism," in Hoffman and Albert, *Religion in a Revolutionary Age*, 244–54; C. O. Loveland, *The Critical Years: The Reconstitution of the Anglican Church in the United States of America: 1780–1789* (Greenwich, CT: Seabury Press, 1956).

[83] S. A. Marini, *Radical Sects of Revolutionary New England* (Cambridge, MA: Harvard University Press, 1982).

[84] Holifield, *Theology in America*, 159–69, quote on 162.

[85] J. Roger Sharp, *American Politics in the Early Republic: The New Nation in Crisis* (New Haven, CT: Yale University Press, 1993).

[86] G. Washington, *Farewell Address* (1796), http://www.yale.edu/lawweb/avalon/washing.htm.

[87] J. Morse, *A Sermon, Exhibiting the Present Dangers, and Consequent Duties of the Citizens of the United States of America. Delivered at Charlestown, April 25, 1799. The Day of the National Fast* (Charlestown, MA, 1799); Bloch, *Visionary Republic*, 202–12.

[88] Jefferson, *Notes on the State of Virginia*, 159.

[89] Quoted in R. M. S. McDonald, "Was There a Religious Revolution of 1800?" in *The Revolution of 1800: Democracy, Race, and the New Republic*, ed. J. Horn, J. E. Lewis, and P. S. Onuf (Charlottesville: University of Virginia Press, 2002), 182.

[90] F. Lambert, "'God—and a Religious President . . . [or] Jefferson and No God': Campaigning for a Voter-Imposed Religious Test in 1800," *Journal of Church and State* 39, no. 4 (1997): 769–89.

[91] Jefferson, *Notes on the State of Virginia*, 159; McDonald, "Was There a Religious Revolution of 1800?" 179.

[92] Leland's address and Jefferson's reply are reprinted in full in Butterfield, "Elder John Leland," 224–25. See also J. L. Pasley, "The Cheese and the Words: Popular Political Culture and Participatory Democracy in the Early American Republic," in *Beyond the Founders: New Approaches to the Political History of the Early American Republic*, ed. J. L. Pasley, A. W. Robertson, and D. Waldstreicher (Chapel Hill: University of North Carolina Press, 2004), 31–56, which is especially insightful about the role of newspapers in playing up the story. "The Mammoth Cheese would have been nothing more than a hefty hors d'oeuvre without the newspaper publicity that grew up around it," Pasley comments (ibid., 42).

[93] The letters from and to the Danbury Baptist Association are reprinted in appendix 6 of D. L. Dreisbach, *Thomas Jefferson and the Wall of Separation between Church and State* (New York: New York University Press, 2002), 142–48. The Danbury Baptists' letter was dated October 7, 1801, but for some reason it only reached Jefferson on December 30 (ibid., 31). Dreisbach notes dissemination of the letters in Republican newspapers in ibid., 24.

[94] Ibid., 148.

[95] Sheridan, "Introduction," 12–30, quote on 19.

[96] N. O. Hatch, *The Democratization of American Christianity* (New Haven, CT: Yale University Press, 1989), quote on 20.

[97] Tocqueville, *Democracy in America*, 423; J. H. Wigger, *Taking Heaven by Storm: Methodism and the Rise of Popular Christianity in America* (New York: Oxford University Press, 1998); Murrin, "Religion and Politics in America from the First Settlements to the Civil War," 26; R. Finke and R. Stark, "How the Upstart Sects Won America: 1776–1850," *Journal for the Scientific Study of Religion* 28, no. 1 (1989): 27–44.

[98] P. K. Conkin, *Cane Ridge: America's Pentecost* (Madison: University of Wisconsin Press, 1990), especially 92–97; Hatch, *Democratization*, 49–55; Butler,

Awash in a Sea of Faith, 236–41; Wigger, *Taking Heaven by Storm*, 106–24, quote on 106.

⁹⁹ J. L. Brooke, *The Refiner's Fire: The Making of Mormon Cosmology, 1644–1844* (New York: Cambridge University Press, 1994); Hatch, *Democratization*, 113–22; Butler, *Awash in a Sea of Faith*, 231, 242–47, quote on 244.

¹⁰⁰ Holifield, *Theology in America*, 197–207, 408–414; J. D. Bratt, "Religious Anti-Revivalism in Antebellum America," *Journal of the Early Republic* 24, no. 1 (2004): 65–106; S. Juster and E. Hartigan-O'Connor, "The 'Angel Delusion' of 1806–1811: Frustration and Fantasy in Northern New England," *Journal of the Early Republic* 22, no. 3 (2002): 375–404.

¹⁰¹ W. Gribbin, *The Churches Militant: The War of 1812 and American Religion* (New Haven, CT: Yale University Press, 1973); J. D. Sassi, *A Republic of Righteousness: The Public Christianity of the Post-Revolutionary New England Clergy* (New York: Oxford University Press, 2001), quote on 103; McLoughlin, *New England Dissent*, vol. 2.

¹⁰² Tocqueville, *Democracy in America*, 282.

¹⁰³ R. R. John, "Taking Sabbatarianism Seriously: The Postal System, the Sabbath, and the Transformation of American Political Culture," *Journal of the Early Republic* 10, no. 4 (1990): 517–67; M. Hershberger, "Mobilizing Women, Anticipating Abolition: The Struggle against Indian Removal in the 1830s," *Journal of American History* 86, no. 1 (1999): 15–40; R. H. Abzug, *Cosmos Crumbling: American Reform and the Religious Imagination* (New York: Oxford University Press, 1994).

¹⁰⁴ Tocqueville, *Democracy in America*, 419.

Response to Sassi

David Barton

I found Jonathan Sassi's piece to be very interesting, filled with useful and instructive information; but in some important areas, I found it far too predictable, often being a repetition of claims made by other modern writers about the Founding Era.

His opening plan to define key words was praiseworthy, but he unfortunately failed to define "secular"—a word he used repeatedly. He admitted that there were various definitions for the word but he never identified the one he embraced. Readers therefore generally default to its meaning as widely used today; and according to current dictionaries, "secular" includes "advocating secularism";[1] the "doctrine that morality . . . [is] without regard to religious belief or a hereafter";[2] and a "doctrine that rejects religion."[3] If Sassi is asserting that the nation and its documents were "secular" within the framework of these definitions, that notion immediately becomes untenable to the overwhelming majority of historians.

A Secular Constitution

Typical of Sassi's thirty-one uses of the word *secular* are his statements that: "The framers of the United States Constitution chose a deliberately secular path." Also, "The federal government would be a secular one." And, "At the national level, they designed a secular Constitution."

To help support his claims, Sassi references *The Godless Constitution*, a work in which two Cornell professors make the same assertions.[4] On what scholarly evidence do these professors rely to prove their claims? Strikingly, in the location where footnotes customarily appear, they candidly acknowledge: "[W]e have dispensed with the usual scholarly apparatus of footnotes."[5]

I remain befuddled over the academic community's recalcitrance to adopt the widely accepted legal rules of evidence used to establish fact and truth. In courts of law, greater veracity is given to an eyewitness or a participant in an event than to a latecomer who simply presents hearsay testimony or his opinion of that event; and if there are a dozen eyewitnesses who say the same thing about an incident, and another says something completely different, the weight of credibility goes to the group, not the anomaly. This remains the preferred method for establishing truth and fact.

Yet many academics today, when seeking to document the Framers' thinking and motivation, make claims but provide little or no documentation (as in the case of *The Godless Constitution*), select quotes from just a handful of Framers with whom they agree while ignoring the opposite position held by dozens of other Framers, or regularly cite each others' works rather than primary documentation from the period they are examining.

For example, in Sassi's 104 footnotes, he admirably cites 76 distinct sources, but when those sources are examined, a disturbing trend appears. Although he is writing about the Founding Era (defined as the period from 1760 to 1805), he cites only two sources from that period (one from the 1770s and one from the 1790s); he cites one source from the 1860s, and the rest are from the 1950s and later, with the heaviest reliance being on the most recent works. Why is it that the works relied on most heavily to establish intent and belief in the period from 1760–1805 are the works farthest away from the actual event?

Significantly, the Framers and early courts provided numerous proofs that the Constitution was *not* secular (i.e., godless), but I will allude to only five.

Consider first the five oath clauses of the Constitution. Numerous Founders affirm that these clauses were inherently religious; in fact the notion of a secular oath was not only oxymoronic but even reprehensible to them:

> [In o]ur laws . . . by the oath which they prescribe, we appeal to the Supreme Being so to deal with us hereafter as we observe the obligation of our oaths. The Pagan world were and are without the mighty influence of this principle which is proclaimed in the Christian system.[6] (RUFUS KING, SIGNER OF THE CONSTITUTION, FRAMER OF THE BILL OF RIGHTS)
>
> [W]here is the security for property, for reputation, for life, if the sense of religious obligation desert the oaths . . . ?[7] (GEORGE WASHINGTON, SIGNER OF THE CONSTITUTION)

The inherently religious nature of oaths was so infused into the Constitution that on the federal oath forms used even during the Civil War, an individual was required to "make oath on the Holy Evangely of Almighty God."[8]

Second, the seventh amendment of the Constitution explicitly incorporates the common law into the procedures of constitutional process. According to James Wilson, a signer of the Constitution and an original justice on the U. S. Supreme Court, "Christianity is part of the common law."[9] The same position is reaffirmed by Justice Joseph Story and Justice James Kent (the two "Fathers of American Jurisprudence") as well as numerous courts. In short, the common law—of which Christianity was legally recognized as an integral part—was directly incorporated into the Constitution.[10]

Third, Article I of the Constitution contains the "Sundays Excepted Clause," and as explained by the U. S. Supreme Court in 1961: "The 'Sundays excepted' clause . . . when incorporated into the U. S. Constitution, carried the same meaning that had been established by traditional usage. . . . Can any impartial mind deny that it contains a recognition of the Lord's Day as a day exempted by law from all worldly pursuits? The Framers of the Constitution, then, recognized Sunday as a day to be observed."[11] No other religion in the world observes a Sunday Sabbath except Christianity, and enshrined in the federal Constitution is the specific recognition of only the Christian Sabbath.

Fourth is the "Attestation Clause" of Article VII declaring that the Constitution was done "in the Year of our Lord." The Framers deliberately linked the Constitution to the birth, death, and resurrection of Jesus Christ, and later courts commented on this clause as evidence of the Christian construction of the Constitution.[12]

A fifth indicator is found in the *Federalist Papers*, which directly invokes multiple references to God to explain various parts of the Constitution and the rights secured therein. In fact, in *Federalist* #20, Madison declared that the Constitution and the means by which it was produced should cause Americans to offer up fervent prayers of thanksgiving to God, and in *Federalist* #37, he even avowed that it was "impossible" for the God-fearing man not to see "the finger of that Almighty Hand" in the writing of the Constitution. Other convention delegates expressed the same view. The Framers simply did not view the Constitution within a secular framework.[13]

Incidentally, Sassi points to one other "proof" of the Constitution's alleged secularity, noting, "The document that they produced said very little at all on the subject of religion. . . . The preamble, for instance, contained no invocation of God's name." When that same argument was raised in 1876 by the National Liberal League,[14] legal writer Samuel Spear promptly rebutted it as nonsensical, noting: "We might as well say that the Constitution is opposed to the Copernican theory of astronomy because it contains no doctrine on the subject of astronomy."[15] In short, there is abundant organic evidence to demonstrate that the Constitution incorporated numerous overtly Christian elements.

Madison and Jefferson: Defining Religion in America

Sassi places almost exclusive reliance on James Madison and Thomas Jefferson, presenting their efforts in the passage of the Virginia statute as the prototype for religious liberty in the new nation, but such a portrayal is not accurate. In fact, much of what Madison and Jefferson so laudably fought for and accomplished in Virginia had already occurred in many other states well prior to the Virginia statute.

For example, New Jersey, North Carolina, and Delaware provided equal denominational protection well before Virginia; and New York, Pennsylvania, Georgia, and Vermont established religious liberty prior to the Virginia statute. Furthermore, as early as 1773 (over a decade before the passage of the Virginia statute) Samuel Chase and William Paca (signers of the Declaration) led Maryland's fight to end the system of state-ordered tithes—something Jefferson and Madison did not even attempt in Virginia until years later. Many other states made progress in the area of religious liberty completely independent of the efforts of Jefferson and Madison in Virginia.[16]

Similarly, Sassi's claim that the efforts of Jefferson and Madison formed the basis for the First Amendment is equally unfounded. Recall that the Constitutional Convention had ended with a proposal for a new federal government, but it had also ended on a very divisive tone. During the convention, Virginian George Mason had advocated that a Bill of Rights be added to the Constitution to provide specific protection for states and individuals,[17] but the other Virginians at the convention—including James Madison—opposed any Bill of Rights, and their position prevailed.[18] For this reason, Virginia delegates such as George Mason and Edmund Randolph refused to sign the new Constitution and returned home to lobby against ratification until a Bill of Rights was added.

In Virginia, the records of its convention make clear that Patrick Henry, George Mason, and Edmund Randolph led the fight for the Bill of Rights over James Madison's opposition. Henry's passionate speeches during the convention resulted in Virginia's motion that a Bill of Rights be added to the federal Constitution. The Virginia convention then selected George Mason to chair a committee to prepare a proposed Bill of Rights, with Patrick Henry and John Randolph as members. Mason incorporated Henry's arguments as the basis of Virginia's proposal on religious liberty.[19]

While Madison had consistently and repeatedly opposed a Bill of Rights, he perceived the political reality that without one, it was unlikely the new Constitution would receive widespread public acceptance.[20] He therefore finally withdrew his long-standing opposition to a Bill of Rights, and in the federal House of Representatives introduced his own versions of the amendments offered by his state. (Several other states had also submitted their proposals.)

The records of Congress make clear that very little of Madison's proposed wording made it into the final version of the First Amendment; and even a cursory examination of the *Annals of Congress* documenting the formation of that amendment quickly reveals the influence of Fisher Ames and Elbridge Gerry of Massachusetts, John Vining of Delaware, Daniel Carroll and Charles Carroll of Maryland, Benjamin Huntington, Roger Sherman, and Oliver Ellsworth of Connecticut, William Paterson of New Jersey, and others on that amendment.[21]

Significantly, the heavy reliance on both Jefferson and Madison (as Sassi has done) is a modern phenomenon.[22] In fact, an important reason that Jefferson was rarely cited as an authority in previous generations was provided by Jefferson himself: "I was in Europe when the Constitution was planned, and never saw it till after it was established."[23]

Jefferson had no hand in the Constitution, and he did not even arrive back in America until months after the First Amendment had been completed. Significantly, by utilizing only these two as the principal spokesmen for the First Amendment, Sassi has chosen one who was out of the country at the time of its formation and another who repeatedly felt it to be unnecessary. Jefferson and Madison did play important roles, but so did a number of other Framers.

Endnotes

[1] Dictionary.com, s.v. "Secular" (at: http://dictionary.reference.com/browse/secular) (accessed August 30, 2010).

[2] Dictionary.com, s.v. "Secular" (at: http://dictionary.reference.com/browse/secular) (accessed August 30, 2010).

[3] Dictionary.com, s.v. "Secular" (at: http://dictionary.reference.com/browse/secular) (accessed August 30, 2010).

[4] See, for example, I. Kramnick and L. Moore, *The Godless Constitution* (New York: Norton, 1996), 22, 27, 12, etc.

[5] Ibid., 179.

[6] *Reports of the Proceedings and Debates of the Convention of 1821, Assembled for the Purpose of Amending The Constitution of the State of New York* (Albany: E. and E. Hosford, 1821), 575. Rufus King made this statement on October 30, 1821.

[7] G. Washington, *Address of George Washington, President of the United States . . . Preparatory to His Declination* (Baltimore: George and Henry S. Keatinge, 1796), 23.

[8] From an original document in our possession ("An Oath of Allegiance taken by John Welles on May 19, 1863."), being a printed oath form with the name and date being handwritten in the blanks. The document declares: "I, John Welles of Washington County, State of Maryland, make oath on the Holy Evangely of Almighty God, that I will bear true Allegiance to the United States of America, and support and sustain the Constitution and Laws thereof . . . further, that I disclaim and renounce all faith and fellowship with the so called Confederate States, Confederate Government, armies and navy."

[9] *Updegraph v. Commonwealth*, 11 Serg. & R 393.4.C (Sup. Ct. of PA, 1824).

[10] J. Story, *Life and Letters of Joseph Story*, vol. 2, ed. W. W. Story (Boston: Charles C. Little and James Brown, 1851), 8; *Reports of the Proceedings and Debates of the Convention of 1821,* 575–76. See, for example, *Church of the Holy Trinity v. U. S.*, 143 U. S. 470–471 (1892); *Updegraph v. The Commonwealth*, 11 S. & R. 394, 399 (Sup. Ct. Pa. 1824); *City Council of Charleston v. S. A. Benjamin*, 2 Strob. 508, 518–521 (Sup. Ct. SC 1846); *Shover v. State*, 10 English 259, 263 (Sup. Ct. Ark. 1850); *Sparhawk v. Union Pass. Ry. Co.*, 54 Pa. 401, 1867 WL 7476 (Pa.), 4 P.F. Smith 401, 15 Pitts.L.J. 49 (Sup. Ct. Penn. 1867); *State v. Chandler*, 2 Harr. 553, 2 Del. 553, 1837 WL 154 (Del.Gen.Sess. 1837); *Zeisweiss v. James*, 63 Pa. 465, 1870 WL 8652 (Pa.), 13 P.F. Smith 465, 3 Am.Rep. 558 (Sup. Ct. Pa. 1870); *Lindenmuller v. The People*, 33 Barb. 548, 21 How. Pr. 156 (Sup. Ct. NY, 1861); *Commonwealth ex rel. Woodruff, Atty. Gen., v. American Baseball Club of Philadelphia*, 138 A. 497, 290 Pa. 136, 53 A.L.R. 1027 (Sup. Ct. Penn. 1927); *Bell v. State*, 31 Tenn. 42, 1851 WL 1952 (Tenn.), 1 Swan 42 (Sup. Ct. Tenn. 1851); *Wylly v. S.Z. Collins & Co.*, 9 Ga. 223, 1851 WL 1417 (Ga.) (Sup. Ct. Ga. 1851); *Strauss v. Strauss*, 148 Fla. 23, 3 So.2d 727 (Sup. Ct. Fla. 1941); and many, many others.

[11] *McGowan v. Maryland*, 366 U.S. 420 (1961), quoting from *State v. Chicago, B. & Q. R. Co.*, 143 S.W. 785, 803 (Mo. 1912).

[12] See, for example, *State v. Ambs*, 20 Mo. 214, 1854 WL 4543 (Mo. 1854); *State v. Barnes*, 22 N.D. 18, 132 N.W. 215, Am.Ann.Cas. 1913E,930, 37 L.R.A.N.S. 114 (N.D. 1911), and others.

[13] A. Hamilton, J. Jay, & J. Madison, *The Federalist* (Philadelphia: Benjamin Warner, 1818), see #2, #20, #37, #43, etc.

[14] See, for example, *Patriotic Address to the People of the United States, Adopted at Philadelphia on the Fourth of July, 1876, by the National Liberal League. Together with the Chief Resolutions of the League, its Constitution and List of Officers, and its Protest Against the Shutting of the International Exhibition on Sundays* (Boston: National Liberal League: 1876).

[15] S. T. Spears, *Religion and the State* (New York: Dodd, Mead & Company, 1876), 149.

[16] *The Constitutions of the Several Independent States of America* (Boston: Norman and Bowen, 1785), 67, 73–74, 77, 91, 138, 166; *The Constitutions of the Sixteen States* (Boston: Manning and Loring, 1797), 250. J. V. L. McMahon, *An Historical View of the Government of Maryland*, vol. 1 (Baltimore: F. Lucas, Jr. Cushing & Sons, and William & Joseph Neal, 1831), 380–400.

[17] See the entry for Wednesday, September 12, 1787, in *The Papers of James Madison*, vol. 3, ed. H. D. Gilpin (Washington: Langress and O'Sullivan, 1840), 1566. See also G. Bancroft, *Bancroft's History of the Formation of the Constitution*, vol. 2 (New York: D. Appleton and Company, 1882), 209–10, and *The Records of the Federal Convention of 1787*, vol. 2, ed. M. Farrand (New Haven: Yale University Press, 1911), 588, 637.

[18] See the entry for September 12, 1787, in *Debates in the Several State Conventions on the Adoption of the Federal Constitution*, vol. 1, ed. J. Elliot (Washington: Printed for the Editor, 1836), 306.

[19] *Debates in the Several State Conventions on the Adoption of the Federal Constitution*, Jonathan Elliot, editor (Washington: Printed for the Editor, 1836), Vol. III, 616–22, James Madison, June 24, 1788. Kate Mason Rowland, *The Life of George Mason* (New York and London: G. P. Putnam's Sons, 1892), Vol. I, 244; *Debates in the Several State Conventions on the Adoption of the Federal Constitution*, Jonathan Elliot, editor (Washington: Printed for the Editor, 1836), Vol. III, 655–56, June 25, 1788. William Wirt Henry, *Patrick Henry: Life, Correspondence and Speeches* (New York: Charles Scribner's Sons, 1891), Vol. I, 430–31. See also Kate Mason Rowland, *The Life of George Mason* (New York: G. P. Putnam's Sons, 1892), Vol. I, 244; and *Elliot's Debates*, Vol. III, 659, June 27, 1788.

[20] *The Debates and Proceedings in the Congress of the United States* (Washington, DC: Gales & Seaton, 1834), 448–50. See also *Wallace v. Jaffree*, 472 U. S. 38, 93–99, Rehnquist, J. (dissenting).

[21] See *The Debates and Proceedings in the Congress of the United States*, vol. 1 (Washington, DC: Gales and Seaton, 1834), 440–948. These pages include debates between June 8 and September 24, 1789.

[22] See, for example, the documentation of this trend by M. D. Hall, "Jeffersonian Wall and Madisonian Lines: The Supreme Court's Use of History and Religion Clauses Cases," *Oregon Law Review* 85, No. 2 (2006): 563–614.

[23] Thomas Jefferson letter to Dr. Joseph Priestly, June 19, 1802, in *The Writings of Thomas Jefferson*, vol 10, ed. A. A. Lipscomb (Washington, DC: The Thomas Jefferson Memorial Association, 1904), 325.

Response to Sassi

William D. Henard

Jonathan Sassi offers a perspective on the role of Christianity in the founding of America that limits the influence of the Christian faith to its smallest degree. Sassi attempts to define America's founding in the most secular and least Christianized manner, referencing the Enlightenment as his primary source of influence. Interestingly enough, he utilizes the same source of influence as does Cornett, only coming to a much different conclusion.

It appears Sassi attempts to defend his position of a purely secular government because of the notion of an expanded pluralism within religion during the eighteenth century. Sassi states:

> If we confine our analysis to constitutional and political matters, then it is the contention of this essay that the framers of the United States Constitution chose a deliberately secular path in the interest of national unity. They designed a government to deal with practical, worldly affairs and not to interfere with the religious realm.

Immediately, I find contradiction in his analysis. Sassi opines, "While there were a variety of Christian influences on American civic life before, during, and after the era of the Revolution, the overall picture was an eclectic and secular one." While he defends his position, I question how Christian influences could be present and yet not be significant in defining the direction of government. The only answer, in my mind, comes from the conclusion that all of the Framers of the Constitution had bad experiences in the church and rejected Christianity. While it is true that their forefathers faced great persecution in England, this fact did not cause them to reject Christianity but became the impetus for why they framed the founding documents with the specific protection of religion. In my chapter, I demonstrate that changes in theology occurred, especially during and immediately following the Great Awakening, that directly influenced the thinking of religious leaders. These changes, however, did not lead them to become great secularists, even though some leaders did not adhere to the Christian faith.

Sassi continues this line of logic, when he explains:

> Both the centrifugal forces of colonization and the centripetal pull of empire yielded the same results, namely greater religious eclecticism and toleration. The religious revivals of mid-century, collectively known as the Great Awakening, only accelerated these trends. The controversies that erupted over the revivals' propriety and legitimacy further divided the denominational landscape. The resulting increase in religious pluralism confirmed the necessity that governments confine themselves to secular matters.

This perspective, in my opinion, is seriously flawed. I focus at this point because he lays much of the foundation of his thought at this juncture. I believe he underestimates the continued impact of the Reformation on eighteenth-century faith. I do not believe that, at this point in American history, a predominant mind-set existed to establish America as an exclusively Christian nation, in opposition to and in persecution of other faiths. As Sassi tries to define pluralism, the issues that divided religion were not Christian versus non-Christian beliefs. Had this matter been at the forefront of discussion, then a preference toward secularism, in order to protect religion, might have been an option. The fact remains, though, that non-Christian religions made up an insignificant number of people, as far as influence was concerned. As I state in my chapter, I believe that these non-Christian religions were taken into consideration as the Framers of the nation examined the issue of religion. Yet the diversity in America was only in Christian theology, not religion itself. Therefore, to conclude that the national sentiment leaned toward secularism is mistaken.

Sassi then attempts to defend his position by referencing the political and theological situation in Rhode Island, indicating that the colony became "home to a diverse array of religious groups." While Rhode Island was open to some diversity, the statement that it became the embodiment of religious freedom

is not totally accurate. Williams discovered that, while total
religious freedom worked in theory, it oftentimes failed in practice. This statement originates out of the fact that Williams,
while on his second trip to England, had to settle a dispute
whereby citizens believed that their government was too harsh
on some transgressors and wanted biblical boundaries set. Williams returned and penned a letter to the town of Providence,
defining the limits for religious toleration. He also penned a
letter to John Cotton in which he called for both the church and
the state to act in a civil manner, based on biblical grounds.
Finally, in 1663, when King Charles finally ratified the charter for the colony, two issues were strikingly present. First, the
inhabitants were granted religious liberty. Second, the civil
state would be best maintained under gospel principles.

Williams's attempt toward religious freedom provides a pivotal look into what it meant for Christianity to influence America's founding. Other influential factors were present, but they
did not provide the strongest stimulus for how church and state
would co-exist. Even in Williams's *Camelot*, the church had significant impact on the direction and activities of the state.

In my opinion, Sassi places far too much emphasis on the
Enlightenment and English behavior and norm in the direction
of American religion and politics. He references how the Great
Awakening brought about an awareness of transatlantic movement, which is true. The problem, however, is that Sassi seems
to imply the emphasis was one-sided. No doubt that English
theologians and philosophers had some impact on American
thinking. These individuals became a source of study in the
American university. The American philosopher and theologian, however, had a strong impact on the mind of the English. Jonathan Edwards became incredibly popular not only in
America but also in Great Britain. His influence was so expansive that book publishers in England reproduced his writings
in large quantities. Edwards was even offered a Scottish pulpit
when he was fired from Northampton.

I would also question a heavy impression of English
Enlightenment on the colonies based on the fact that, outside
the Anglican churches, most Congregational and Puritan pastors rejected English influence. Yet even Sassi admits that the

Anglican churches in the South were sympathetic to the Revolutionary cause. When the Puritans came to the New World, they brought the Geneva Bible, not the King James Bible. When John Witherspoon helped publish two American editions of the Bible, although it was similar to the King James Bible, he refused to use the name "King James." Witherspoon, a signer of the Declaration of Independence, obviously refused to use the King James Bible because the war for independence was waged against kings. If the Americans waged war against the English, why would they allow English thought to be profoundly influential for them? As Sassi quotes Witherspoon, "There is not a single instance in history in which civil liberty was lost, and religious liberty preserved entire. . . . If therefore we yield up our temporal property, we at the same time deliver the conscience into bondage." These words demonstrate the mind-set of many colonials with regard to liberty. Witherspoon no doubt saw a direct connection between civil liberty and religious liberty. If the two were to be totally separate, with civil law being totally secular, then why make the connection? In my opinion, Witherspoon demonstrates a prevailing attitude that carried into the Declaration and into the Bill of Rights.

Finally, Sassi does an excellent job demonstrating how the preaching of colonial pastors influenced the thinking of those who would be leaders in the Revolution and the future politicians and writers of the official documents. He also documents the cost to the colonial church, specifically for some of those that supported the Revolution. As I evaluated these findings, it seems that his conclusions actually lean more toward showing why Christianity had a greater influence on America's founding than Sassi gives credit. If the church had been far removed from the Revolution and was able to isolate itself from involvement, one might easily conclude that the Founders would have been mostly secular in their approach to the founding documents. If, however, a direct connection occurred, and the Founders were inspired by their pastors to move toward revolution, and if the churches were intricately involved in the Revolution both in cost and manpower, then I do not think one can conclude that the church became silent when America was founded.

I will once again reference the impact of Pastor John Leland on Thomas Jefferson. In my chapter, I tell of Leland's trip to Washington to congratulate Jefferson on his reelection as president. Leland preached in the House of Representatives (a fact that is astounding considering those who propose an absolute separation of church and state) with Jefferson in attendance. Culturally, the church had a much greater impact on society in colonial days than it does today. I am afraid that modern interpreters of history attempt to intertwine contemporary models of faith and culture into the environment of history. I must also exhibit caution, for those of us who hold to the belief that Christianity held a much higher position in the political circles can be guilty of making more of faith than what actually took place. Yet I am compelled to believe, based on the culture of the day and the record of history, that Christianity's role in America's founding made a much greater impact than Sassi credits. A wall of separation did occur, but it was a wall that kept government out of the hands of religion, not religion from influencing government. The Founders were far more than just enlightened secularists who winked at religion. Many of them were strong men of faith whose ideas were shaped and developed through their relationship with Christ and the church.

Response to Sassi
Daryl C. Cornett

Jonathan Sassi gives a more micro-historical treatment of the crucial Founding Era of America's past. Rather than a more general view from 30,000 feet (like my chapter), he zooms in for a more detailed treatment focused on the 1760s through the 1830s. His reasoning for this approach is to demonstrate that American culture was diverse from the beginning of this timeframe and religious pluralism only continued to increase as time proceeded.

First, he chooses to limit his discussion to the late colonial period from around 1760 through the American Revolution and Founding Era, roughly examining American politics and religion through the 1830s. Second, he focuses on government and its relationship to religion, particularly the issue of the relationship between church and state. Third, he argues that America was religiously eclectic during the founding period in the late eighteenth century, rather than distinctly Christian. Sassi neatly frames his discussion with a straightforward chronological treatment. He examines the ideas that permeated the years just prior to the American Revolution (1763–76), the period of the Revolution itself, and the following years of the early republic.

Sassi provides adequate examples to make his point about the religious diversity that already existed in the decades just prior to the American Revolution. He is correct in pointing out that the shifting relationship of the church to government in England was impacting the British colonies in America, most notably the political consequences of the 1698 Act of Toleration. Those established groups such as New England Puritans or Virginia Anglicans during this time had to increasingly concede more rights to individuals and increase their toleration for marginalized, dissenting groups such as Baptists and Quakers. However, there still existed for some groups a second-class citizen status, real discrimination, and occasional persecution.

Sassi demonstrates the role of patriot clergy in the struggle for independence and how freedom-seeking evangelicals and politicians seeking consensus and unity for a fragile new country found common ground in the intentional secularization of the national government. Sassi correctly points out that the Constitution and the Bill of Rights sought to secure individual religious freedom and restrict the federal government from making policy in regard to religious practice. This solution did not automatically translate to state governments, some of which kept religious tests into the 1830s. It is interesting that he observes that some Christians objected to this secularization during the ratification process of the Constitution, demonstrating that religion was a point of contention during this time.

Sassi observes that during the period of the new republic, religious diversity only increased in response to increased religious freedom. Deism continued to grow and fringe groups emerged, such as Shakers and Universalists. He uses the example of Thomas Jefferson's religious and political views as the victorious paradigm emerging during this time. Many orthodox Christians opposed Jefferson's campaign for president based on the fact that he did not adhere to basic Christian tenets of faith. However, Jefferson's view that religion should be private and that the federal government should not be concerned with religion won the day. Sassi observes that more marginal groups such as Baptists supported Jefferson, seeing him as one committed to religious liberty. His personal religious views appeared to be inconsequential to John Leland. The early nineteenth century evidenced an increasing diversity as new groups continued to emerge, such as the Mormons.

That the Framers of the founding documents intentionally chose a secular path for the sake of national unity seems to be a reasonable observation, though I would add that many of them were not secular-minded themselves. There was no hostility toward religion by most. On the contrary, most of the Founders seemed to hold personal views that valued the role of religion in the public arena in regard to maintaining a virtuous society. However, this is not to say that they were all orthodox Christians.

What I find most helpful about Sassi's essay is the fact that he opens and concludes with reference to the comment made by Alexis de Tocqueville, who was reflecting on his experience of America in 1830. Tocqueville marveled that in the United States he observed religion and the spirit of freedom, "united intimately with one another: they reigned together on the same soil." Sassi has produced a compelling argument that posits that it was the intentional secularization of government that ironically led to a more vibrant religious society, albeit full of heterodoxy and cult movements.

Although I would agree with Sassi's overall observation of the religiously eclectic nature of early America, I believe he does not attach sufficient significance to the fact that the umbrella under which that diversity overwhelmingly operated was the Christian faith. This fact in itself should be counted as significant because the eclecticism he emphasizes was still overwhelmingly within the bounds of Protestant Christian tradition during the founding period, and non-Christian groups (e.g., Jews, Muslims, pagans) and Roman Catholics were inconsequential in numbers. However, a century later would be a different story.

In taking such a narrow slice of American history (which is helpful in some ways), he does not take into account the ebb and flow of Christian presence and influence. America's relationship to Christianity is not defined merely by the period of time Sassi has chosen to examine. He is correct in that the founding period is key to understanding politically what the Founders envisioned for America as evidenced in their own rhetoric and the founding documents. However, for me this is only one part of the discussion and certainly not the defining part of the debate. One could argue that vestiges of the highly Christianized early nineteenth century continue to resonate in American culture in evangelicalism and challenge the initial step toward secularization taken at the founding. I believe the pull and tug between these two forces is what has actually defined America through its history. Even though a good discussion of American politics in crucial to the overall discussion, it is not the only item. If it is, then it does beg the question of whether *Christian nation* must be defined merely by what one finds in the Constitution.

I continue to assert that what ultimately makes a country Christian or not is the presence and activity of Christian people. Just as Barton (according to my thinking) cannot prove America to be a Christian nation based on scores of favorable quotes from the Founding Fathers, Sassi cannot prove America not to be Christian simply because he can demonstrate the ideas enshrined in the founding documents had a primarily secular foundation. Whether or not a country *is* Christian is determined by what kind of influence Christians are making on their culture in matters of belief and behavior that is congruent with God's precepts and principles contained in the Bible. When you look at the debate in this way, you can observe that America has been more and less Christian at different times. My hope is that I and my children get to see it more Christian again.

America Essentially Christian

William D. Henard

In 2008, America made a bold change of direction as she elected her first African American president. It was, by many accounts, an important step in healing the past and moving toward a viable future for the nation. While some would disagree with that assessment, it takes very little observance to discover that the United States of America comprises an incredibly diverse population, not only in age but in race, color, and religion. From an evangelical perspective, this diversity positively allows the church to more completely fulfill the Great Commission because the world has come to America.

Many evangelical Christians, however, expressed shock at statements made by President Barack Hussein Obama in his attempts to boost U. S. relations with other countries, especially those of Muslim population. Speaking to a Turkish press conference on April 8, 2009, Obama opined, "Although . . . we have a very large Christian population, we do not consider ourselves a Christian nation, or a Jewish nation, or a Muslim nation. . . . We consider ourselves a nation of citizens who are bound by ideals and a set of values."[1]

In 2007, presidential hopeful Obama made a similar remark in an email to CBN News's senior national correspondent, David Brody. To his defense, he was attempting to show how religious/moral issues provide an important component in the solution to certain problems people face—problems that government cannot fix. In Brody's opinion, Obama made some unfortunate inflammatory remarks to a church convention in 2007 when he proffered, "Somehow, somewhere along the way, faith stopped being used to bring us together and started being used to drive us apart. It got hijacked. Part of it's because of the so-called leaders of the Christian Right, who've been all too eager to exploit what divides us."[2]

Obama attempted to explain these remarks to Brody, suggesting:

> I think that the Right might worry a bit more about the dangers of sectarianism. Whatever we once were, we're no longer just a Christian nation; we are also a Jewish nation, a Muslim nation, a Buddhist nation, a Hindu nation, and a nation of unbelievers. We should acknowledge this and realize that when we're formulating policies from the state house to the Senate floor to the White House, we've got to work to translate our reasoning into values that are accessible to every one of our citizens, not just members of our own faith community.[3]

According to Gilbert and Westen, people from bloggers to magazine editors jumped on the proverbial "America is not a Christian nation" bandwagon. They cite a *Newsweek* article titled "The End of Christian America," which references the 2009 American Religious Identification Survey. In this survey, only 62 percent of respondents considered the United States to be a Christian nation. The writer concludes that the survey demonstrates a clear decline in religious values over the past decade.[4]

Christian educators and adherents did not remain silent, however. In an interview with LifeSiteNews.com, Dr. Timothy O'Donnell, president of the predominantly Catholic Christendom College, asserted:

> I think he [Obama] was using the editorial "we" there. I don't know who he's talking to. . . . While it is clear America was not instituted as an explicitly Christian nation, it's an inconvertible fact of history that the overwhelming population of people who were involved in the drafting of the

Constitution . . . came out of the tradition of Western Christian civilization.[5]

Dr. Albert R. Mohler, president of the Southern Baptist Theological Seminary in Louisville, also quickly responded to the remarks. He clarified Obama's remarks by reminding critics that Obama was initially addressing the issue of America's relationship with Muslim nations, specifically Turkey. Mohler stated, "I think President Obama rightly said that the United States is not at war with Islam. . . . Classical Islam understands no real distinction between religion and the state, but instead establishes a unitary society. Thus, when a foreign power like the United States invades a Muslim nation like Iraq, most Muslims see this as a war against Islam."[6]

Mohler additionally offered two important observations. First, he surmised:

> In this light, President Obama's statement that America is not a Christian country is also both accurate and helpful, though he is being criticized by many conservative Christians for making the claim. His clarification, offered in Muslim Turkey, establishes as a matter of public fact the reality that our American constitutional system is very different from what is found in the Muslim world—and even in Turkey itself.[7]

He then went on to offer this reminder:

> Beyond any historical doubt, the United States was established by founders whose worldview was shaped, in most cases quite self-consciously, by the Christian faith. The founding principles of this nation flow from a biblical logic and have been sustained by the fact that most Americans consider themselves to be Christians and have operated out of a basically Christian frame of moral reference. America is a nation whose citizens are overwhelmingly identified as Christians and the American experiment is inconceivable without the foundation established by Christian moral assumptions.[8]

The most interesting response to Obama's conclusions, perhaps, came from the congressman from Virginia's 4th District, Randy Forbes. On May 4, 2009, Congressman Forbes introduced House Resolution 397, titled "America's Spiritual Heritage Resolution," which "recognizes the rich spiritual and religious history of our nation's founding and subsequent history. The resolution would also designate the first week in May of every year as America's Spiritual Heritage Week."[9]

On May 6, 2009, Forbes addressed the United States House of Representatives. In his speech, the congressman posited these remarks:

Mr. Speaker, on April 6th of this year, the President of the United States traveled halfway around the globe, and in the nation of Turkey, essentially proclaimed that the United States was not a Judeo-Christian nation. I don't challenge his right to do that or dispute the fact that it is what he believes, but I wish he had asked and answered two questions when he did that. The first question was whether or not we ever considered ourselves a Judeo-Christian nation, and the second one was, if we did, what was the moment in time where we ceased to be so? If asked the first question, Mr. Speaker, you would find that the very first act of the first Congress in the United States was to bring in a minister and have Congress led in prayer, and afterwards read four chapters out of the Bible. A few years later, when we unanimously declared our independence, we made certain that the rights in there were given to us by our Creator. When the Treaty of Paris was signed in 1783, it ended the revolutionary war and birthed this nation. The signers of that document made clear that it began with this phrase, "in the name of the most holy and undivided Trinity."

When our constitution was signed, the signers made sure that they punctuated the end of it by saying, "in the year of our Lord, 1787," and 100 years later in the Supreme Court case of *Holy Trinity Church v. United States*, the Supreme Court indicated, after recounting the long history of faith in this country, that we were a Christian nation. President George Washington, John Adams, Thomas Jefferson,

Andrew Jackson, Abraham Lincoln, Teddy Roosevelt, Woodrow Wilson, Herbert Hoover, Franklin Roosevelt, Harry Truman, John Kennedy, and Ronald Reagan, all disagreed with the President's comments, and indicated how the Bible and Judeo-Christian principles were so important to this nation. Franklin Roosevelt even led this nation in a six-minute prayer before the invasion of perhaps the greatest battle in history, in the Invasion of Normandy, and asked for God's protection. After that war, Congress came together and said, "Where are we going to put our trust?" It wasn't in our weapons systems, or our economy, or our great decisions here. It was in God we trust, which is emboldened directly behind you. So, if in fact we were a nation that was birthed on those Judeo-Christian principles, what was that moment in time when we ceased to so be? It wasn't when a small group of people succeeded in taking prayer out of our schools, or when they tried to cover up the word referencing God on the Washington Monument. Or, when they tried to stop our veterans from having flag-folding ceremonies at their funerals on a voluntary basis because they mentioned God, or even when they tried in the new visitor's center to change the national motto, and to refuse to put "in God we trust" in there. No, Mr. Speaker, it wasn't any of those times because they can rip that word off of all of our buildings and still those Judeo-Christian principles are so interwoven in a tapestry of freedom and liberty, that to begin to unravel one is to unravel the other.

That's why we have filed the Spiritual Heritage Resolution, to help reaffirm that great history of faith that we have in this nation and to say to those individuals who have yielded to the temptation of concluding that we are no longer a Judeo-Christian nation, to come back. To come back and look at those great principles that birthed this nation, and sustain us today. We believe if they do, they will conclude as President Eisenhower did and later Gerald Ford repeated, that "without God, there could be no American form of government. Nor, an American way of life." Recognition of the Supreme Being is the first, the most basic expression of Americanism. Thus the Founding Fathers of

America sought and thus with God's help, it will continue to be.[10]

Forbes's conclusions, as compared with Obama's interpretation, beg for a solution. Where does Christianity fit into the founding of America? Are we an exclusively Christian nation, established for the propagation of the gospel and in opposition to all other religions? Or was America founded on principles grounded in secular governmental polity, with little or no regard to the Christian faith?

The need for this discussion looms as one that is, perhaps, more necessary now than it has ever been. Take into consideration two cases in point. First, the Nashville, Tennessee, area Wilson County school system issued a ruling that would ban any organization from distributing Bibles on school grounds. A fifth-grade student told her parents that she had accepted a Bible from a Gideons International missionary during a school assembly. The principal of Carroll-Oakland Elementary School in Lebanon told the students of the first time she had received a Bible from the Gideons, then instructed the children to come and receive a Bible of their own. According to reports, children were not forced to take a Bible but all of them did. The child reported to her parents that she took the Bible out of fear of being ostracized. In reaction, her parents contacted the ACLU, which promptly contacted the school system with a threatened lawsuit regarding the violation of the girl's rights. Historically, the Gideons International has been distributing Bibles in schools for more than sixty years, handing out more than eleven million in the United States in 2009. The Bibles are simple New Testaments and include the Psalms and Proverbs from the Old Testament.[11]

While the assertion can be offered that the principal may not have shown good judgment in assembling the children in the way that she did and in instructing them to line up to receive a Bible, the entire scenario illustrates the dilemma facing America regarding the issue of religious freedom and the founding of the nation. Groups such as the ACLU want to interpret history to say that America intentionally governs out of a purely secular mind-set that is devoid of any religious context.

Religion and faith seemingly have no place in corporate settings, at least where government and education are involved.

A second test case for religious freedom looms from the military. In 2009, it was discovered that Trijicon, Inc., which supplies high-powered rifle sights for the Marine Corps and the Army, had been inscribing Bible verses on the gun scopes. The first inscription reads 2COR4:6, which stands for 2 Corinthians 4:6 and states, "For God who said, 'Let light shine out of darkness,' has shone in our hearts to give the light of the knowledge of God's glory in the face of Jesus Christ."[12] The second inscription reads JN8:12, referencing John 8:12 which declares, "Then Jesus spoke to them again: 'I am the light of the world. Anyone who follows Me will never walk in the darkness but will have the light of life.'"

The firestorm of complaint originated from Mikey Weinstein, founder of the Military Religious Freedom Foundation, an organization committed to a "fierce separation of church and state."[13] Weinstein told ABC News that his opposition stems from the fact that this type of violation will allow insurrectionists to claim that they are being shot by Jesus rifles and that this type of activity "plays into the hands of those who are calling this [war with Iraq] a Crusade."[14]

Trijicon ceased the practice on January 21, 2010, and will provide the Pentagon with modifications kits for the removal of previous inscriptions. The company has maintained a working relationship with the military for more than two decades, an agreement that currently encompasses a $660 million multi-year contract. A spokesman for Trijicon said that the idea for the Bible verses originated with their company's founder, Glyn Bindon, a devout Christian who died in a 2003 plane crash. The corporation's website includes this statement, "We believe that America is great when its people are good. This goodness has been based on biblical standards throughout our history, and we strive to follow those morals."[15]

With this situation, one might question the wisdom of inscribing Scripture verses on gun sights, especially with the onslaught of the Islamic *jihad*. To some, even Christians, this practice might be considered offensive. The issue, however, does not originate in the hallways of offensive behavior. The real crux of the matter stems from the meaning of religious freedom and the role that Christianity played in the founding of America.

The argument I plan to present in this chapter grows out of the conviction and conclusion that, while America was not founded to be a Christian nation, in that other religions were not welcome, it certainly was not established as a secular society that only included some Christians as signers of its original documents. In order to defend this position, I wish to examine the origins of American democratic thought, trace those beginnings through the early stages of governmental development in the colonies, and finally demonstrate how theology played an important role in the framing of the United States Constitution and in the formation of the government at large. My conclusion is simple: since Christianity played such a vital role in the founding of the American system of government, the original intention of the signers of the Declaration of Independence and the authors of the Constitution was not to form a government that was free from religion but to protect religion from the tyranny and control of government.

John Calvin and the Separation of Church and State

In order to best understand where the eighteenth-century American constitutionalists developed their thought and process regarding the relationship of religion and society, one must travel back to sixteenth-century Geneva and John Calvin. While Calvin has been responsible for much of the refinement of theology in ecclesiastical circles, his theology also played an important role in the way that governments were developed, especially those in colonial America.

An Important Look at Calvin's Life and Work

John Calvin was born in Noyon, in the Picardie region, a small town about sixty miles northeast of Paris, France, on July 10, 1509. His father, Gérand Cauvin, worked as the cathedral notary and registrar, serving the bishop of Noyon. As a result, Calvin received a canonry that included a scholarship to pay for his education. His mother, Jeanne le Franc, was an innkeeper's daughter from Cambrai and died only a few years after Calvin's birth.

Calvin began training for the priesthood at the College de la Marche in Paris, then transferred to the College de Montaigu to study philosophy. His father, however, decided that Calvin should become a lawyer and had his son move his studies to the University of Orleans. Some disagreement exists as to the reason for the change in vocational direction. Some believe that Calvin's father moved him to law because he would make more money in that profession.[16] Others believe that Calvin's father made this decision in reaction to a dispute with the bishop and clergy of the Noyon cathedral. Regardless, Calvin made the move to Orleans, then eventually transferred to the University of Bourges in 1529 to study under humanist lawyer Andrea Alciati.

On May 26, 1531, Calvin's father died, an event that became a turning point in Calvin's life. Liberated from his father's oversight, Calvin moved to Paris to engage in humanistic studies. Debate surrounds the circumstances of Calvin's salvation experience, since Calvin wrote little about his own personal spiritual pilgrimage. His time in Paris, however, brought him in contact with ideas surrounding reformation. Shortly thereafter, Calvin's life turned to a new direction. Insight can be gained from a quote from his *Commentary on the Book of Psalms*, where he posited:

> God by a sudden conversion subdued and brought my mind to a teachable frame, which was more hardened in such matters than might have been expected from one at my early period of life. Having thus received some taste and knowledge of true godliness, I was immediately inflamed with so intense a desire to make progress therein, that although I did not altogether leave off other studies, yet I pursued them with less ardour.[17]

The date of Calvin's break with Rome also remains a mystery, but sometime in the fall of 1533, Calvin linked up with his friend Nicolas Cop, rector of the Collège Royal. On November 1, 1533, Cop delivered a strongly Protestant address, advocating the need for reform in the Catholic Church to the faculty and students. The faculty denounced the speech as heretical, forcing Cop to flee to Basel. Interestingly enough, Calvin was implicated in the transgression, many believing that he was the actual author of the discourse. Calvin fled to Noyon and Orleans, eventually joining Cop in Basel in 1535. In March 1536, Calvin published the first edition of his exposition of Protestant doctrine, titled *Institutes of the Christian Religion*. Calvin eventually fled France. After some months of travel, he was headed to Strasbourg, a city of refuge for Reformers, but was forced to detour to Geneva because of military maneuvers. The trip brought him to the home of William Farel, who enlisted Calvin to assist him in the task of reformation. The city councils offered him the position of Professor of Sacred Scripture, and Calvin began his work of preparing a confession of faith that would be required for those wishing citizenship and would establish the spiritual standards necessary for admission to the eucharist. Opposition arose regarding those who had the power to excommunicate, the church or the magistrates. Issues also surfaced with respect to certain requirements for the eucharist, such as the use of unleavened bread, standards that Calvin thought were too legalistic. Additionally, the councils became alarmed concerning the fact that few citizens were meeting the requirements set by Calvin. After a year of struggle, the councils finally voted to exile both Farel and Calvin.

Calvin fled to Strasbourg, where he was installed as pastor of a church of French refugees. The church had about five hundred members. During the years of his pastorate, the congregants worshipped in several locations, first in the Nicholas church, then in the Magdalene church, and finally in the chancel of the Dominican church. While in Strasbourg, Calvin revised his *Institutes* in 1539, enlarging the book from six chapters to seventeen. He also wrote his *Commentary on Romans*, published in March 1540.

Friends began to encourage Calvin to marry. At first he reluctantly agreed to wed a young woman from a nobleman's family but he later reneged on this arrangement. At his church in Strasbourg, he met and married the widow of Anabaptist Jean Stordeur, who died of the plague in 1540, with Calvin having provided pastoral care for him during his illness. Along with her two children, Idelette de Bure served as a woman of faithful companionship for Calvin until her death in March 1549. She and Calvin had several children together, all of whom died in infancy.

The situations in Geneva, however, were beginning to unsettle. Church attendance dwindled and the political scene changed with the installation of a new government. An emissary for the city council, Ami Perrin, was commissioned in September 1540 to recall Calvin to Geneva, a request to which Calvin responded in horror, saying, "Rather would I submit to death a hundred times than to that cross on which I had to perish daily a thousand times over."[18] Calvin reconsidered, and on September 13, 1541, he returned to Geneva, this time under official escort rather than as a refugee.

While in Geneva, Calvin began to flesh out his perspective on the relationship between the church and government. On November 20, 1541, the city council passed the *Ecclesiastical Ordinances*, a series of rules developed by Calvin that defined ministerial functions in four specific orders, namely: pastors were to preach and to administer the sacraments of baptism and the Lord's Supper; doctors were to instruct believers in the faith; elders, with the pastors, were to provide discipline; and deacons were to care for the poor and needy. The government of the church was placed under the supervision of a group of individuals known as the Consistory, which consisted of five pastors and twelve lay elders. Calvin's *Institutes* provided the historical and theological foundation for the *Ordinances*. Bruce Gordon notes:

> What was proposed was a decidedly mixed form of government in which ministers and laity were bound together under mutual responsibility for building the godly society. Church and government were linked but separate entities, with the laity responsible for the election and correction of ministers, who in turn were to teach the Word of God and oversee the Christian life of the community. . . . With the *Ordinances* he crafted a particular view of the Church, but one not entirely shared by the magistrates. He envisaged a clearer separation of the church from the authority of

the magistrates than the Genevan rulers were prepared to accept. . . . On the issue of disputes over doctrine, for example, Calvin's text had originally proposed that contested points should be resolved by ministers, who could then call in the elders. The council insisted that the amended version read that the elders were appointed by the magistrates. Calvin's visceral distaste for any involvement by theologically untrained politicians in matters of doctrine was not to prevail.[19]

This arrangement provides a critical look into Calvin's perspective on church/state issues. It appears that Calvin expected the church to influence the state, especially in partnering with the government in providing for the moral climate of the whole society. Calvin, however, bristled at the idea that the government would have any dealings with the theological or ecclesiastical issues facing the church. This perspective can be seen in his establishment of the Company of Pastors, a meeting of all of the urban and rural pastors who worked within the confines of the Genevan parishes that comprised the territory that fell under the city council's authority. Between 1541 and 1546, Calvin initiated the process of replacing those ministers who had earlier been ousted from the city. These new pastors were educated Frenchmen, close to Calvin and passionate in supporting his vision of reform. The Company met each Friday, existing to oversee the doctrine of fellowship of the Genevan church.

Closely connected to the Company was the aforementioned Consistory. While the Company governed the clergy of Geneva, the Consistory oversaw the laity. Assembling for the first time in December 1541, the twelve lay elders were particularly responsible for governing the residents of their neighborhoods and for settling disputes. The pastors additionally carried the responsibility of community oversight. William G. Naphy offers this observation:

> Calvin's ideas of a true church had nearly come to full flower in Geneva. The Company of Pastors (basically, the Genevan national synod) met weekly for discussion, improvement, admonition, and support. The Consistory was an ecclesiastical court that became the governing body of the national

congregation. The physical buildings of Geneva's churches were always branches of *one* Geneva church. Individuals were not assigned to parishes and could attend any service in any building they wished, though most went to the nearest. The local school system remained under state control, but the ministers were involved in the hiring of teachers (doctors). . . . Although always under secular control, the provision of poor relief through the Hôpital provided a model for other Calvinist communities and governments.[20]

Calvin's Formation of Church and State

From this arrangement, one can see how Calvin depicted the relationship between church and secular government. Calvin believed that both held particular duty and responsibility with regard to the oversight of religious and secular duties. The government, in particular, was responsible for the education, relief, and behavior oversight of the citizenry.[21] The church provided guidance in the religious and theological training of its members. It also possessed the right to engage in the supervision of such secular activities as formal education and pronouncing judgment on behavior or lawbreaking. As Naphy opines, "The ministers were on level footing with the magistrates and, in the religious realm, they claimed full competence and responsibility. Thus, the Consistory asserted its absolute right to excommunicate, a view resisted by the magistracy. In effect, Calvin had freed the ministers from magisterial control in most religious areas."[22] The church was more involved in influencing and directing the affairs of the state than the state was in engaging the issues facing the church. Calvin was attempting to build a one-sided wall, one in which the church could cross but not the secular government.

This arrangement did not develop without resistance. There were those within the magistrate who did not cater to this form of government. The Consistory and the city government clashed repeatedly over the next twelve years, specifically regarding Calvin's promptings for the ecclesiastical body to "regulate the customs of the citizens—who were also the members of the church—with a severity not always shared by the government."[23] Thus, the one-sided wall, though espoused by Calvin, was not built without opposition.

The Rise of Opposition

By 1547, opposition to Calvin and the other French pastors had spread to a majority of the magistrates in Geneva. On June 27, 1547, an unsigned letter written in Genevan dialect was discovered in the pulpit of St. Pierre Cathedral, where Calvin preached. Upon investigation by a special commission appointed by the city council, it was discovered that the letter had been written by Jacques Gruet. Gruet was associated with Francois Favre, a well-established Genevan merchant who led a group into open opposition of both Calvin and the Consistory. Ami Perrin, the man responsible for bringing Calvin back to Geneva, had joined this group, having married Favre's daughter, Francoise. Perrin, his wife, and Favre all had expressed disagreements with the Consistory. They were all a part of a group that Calvin called Libertines, because they believed that they had been liberated through grace and were exempt from both ecclesiastical and civil law. Perrin, along with several of Geneva's notable citizens, had been cited for breaching a law against dancing. Pierre Ameaux, a merchant who made playing cards, had run afoul of the Consistory because he called Calvin a "Picard," an unflattering calumny criticizing Calvin's French heritage. The civil court found Gruet guilty and condemned him to death. He was beheaded, with Calvin's approval, on July 26, 1547.

Opposition to Calvin also arose because of his preaching. Calvin's preaching was pointed, speaking to the masses in clear and forceful language. He even confronted the elected officials in his congregation with sermons that were "at times direct, confrontational, and politically informed."[24] David Hall remarks, "One 1552 sermon so irritated the Council that they inquired just why Calvin spoke of the Senators and other civil rulers as 'arguing against God,' 'mocking him,' 'rejecting all the Holy Scriptures [to] vomit forth their blasphemies as supreme decrees,' and as 'gargoyle monkeys [who] have become so proud.' Calvin's rhetoric was certainly not so academic or technical as to elude his audience."[25] His opposition continued, with the Libertines continuing in their insults of Calvin and the other pastors and in their defiance of the Consistory. On July 24, 1553, Calvin asked the council for permission to resign but the request was refused, his opposition recognizing that, while they could diminish his authority, they did not possess enough power to banish him for a second time.[26]

The Test Case of Michael Servetus

On August 13, 1553, Michael Servetus, a Spaniard fugitive from ecclesiastical authorities, arrived in Geneva. Suspicions of Servetus arose over his criticism of Christian dogma in general, and in his denial of the doctrine of the Trinity in particular. Calvin had encountered Servetus in 1546 through a series of letters in which they debated doctrine, and finally through the return by Servetus of a copy of Calvin's *Institutes* in which he heavily annotated it with arguments pointing out supposed errors in the book. Servetus had already been condemned by Catholic authorities *in absentia* for his heretical views, and Calvin assured him that he would not give him safe passage if he traveled to Geneva.

For some unknown reason, Servetus stopped in Geneva and attended one of Calvin's sermons in St. Pierre. He was immediately arrested, and a list of thirty-nine accusations drawn from his writings concerning the Trinity, pantheism, baptism, and the denial of immortality was submitted to the court. Claude Rigot, a member of the Libertines, served as city prosecutor, and Pierre Tissot, Ami Perrin's brother-in-law, led the court sessions. The Libertines desired to embarrass Calvin by extending the trial beyond reason, with the hopes of using Servetus as a weapon against Calvin since opposition quickly arose within the city against him with Servetus's arrest. Their dilemma, however, arose out of the interest others showed in this trial. Servetus's heretical views were well known among many of the cities of Europe, with keen interest and observation being drawn toward the outcome of these court proceedings.

Wishing to avoid embarrassment, the council decided to write other Swiss churches for their opinions. They also asked Servetus if he wished to remain on trial in Geneva or be moved to Vienne; Servetus chose to stay in Geneva. On October 20,

1553, the council received replies from Zürich, Schaffhausen, Bern, and Basel, all concurring with the court's findings. As a result, Servetus was found guilty of heresy and was condemned to death by being burned at the stake. Calvin requested that he be beheaded as a more humane means of death. The court refused, and on October 27, 1553, Servetus was burned to death at the Plateau of Champel at the edge of Geneva, atop a pyre of his own books.[27]

One discovers the importance of these proceedings through examining the connection between this condemnation and the act of excommunication in this cultural context. Bruce Gordon ascertains:

> By the early 1550's the Protestant Reformation was facing a resurgent Catholic church which at the Council of Trent was clearly defining its theology and discipline. The Protestant churches continue to be severely damaged by accusations that they were spawning heresy and heretics. The unwanted Servetus case came at a vital moment when Protestantism was forced to define itself against heresy. Failure to condemn Servetus and his evident denial of fundamental doctrines of the Christian Church would have been catastrophic. Having waged a long battle against what he regarded as idolatry, Calvin could not have turned a blind eye. To the Protestant churchmen of the sixteenth century, of all the plagues that struck their cities heresy was the most heinous.[28]

The real issue stemmed from the desire of the church for discipline and its autonomous ability to enact it upon its members. Obviously, Calvin wanted Servetus executed for his heresy. The trial only escalated the hostility between Calvin and the magistrates. The council alone had the authority to put Servetus to death, and it exercised its authority by executing him by burning rather than by the sword, as requested by Calvin. The Consistory had been kept totally out of the proceedings, enabling the magistrates to exert their control. The conviction of Servetus was an apparent victory for the council. Next, it tried to assert authority in matters of the church.

The Test Case of Philibert Berthelier's Excommunication

During Servetus's trial, Philibert Berthelier, a Libertine, had requested the council remove his excommunication, a decision rendered the previous year by the Consistory for insulting one of the pastors. Calvin believed that church discipline provided an effective means of combating sins and shortcomings, a point even agreed upon by the council itself. In 1549, the council issued a decree urging citizens to abide by the regulations of God's law.[29] Berthelier refused to acknowledge the authority of the Consistory, thus justifying his appeal to the council for reinstatement. The council first approved his ability to appeal, though it cautioned him not to attend the Lord's Supper. Calvin made it immediately known that he would oppose this decision if approved. In a sermon on September 2, 1553, Calvin preached that he would only administer the sacrament according to the prescription of Christ. He declared that he would defend the Lord's Table with his life. The following day, Calvin appeared before the council and debated with the magistrates the details of the *Ordinances*. Several days later, other pastors without Calvin being present argued for the protection of the Lord's Supper, insisting that they would choose death or banishment before they would allow this sacrament to be desecrated. In November, Berthelier petitioned the secular council for permission to receive the sacrament. Bruce Gordon posits, "Calvin and the other members of the Consistory were summoned before the syndics on 7 November to be told that denial of the Lord's Supper was a matter for the magistrates and that the Consistory had no choice but to acquiesce. Calvin protested and demanded to speak before the General Council. Once more the Swiss cities were to be consulted."

The connectionalism between church and state offers an interesting dilemma. In Calvin's day, both the secular government and the church government wanted authority in both realms of life. Neither saw an exact barrier between church and state. For the people of sixteenth-century Geneva, church and government were so intricately intertwined that sometimes one would be pressed to find the distinction. Calvin had attempted to define the roles of each, but he also saw that both stood before a delicate bridge that linked the two concepts together. The issue of excommunication demonstrated this fragile balance between church and state, one that would continue for centuries up to the founding of the United States. In Calvin's day, the church needed the ability to control its members, but the government also wanted to have its say in the matters of church discipline.

While individuals today may not understand this strong connection between church and state, one must realize that, prior to the Reformation, the church was essentially the state in most areas. Under Catholicism, those who ruled in the church were also those who ran what would be called the secular government. This fact was particularly true in Rome. Robert A. Baker and John M. Landers offer this intellection, "By the fifth century Roman popes were beginning to assert their right to rule not only the spiritual world but also the secular world. Such assertions, later supported by ecclesiastical weapons, kept the papacy in constant struggle with secular power."[30] Justo L. González adds, "When Luther nailed his theses on the Wittenberg door, the papacy was in the hands of Leo X, who was more interested in embellishing the city of Rome, and in furthering the interests of the house of Medici, than in religious matters."[31] Although the Holy Roman Empire during the Renaissance did not control all of Europe, even those cities that stood outside Rome established their own independent republics. In most of these independent cities, a strong connection existed between the work of the government and the religious training of the people.[32] Today, the Vatican stands as essentially its own country; literally, it is a country within a country.

As cities determined whether they would maintain ties to Rome or would embrace the theology of the Reformers, Calvin sought to bring balance to this most important decision regarding church and state. He obviously favored the influence of the church over the state, especially in ecclesiastical decisions. He also believed, however, that the church must direct and correct the daily affairs of people, especially as these decisions affected their behavior. The case of Michael Servetus demonstrates the extent of Calvin's belief with regard to rule, court, and theology. The secular court determined that Servetus was a theological heretic. Here one discovers from the position of the operation of the government the connection of church and state. Calvin agreed with the assessment and gave credence to the death penalty, a step that might seem unchristian today, but one that was not out of character for those in Calvin's time. It is this connectionalism that was passed on to the Puritans and became an essential element in the founding of the United States and the First Amendment. Calvin would not be the only source of thought for the Puritans, but he would hold a significant influence. Francis Bremer explains that "Calvin was the single most important theological influence on English Reformation thought (the *Short-Title Catalogue* of books printed in England reveals that between 1548 and 1660 more of Calvin's works were published than of any other author)" but "he was not the only one."[33]

Calvin's Death

After these long struggles, it became evident that the Libertines had lost favor and power. They had attempted to prevent "refugees" from holding any office and citizenship, but these asylum seekers eventually moved into a majority. Ami Perrin and his followers, the native-born citizens, lost their influence, and the city of Geneva finally began to move in the direction Calvin had originally envisioned, for "he now had the opportunity to focus completely on the rule of Christ and his Word."[34] Justo González adds that "after Servetus' execution, Calvin's authority in Geneva had no rival. This was especially true since the theologians of all the other Protestant Canons had supported him."[35]

In 1559, Calvin opened the Genevan Academy, under the direction of Theodore Beza. Students from all over Europe attended, learning Calvinist principles in equivalence with the royal lectureships in Paris.[36] On December 25, 1559, Calvin received an invitation to become a citizen of Geneva. Five years later, on April 27, 1564, he gave his farewell address to the Small Council, speaking to the Company the following day. In giving a concluding observation, Willem van't Spijker states, "Calvin knew all too well where his weaknesses and shortcomings lay. He sometimes had such a violent temper that he was completely powerless to control himself. He was impatient and occasionally very unreasonable. . . . It is possible that the frailty of his body played a role in all of this."[37] His friend Farel visited with him one final time, then at eight o'clock in the evening, May 27, 1564, at the age of 54, John Calvin died. He was buried the next day in an unmarked grave, per his request.

The Particulars of Calvin's Belief in Church and State

The issue of church and state relations was obviously not foreign to Calvin. Robert M. Kingdon elaborates:

> John Calvin often thought about the state and church and how they should be connected. The last of the four books that make up his masterwork, the *Institutes of the Christian Religion*, deals entirely with that subject. So do some of the laws he drafted for the city of Geneva, where he spent most of his working career, including the *Ecclesiastical Ordinances*, which Calvin alone wrote as a constitution for its Reformed Church, and the *Ordinances on Offices and Officers*, which a committee on which Calvin served wrote to codify the legislation governing the functioning of its state. He devoted far more time and thought to the church than to the state, of course, dedicating nineteen of the chapters in the crucial book in the *Institutes* to the church and only one, the last, to civil government.[38]

One can discover just how much Calvin believed in a negative impact made by the Roman Catholic Church on the religious world in that, in book four of the *Institutes*, he uses at least seven of the twenty chapters to address the fallacies he saw in the Catholic Church, specifically in the abuses of the papacy. Calvin does not particularly speak to the Catholic Church's role in secular matters as much as he shows the corruptions within the church. For example, Calvin lamented:

> Here is the noble calling, but reason of which bishops boast that they are the apostles' successors. But they say that the right to create presbyters belongs to them alone. In this they very wickedly corrupt the ancient institution, because they create by their ordination not presbyters to lead and feed the people, but priests to perform sacrifices. Similarly,

when they consecrate deacons, they do nothing about their true and proper office, but ordain them only for certain rites concerned with chalice and paten.[39]

Thus, Calvin recognizes that the church can misuse its authority; therefore, preventative measures must be in place to guard the church and the state from such abuses.

The topic of government and its role in thought and action were ideas that presented very favorable concepts to Calvin. His concern over politics obviously grew out of the fact that he had been persecuted by those representing the official government. Calvin also believed that the lordship of Christ must rule all forms of life, civil and religious. William Johnson explains, "Among other things, this meant that both rulers and their subjects were accountable to God. Religious beliefs have public consequences. Religious reform was meant to lead to social, political, and economic reform. And all of this was to be pursued for the glory of God."[40] Interestingly enough, Calvin included chapters concerning civil government in both his *Institutes*, to be used for educating adults, and in his first catechism, a learning tool for children. Calvin developed a sharpness in political thought and organization, always calling on political leaders to "consider their actions in the light of the Word of God."[41] In Calvin's thought, one can even find the concept of a decentralized government and the early makings of a republic. This rationale was evident in structures for both ecclesiastical and civil government. David Hall explains:

> One of the procedural safeguards of the 1543 civic reform—a hallmark of Calvinistic governing ethos—was that the various branches of local government (councils) could no longer act unilaterally; henceforth, at least two councils were required to approve measures before ratification. This early republican mechanism, which prevented consolidation of all government power into a single council, predated Montesquieu's separation of powers doctrine by two centuries. . . . This kind of thinking, already incorporated into Geneva's ecclesiastical sphere (imbedded in the 1541 *Ecclesiastical Ordinances*) and essentially derived from biblical

sources, anticipated many later instances of political federalism.[42]

The Belief in Two Kingdoms

An important doctrine in the mind of Calvin regarding the relationship between church and state originates out of his understanding of the two kingdoms. Calvin advocated the freedom of Christians, not that believers can use their freedom to sin, but that Christians have a privilege to live above law because "Christ's death is nullified if we put our souls under men's subjection."[43] Calvin addressed extensively how Christians should behave in the previous sections of chapter nineteen in Book 3 in his *Institutes*. He then expounded:

> Therefore, in order that none of us may stumble on that stone, let us first consider that there is a twofold government in man: one aspect is spiritual, whereby the conscience is instructed in piety and in reverencing God; the second is political, whereby man is educated for the duties of humanity and citizenship that must be maintained among men. These are usually called the "spiritual" and the "temporal" jurisdiction (not improper terms) by which is meant that the former sort of government pertains to the life of the soul, while the latter has to do with the concerns of the present life. . . . Now these two, as we have divided them, must always be examined separately. . . . There are in man, so to speak, two worlds, over which different kings and different laws have authority. . . . Let this be the conclusion of the present discussion. The question, as I have said, is not of itself very obscure or involved. However, it troubles many because they do not sharply enough distinguish the outer forum, as it is called, and the forum of conscience.[44]

Calvin argues that all humanity is a part of the first kingdom. Those who believe in Christ and have become followers of him become a part of the second kingdom. The primary distinction between the two kingdoms derives out of Christ's redemptive rule in the spiritual kingdom and his providential rule in the political kingdom. The political kingdom comprised the state and other areas of life outside the church and the spiritual kingdom.[45]

Calvin's doctrine provides an initial inference that a connection exists between the two kingdoms, both secular and spiritual, because God serves as the source for both. It is this relationship that gives ground to the belief that Christianity played an important role in the founding of America and in its impact in law and secular documents. If God functions as the impetus for all discipline, both ecclesiastical and secular, then one can discover the importance of both civil and church governments. Like Calvin, both forms of discipline provide a specific need and some separation must exist. The two governments or kingdoms, however, are not mutually exclusive and are part of a much bigger picture, that being Christ's rule and reign. Obviously, part of the problem with regard to the concept of church and state arises out of one's theological and even eschatological formations. Logically, if someone denies the existence of God or holds to a more deistic mind-set of God's intentional separation from the affairs of humanity, that person would probably be more inclined to deny a connection between the two worlds. Those who believe in God's role in creation would most probably deduce a more active alliance between the two kingdoms. The fact is, though, that one must be careful not to introduce personal theological convictions in reading history. Thus, if one believes that Calvin influenced greatly the Framers of the U.S. Constitution, then a connection can be made regarding Christianity's positive role in the founding of the nation.

The Role of Ecclesiastical and Civil Government

Calvin recognized that the need existed for two governments, one that ruled the church and one that handled issues relating to morality and civil justice. Ideally, if people came to Christ, a need would not exist for civil jurisdiction. Calvin wisely understood, however, that such a utopia did not exist. Therefore, two forms of government were necessary.[46] Additionally, he did not perceive either form of government to be in opposition to the other, or what he called antithetical. He reasoned the need for civil government out of the theological perspective of the depravity of humanity, explaining:

Our adversaries claim that there ought to be such great perfection of the church of God that its government should suffice for law. But they stupidly imagine such a perfection as can never be found in a community of men. For since the insolence of evil men is so great, their wickedness so stubborn, that it can scarcely be restrained by extremely severe laws, what do we expect them to do if they see that their depravity can go scot-free when no power can force them to cease from doing evil?[47]

The primary function of both church and state government was the discipline of people. Under Martin Luther's call for justification by faith alone, a fear arose among church leaders that Christians themselves would fall into an antinomianism. The solution came through the establishment of rules of discipline.[48]

Because he saw a biblical foundation for civil government, Calvin did not view these two forms as mutually exclusive. He divided law into three categories: "The moral law . . . which commands us to worship God with pure faith and piety. . . . The ceremonial law [which] was the tutelage of the Jews. . . . The judicial law, given to them for civil government, imparted certain formulas of equity and justice, by which they might live together blamelessly and peaceably."[49] When many people think of church and state, they determine church being purely religious and state being purely secular. In modern America, a constant battle wages between the church setting moral standards for all and the state getting involved in religious matters. Calvin did not see as much of a conflict in these two roles, for he believed that the civil government received its authority from God. He did believe that each form of government had its particular responsibilities, but those duties were not self-exclusive. Calvin explained, "The Lord has not only testified that the office of magistrate is approved by and acceptable to him, but he also sets out its dignity with the most honorable titles and marvelously commends it to us."[50]

To the disbelief of some, Calvin wrote:

Let no man be disturbed that I now commit to civil government the duty of rightly establishing religion, which I seem above to have put outside of human decision. For, when I approve of a civil administration that aims to prevent the true religion which is contained in God's law from being openly and with public sacrilege violated and defiled with impunity, I do not here, any more than before, allow men to make laws according to their own decision concerning religion and the worship of God.[51]

In this particular quote, one discovers that Calvin believed that civil government had a responsibility to promote religious activity, not to hinder it or be separate from it. He again established a wall of separation, but one that distinctively protected the church, or what he called "true religion," from the activity or decision of human beings. These statements are significant because they become the basis for the belief system of those who would later become some of the primary settlers and Founders of America, specifically the Puritans and the Separatists, and the Framers of the Constitution of the United States. William Johnson concurs, adding:

In the wake of the St. Bartholomew's Day Massacre, the survivors among the Huguenot leadership become more politically radical. Although Calvin was no longer alive to provide guidance, his brief comments about resistance against tyranny were pushed in a revolutionary direction by some of the Huguenot leaders.

Almost two hundred years later, in the years leading up to the events of 1776, similar arguments were made in the American colonies. This is not surprising, since some 70 percent of the population at the time of the revolution had been influenced by Calvinism. Revolutionary leaders such as the Calvinist minister John Witherspoon . . . looked to Calvin and the later Huguenot writers to buttress their belief in the power of the people and the right to oppose tyrannical government. They also drew to some extent upon Calvin's writings about the centrality of freedom.[52]

Additionally, the importance of Calvin's perspective comes in the fact that he saw the church and state as entities that worked together for the mutual good of the society. In his section on civil and ecclesiastical jurisdiction, he opined:

The church does not assume what is proper to the magistrate; nor can the magistrate execute what is carried out by the church. An example will make this clearer. Suppose a man is drunk. In a well-ordered city, imprisonment will be the penalty. Suppose he is a fornicator. His punishment will be similar or, rather, greater. So will the laws, the magistrate, and outward justice be satisfied. Yet he may happen to show no sign of repentance, but, rather, murmur or grumble. Shall the church stop there? Such men cannot be received to the Lord's Supper without doing injury to Christ and his sacred institution. And reason requires that he who offends the church by a bad example remove, by a solemn declaration of repentance, the offense he has caused.[53]

He then explicated:

First, this is the aim of ecclesiastical jurisdiction: that offenses be resisted, and any scandal that has arisen be wiped out. In its use two things ought to be taken into account: that this spiritual power be completely separated from the right of the sword; secondly, that it be administered not by the decision of one man but by a lawful assembly. Both of these were observed when the church was purer [1 Cor 5:4–5].

Now the holy bishops did not exercise their power through fines or prisons or other civil penalties but used the Lord's Word alone, as was fitting. For the severest punishment of the church, the final thunderbolt, so to speak, is excommunication, which is used only in necessity.[54]

Calvin offered a clear explanation for some of the responsibilities civil government held, specifically those of waging war and levying taxes or tributes. Speaking of the right of civil government to engage in war, he explained, "If they ought to be the guardians and defenders of the laws, they should also overthrow the efforts of all whose offenses corrupt the discipline of the laws."[55] In this statement, one discovers again the perspective that Calvin had regarding the responsibility of civil government to ensure discipline, not only in the citizenry, but also in those who would openly oppose that discipline.

In reading Calvin and his interpreters, the opinion can easily be reached that Calvin clearly defended the need for both
church and civil governments. Each had its own nuances and
responsibilities, but they did not stand in opposition to the
other. Calvin certainly would never have called for a separation
of church and state, whereby a wall existed that prohibited the
church from influencing the state or the state furthering the
work of the church. In Calvin's mind, the state, in many ways,
became the servant of the church, since the civil government
has the responsibility of upholding the moral code established
by the church leaders. Moral law originates through Scripture,
and the authority of the magistrate came directly from God.

It is this perspective that is passed on to the generations
to follow. Calvin's understanding of the connection between
church and state can be understood in this final quote:

> Let no man deceive himself here. For since the magistrate
> cannot be resisted without God being resisted at the same
> time, even though it seems that an unarmed magistrate
> can be despised with impunity, still God is armed to avenge
> mightily this contempt toward himself. . . . But in that
> obedience which we have shown to be due the authority
> of rulers, we are always to make this exception, indeed, to
> observe it as primary, that such obedience is never to lead
> us away from obedience to him, to whose will the desire of
> all kings ought to be subject, to whose decrees all their com-
> mands ought to yield, to whose majesty their scepters ought
> to be submitted.[56]

The Puritan Perspective and the Settlement of America

The influence of Calvin and the connectionalism of the role
of the church and the state can be seen in the theology of the
Puritans and the Separatists who ventured to the New World.
No greater evidence for the influence of Christianity in the
founding of America can be discovered, perhaps, than examining the history of the early settlement of the colonies. When
one understands Puritan theology, especially its eschatological
implications and Old Testament typology as they relate to this
nation's founding, greater discernment can be achieved in see-

ing how, for them, no conflict existed in balancing the Christian faith in both ecclesiastical and political circles.

John Winthrop and the Massachusetts Bay Colony

One of the clearest perspectives on the purpose of the founding of America and where religion connected to the political world can be found in the mind of John Winthrop. Winthrop was born in Edwardstone, Suffolk, in 1588. A lawyer by trade, early in his life he became a passionate adherent to Puritanism. This fire served as a primary factor in his decision to migrate to America. In a letter written to his wife on May 15, 1629, he espoused:

> My dear wife, I am verily persuaded God will bring some heavy affliction upon this land, and that speedily: but be of good comfort, the hardest that can come shall be a means to mortify this body of corruption, which is a thousand times more dangerous to us than any outward tribulation, and to bring us into nearer communion with our Lord Jesus Christ and more assurance of his kingdom.[57]

As he studied Puritan thought, he became increasingly discouraged about the future of the Christian faith in England. Politically, King Charles asserted his authority over Parliament, eliminating its political influence through dissolution and reducing any hope of Puritan grievances against the crown being heard. Religiously, Puritan beliefs were increasingly coming under attack. Joel Beeke and Randall Pederson note, "Laud, the bishop of London, was already showing the intolerance that he enforced a few years later as archbishop of Canterbury."[58]

The very issue of the political/religious ramifications gives impetus for comprehending the Puritan mind-set and the perspectives that led up to the founding of America. While one notes that another 150 years would pass before the signing of the Declaration of Independence, the recognition must be made as to the theological thoughts guiding those who served as the forefathers of the United States. Church and state were theologically and politically intertwined. No attempt was made to build a wall of separation. The Puritans traveled to America through what they considered to be a biblical mandate. Francis Bremer expostulates:

> Most Englishmen of the seventeenth century accepted without question that their country was an "elect nation," chosen by God to play a great role in human destiny. The Puritans, however, were firmer adherents of this notion than most; it colored their view of domestic events and foreign affairs and was influential in determining Puritan views of the possibilities offered by New World settlement.
>
> The Puritan view of England's mission rested heavily upon an interpretation found, among other places, in John Foxe's *Book of Martyrs*. In that catalogue of sufferings, Foxe had argued from reading the book of Revelation that there were five distinct periods of church history. The first four had passed: that in which the church in all its purity was persecuted by heathen emperors; that in which the church was supported by the post-Constantine Roman state; that reaching from A.D. 600 to the Norman Conquest, during which time the church was retarded by the influence of the Roman primates; and the reign of Antichrist, inaugurated by the accession of Hildebrand to the papacy. The fifth period, initiated by the Reformation, was that in which Puritan Englishmen lived. It was a time when the forces of Christ and the forces of Antichrist did battle; the ultimate outcome would be the final triumph of the true reformed church.[59]

Winthrop prepared a statement, speaking to his dissatisfaction with current conditions and justifying the need for a new start, in a pamphlet titled, "Reasons to be Considered for Justifying the Undertakers of the Intended Plantation in New England, and for Encouraging Such Whose Hearts God Shall Move to Join with Them in It."[60] He lost his attorneyship, leading him to an interest in the Massachusetts Bay Colony. The corporation received its charter under royal seal on March 4, 1629, with Matthew Craddock being chosen chairman of its board of directors under its new patent. Winthrop, along with eleven others, became the charter signatories to an agreement whereby they promised to migrate to America with the stipulations that the charter could be transferred and that the government could be established in New England. The accord was signed on August 16, 1629, at Cambridge. Bremer explains:

> When Craddock had suggested transferring the government to the colony his expectation was that the company's government—and control of the business aspects of the venture—would remain in London. The Cambridge Agreement signified the determination of men in the process of deciding to emigrate to safeguard themselves as much as possible. If Massachusetts was to become a Puritan state it was imperative that the colony's future and that of the individuals settling there be safeguarded against any later change in the faction controlling the company. The decision to move the charter was a pragmatic one taken after the signatories' decision to migrate.[61]

The group elected Winthrop governor on October 26, 1629, replacing Matthew Craddock, giving him authority to supervise their departure. Winthrop undertook the task of securing and supplying a sizable fleet to transport their families and hundreds of followers to the Bay Colony. John Cotton traveled to Southampton to preach the departure sermon, and on March 29, 1630, seven vessels left port, led by the flagship *Arbella*.

The Separatists of Plymouth Colony

While some might try to explain this event as either obscure or unique, to better understand how this process was more rule than exception, an evaluation must be made of a similar trek that took place almost a decade earlier. The journey of the Pilgrims, who landed on Cape Cod in 1620, began in the small Nottinghamshire village of Scrooby in 1606. These believers were not Puritans but joined a group of churches known as Separatists. They believed that their souls were at stake by remaining a part of the Church of England, which was beyond reform and was too impure to be the true church; therefore, they separated themselves. Originally an insignificant movement, they began to grow in numbers after the death of Queen Elizabeth I, and eventually provided the background for "the emergence of Congregationalists and Baptists."[62] Their dissent led them to the Netherlands, where they eventually settled in Leyden. Because they were Englishmen, they could not join the guilds. Exiles from England, they found it difficult to return to their homeland. Finally, the decision was reached to sail to the New World. Bremer notes:

> After two false starts from England in which the *Speedwell* and her companion ship *Mayflower* had to put back to England because of the former's lack of seaworthiness, on 6 September 1620 *Mayflower*, now overcrowded with 102 passengers, set sail alone for the New World. Only thirty-five of the passengers were actually members of the Leyden congregation, and although many of the others were London and Southampton relatives and friends of the Separatists, the body of "saints" was significantly augmented by a party of "strangers"—non-Separatists engaged by the London adventurers to provide the colony with needed skills. The most famous of these were militia captain Miles Standish and cooper John Alden.[63]

The importance of the settlement of the Pilgrims in Plymouth lies in the fact that they set up not only a political system, but a religious one as well. The Pilgrims had no legal right to settle in New England; therefore, they had no governing documents. In order to remedy this situation, the leaders drew up the Mayflower Compact, a political covenant signed by forty-one men, including all free adult male passengers. This charter, though intended for their settlement in Virginia, clearly elucidated a Christian intention of their priorities. In part, the covenant declared:

> We, whose names are underwritten, the loyal subject of our dread sovereign Lord King James . . . having undertaken, for the glory of God, and advancement of the Christian faith . . . a voyage to plant the first colony in the northern parts of Virginia do, by these presents, solemnly and mutually, in the presence of God and one of another, covenant and combine ourselves together into a civil body politic. . . .[64]

Like the Puritans of the Massachusetts Bay Colony, a strong connectionalism existed between the colony and its religious heritage. Though one might not be proud of these decisions, the Separatists actually demonstrated intolerance for others outside of their brand of religion. When Roger Williams moved to Plymouth after his banishment from Massachusetts, he was asked to move on by the leaders of the colony. William Bradford, who became governor in 1621, refused to take into consideration a petition for religious toleration in 1645. In 1649, the Plymouth authorities blocked the attempt by some Baptists to plant a church in Rehobeth and, in following the examples of Massachusetts and Connecticut, they passed legislation to restrict the work of the Quakers. In 1667, the Plymouth church issued a call to John Cotton the younger to be their pastor and ordained him the following year. For the first time, this church would have someone with religious distinction to lead them. The Bay Colony would eventually absorb the Plymouth Colony into its numbers in 1691, as the distinctions between the Massachusetts Puritans and the Plymouth Separatists lost their significance.

These events provide an understanding into the relationship between the secular government and the ecclesiastical particulars of early New England. Essentially, no real separation existed, even though many of the settlers themselves were Separatists. A church was immediately established, even though they did not have a pastor and did not offer the sacraments. In spite of these issues and the fact that it would be nearly a decade before they would have an ordained pastor, they still considered themselves as having established a true church. They even built a fort after their first year that also served as their meetinghouse. One immediately discovers that the faith of the Separatists and the governance of their colony were intertwined without any necessary conflict. The governance of the colony allowed for the settlers to carry on business and to survive, but the political leaders also assisted the church in protecting its territory, even to the point of intolerance of others. All of these things took place despite the fact that some within the group were non-Separatists. Standish and Alden must have acquiesced to these religious requirements, or at least ignored them. The fact remains that the Plymouth colony was both political and religious. In agreement with Calvin, the government of the colony held certain responsibilities, but it was not in competition with or in opposition to the religious activities of the people. In other words, a conspicuous connectionalism occurred. As one studies the progress of the settlement of the New World, one discovers that adjustments were made through the course of the establishment of new colonies. One can conclude, however, that the establishment of these church/states affected and influenced the founding of America. Rudolf Heinze elaborates:

> As Separatists, the Pilgrims were convinced that the Church of England could not be reformed, so they decided they must separate from the Church of England and establish a gathered church. In contrast, the settlers in the Massachusetts Bay Colony were committed to staying in the Churches of England and working for reform from within. Both groups believed in the ideal of a Christian commonwealth in which the society would be governed by Christian principles. In America they sought to achieve the earthly prototype of the heavenly city, and their model was in many respects Calvin's Geneva.[65]

John Winthrop's Sermon "A Model of Christian Charity"

A clear indication of the Puritan perspective on the establishment of a Christian commonwealth comes from John Winthrop's sermon, "A Model of Christian Charity," also referred to as "A City on a Hill," that he preached to the Puritan settlers aboard the *Arbella*. To better interpret the meaning of this sermon, one must understand two things: first, Puritan eschatology, and second, their hermeneutical use of typology.

From an eschatological perspective, many of the earliest theologians held to a form of premillennialism, including Irenaeus, Justin Martyr, Tertullian, and Hippolytus. This theology taught that "Jesus Christ would reign on earth either in person or through His saints for one thousand years at the end of the present age."[66] By the time of Augustine of Hippo, this belief system was considered to be superstition, as expressed at the Council of Ephesus in AD 431. Augustine, in book 20 of his *City of God*, explained that the thousand years represented a perfect number to be understood as expressing:

> the whole period of years from the time of Christ's first coming to the time of His second coming when the Last Judgment would occur. The binding of the devil in this period is the power of God restraining Satan from using his power to prevent the elect believing in Christ for salvation. . . . This Augustinian eschatology which taught that the present gospel age is the millennium and that it is to come to an end with a brief period of persecution, the Second Coming of Christ, the resurrection of the dead, and the Last Judgment, reigned supreme in the Church from 431 to the time of the Reformation."[67]

John Calvin also held to this idea of the present millennial reign of the true church, not a future millennial kingdom. Calvin wrote, "Those who assign the children of God a thousand years in which to enjoy the inheritance of the life to come do not realize how much reproach they are casting upon Christ and his kingdom."[68] The reason for his rejection of this belief stemmed from his understanding of the immortality of the soul. Calvin believed that teaching a future millennial reign denied the theology of the immortality of the soul, the glory received in being transformed by Christ, and the promised rest for the Christian.

This millennial thought carried to the seventeenth-century Puritans, as they saw themselves as living within the timeframe of these thousand years. Several views existed as to how the particulars of the millennium would play out, but the Puritans utilized this eschatological belief to further their connectionalism between church and state.[69] Bremer explains:

> It was England's task to redeem Christendom, to restore the medieval unity of Europe by bringing all men under the Reformed Protestant banner. The Puritans tended in this fashion to be what would now be called postmillennialism. . . . In that the Puritan view of history tended to define national interests in terms of international reform, it was increasingly incompatible with the developing nationalism

of the Anglican establishment, for it led to an indictment of the government for failure to advance reform at home and failure to champion Protestantism abroad.[70]

The Puritans believed that Scripture mandated the expansion of the true church, and they saw no conflict in believing that God held the secular government responsible for assisting in this evangelization process.

Coupled with the theological belief in the millennium, the Puritans also used typology in interpreting the Scripture. This method provides an understanding into the manner in which the Puritans unified and preached from the Old and New Testaments. Allen Carden illuminates:

> The use of "types" was in itself a biblical concept whereby OT characters, rituals, places, etc., were viewed as symbols or foreshadowings of NT realities. Thus most OT passages were interpreted with a dual meaning—a past reality or symbol which served as a type and pointed to the antitype, or a later or still future reality, which was always "something more glorious than the type."[71]

Carden goes on to explain that Christ served as the most frequent antitype in Puritan preaching. Puritans interpreted Scripture Christologically. Christ and his plan of salvation provided the primary subject matter of the Bible. Carden continues:

> Some of the OT types seen as prefiguring Christ included Samson, the Mosaic Tabernacle and the later temple, and the "tree of life" in the Garden of Eden, as well as Moses, Joseph, Adam, and Solomon. King David was viewed as typifying Christ as the head of the Church, the OT high priest was seen as a type of Christ's making intercession to God for the saints, and the penitential sacrifices of the Mosaic Law were considered as prefiguring Christ's sacrifice.[72]

Conrad Cherry surmises that the use of typology by the Puritans struck them "as a reasonable alternative to both an unimaginative literalism and a fanciful allegorizing, for the typological method aimed first of all to take a text for what it said and then, without abandoning its plain meaning, sought to discern its prefiguring of a later historical meaning."[73] Cherry offers an interesting proposal of how the Puritans' use of typology connected to their hermeneutics. He says, "New England Puritans were convinced that they were a new Israel commissioned to complete what the Israel of the Old Testament had prefigured: A Holy Commonwealth which would be—in its own religion, its governance, and its social order—a model to the nations. The Puritans thus extended their own typological method to their own history."[74]

Charles Cohen draws this conclusion, "Typological analysis deepened a verse's plain sense while linking the two canons into a unitary revelation. The ghost of the New Testament hovers over the Old, clothing its incidents with more specifically Christian meaning than the bare narrative alone could possibly show."[75]

With these concepts of postmillennialism and typology in mind, one can better interpret Winthrop's sermon. In 1630, he preached:

> for the worke wee haue in hand, it is by mutuall conset through a speciall overruleing providence, and a more then an ordinary approbation of the Churches of Christ to seeke out a place of Cohabitation and Consorteshipp vnder a due forme of Government both ciuill and ecclesiasticall. In such cases as this the care of the publique must oversway all private respects, by which not onely conscience, but meare Ciuill pollicy doth binde vs; for it is a true rule that perticuler estates cannot subsist in the ruine of the publique.
>
> The end is to improue our liues to doe more seruice to the Lord the comforte and encrease of the body of christe whereof wee are members that our selues and posterity may be the better preserued from the Common corrupcions of the euill world to serue the Lord and worke out our Salvation vnder the power and purity of his holy Ordinances.
>
> . . . for wee must Consider that wee shall be as a City vpon a Hill, the eies of all people are vppon vs; soe that if wee shall deale falsely with our god in this worke wee haue

vndertaken and soe cause him to withdrawe his present help from vs . . .[76]

Winthrop believed that society had been ordained by God, and this providential choosing demanded that everyone cooperate for the betterment of the society at large. This relationship manifested itself through a national covenant with God. As God had brought Israel to the Promised Land, so had he brought these Puritans to this new land of promise to become "a people of God with a political identity, and so they stood in precisely the same relationship to God as did Old Testament Israel."[77] The key factor to experiencing God's blessings was obedience to his law, specifically as it related to relationships among believers within the community and how those members worked for the success of the society at large. Winthrop promulgated:

> Now the onely way to avoyde this shipwracke and to provide for our posterity is to followe the Counsell of Micah, to doe Justly, to loue mercy, to walke humbly with our God, for this end, wee must be knitt together in this worke as one man, wee must entertaine each other in brotherly Affection, wee must be willing to abridge ourselves of our superfluities, for the supply of others necessities, wee must uphold a familiar Commerce together in all meekenes, gentleness, patience and liberlaity, wee must delight in eache other, make others Condicions our owne, rejoyce together, mourne together, allwayes haveing before our eyes our Commission and Community in the worke, our Community as members of the same body.[78]

For Winthrop, a common bond existed between the function of the state and the Church, a bond that was not mutually exploitive, but one that worked for the advance of the Kingdom of God. The church set the standards, and the government enforced these standards, even to the point that some were excluded from their society. Bremer explains:

> The American Puritans believed in a strong and active government. It was the responsibility of the state to oversee the conduct of the citizens, seeing to it that they adhered to

the path of righteousness or were punished for wandering from it. If the government failed to maintain proper standards, God would punish the whole people. The magistrates and legislatures established wage and price controls so that no individual could seek his own enrichment at the expense of the common good. They provided for school systems to provide future generations of leaders. Local government by town meetings and boards of selectmen prevented the admission to communities of undesirable newcomers. . . . Town meetings also regulated the personal conduct of community inhabitants with a sharp eye and a heavy hand.[79]

Winthrop, through his Puritan theological lenses, did believe in liberty, but it was not a liberty that espoused a freedom to step away from Christian principle or practice. The distinction came in what he termed as civil liberty and natural liberty. Civil liberty, which represents the only true form of liberty, is that which is good, just, and honest. Natural liberty represents the mind-set of doing what a person pleases to do, a perversion of liberty according to Winthrop.[80] This distinction represents an important understanding as one moves to interpret the intentions of the Founding Fathers. What has taken place is that some have sought to rewrite history in order to gain a greater audience for their position. George McKenna explains this phenomenon quite well, as he demonstrates how later generations have sought to change the meaning of Winthrop's words. He writes:

By the 1920's, major writers and opinion leaders were letting everyone know that they had wearied of Gilded Age preaching about liberty only for "good, just and honest" purposes. They celebrated "natural" liberty, the liberty to do what you please. They knew that this new attitude ran counter to America's Puritan heritage, and so they reexamined that inheritance in a harshly critical light. Quite consciously, they set out to debunk the Puritan legacy.[81]

In the end, however, the Massachusetts Bay Colony essentially failed. Some interpreters credit this blunder to the establishment of the church by the state, thus leading later settlers to establish a wall of separation—a conclusion this chapter seeks to dispute.[82] The Bay Colony did come under scrutiny by Archbishop of Canterbury William Laud of the Anglican Church and by King Charles II, who revoked its royal charter in 1684 but was unable to take over its government because of financial constraints in England. The Bay Colony's charter had lavishly left out the standard clause that required the documents to stay in London, allowing for the Puritans to set up an organization dedicated to the worship of God in the prescribed manner by their doctrine. The Bay Colony also remained as the only English-chartered colony whose Board of Governors did not reside in England.

Another interpretation of this lack of success stems not from the connectionalism between church and state, but in the fact these Puritans failed in their continued evangelization of the colony. The colony grew an adult population that was increasingly non-Christian in its commitments, at least to the point that men were not adhering to the principles necessary for them to become members of the church. Bremer indicates that as of

> May of 1631 there were 118 adult males, Puritans and non-Puritans, who presented themselves at the election meeting of the General Court to take the oath as freemen. At the same session the court placed a restriction on the franchise, requiring all freemen to be church members. This was a concession to the colony's mission, intended as a guarantee of godly government.[83]

The reasons for their lack of evangelism, whether theological or pragmatic, are beyond the scope of this essay. Their goals may have been set too high, assuming that the vast majority of colonists would adhere to Christianity. That reality never occurred. It may be that the colony was distracted by the problems they faced or that they lacked the skills or passion necessary in evangelism. Regardless of the reasons, the basic premise for the success of the colony stemmed from the propagation of the Christian faith. Mark Noll, Nathan Hatch, and George Marsden remark, "In Massachusetts Bay the voting franchise was limited to church members, with the corollary that only church members were eligible for public office."[84] It would be this same problem that would plague other communities as well, even a century later.[85] Yet the Bay Colony constructed a political image that would impact the establishment of later governments. Bremer explains:

> Through conflict with the English government and among themselves the colonists had come to define what they meant by a godly society in church and state and guarded their "city on a hill" against external and internal threats. The very survival of the colony as a Puritan state was frequently in jeopardy, but the settlers had succeeded not only in surviving but in erecting a civilization that could serve as a model for seventeenth-century England and for later generations of New Englanders.[86]

It must be noted that, while the Puritans did attempt to develop a political system distinctly different from their English forefathers, a very slight difference can be detected in the church/state connection of the Puritans and that of Geneva, demonstrating that the religious connection to Geneva was much closer in Puritanism than it was to the Church of England. One might theorize that a slow, progressive change was taking effect in the way in which people viewed church/state relations. Improvements or adjustments were being made as time passed, based mostly on abuses seen or experienced. These adjustments would culminate at the writing of the Declaration of Independence, the Constitution, and the Bill of Rights. These documents as written, however, did not call for a secular government devoid of religious implications. History shows that, just a century earlier, a definite connection occurred. This connectionalism had not dramatically changed between the sixteenth and seventeenth centuries. One can surmise that the degree of change between the seventeenth and eighteenth centuries, though more rapid than the previous century, was not so great as to alter completely the premise set by Calvin or the Puritans. Bremer offers an important interpretation at this point:

> The assumption by numerous historians that the Bible Commonwealths were theocracies still clouds our

understanding. The fact is, of course, that the men who founded Massachusetts Bay and her sister colonies (Rhode Island excepted) believed that there was one true faith, one true way to worship according to God's wishes, and that it was possible to determine what that path of truth was. As a result, they felt it to be the duty of the magistrates to punish open expressions of heresy. Paradoxically, the Puritans arrived at this view as a result of their belief in the separate spheres of church and state. Drawing heavily upon the Bible, the colonists contended that the visible church, representing Christ's kingdom on earth, was the spiritual organization dealing with matters of the spirit and limited in its authority to spiritual powers. Thus, in dealing with those who held erroneous views in matters of faith, the church was and should be limited to attempting to persuade the individual of his error, to warn him of the dangers he faced if he publicly persisted in it, and— as a last resort—to expel him from the spiritual society by excommunication. The state, however, was an institution of the world and thus empowered to use secular weapons: corporal punishment, banishment, execution. Like the church, the state had a responsibility to uphold the true religion lest the public heretic prove to be a threat to the stability and purity of the commonwealth.[87]

One sees in Bremer's assessment that the Puritans continued very closely to Calvin's perspective and process in government and society. Though the Massachusetts Bay experiment failed, it set the tone for the direction of the colonies to come.

Thomas Hooker and the Settlement of Connecticut

In 1633, Thomas Hooker arrived in Massachusetts. He had come under persecution by the Anglican Church in England and longed to be a part of a biblically modeled church. He was born in Marfield, Leicestershire, and received his education at Emmanuel College, receiving both his B.A. and M.A. Hooker, though a Puritan, had befriended many Separatists and, like several others, had accepted a modified form of Separatism called, according to Perry Miller, Nonseparating Congregationalism. These adherents advocated a Congregational form of church government, rather than a Presbyterian one.[88] Hooker had already established a reputation in England, one not ignored by the religious powers. Perry Miller explains:

> Hooker was a man of mark long before he left England. According to Samuel Collins, vicar of Braintree and agent of Laud, it was high time in 1629 that something be done about him:
> "I have lived in Essex to see many changes, and have seen the people idolizing many new ministers and lecturers; but this man surpasses them all for learning, and some other considerable parts, and . . . gains more and far greater followers than all before him."[89]

William Laud, who served at the time as a bishop in the Anglican Church, forced Hooker to retire as lecturer at St. Mary's, Chelmsford, in Essex, because "he had become one of the most conspicuous leaders of Puritan sentiments in the land."[90] The High Commission held him on charges, so he fled to Holland in 1630. He eventually pastored an English Puritan church in Rotterdam, where he became acquainted with William Ames, a strong leader and theologian of the Puritans.[91] Two years later, he boarded a New England-bound ship with Samuel Stone and John Cotton, upon the urging of friends from Chelmsford.

When Hooker reached Newtown, Massachusetts, in the fall of 1633, the townspeople chose and ordained him to be their pastor. Within six months, a restlessness arose among the people concerning the amount of land they owned, whereby they petitioned and were granted by the General Court permission to find a new place of settlement. By 1635, several other Massachusetts towns either requested permission or on their own authority relocated to the Connecticut Valley.

Connecticut faced similar polity problems as did the Bay Colony. As a tenet of Congregationalism, the colony held to the position that only the elect should obtain church membership. Early on, they recognized some of the problems this doctrine created, as they struggled in determining the most effective means of examining congregants. Hooker and others realized that "if there were those being admitted who turned out to be hypocrites, there were probably others who were actually elected but were unable to give satisfactory evidence."[92] This same problem plagued later congregations, even into the eighteenth century, and would become a foundational element for the spread of Arminianism and the beliefs in personal freedom and human ability.

Even Hooker's understanding of free consent and covenant relationship played an important role in the future of American religious thought, specifically in the concept of religious freedom. Miller and Johnson explain, "Though every resident was obliged to attend and to pay taxes for the support of the churches, no one became an actual member who did not signify his strong desire to be one. . . . No doubt the Puritans maintained that government originated in the consent of the people."[93] Hooker promoted the concept of voluntary submission and mutual respect among citizens, positing, ". . . there must of necessity be a mutuall ingagement, each of the other, by their free consent, before by any rule of God they have any right or power, or can exercise either, each towards the other."[94] This belief in free consent must be taken into account when evaluating the Founding Fathers' ideas on the separation of church and state and religious freedom. As this theology germinated and grew, one can imagine that it had some effect on the Framers of the Constitution, as they considered the extent of control that religion or government should maintain.

Hooker sought to resolve this problem by promoting the doctrine of preparationism, a method by which one takes steps to be prepared for salvation. This theology was also not without controversy. Perry Miller, in his book *Nature's Nation*, makes the claim that those Puritans who embraced preparationism quite possibly were guilty of Arminianism. He writes:

> We should not be surprised that Thomas Hooker, the virtual dictator of Connecticut and one of the most socially minded among the early ministers, should be also the greatest analyst of souls, the most exquisite diagnostician of phases of regeneration, and above all the most explicit exponent of the doctrine of preparation. Thomas Shepard and Peter Bulkeley followed his lead. All three agreed that

preparation was not a meritorious work; they took infinite precautions lest their doctrine be construed in any Catholic or Arminian sense. . . . However, his teachings were not universally accepted by all Puritans. They were opposed even by some federalists, who saw in them, despite Hooker's elaborate safeguards, a sophistical form of Arminianism.[95]

Hooker and the Connecticut Colony sought to resolve this problem as it related to government by allowing men to vote, regardless of their church membership status, but to require magistrates to be members of some local congregation. They accepted the concept of establishing a Bible commonwealth, as well as levying taxes for church membership on both members and nonmembers. With regard to the connection of church and state, Perry Miller quotes from the *Connecticut Records*, "It is ordered by this Courte and decreed, that the Ciuill Authority heere established hath power and liberty to see the peace, ordinances and rules of Christe bee obserued in euery Church according to his word."[96] While Connecticut differed from Massachusetts, in that it applied congregational rule in its electorate of civil authorities, the conservatism of the Connecticut Colony was greater than that of Massachusetts, as evidenced by the passing of the *Saybrook Platform* of 1708, an agreement that allowed for a more centralized control of and a restoration of discipline among the churches and their pastors.

William Penn, Roger Williams, and the Concept of the Separation of the State from the Church

Two individuals often cited in promoting the separation of church and state are William Penn and Roger Williams, the founders of Pennsylvania and Rhode Island respectively. William Penn adhered to a Quaker form of Christianity known for its adherence to pacifism and the "inner light," a belief that each individual Christian listens to God's voice for instruction. The Quakers tended to disregard biblical authority for the mystical relationship of having Christ within them.[97] They rejected "formal worship, singing, the ordinances of baptism and the Lord's Supper, ministers, and special theological training."[98] As a result of these beliefs, Quakers often found themselves as the recipients of persecution.

The firmness of Penn's convictions not only resulted in his father ousting him from their house, but also landed Penn in jail in the Tower of London for seven months. While there, he wrote his opus on suffering for Christ, *No Cross, No Crown*, a work in which he cited sixty-eight authors from memory. After his release, he continued preaching his views of religious toleration and freedom, landing in jail on occasion. Years later, he presented King Charles II with a plan for the mass emigration of Quakers to the New World and negotiated with him for a parcel of land in what is today Pennsylvania, as a means for settling a debt owed to Penn's now deceased father.[99] While other British colonies had been established, all were intolerant of other sects with the exception of Rhode Island. González notes that in "Massachusetts, the most intolerant of the colonies, Quakers were persecuted, condemned to exile, and even mutilated and executed. What Penn now proposed was a new colony in which all would be free to worship according to their own convictions."[100] Thus, in 1681, Penn launched his "holy experiment," appealing to any who suffered religious persecution to join him. Many from all over Europe, dissenters of every kind, not just Quakers, immigrated to "Penn's Woods."

The interesting issue regarding Penn's colony was the fact that religion and government still went hand in hand, as in other colonies. Penn did not establish a colony that separated church from government. The Pennsylvania charter from England stipulated that they must follow an episcopal form of worship, and that they must provide a representative agent to London. The government established that murder and high treason were the only reasons for capital punishment, and they debated issues concerning the defense of the colony and the need for a militia.

A cursory reading of some of Penn's writings and formulations clearly enunciates the Christian connection between church and government and the call for religious freedom. In Penn's *Fundamental Constitutions of Pennsylvania*, he writes:

Considering that it is impossible that any People or Government should ever prosper, where men render not unto God, that which is Gods, as well as to Caesar, that is Caesars; and also perceiveing that disorders and Mischiefs that attend those places where force in matters of faith and worship, and seriously reflecting upon the tenure of the new and Spirituall Government, and that both Christ did not use force and that he expressly forbid it in his holy Religion . . . therefore, in reverrence to God the Father of lights and Spirits the Author as well as object of all diving knowledge, faith and worship, I do hereby declear for me and myn and establish it for the first fundamental of the Government of my Country that every Person that does or shall reside therein shall have and enjoy the Free Possession of his or her faith and exercise of worship towards God, in such way and manner As every Person shall in Conscience believe is most acceptable to God and so long as every such Person useth not this Christian liberty to Licentiousness, that is to say to speak loosely and prophainly of God Christ or Religion, or to Committ any evil in their Conversation, he or she shall be protected in the enjoyment of the aforesaid Christian liberty by the civill Magistrate (very good).[101]

While Penn was establishing the need for religious freedom, he obviously did not recognize as problematic allowing the civil government to enforce religious standards. Even Penn's religious freedom has some limitations, especially for those who would make a mockery of the Christian faith. Additionally, while Penn believed in the protection of one's worship expression, he established the need for Christians to be directly involved in government, stating in his *Charter of Privileges* that "all persons who also profess to believe in Jesus Christ, the Savior of the World, shall be capable to serve this government in any capacity, both legislatively or executively."[102] Whatever wall of separation Penn conceived, it certainly did not involve keeping Christianity out of government. In his *Frame of Government*, Penn revealed how he even believed that the government, specifically the school system, had the responsibility of teaching children to read and write so that "they may be able to read the Scriptures and to write by the time they attain to 12 years of age."[103]

The failure of Penn's holy experiment came, not from the connectionalism of the two entities, but possibly from the consequences of religious toleration. Quakers eventually found themselves in a religious minority, an enigma that resulted in a spiritual climate less narrow than Penn had intended. Although the Quakers "dominated the political life of the colony for some time . . . much later [they] resigned their positions in government."[104] González concludes, however, that this religious tolerance "eventually was imbedded in the Constitution of the United States, as well as in those of many other countries."[105]

In similar fashion, Roger Williams suffered persecution at the hands of the Puritans. Born in London, England, in 1603, Williams was raised in the Church of England but experienced what he considered to be his conversion at age twelve. While a student at Cambridge University, Williams became acquainted with Puritan doctrine and renounced his Anglican beliefs, even though he had taken Holy Orders. Eventually he would move from a Puritan form of reform within the church to a Separatist view, believing that the Church of England was corrupt.

Williams's views were greatly influenced by Separatist English Baptist pastors John Murton and Thomas Helwys. Both had fled to Amsterdam but returned to England to form the first Baptist church on English soil around 1611–12. Their distinctiveness came in the fact that they held to a general view of the atonement, the idea that Christ died for all. They also became champions of religious liberty. Helwys wrote most probably the first book in England to call for freedom of worship, in 1612, titled *A Short Declaration of the Mistery of Iniquity*. In this treatise, Helwys declared, "Let the King judge, is it not most equal that men should choose their religion themselves, seeing they only must stand themselves before the judgment seat of God to answer for themselves."[106] In the same publication, he admonished the King, "The King is a mortall man and not God, therefore hath no power over y [sic] immortall soules of his subjects to make lawes and ordinances for them and to set spirituall Lords over them."[107] These words followed Williams as he left for New England, arriving in 1631, six months after Boston was settled. William Estep contends that Williams was also influenced by Anabaptist Balthasar Hübmaier, comparing excerpts from Williams's *The Bloudy Tenet of Persecution* with Hübmaier's *Concerning Heretics*, published in 1524. Estep's point is that Williams's concept of religious freedom was not new, nor was it a position at which he arrived without proper thought, study, and precedence.[108]

Some disagreement exists among historians with regard to Williams's activities upon arriving in Massachusetts.[109] It appears that Williams arrived in Massachusetts and was approached by a church in either Salem or Boston with the request that he become their teaching elder. He refused because the church had not sufficiently separated itself from the Church of England, a move that did not set well with the Massachusetts leadership. He relocated to Plymouth, where he ministered for over a year, and then moved to Salem, where he accepted the ministerial position of the church.

While in Salem, he continued his agitation of the political and religious leadership of the colony. Miller and Johnson explain:

> He continued to demand that the churches of New England, at a time when all the ingenuity of authorities could muster was being expended in proving that they never had seceded from the Church of England; he attacked the charter on the ground that the King of England had no title to the land and that the colonists needed only to purchase Massachusetts from the Indians; he denied that a magistrate could tender an oath to an unregenerate man, thus promising to upset the whole judicial system of the colony; finally, when he was being dealt with for these heresies, he broached the idea that the civil magistrates had no power to punish persons for their religious opinions. Sentence of banishment was pronounced upon him in October, 1635, but he was allowed to remain in Salem for the winter on condition that he keep quiet; in January the Court heard that people of Salem were resorting to his house and sent Captain Underhill to arrest him; probably John Winthrop

sent him a warning, and he fled to the Narragansett country in the dead of winter.[110]

Williams purchased land from Canonicus and Miantonomi,
chiefs of the Narragansett Indians, and founded the colony
of Providence in 1636, with a few families from Salem. As a
result of his growing dissatisfaction with the Puritan religion,
he became an adherent to Baptist doctrine, accepting believer's
baptism in 1639. His spiritual restlessness continued as he
later believed that his baptism originated out of a hasty decision. He finished his ministry as a Seeker.

In late 1637, Anne Hutchinson was banished from Massachusetts because of her claim to have received personal revelations. She and eighteen others founded the settlement of
Portsmouth on an island near Providence, with some settlers
moving later to the other end of the island to establish the
town of Newport. In 1643, she, her children, and her servants
would all be scalped by the Siwanoy Indians, "who were taking revenge on the whites for a massacre of eighty Siwanoy
men, women, and children by Dutch soldiers a few months earlier."[111] All of these townships experienced growth from Baptists, Quakers, and others because of the emphasis of each on
religious toleration.[112]

The relationship between Williams and the Massachusetts Puritans continued to deteriorate, as the new settlement
became a refuge for "religious radicals and dissenters from the
New England way. Providence quickly put into law Williams's
convictions concerning liberty of conscience."[113] Because they
had only bought their land from the Indians, charges were
made by other colonies that they had no legal claim to the area.
Therefore, Williams sailed for England and, in 1644, obtained a
charter for the Colony of Rhode Island and Providence Plantations from the Long Parliament, a ruling eventually to be confirmed by Charles II in 1663.

While in England, Williams penned *The Bloudy Tenet of
Persecution for Cause of Conscience* in 1644, a work that sheds
light on his views on religious liberty and the separation of
church and state. He had entered into a writing debate with
Massachusetts pastor John Cotton, who was known as the

"spokesman for the orthodox theory of persecution."[114] Miller and Johnson note:

> To allow no dissent from the truth was exactly the reason they had come to America. They maintained here precisely what they had maintained in England, and if they exiled, fined, jailed, whipped, or hanged those who disagreed with them in New England, they would have done the same thing in England could they have secured the power.[115]

Yet, Williams's influence can be seen in the fact that, forty years from this point, Puritan pastor Increase Mather and his son Cotton would participate in an ordination of a Baptist minister in Boston. Increase Mather would then preach a sermon calling for increased toleration toward Quakers, Anabaptists, and other nonconformists.

John Eidsmore argues that Williams's position stemmed from his belief that "of the 'two tables' on which the law of God had been given to man, only the second (Thou shalt not kill, steal, etc.) was within the jurisdiction of civil government, because those laws dealt with man's relationship with his fellow man."[116] The other table, which defines God's command to have no other gods before him, dealt specifically with humanity's relationship with God. Therefore, this table stood outside civil government's jurisdiction. One discovers this same argument from Noll, Hatch, and Marsden, who reason that, because of Williams's concern with preserving the purity of the church, "he came to the conclusion that this could be accomplished only by the clear separation of the church from the state and society."[117] In differing with his Puritan counterparts, Williams did not interpret the church as the fulfillment of Israel but as an antitype. The state, since it stood farther away from God than did the church, had no spiritual right to enforce principles of true religion. Williams wrote: "The *Antitype* to this state I have proved to be the *Christian Church* which consequently hath been and is afflicted with spirituall *plagues, desolations,* and *captivities,* for corrupting of the *Religion* which hath been revealed unto them."[118]

Williams's position stood essentially alone, specifically with regard to the theory of the two tables. Other Puritans interpreted that the government had the responsibility, under God's law, to punish transgressions and to actively promote the preaching of God's Word by compelling church attendance and by providing support for the church meetinghouse and its minister.[119] Religious freedom would be tolerated "no further than the boundaries of 'gospel order' determined by the Congregational churches. Those who were not prepared to accept those boundaries were free to live elsewhere."[120] Williams and many others did just exactly that.

Interpreting Williams presents an interesting challenge. While some hold that he held unwavering views regarding religious toleration, one discovers some variance in his opinions, especially as time passed and situations changed. In examining Williams's *Bloudy Tenet*, the treatise certainly provides his strongest apologetic for religious toleration. In it he stated:

> It is the will and command of God that, since the coming of his Son the Lord Jesus a permission of the most paganish, Jewish, Turkish, or Antichristian consciences and worships be granted to all men in all nations and countries. . . . God requireth not an uniformity of religion be enacted and enforced on any civil state; which enforced uniformity, sooner or later, is the greatest occasion of civil war, ravishing of conscience, persecution, of Christ Jesus in his servants, and of the hypocrisy and destruction of millions of souls.[121]

Yet during Williams's second trip to England in 1651 to defend the colony's charter, internal dissension arose within the ranks of the people regarding the fact that it was contrary to the gospel to execute judgment upon lawbreakers outside the public will. Williams returned to Rhode Island in 1654, and penned a letter to the town of Providence in order to define the limits of toleration. It is interesting to note that, while in theory the idea of complete separation seemed to work, in practice it did not. Williams wrote, using the analogy of a ship as a commonwealth:

> I affirm, that all the liberty of conscience, that ever I pleaded for, turns upon these two hinges—that none of the papists, protestants, Jews, or Turks, be forced to come to the ship's

prayers or worship, nor compelled from their own particular prayers or worship, if they have any. I further add, that I never denied, that notwithstanding this liberty, the commander of this ship ought to command the ship's course, yea, and also command that justice, peace, and sobriety, be kept and practiced, both among the seamen and all the passengers . . . if any should preach or write that there ought to be no commanders or officers, no laws nor orders, because all are equal in Christ . . . I say, I never denied, but in such cases, whatever is pretended, the commander or commanders may judge, resist, compel and punish such transgressors, according to their deserts and merits.[122]

Obviously, Williams did not want groups to be persecuted because of religious belief or unbelief. Nor did he desire a forced worship. He wished for a state separate from the church, but one that would maintain order. A separation of church and state did not mean that morality did not exist. One must ask, though, "Where did the standards of morality originate then?" The answer lies, perhaps, in Williams's arguments with Cotton, for he admonishes both the church and the state to act civilly and morally on biblical grounds. Though he interprets the Bible as calling for separation, he still uses the Bible as his source for both civil and religious direction.

Most vivid as to the connection between Christianity and Rhode Island originates in a reading of the charter for the colony. In 1663, King Charles II ratified the charter after several aforementioned attempts to discredit the patent. In the final rendering of the document, one finds this quote:

> . . . that they, pursueing, with peaceable and loyall mindes, their sober, serious and religious intentions, of godlie edifieing themselves, and one another, in the holie Christian ffaith and worshipp as they were perswaded; together with the gaineing over and conversione of the poore ignorant Indian natives, in those partes of America, to the sincere professione and obedienc of the same ffaith and worship . . . theire different apprehensions in religious concernements, and in pursueance of the afforesayd ends, did once againe leave theire desirable stationes and habitationes,

and with excessive labor and travell, hazard and charge, did transplant themselves into the middest of the Indian natives . . . there may, in due tyme, by the blessing of God upon theire endeavors, bee layd a sure ffoundation of happinesse to all America: And whereas, in theire humble addresse, they have ffreely declared, that it is much on their hearts (if they may be permitted), to hold forth a livelie experiment, that a most flourishing civill state may stand and best bee maintained, and that among our English subjects, with a full libertie in religious concernements; and that true pietye rightly grounded upon gospell principles, will give the best and greatest security to sovereignetye, and will lay in the hearts of men the strongest obligations to true loyaltye.[123]

One observes in the charter two things: first, King Charles took note of the desire for religious liberty of the inhabitants and granted such a request, and, second, the civil state would be best maintained under gospel principles. The colony was obviously established for the purpose of the propagation of Christian principles and conversion. William MacDonald adds that "this charter continued to be the fundamental law of Rhode Island until the adoption of a state constitution in 1842."[124]

Therefore, one discovers that Williams did not advocate, nor practice, an absolute separation. Although Williams would not call for a Christian nation, he did not seem to be in opposition to a direct influence of Christianity on the state. In a sermon he preached, Williams introduced the idea of separation as a wall. This designation would later be quoted by Thomas Jefferson in a letter to the Danbury Association of Baptists in Connecticut. Notice that Williams's intention was to protect the church from the state, not the state from the church. He opined:

when they have opened a gap in the hedge or wall of separation between the garden of the church and the wilderness of the world, God hath ever broke down the wall itself, removed the candlestick, and made His garden a wilderness, as at this day. And that therefore if He will err please to restore His garden and paradise again, it must of necessity be walled in peculiarly unto Himself from the world.[125]

While some champion Williams as a model for complete separation, Malcolm Yarnell presents a differing conclusion, explaining, "Williams's Rhode Island granted citizenship only to Christians, discriminated against both blacks and Roman Catholics, and used state funds to construct the First Baptist Church sanctuary. 'A degree of religious toleration existed from the beginning but there was no complete separation of church and state.'"[126]

While some differences might exist in the founding of various colonies, one overarching characteristic prevails. In New England, colonies were established with a primary objective to provide some kind of religious liberty and the avoidance of persecution by others. This fact must be taken into consideration when examining the motives of the Founding Fathers and the writing of the early documents of the United States. All of the colonies maintained some direct connection with Protestant, Evangelical, or Catholic Christianity. Williams acknowledged both the Jewish and Muslim (Turkish) faith, but neither of those religions was instrumental in the founding of any colony. In the seventeenth century, deism had not become prominent, although Arminianism was on the rise, especially among the Baptists.

Yet, by the end of this century, no conclusion can be reached that says that America was moving toward an absolute separation of church and state whereby Christianity had little or no influence on the founding of the nation. If any conclusion can be reached, it must be that, for all of the colonies, their desire was to protect themselves from the persecution of other denominations and to propagate their interpretation of the gospel. Ruling that a national day of prayer was unconstitutional would seem not only foreign to all colonial inhabitants but blasphemous to most.[127]

Paul Pressler offers an intriguing interpretation of the purposes of the original colonies. He writes:

The Puritans settled in New England to escape religious persecution in England by the Anglicans. . . . What did the Puritans do when they came to New England? They established regulations requiring membership in a

Congregationalist church in order to vote. They denied religious freedom to the people in their communities. That is why Roger Williams was a Baptist and had to leave Massachusetts because he did not have the freedom to worship there. The Quakers were also persecuted in England. Roman Catholics who did not have freedom to worship in England settled in Maryland where they found freedom. William Penn founded Pennsylvania. . . . Virginia became a haven for Episcopalians. . . . In order to preach in Virginia, one had to get a license from the state which was controlled by the Episcopalians. The local Baptist preacher could not get a license to preach, and when he kept on preaching, they put him in jail. The preacher was a friend of Daniel Boone, so the whole congregation migrated to the Kentucky territory under Boone to obtain religious freedom. They became known as the "Traveling Church." . . . South Carolina was a haven for Huguenots. . . . the Huguenots (French Protestants) had grown greatly, and many in the middle classes in France had become Huguenots, forsaking the Roman Catholic Church. The grandson of Henry IV, Louis XIV, would revoke the Edict of Nantes eighty-seven years after its establishment, making Protestantism illegal. The revocation did not start new wars, but it did result in a mass exodus of French Protestants.[128]

In evaluating the role of Christianity in the founding of America, one discovers how the Christian faith provided an instrumental, if not unequivocal, impact in all of the colonies. Their goal was not to build a secular state but to provide protection from persecution. Though the system employed to accomplish this task varied from colony to colony, they all held to some form of religious connectionalism.

The Eighteenth Century and the Acceleration Toward Personal Freedom

As the country moved into a new century and headed toward its founding, several factors must be examined. The nation was changing, moving toward the establishment of a centralized government and formulating ways to rid itself of the political and economic tyranny of England. The Christian faith, however, remained at the forefront of the movement.

Jonathan Edwards and the First Great Awakening

Jonathan Edwards was born in what could be described as precarious times.[129] New England had come under the consistent attack of the French army and Indian warriors. Shortly after his birth on October 5, 1703, in East Windsor, Connecticut, the French and Indians attacked neighboring Deerfield, Massachusetts, killing thirty-nine people. This number included Edwards's aunt and two of his cousins. The Indians captured his uncle John Williams and took him to Canada. A crucial perspective of this tragedy was offered by Edwards's grandfather, Solomon Stoddard. Stoddard, pastor of the Congregational church in Northampton, Massachusetts, related this attack and others as judgments from God. He believed that "God had brought this people to this promising land with an eternal purpose," preaching that God was judging the people because of sin. Biographer George Marsden writes, "The far deeper problem, Stoddard declared, was moral and spiritual. God was punishing New England because its people violated his commandments. The evidence was clear. 'God has had a great controversy with the country for many years,' Stoddard warned in familiar terms."[130] Considering the fact that Edwards would one day serve as an assistant to his grandfather, and later would become the pastor of the Northampton church, one might conclude that his penchant for prophetic preaching must have come naturally.

Edwards began his formal educational development as a thirteen-year-old student at the Collegiate School of Connecticut in Wethersfield, eventually moving to Yale College in New Haven. While the passion for reading evidently impacted his intellectual development, Edwards's conversion provided the greatest conduit for change and theological development.

While a seventeen-year-old college student, he came to realize that something was wrong in his state of being. A bout with pleurisy and the realization that he could die led him to ponder his eternity and the question of evil in this world. Henry Parkes writes, "The theology of his forefathers gave him an explanation: God had given man a law; man had disobeyed God and broken the law; God was therefore angry with man and with the world."[131]

Edwards called his conversion "a delightful conviction," his "sense of divine things," explaining:

> The first instance that I remember of that sort of inward, sweet delight in God and divine things that I have lived much in since, was on reading those words [1 Tim.1:17] "Now unto the King eternal, immortal, invisible, the only wise God, be honour and glory for ever and ever, Amen." As I read the words, there came into my soul, and as it were diffused through it, a sense of the glory of the Divine Being; a new sense, quite different from any thing I ever experienced before.[132]

In 1726, he was called to serve as his grandfather's assistant in Northampton.

Under the ministry of Solomon Stoddard, at least five periods of revival had taken place, all of which resulted in a number of conversions. Murray explains:

> In each of these times, writes Edwards, "I have heard my grandfather say, the greater part of the *young* people in the town seemed to be mainly concerned for their eternal salvation" (1,347). In part, as a consequence of these revivals, the percentage of communicant members in Northampton was very different in 1727 from what it had been in the town fifty years earlier.[133]

Edwards had little time under the tutelage of his grandfather, as Stoddard died on February 11, 1729. Stoddard had served sixty years in the same town and church. At the age of twenty-six, Jonathan Edwards accepted the call as the Northampton pastor and served there for twenty-three years.

During his time at Northampton, Edwards experienced the arrival of the First Great Awakening. The awakening began through the ministries of Dutch Reformed pastor Theodore J. Frelinghuysen and Presbyterian minister Gilbert Tennent. Tennent, son of William Tennent of the Log College, would also be instrumental in the reprisal of the awakening during the next decade. Edwards had become personally burdened about the lack of moral concern by the members of his church. Five years after assuming the pastorate in Northampton, Edwards preached four sermons that led to the first wave of the revival in his church. He published these sermons as *Five Discourses on Important Subjects, Nearly Concerning the Great Affair of the Soul's Eternal Salvation.*[134] Delivering these sermons during the years 1734 and 1735, they represent his philosophy about the importance of theology in bringing about the revival. According to Edwards, the revival began as he preached doctrinal answers for the rising problem of Arminianism.[135] Edwards explained:

> About this time began the great *noise*, in this part of the country, about Arminianism, which seemed to appear with a very threatening aspect upon the interest of religion here. The friends of vital piety trembled for fear of the issue; but it seemed, contrary to their fear, strongly to be overruled for the promoting of religion. Many who looked on themselves as in a Christless condition, seemed to be awakened by it, with fear that God was about to withdraw from the land, and that we should be given up to heterodoxy and corrupt principles; and that then their *opportunity* for obtaining salvation would be past.[136]

Thus, as Edwards proclaimed messages which explained God's sovereignty and the means by which a person sought salvation, the initial stirrings of the awakening began. While his intentions originated more out of correction and instruction than revival, the results of the sermons proved astounding. In evaluating this revival, Randall Balmer explains, "Three hundred people were added to the church. . . . Religion, according to Edwards, became the dominant topic of conversation among townspeople."[137]

The revival began to wane in the late 1730s but was reignited through the preaching of George Whitefield and the aforementioned Gilbert Tennent. Whitefield arrived in Northampton on October 17, 1740, and stayed at Edwards's home for three nights. He preached four times from the Northampton pulpit.

Because of this outbreak of revival at his church, Edwards became known as a leader of the awakening throughout New England. He was invited to preach in surrounding churches in order to promote the revival. It was during one of these preaching tours that he preached his sermon, "Sinners in the Hands of an Angry God."

As Edwards studied further his stance on revival and evangelism, he became increasingly convinced about the distinction between the saved and the unsaved. He concluded that the unregenerate must not partake in the Lord's Supper. In 1748 he resolved that he could "no longer support the church's traditional method of bringing applicants into full membership."[138] First and foremost stood the Half-Way Covenant, a policy promoted heavily by Solomon Stoddard. Stoddard followed an Old Testament model that emphasized a territorial church. Marsden posits:

> Anyone who was upright and would affirm Christian principles should be a full member of the church. Conversion could come later. That was what the church ordinances, the Lord's Supper as well as Gospel preaching, were designed to promote. . . . Most adults would become communicants, even if some stayed away because of moral failings, scruples, or mere indifference. Clergy would thus retain moral authority over almost the whole community. The nation would be, like Israel of old, standing before God as a people who observed his ordinances.[139]

Edwards, though influenced by his Puritan roots, believed that the true model for church polity must come from the New Testament. His resolve grew stronger as he studied more intently the Scriptures that addressed the church. He requested permission to address the issue through a series of sermons, but the request was denied. Edwards then labored for several months writing a treatise that would provide the scriptural basis for his position. He finished *An Humble Inquiry* in early 1749, but the work was not published until August of that same year. In the treatise, Edwards explained:

The name and visibility, that nominal or visible Christianity had in the days of the New Testament, was of saving Christianity, and not of moral sincerity; for they had a name to live, though many of them were dead (Rev. 3:1). Now it is very plain what that is in religion which is called by the name of life, all over the New Testament, viz. saving grace; and I don't know that anything else, of a religious nature, is ever so called. ... It is evident, that it is not only a visibility of moral sincerity in religion, which is the scripture qualification of admission into the Christian church, but a visibility of regeneration and renovation of heart, because it was foretold that God's people and the ministers of his house in the days of the Messiah, should not admit into the Christian church any that were not visibly circumcised in heart.[140]

Edwards built his entire appeal and response on the Scripture. He passionately held the desire to respond to his critics with more than just reason. As would be true in the development of his conversion theology, a high view of Scripture guided his thought process. Marsden opines, "Edwards' reverence for Scripture enhanced his sense of the authority of whatever beliefs he derived from it. His conviction that the life or death of eternal souls was at stake made him willing to risk his own welfare."[141]

One might find fault with Edwards for not expressing his convictions sooner than he did. He could be accused of cowardice for not taking an early stand against his grandfather's erroneous position, but for many years Edwards had warned parishioners about hypocrisy in taking the Lord's Supper.[142] Kimnach, Minkema, and Sweeney believe that Edwards came to his conclusions as a result of the awakening. They explain:

His decision was in theory the result of a long process of study and contemplation that took into account the lessons learned during the revivals. In practice, it was also fueled by a failed relationship. Shepherding hundreds of souls, and seeing many fall away after supposed conversions and admission to the church, led Edwards to the conclusion that the requirements for entering the church needed to be stricter. Rather than reciting a short formulaic statement that had been used since Stoddard's time, Edwards wished applicants to give a profession "of the things wherein godliness consists." The townspeople, as well as his opponents in surrounding towns, interpreted his change of position to mean that he required proof of conversion and that he, as minister, was the only person qualified to judge.[143]

Thus, Edwards's positions and conflicts led to his dismissal from the church on June 22, 1750. In his own account, he recorded:

> When the church was convened, in order to the council's knowing their minds with respect to my continuance, about twenty-three appeared for it, others staid away, choosing not to act either way; but the generality of the church, which consists of about 230 male members, voted for my dismission. My dismission was carried in the council by a majority of one voice. The ministers were equally divided, but of the delegates one more was for it than against it, and it so happened that all those of the council, who came from the churches of the people's choosing, voted for my dismission; but all those who came from the churches that I chose, were against it, and there happening to be one fewer of these than the other, by the church of Cold Spring not sending a delegate (which was through that people's prejudice against my opinion,) the vote was carried that way by the voice of one delegate.[144]

In 1751, shortly after his firing, Edwards moved to Stockbridge, Massachusetts, to take charge of a seventeen-year-old mission to the Mohawk and Housatunncock Indians and to pastor the church in Stockbridge. During these years of proverbial exile, Edwards wrote some of his most prolific works, including *Freedom of the Will*, *The End for Which God Created the World*, *The Nature of True Virtue*, and *Original Sin*.[145] On September 29, 1757, the College of New Jersey contacted Edwards about accepting the presidency. After much prayer and council, Edwards accepted their invitation and was inaugurated as president on February 16, 1758.[146] On February 13, on the advice of his physician, William Shippen, Edwards had taken a smallpox inoculation because of an outbreak of the pox in Princeton. Unfortunately, he contracted smallpox on the roof of his mouth and his throat, making it impossible for him to swallow. As he lay dying, his last words were, "Trust in God, and ye need not fear."[147] Jonathan Edwards died on March 22 of that same year, one month after assuming the presidency of the College of New Jersey, at the age of fifty-four.

Arminianism, Church Membership, and the Freedom of Conscience

One must notice that the issues of both Arminianism and the Half-Way Covenant escalated during the Edwards years. These issues plagued the colonies from early on. The Massachusetts Bay Colony failed partly because it could not reproduce itself and had to compromise in its convictions regarding membership. Other colonies followed suit. The increase in Arminian theology moved people to a greater understanding of personal will and choice. Many of the pulpits of America that would call for liberty and freedom had already embraced a theology that called for sensibility with principles of equity and justice. Jonathan Mayhew, pastor of the Old West Church in Boston, vehemently opposed the Stamp Act of 1765, and preached an inflammatory sermon from Gal 1:7–9 that led some parishioners to violence. Even noted Boston pastor Charles Chauncy, who openly opposed the revival and Jonathan Edwards, was known to have penned Libertarian letters to the *Boston Gazette*. Harry S. Stout notes:

> The radical voices did not go unheeded. In Boston, Samuel Adams was elected to replace the recently deceased Oxenbridge Thacher in the house where he took his seat alongside Thomas Cushing, James Otis, Jr., and John Hancock. Outside Boston the results were similar. In Windham, Connecticut, for example, the town inhabitants took the unusual step of electing one of their Whig pastors, Ebenezer Devotion, to a term as deputy to the Connecticut Assembly. . . . While few ministers followed Ebenezer Devotion's course of direct political participation in the assemblies,

most participated enthusiastically at the local level in town meetings and in the occasional pulpit.[148]

One additional reason for this rise in personal freedom can be attributed to Edwards himself and his belief in the spiritual sense of Scripture. In this one critical area, Edwards made a categorical break with his Puritan counterparts regarding his theology of the Holy Spirit and the Holy Spirit's role in interpretation. The Plain Style of hermeneutics and homiletics arose out of the "prevailing rationalistic, over-intellectualized faith which it tended to engender."[149] Edwards reacted to this stale form of interpretation as he further explored the role of the Holy Spirit in the life of the believer. Yet, it was this very concept of individual freedom that helped set the stage both for his own firing, as the congregation found liberty in making its own decisions rather than following the monarchial style of the Puritan pastor, and for the rise of rebellion against the monarchy of England.

Samuel Logan notes that "Edwards sought more than anything to make Christ a totally engaging Person for his people."[150] Because of this desire, Stein opines, "Edwards began to part company with the prevailing tradition of Protestant hermeneutics."[151] This fact became most evident in his work *Religious Affections*. Edwards explained:

> There is such a thing, if the Scriptures are of any use to teach us anything, as a spiritual, supernatural understanding of divine things, that is peculiar to the saints, and which those who are not saints have nothing of. . . . And that there is such a thing as an understanding of divine things, which in its nature and kind is wholly different from all knowledge that natural men have, is evident from this, that there is an understanding of divine things, which the Scripture calls spiritual understanding. . . . It has already been shown, that that which is spiritual, in the ordinary use of the word in the New Testament, is entirely different in nature and kind, from all which natural men are, or can be the subjects of.[152]

People in their natural state possess the ability to specu-
late about the Bible. The spiritual understanding, though,
comes only to those who have the Holy Spirit within, or as Stein
records, quoting Edwards, "'a new sense of the heart' produced
by the presence of the Holy Spirit and a 'spiritual supernatural
sense' implanted by God at the time of conversion."[153]

The importance of the spiritual sense, for Edwards, came in
the fact that it allowed him to discover the deeper insights of
the text. For Edwards, grammar, history, and prophesy were not
enough. Stein comments that "he seldom rested content with an
explanation of the literal meaning of a passage. . . . At best the
literal sense provided the materials for reflection and medita-
tion."[154] The spiritual sense, however, did not eliminate the need
for a literal interpretation of the Bible, because a "person cannot obtain a spiritual sense of the excellency of Christ without
such a notion being conveyed to the mind through speculative
knowledge."[155]

Once an individual obtains the spiritual sense as implanted
in the heart, it produces a spiritual understanding. Spiritual
sense and spiritual understanding occupy different perspectives, in that the first defines the process of God's grace, while
the latter provides the product of God's grace. For Edwards,
spiritual understanding became the goal of the hermeneutical
effort.

The overall purpose of the spiritual sense, and why God
would communicate such an understanding, relates directly
to the glory of God and specifically the Trinity. A key element
within the theology of Edwards was his belief in the Trinitarian
nature of God. For Edwards, the salvation of humanity involved
the entire Trinity. He preached:

> All the persons of the Trinity are now seeking your salva-
> tion. God the Father has sent the Son, who hath made way
> for your salvation, and removed all difficulties, except those
> which are with your own heart. And he is waiting to be gra-
> cious to you; the door of his mercy stands open to you; he
> hath set a fountain open for you to wash in from sin and
> uncleanness. Christ is calling, inviting, and wooing you; and

the Holy Ghost is striving with you by his internal motions and influences.[156]

God now glorifies Himself as He conveys truth through His Spirit. Stephen Holmes explains how the Father "glorifies Himself by communicating truth to His intelligent creatures through the gift of His Son and communicating delight or love to His intelligent creatures through the gift of His Spirit."[157] The ability to discover the spiritual sense originates out of the interaction of the Trinity, specifically in the connection of God's word with God's Spirit. Conrad Cherry references this Edwardsean doctrine as "the Spirited Word of God that produces faith."[158] Apart from the Spirit, one cannot understand the excellency of Christ or the infinite understandings of God. The Scripture serves as nothing more than a "dead letter" without the work of the Holy Spirit.[159] Samuel Logan explains, "The Holy Spirit is the necessary and sufficient hermeneutical principle for both the analytic and the existential elements of true Christian knowledge."[160]

Couple this ability to now personally encounter Christ and interpret Scripture with the belief in individual freedom and liberty, and one can understand the makings for the American Revolution. Many of those involved in the Revolution were directly connected to Edwards, including Joseph Bellamy, who helped, though somewhat reluctantly, his parishioners fight the British in Connecticut; Samuel Hopkins, who called for independence from his Congregational pulpit in Newport, Rhode Island; and Isaac Backus, who fought for freedom for Baptists against religious establishments and used that analogy in his challenges to those who fought the Revolution.[161] The Great Awakening brought about an understanding of and acceptance of some sense of religious pluralism and especially personal autonomy. Notice, however, that the emphasis at this time rested in religious matters. The Revolution did not grow out of a secular call for freedom but from a religious one. Meic Pearse explains, "By this circuitous means it may be argued that the rise of evangelicalism helped prepare minds for republican and democratic ideals."[162]

The increased interest in and adherence to Arminianism, along with the acceptance of the Half-Way Covenant, certainly moved some of the colonists away from the Winthropian belief in "a city on a hill," but the emphasis remained in a spiritual realm. Their desire became not so much to establish a church-run state but to have churches that directly impacted the state. They offered little fear in proclaiming the call for political freedom, a conviction that would not have resonated had they only watched the Revolution and the founding of America from a distance. Even the Arminian churches participated directly in the call for Revolution and the establishment of a new nation.

The death of Edwards, who quite possibly could have helped the remaining colonists to maintain some balance in the midst of the Revolution fervor, left a theological void in Puritan Christian circles. As a result, those with Calvinist leanings saw the coming Revolution as another millennial fulfillment of Scripture. They believed that their evangelistic passion, as developed through the awakening, would eradicate the problems of politics. Noll, Hatch, and Marsden explain, "Christian patriots, with no self-consciously Christian moorings to anchor their approach to politics, were swept along with the nationalistic tide."[163]

CONCLUSION

Some historians have attempted to deny the role of Christianity in the founding of America and to point to a two-sided wall of separation between the federal government and the church by appealing to the faith, or the lack thereof, of the Founding Fathers. They point to the fact that some, like Thomas Jefferson and Benjamin Franklin, were deists and were greatly influenced by the Enlightenment.[164] They argue that these men, as well as others, had little or no interest in religious matters, and, therefore, the tenets of the Constitution came more from the secular mind with little regard for religion. Religious references were generally made, not specifically intended toward Christianity. They point out that few of the Founding Fathers actually adhered to orthodox teachings of the traditional Christian faith.[165] Yet other historians disagree and provide a different interpretation. George McKenna writes:

> Even Jefferson wasn't much of a Deist, if by Deism we mean the notion that God is a celestial watchmaker who wound up the universe one day and then let it run by its own laws. In his Second Inaugural address Jefferson professed the need for "the favor of that Being in whose hands we are, who led our fathers, as Israel of old, from their native land and planted them in a country flowing with all the necessities and comforts of life, who has covered our infancy with his providence and our riper years with his wisdom and power." Jefferson's God, at least the one he publicly professed, was not a detached watchmaker but a God who actively intervenes in history. Franklin, another supposed Deist, recalled that he had toyed with it in his youth but ultimately rejected it because it was not "useful"—it seemed to lack any moral compass. In his later years he expressed very emphatically his belief in an interventionist God. "The longer I live," he said at the Constitutional Convention of 1787, "the more convincing proofs I see of this truth—that God governs the affairs of men. And if a sparrow cannot fall to the ground without his notice, is it probable that an empire cannot rise without his aid?" . . . The men who led the American Revolution and drafted the Constitution may not have been punctilious about specific tenets of Christian orthodoxy, but virtually to a man they were convinced that God had a hand in the "new order of the ages" called America and hoped that they were doing it according to his will.[166]

One must admit that all interpreters may falter in defining what others believe based on personal bias and desired outcome. This conundrum holds very true with regard to American history and the issue of the separation of church and state. It becomes a simple task to quote individuals fully or partially, depending on how those quotes play into the interpreter's hands.

For that reason, this essay has intentionally dwelt upon historical data. While not exhaustive, the issue presented has been that one can find the roots of the connection of church and state in a study of John Calvin. Calvin left an indelible impression on those who came and settled America. Through the call for religious freedom and the desire to stem the tide of persecution, coupled with the coming of the First Great Awakening, one discovers that theological adjustments occurred in the Puritan ideal. Thus, while America's founding was not purely Christian, it was distinctively influenced by the Christian paradigm and theology.

Furthermore, American politics did not become purely secular. The call for freedom rang from the pulpits of America. The Midway Church became known as "Georgia's Cradle of Liberty," as two signers of the Declaration of Independence were members. Up and down the rural back roads of Connecticut, one finds the Black Regiment, the dissenting clergy who were responsible for making their people "all politicians and Scripture learnt."[167] If one follows the progression of religious liberty, it becomes easy to understand why the Founders did not specifically refer to certain tenets of the Christian faith. America was not being founded as a purely Christian nation; in that, it would persecute or condemn those who adhered either to another religion or to no religion at all. The issue also did not surround the concept of a fully secular society, as some try to interpret the Constitution. Even Noll, Hatch, and Marsden have to admit that the Judeo-Christian ethic provided a strong foundation for American government. In *The Search for Christian America*, these three authors attempt to downplay the role of Christianity in the founding of America, opting for a more moralistic perspective. While trying to relegate the impact of even Puritanism as compared with the Enlightenment, they admit that the "Judeo-Christian tradition made an important and probably quite laudable contribution."[168]

Understanding the historical progression thus leads to a better reasoning with the establishment clause. Congress, in making no law regarding an establishment of religion, is the prohibition. That wall, however, is one-sided. It does not mean that Christianity is thrown out of Congress, the school system, or the National Day of Prayer. The First Amendment was intended to protect the church from the federal government, not the federal government or the state government or the local government from the church. To come to the conclusion otherwise would mean that one would have to make a light-year jump in history. Consider where the American pulpit was in 1776 and compare that time with 1787. Stout notes, "However much themes of civil liberty and resistance to tyranny dominated the occasional pulpit, they did not come at the expense of personal salvation, nor did they signal a new 'civil religion' replacing the old otherworldly religion."[169] In fact, the First Amendment was not originally drafted until the states wanted affirmation that the federal government would not interfere with their religious affairs or the affairs of the churches.

To better understand this perspective and even the position of Thomas Jefferson, one must recall Jefferson's letter to the Danbury Connecticut Association of Baptists and specifically his encounter with Pastor John Leland. Baptists stood at the forefront because they were under heavy persecution by state established churches. Nine of the original thirteen states had tax-supported, state-established churches. Oftentimes, these state churches persecuted those of dissenting religious opinions. In Connecticut and Massachusetts, the established churches were Congregational. Farther south, Episcopalians, who were more directly connected with the Anglican church of England, were state funded.[170]

John Leland became a leading opponent to ratification of the Constitution. Baptists living in Virginia, North Carolina, Massachusetts, and Connecticut expressed resistance, fearing that the establishment of a federal government would add to their difficulties in religious freedom. The primary state in question was Virginia, being the home of Thomas Jefferson, George Washington, James Madison, and James Monroe. Four of the first five presidents of the United States hailed from Virginia. If the Constitution was going to come into existence, it would demand the support of Virginia.

The first test case occurred in Virginia itself. Jefferson introduced to the Virginia legislature his "Bill for Establishing Religious Freedom," which would be debated between 1779 and 1785. Baptists took the lead in wanting their religious rights protected. Finally, on December 17, 1785, the bill passed, stating in part:

> We the General Assembly of Virginia, do enact that no man shall be compelled to frequent or support any religious worship, place or ministry whatsoever, nor shall be enforced, restrained, molested or burdened in his body or goods, nor shall otherwise suffer on account of his religious opinions or belief; but that all men shall be free to profess, and by argument to maintain, their opinions in matters of religion, and that the same shall in no wish diminish, enlarge or affect their civil capacities.[171]

With this test case in place, Leland met with James Madison in Orange County, Virginia, and struck a deal whereby Leland would withdraw as an antiratification candidate for the Constitutional Convention and Madison would introduce an amendment reading, "Congress shall make no law affecting an establishment of religion, nor interfering with the free exercise thereof."[172] More than a decade after the ratification of the Bill of Rights and following Jefferson's reelection as president of the United States, Leland would travel to the White House to bring congratulations from the Democrats of western Massachusetts, having relocated there in 1791 from Virginia. Note that the political party chose a pastor as its representative. Leland brought Jefferson a gift of cheese and prayed for the president. Jefferson had lunch, then penned his letter to Nehemiah Dodge, Ephraim Robbins, and Stephen S. Nelson of the Baptist churches of Danbury, Connecticut, on January 1, 1802. Two days later, on Sunday morning, Jefferson attended a Christian worship service in the House of Representatives. Richard Land explicates:

> With about half the members of Congress in attendance, as well as the president of the United States, John Leland, a Baptist evangelist, preached a revival sermon from the speaker's rostrum of the House of Representatives.
>
> One account from an Episcopal congressman said Leland preached like an untutored frontier preacher. Yet, no matter his style of delivery, he was afforded the opportunity

to preach in what was apparently a regularly scheduled worship service, with Jefferson (who was evidently not a regular attendee) sitting on the front row. Clearly Thomas Jefferson did not intend for a wall of separation between the church and state to mean the segregation of religious expression from public life in public places, including the House of Representatives.[173]

One might add that the fact this event took place demonstrates further the intricate influence that Christianity, and not just religion, had on the founding of America. Additionally, this impingement was much more than just moral. It involved a deep, spiritual value. For example, the very idea that the First Amendment addresses the issue of church and state demonstrates the impact that the church had on the founding of America. If Christianity was merely a side thought, why would the Framers of the Constitution even include this clause? The fact that church and state issues, even to this day, are debated shows the effect of Christianity on American government.

One must also remember that while Jefferson certainly played an important role in both the Constitution and the Bill of Rights, he did not sign the Constitution, nor was he present when the First Amendment was debated in the first session of Congress in 1789. Jefferson was out of the country, representing the United States in France.

Finally, the whole pretext of the church-state argument really surrounds the issue of denominationalism, not the plurality of religion. As already noted, Roger Williams recognized the presence of the Jews and the Turks (Muslims). The earliest settlement of Jews can quite possibly be traced back to New England in 1649, with another congregation meeting in Newport, Rhode Island, around 1658. Other congregations arose in Savannah in 1733, Philadelphia in 1747, and Charleston in 1749, but none of these gatherings had a rabbi until the nineteenth century. Islam was essentially nonexistent in the colonies through the eighteenth century. The one compelling argument for how the First Amendment connects with other religions comes from James Madison's *Memorial and Remonstrance* of 1784, whereby he said, "The same authority which can establish Christianity in exclusion of all other religions may establish with the same ease any particular sect of Christians in exclusion of all other sects."[174] This statement helps interpreters to note that America was not established as a purely Christian nation. Yet the fact remains, as modern church/state advocates try to discern Christianity's role, they must take into account what issues were at hand. To deny Christianity's part in the founding of this nation is to deny America's very existence.

As further proof, it is interesting to note that many of the states had specific Christian jargon included in their documents and constitutions. Massachusetts included a clause in its Declaration of Rights of 1780 that upheld the right of its citizens for the public worship of God and for public instructions in piety, religion, and morality. Both Delaware and North Carolina determined in 1776 that the conditions of an acknowledgment of the divine inspiration of the Scriptures and a Trinitarian declaration of faith be given for public appointments. Delaware annulled this stipulation in 1790. Pennsylvania imposed a somewhat broader test for members of its legislature, while Tennessee excluded only atheists and those who denied the future spiritual state of humanity. Georgia ruled that members of its legislature had to be Protestants, while New Jersey, in 1776, extended religious toleration only to Protestants. In 1784, New Hampshire allowed local authorities to make provision for the maintenance of Protestant public teachers, who would teach piety, religion, and morality. It added a concession that adherents to one denomination did not have to pay for the teachers of another denomination. Massachusetts succeeded in maintaining a state-established church until 1833. On December 21, 1780, a group of Baptists on Martha's Vineyard petitioned their town council, wishing to stop paying taxes to the established Congregational clergy so that they might employ a Baptist preacher. Their petition was denied, and these taxes were required until 1804. Paul Pressler notes, "This occurred after the Bill of Rights was approved. Obviously, if this could be done after the Bill of Rights was approved, it was not considered in violation of the Bill of Rights."[175]

Thus, Christianity provided an indelible impression on the founding of America and its establishing documents. Because of persecution, both previously experienced and presently enacted, little desire existed to create a Christian federal government that would demand that all adhere to the Christian faith in order to maintain citizenship or voting rights. Outside of the Anglicans of the South and the Congregationalists of Massachusetts and Connecticut, Christian groups did not want a denominationally led federal government. The nation, however, and its documents were profoundly influenced by Christianity. The nation was not just religious; it was Christian.

Endnotes

[1] K. Gilbert and J. Westen, "Obama: 'We Do Not Consider Ourselves a Christian Nation,'" Life Site News, available online at http://www.lifesitenews.com/1dn/printerfriendly.htlm?articleid=09040809 (accessed August 7, 2009).

[2] D. Brody, "Obama to CBN News: We're no Longer Just a Christian Nation," CBN News, available online at http://www.cbn.com/CBNnews/204016.aspx (accessed August 7, 2009), emphasis mine.

[3] Ibid.

[4] Gilbert and Westen, "Obama: 'We Do Not Consider Ourselves a Christian Nation.'"

[5] Ibid.

[6] R. A. Mohler, "The Challenge of Islam—A Christian Perspective," available online at http://www.Albertmohler.com/blog_print.php?id=3579 (accessed April 4, 2009), emphasis original.

[7] Ibid.

[8] Ibid.

[9] J. R. Forbes, "Judeo Christian Nation," available online at http://forbes.house.gov/judeochristiannation (accessed November 8, 2009).

[10] Ibid.

[11] "School system agrees to curb Gideons," Baptist Press (January 29, 2010), available online at http://www.baptistpress.org/BPnews.asp?ID=32173 (accessed January 30, 2010).

[12] Unless otherwise noted, all Scripture quotations are from the Holman Christian Standard Bible.

[13] "Weapons Inscribed with Scripture Halted," Baptist Press (January 29, 2010), available online at http://www.baptistpress.org/BPnews.asp?ID=32172 (accessed January 30, 2010).

[14] Ibid.

[15] Ibid.

[16] For biographical information on John Calvin see T. H. L. Parker, *John Calvin* (Hertfordshire, England: Lion Publishing, 1995); W. S. Reid, "Calvin, John," in *Evangelical Dictionary of Theology*, 2nd edition, ed. W. A. Elwell (Grand Rapids: Baker Academic, 2001); B. Cottret, *Calvin: A Biography* (Grand Rapids: Eerdmans, 2000); W. H. Neuser, "Person: Stations—France and Basel," in *The Calvin Handbook,* ed. H. J. Selderhuis, trans. H. J. Baron, J. J. Guder, R. H. Lundell, and G. W. Sheeres (Grand Rapids: Eerdmans, 2009).

[17] J. Calvin, "Preface," in *Commentary on the Book of Psalms*, vol. 1, trans. J. Anderson (Grand Rapids: Eerdmans, 1948), xl-xli.

[18] Parker, *John Calvin*, 105.

[19] B. Gordon, *Calvin* (New Haven: Yale University Press, 2009), 126–27.

[20] W. G. Naphy, "Person: Stations—Geneva II," in *The Calvin Handbook*, 45.

[21] Geneva had a complex system of government councils: the Little Council, the Two Hundred, and the General Council. See S. Wellman, *John Calvin: Father of Reformed Theology* (Uhrichsville, OH: Barbour Publishing, 2001), 120. The Little or Small Council was made up of twenty-five native-born citizens who were reelected every year. They were supervised by four executives called syndics, who were elected every year for a single term of only one year. See R. M. Kingdon, "Work: Themes—Church and State," in *The Calvin Handbook*, 356.

[22] Ibid.

[23] J. L. González, *The Story of Christianity: The Reformation to the Present Day*, vol. 2 (San Francisco: Harper, 1985), 67.

[24] D. W. Hall, *The Legacy of John Calvin: His Influence on the Modern World* (Phillipsburg, NJ: P&R, 2008), 61.

[25] Ibid. It is estimated that Calvin preached over two thousand sermons during his ministry at Geneva. At his height, he preached twice on Sunday and three times during the week. His sermons lasted more than an hour, and he preached without the use of notes. Calvin was very consistent in his preaching, with his style changing little over the years. See Parker, *John Calvin*, 116–23.

[26] Parker, *John Calvin*, 139–45.

[27] Cottret, *Calvin*, 222–25.

[28] Gordon, *Calvin*, 224.

[29] Willem van 't Spijker, *Calvin: A Brief Guide to His Life and Thought*, trans. Lyle D. Bierma (2001; repr., Louisville: Westminster John Knox, 2009), 99.

[30] R. A. Baker and J. M. Landers, *A Summary of Christian History*, 3rd ed. (Nashville: B&H, 2005), 115.

[31] González, *The Story of Christianity*, 118.

[32] J. Hill, *Zondervan Handbook to the History of Christianity* (Oxford, UK: Lion, 2006), 240.

[33] F. J. Bremer, *The Puritan Experiment* (London, UK: St. James Press, 1976), 18–19.

[34] Spijker, *Calvin*, 102.

[35] González, *The Story of Christianity*, vol. 2, 68.

[36] Gordon, *Calvin*, 299–300.

[37] Spijker, *Calvin*, 123–24.

[38] Kingdon, "Work: Themes—Church and State," 355–56.

[39] J. Calvin, *Institutes of the Christian Religion*, vol. 2, ed. J. T. McNeill, trans. F. L. Battles (Louisville: Westminster John Knox, 1960), 1087–88.

[40] W. S. Johnson, *John Calvin: Reformer for the 21st Century* (Louisville: Westminster John Knox, 2009), 109.

[41] Ibid., 110.

[42] Hall, *The Legacy of John Calvin*, 24–25. Hall adds in a footnote, "In 1542 the General Council adopted this proviso: 'Nothing should be put before the Council of Two Hundred that has not been dealt with in the Narrow Council, nor before the General Council before having been dealt with in the Narrow Council as well as the Two Hundred' (translation by Kim McMahan). E. William Monter, *Calvin's Geneva* (Huntington, NY: R. E. Krieger, 1975), 72." Ibid.

[43] Calvin, *Institutes of the Christian Religion*, 1:846.

[44] Ibid., 1:847.

[45] D. Vandrunen, "The Context of Natural Law: John Calvin's Doctrine of the Two Kingdoms," available online at http://www.britannica.com/bps/additionalcontent/18/29385382/The-Two-Kingdoms-Doctrine-and-the-Relationship-of-Church-and-State-in-the-Early-Reformed-Tradition (accessed December 13, 2009).

[46] Calvin, *Institutes of the Christian Religion*, 2:1485.

[47] Ibid., 2:1489.

[48] Kingdon, "Work: Themes—Church and State," 356–57.

[49] Calvin, *Institutes of the Christian Religion*, 2:1503.

[50] Ibid., 2:1489.

[51] Ibid., 2:1488.

[52] Johnson, *John Calvin*, 112.

[53] Calvin, *Institutes of the Christian Religion*, 2:125.

[54] Ibid., 2:1217.

[55] Ibid., 2:1499.

[56] Ibid., 2:1511–20.

[57] J. R. Beeke and R. J. Pederson, *Meet the Puritans: With a Guide to Modern Reprints* (Grand Rapids: Reformation Heritage Books, 2006), 621–22.

[58] Beeke and Pederson, *Meet the Puritans*, 623.

[59] Bremer, *The Puritan Experiment*, 33–34.

[60] Beeke and Pederson, *Meet the Puritans*, 622.

[61] Bremer, *The Puritan Experiment*, 33.

[62] R. W. Heinze, *Reform and Conflict: From the Medieval World to the Wars of Religion, AD 1350–1648*, The Baker History of the Church, vol. 4, ed. Tim Dowley (Grand Rapids: Baker, 2005), 248–49.

[63] Ibid., 49.

[64] C. Millard, *The Rewriting of America's History* (Camp Hill, PA: Horizon House Publishers, 1991), 19.

[65] Heinze, *Reform and Conflict*, 324–25.

[66] P. Toon, "Puritan Eschatology: 1600–1648," in *Puritan Papers: 1968–1969*, vol. 5, ed. J. I. Packer (Phillipsburg, NJ: P&R Publishing, 2005), 63.

[67] Ibid., 63–64.

[68] Calvin, *Institutes of the Christian Religion*, 2:995.

[69] For a more extensive explanation of these views, see Toon, "Puritan Eschatology: 1600–1648," 63–79.

[70] Bremer, *The Puritan Experiment*, 34.

[71] A. Carden, "Biblical Texts and Themes in American Puritan Preaching, 1630–1700," *Andrews University Seminary Studies* 21 (1983): 116–17.

[72] Ibid., 118.

[73] C. Cherry, "Symbols of Spiritual Truth: Jonathan Edwards as Biblical Interpreter," *Interpretation* 39 (1985): 264.

[74] Ibid., 265.

[75] C. L. Cohen, "Two Biblical Models of Conversion: An Example of Puritan Hermeneutics," *Church History* 58 (1989): 185.

[76] Miller and Johnson, *The Puritans: A Sourcebook of Their Writings*, 195–99.

[77] Mark Noll, Nathan O. Hatch, and George M. Marsden, *The Search for Christian America* (Colorado Springs, CO: Helmers & Howard, 1989), 34.

[78] Ibid., 198.

[79] Bremer, *The Puritan Experiment*, 93.

[80] Miller and Johnson, *The Puritans*, 206–7.

[81] G. McKenna, *The Puritan Origins of American Patriotism* (New Haven, CT: Yale University Press, 2007), 208.

[82] Noll, Hatch, and Marsden, *The Search for Christian America*, 36.

[83] Bremer, *The Puritan Experiment*, 62.

[84] Noll, Hatch, and Marsden, *The Search for Christian America*, 36.

[85] One of the reasons that Jonathan Edwards was fired as pastor of Northampton stemmed from his refusal to back the Half-Way Covenant espoused by his grandfather Solomon Stoddard. This doctrine allowed for the unconverted to take communion as a converting ordinance. As Edwards studied further his stance on revival and evangelism, he became increasingly convinced about the distinction between the saved and the unsaved. He concluded that the unregenerate must not partake in the Lord's Supper. Of this time, Malcolm McDow and Alvin Reid write, "In 1748 he refused to admit an applicant without a public profession of faith. In 1749 he published his *Humble Inquiry* to explain his views on requirements for church membership. The treatise provided a glimpse into the pastoral nature of Edwards. However, he was unable to win most church members to his side. After two stormy years, a council was summoned with the result that Edwards was dismissed in 1750." M. McDow and A. L. Reid, *Firefall: How God Shaped History through Revivals* (Nashville: B&H, 1997), 216.

[86] Bremer, *The Puritan Experiment*, 74.

[87] Ibid., 93–94.

[88] Miller, *Errand in the Wilderness*, 18. To explain Congregationalism, Miller quotes from John Robinson's *Works*, "Wise men having written on this subject, have approved as good and lawful, three kinds of polities,—monarchial, where supreme authority is in the hands of one; aristocratical, when it is in the hands of some few select persons; and democratical, in the whole body or multitude. And all these three forms have their places in the Church of Christ. In respect of Him, the Head, it is a monarchy; in respect of the eldership, an aristocracy; in respect of the body, a popular state." Miller, *Errand in the Wilderness*, 22. Miller additionally notes, "Hooker was joint moderator with [John] Cotton at the synod of 1643, which condemned Presbyterianism." Ibid., 29.

[89] Ibid., 19.

[90] Miller and Johnson, *The Puritans*, 290–91.

[91] Ames authored a theological work titled *Medulla Sacrae Theologiae*, which become the standard textbook for theology in New England. See Miller, *Errand in the Wilderness*, 52.

[92] Miller, *Errand in the Wilderness*, 32.

[93] Miller and Johnson, *The Puritans*, 195–99, 188.

[94] Ibid.

[95] P. Miller, *Nature's Nation* (Cambridge, MA: Harvard University Press, 1967), 58–60. See also C. E. White, "Were Hooker and Shepard Closet Arminians?" *Calvin Theological Journal* 20 (1985): 33–42.

[96] Ibid., 35.

[97] D. M. Lloyd-Jones, *The Puritans: Their Origins and Successors* (Carlisle, PA: The Banner of Truth Trust, 1987), 398.

[98] Baker and Landers, *A Summary of Christian History*, 321.

[99] M. Pearse, *The Age of Reason: From the Wars of Religion to the French Revolution, 1570–1789*, The Baker History of the Church, vol. 5, ed. Tim Dowley (Grand Rapids: Baker, 2006), 315. Penn eventually decided to buy the land from the Indians in order to establish good relations with them. See González, *The Story of Christianity*, 202.

[100] González, *The Story of Christianity*, 202.

[101] Cited in Millard, *The Rewriting of American History*, 43–44.

[102] Ibid., 44.

[103] Ibid.

[104] González, *The Story of Christianity*, 202–3.

[105] Ibid., 203.

[106] R. G. Torbet, *A History of the Baptists*, 3rd ed. (Valley Forge, PA: Judson, 2000), 519.

[107] Ibid.

[108] W. R. Estep, *The Anabaptist Story* (Grand Rapids: Eerdmans, 1975), 226–27.

[109] See T. S. Kidd, "Williams, Roger," in *Biographical Dictionary of Evangelicals*, ed. Timothy Larsen (Downers Grove, IL: InterVarsity, 2003), 741; González, *The Story of Christianity*, 224–25; Miller and Johnson, *The Puritans*, 214.

[110] Miller and Johnson, *The Puritans*, 215.

[111] Pearse, *The Age of Reason*, 310.

[112] Debate surrounds which church in Rhode Island serves as the oldest Baptist church in America, the First Baptist Church of Providence or the Baptist church founded by John Clarke in Newport. See Torbet, *A History of the Baptists*, 202–3.

[113] Kidd, "Williams, Roger," 741.

[114] Miller and Johnson, *The Puritans*, 215.

[115] Ibid., 185.

[116] J. Eidsmoe, *Christianity and the Constitution: The Faith of Our Founding Fathers* (Grand Rapids: Baker, 1987), 37–38.

[117] Noll, Hatch, and Marsden, *The Search for Christian America*, 37.

[118] Quoted in E. S. Morgan, ed., *Puritan Political Ideas: 1558–1794* (Indianapolis: Hackett, 2003), 208, emphasis original. Quotation comes from *The Bloudy Tenet of Persecution for Cause of Conscience*, Williams's response to a tract titled "A Model of Church and Civil Power," which was published by a group of Massachusetts ministers. See Ibid., 203–4.

[119] These sins, as specified in the *Cambridge Platform*, included "idolatry, blasphemy, heresy, venting corrupt and pernicious opinions . . . open contempt of the word preached, prophanation of the Lord's Day, [or] disturbing the peaceable administration and exercise of the worship and holy things of God." Quoted in H. S. Stout, *The New England Soul: Preaching and Religious Culture in Colonial New England* (New York: Oxford University Press, 1986), 20–21.

[120] Ibid., 21.

[121] R. Williams, *The Bloudy Tenet of Persecution for Cause of Conscience Discussed: And Mr. Cotton's Letter Examined and Answered* (London: The Hanserd Knollys Society, 1848), 2.

[122] Roger Williams, *Letter to the Town of Providence, January, 1655*, in *The Puritans: A Sourcebook of their Writings*, ed. P. Miller and T. H. Johnson, vol. 1 (New York: Harper and Row, 1938), 225.

[123] W. MacDonald, ed., *The Documentary Source Book of American History, 1606–1913* (New York: The MacMillan Company, 1916), 67–68.

[124] Ibid., 67.

[125] Quoted in L. R. Buzzard and S. Ericsson, *The Battle for Religious Liberty* (Elgin, IL: David C. Cook, 1982), 51.

[126] M. B. Yarnell III, "Political Theology at the Foundation of the Southern Baptist Convention," in *First Freedom: The Baptist Perspective on Religious Liberty*, eds. T. White, J. G. Duesing, and M. B. Yarnell III (Nashville: Broadman & Holman Academic, 2007), 69.

[127] On April 15, 2010, U. S. District Judge Barbara Crabb ruled that the National Day of Prayer, set up by Congress in 1952 and reaffirmed in 1988 as the first Thursday in May, was unconstitutional because it calls for "religious exercise that serves no secular function." "Federal Judge Rules Day of Prayer Unconstitutional," available online from http://www.newstribune.townnews.com/articles/2010/04/16/news_national/nt260nat30prayer10.txt (accessed April 21, 2010).

[128] P. Pressler, "Contemporary Religious Liberty and Judiciary in America: A Southern Baptist Jurist's Personal Perspective," in *First Freedom*, 172–73.

[129] The definitive biographical work on Edwards is G. Marsden, *Jonathan Edwards: A Life* (New Haven, CT: Yale University Press, 2003), 13–15.

[130] Ibid.

[131] H. B. Parks, *Jonathan Edwards: The Fiery Puritan* (New York: Minton, Balch, and Company, 1930), 60.

[132] J. Edwards, "Memoirs of Jonathan Edwards," *The Works of Jonathan Edwards*, vol. 1, ed. Edward Hickman (Peabody, MA: Hendrickson, 2003), lv.

[133] I. H. Murray, *Jonathan Edwards, A New Biography* (Carlisle, PA: Banner of Truth, 1987), 88, emphasis original.

[134] J. Edwards, "Preface to Five Discourses on Important Subjects, Nearly Concerning the Great Affair of the Soul's Eternal Salvation," The Works of Jonathan Edwards, 1:620. Edwards mentioned in his preface to these sermons that a fifth sermon titled "The Excellency of Christ" was actually ". . . added on my own motion, thinking that a discourse on such an evangelical subject, would properly follow others that were chiefly legal and awakening, and that something of the excellency of the Savior, was proper to succeed those things that were to show the necessity of salvation." M. X. Lesser, "Editor's Introduction: The Excellency of Christ," in *Sermons and Discourses, 1734–1738*, The Works of Jonathan Edwards, vol. 17, ed. M. X. Lesser (New Haven, CT: Yale University Press, 2001), 560.

[135] Unfortunately, this same controversy over Arminianism led to a decline in the revival fever. In recording his recollections of the revival in a letter to Benjamin Colman, Edwards requested prayer for Hampshire County and Northampton because "in its present melancholy circumstances into which it is brought by the Springfield quarrel, which doubtless above all things that have happened, has tended to put a stop to the glorious work here, and to prejudice this country against it, and hinder the propagation of it." J. Edwards, "The Great Awakening," in The Works of Jonathan Edwards, vol. 4, ed. C. C. Goen (New Haven, CT: Yale University Press, 1972), 211.

The controversy about which Edwards spoke developed out of a debate over the call of Harvard graduate Robert Breck to a pastorate in Springfield, Massachusetts, in 1735. The Hampshire Ministers Association opposed his installation because of his Arminian and heterodox views. Church authorities in Boston intervened and allowed the church members to call Breck as their pastor. P. F. Gura, *Jonathan Edwards: America's Evangelical* (New York: Hill & Wang, 2005), 63–65.

Although he took little part in this particular struggle between Calvinism and Arminianism, Edwards faced significant opposition in the Northampton church and throughout his ministry because of the Arminian controversy. Eventually he broke ranks with some of the members of his church, specifically the Williams family and their descendants. A major part of their disagreement with Edwards originated out of the Williamses' willingness to embrace Arminianism. Perry Miller explains, "That the Williams were lax on certain doctrines was probably public knowledge; it is significant that [Charles] Chauncy liked the head of the clan, William Williams, and thought him greater than Stoddard." P. Miller, *Jonathan Edwards* (Westport, CT: Greenwood, 1949), 105.

Edwards's contention with Arminianism developed out of his biblical hermeneutics and soteriology. As he evaluated the theology of Arminianism, he concluded, "If there be any part of the scheme here laid down, or any distinction here used, not warranted by Scripture, let it be rejected, and if any opposite scheme can be found that is more easy and plain, having fewer and more rational distinctions, and not demonstrably inconsistent with itself and with the Word of God, let it be received. Let the Arminian scheme of justification by our own virtue be as *plain* and natural as it will. If at the same time it is *plainly* contrary to the certain and demonstrable doctrine of the gospel, as contained in the Scriptures, we are bound to reject it, unless we reject the Scriptures themselves as perplexed and absurd, and make ourselves wiser than God, and pretend to know his mind better than himself." J. Edwards, "Preface to Five Discourses on Important Subjects," The Works of Jonathan Edwards, 1:621, emphasis original.

[136] J. Edwards, "A Narrative of Surprising Conversions," in *Jonathan Edwards on Revival* (Carlisle, PA: Banner of Truth, 1984), 11, emphasis original.

[137] R. Balmer, "Jonathan Edwards (1703–1758)," in *Encyclopedia of Evangelicalism*, ed. R. Balmer (Louisville: Westminster John Knox Press, 2002), 189.

[138] W. H. Kimnach, K. P. Minkema, and D. A. Sweeney, "Editors' Introduction," in *The Sermons of Jonathan Edwards: A Reader*, eds. W. H. Kimnach, K. P. Minkema, and D. A. Sweeney (New Haven, CT: Yale University Press, 1999), xxxii.

[139] Marsden, *Jonathan Edwards*, 351.

[140] J. Edwards, "An Humble Inquiry," in *Ecclesiastical Writings*, in The Works of Jonathan Edwards, vol. 12, ed. D. D. Hall (New Haven, CT: Yale University Press, 1994), 194–96.

[141] Marsden, *Jonathan Edwards*, 349.

[142] See J. Edwards, "A Warning to Professors, or the Great Guilt of Those Who Attend on the Ordinance of Divine Worship and yet Allow Themselves in Any Known Wickedness," in The Works of Jonathan Edwards, vol. 2, ed. Edward Hickman (Peabody, MA: Hendrickson, 2003), 185–90. This sermon dates prior to 1733. See also J. Edwards, "Self-Examination and the Lord's Supper," in *Sermons and Discourses, 1730–1733*, in The Works of Jonathan Edwards, vol. 17, ed. Mark Valeri (New Haven, CT: Yale University Press, 1999), 264–72. Edwards preached this sermon in March 1731.

[143] Kimnach, Minkema, and Sweeney, "Editors' Introduction," xxxiii.

[144] Edwards, "Memoirs," clxii.

[145] Gura, *Jonathan Edwards*, 182–85.

[146] K. P. Minkema, "A Chronology of Edwards's Life and Writings," Jonathan Edwards Center at Yale University, available online at http://edwards.yale.edu/files/JE%20Chronology.pdf (accessed January 27, 2010).

[147] Gura, *Jonathan Edwards*, 218. Marsden dates the inoculation on February 23. See Marsden, *Jonathan Edwards*, 493.

[148] Ibid., 264.

[149] S. T. Logan, "The Hermeneutics of Jonathan Edwards," *Westminster Theological Journal* 43 (1980): 91.

[150] Logan, "The Hermeneutics of Jonathan Edwards," 91.

[151] S. J. Stein, "The Quest for the Spiritual Sense: The Biblical Hermeneutics of Jonathan Edwards," *Harvard Theological Review* 70 (1977): 108.

[152] Jonathan Edwards, *Religious Affections*, The Works of Jonathan Edwards, vol. 2, ed. J. E. Smith (New Haven, CT: Yale University Press, 1959), 270–71.

[153] Stein, "The Quest for the Spiritual Sense," 109.

[154] Ibid., 110.

[155] Ibid., 109.

[156] J. Edwards, "The End of the Wicked Contemplated by the Righteous: The Torments of the Wicked in Hell, No Occasion of Grief to the Saints in Heaven," in The Works of Jonathan Edwards, 2:212.

[157] Holmes, *God of Grace & God of Glory*, 177.

[158] C. Cherry, *The Theology of Jonathan Edwards: A Reappraisal* (Bloomington: Indiana University Press, 1966), 50.

[159] Stein, "The Quest for the Spiritual Sense," 109.

[160] Logan, "The Hermeneutics of Jonathan Edwards," 92.

[161] Noll, Hatch, and Marsden, *The Search for Christian America*, 56–58.

[162] Pearse, *The Age of Reason*, 329.

[163] Noll, Hatch, and Marsden, 65.

[164] Pearse, 330–31.

[165] Noll, Hatch, and Marsden, *The Search for Christian America*, 72–73.

[166] McKenna, *The Puritan Origins of American Patriotism*, 46.

[167] Hudson and Corrigan, *Religion in America*, 96–97.

[168] Noll, Hatch, and Marsden, *The Search for Christian America*, 39.

[169] Stout, *The New England Soul*, 271. Stout provides strong evidence of the role of the pulpit in calling America to revolution and liberty. The fact that the American pulpit was so intricately involved in the movement of American freedom clearly demonstrates that, by the time of the signing of the Declaration of Independence and the Constitution, Christianity played an indelible role in the nation's founding. Care was given to distinguish the difference between spiritual and political freedom, but it is a far-fetched idea that, by the time of the writing of the Constitution, America had become purely secular, with only a smattering of religious influence. Stout writes, "By explaining their terms carefully and distinguishing regular sermons from occasional, ministers could praise both spiritual and political liberty. Depending on the subject matter and occasion, the same text could be made to elicit political or spiritual meanings in the same way earlier generations distinguished federal and personal covenant. Rather than substituting political for spiritual meanings, they retained both through the exegetical technique of extracting 'double applications.'" Ibid., 297.

[170] R. D. Land, "The Role of Religious Liberty in the Founding and Development of America," in *First Freedom*, 105.

[171] W. W. Sweet, *The Story of Religion in America* (Grand Rapids: Baker, 1930), 192.

[172] Land, "The Role of Religious Liberty in the Founding and Development of America," 106.

[173] Ibid., 108.

[174] Quoted in Hudson and Corrigan, *Religion in America*, 103.

[175] Pressler, "Contemporary Religious Liberty and Judiciary in America," 174.

Response to Henard

David Barton

I thoroughly appreciated William Henard's approach, especially the effort he made in documenting the religious thinking that predominated among the prevalent Christian groups leading up to American colonization and the subsequent American founding. Having thus identified the seeds from which the American tree of liberty sprang, and the beliefs undergirding the government that grew up in the nurturing shade of that tree, he has arrived at historical conclusions fully warranted by any objective study of the primary documents of the Founding Era and the two centuries preceding it. He has shown the spiritual roots of what later manifested itself politically.

I find myself in strong agreement with so many of his historically derived conclusions, including the idea that government in early America was not viewed as a secular institution; that the American colonies "all held to some form of religious connectionalism"; that "the Revolution did not grow out of a secular call for freedom but from a religious one"; that separation of church and state in America was always historically directed at the government, not the church, and thus the First Amendment limited Congress, not citizens or churches; etc.

Henard also correctly observes that militant secularist groups today claim to be committed to a "fierce separation of church and state." They proudly strut about in front of the issue as though the concept were their own progeny, but as Henard rightly notes, it was Calvin and other Reformers who envisioned the separation of church and state as a result of their study of the Scriptures. After all, in ancient Israel, God placed Moses over the civil affairs and Aaron over the spiritual ones—the nation was one, but the jurisdictions were two. In fact, in 2 Chronicles 26, when King Uzziah of Judah attempted to enter the temple and perform the duties of a priest (thus crossing a line established by God), God Himself directly opposed Uzziah. Significantly, the doctrine for which secularists are responsible is the fiercely coercive "secularization of church and state"—an absurd perversion of the original scriptural doctrine of separation of church and state.

Henard does an excellent job of tracing the teaching of separation of church and state back to the Bible and the Reformers, and then of providing its proper historical context and usage in American history—something that writers today rarely do.

Calvin, Edwards, and the Puritans

In tracing the origins of important concepts back to Calvin and his disciples (such as Jonathan Edwards), Henard does a superb job of citing extensively from their primary source documents. For example, in establishing Calvin's views on various topics, he heavily cited Calvin's own writings. Thus, when he later invoked a number of statements about Calvin from modern biographers (e.g., Parker, Naphy, Wellman, Kingdon, etc.), it was clear that their conclusions about Calvin comported with Calvin's own previously presented words. Henard also followed this same praiseworthy practice in his review of Jonathan Edwards.

However, I did not find this admirable habit to be repeated in his analysis of the Puritans. With only rare allusions to primary sources, Henard instead says "Bremer explains . . ."; "Cherry surmises . . ."; "Cohen draws this conclusion . . ."; etc. Perhaps not surprisingly, it is also in this one area that I found my greatest disagreement with Henard (although "disagreement" is much too strong a word; it is more like "difference"), specifically in his repeated assertions regarding the impact of eschatology and millennialism on the Puritans thinking and actions.

Part of my difficulty with the portions of his chapter may stem from Henard's frequent use of theological terms without first defining them (e.g., Arminianism, eschatology, millennialism, postmillennialism, premillennialism, etc.). I have noticed that when a Calvinist defines "Calvinism," he does so in a manner very different from the way that an Arminian defines that same term (and vice versa), thus making intelligent discussions difficult and agreement virtually impossible unless a definition has been set forth before discussion begins.[1]

Nevertheless, he asserts that "millennial thought carried to the seventeenth-century Puritan" and that they "utilized this eschatological belief to further their connectionalism." Henard also states that, "With these [Puritan] concepts of postmillennialism and typology in mind, one can better interpret Winthrop's sermon. In 1630, he preached . . ." He then admirably cites at length from that 1630 sermon (one of the few instances when he cited original Puritan sources). But in reading his excerpts from that sermon (or even the full sermon), I see no eschatological or millennial considerations expressed as either an overt or even a suggested strand. To the contrary, the passage sounds more like a group of Christians trying to emulate the body of believers in the book of Acts than it does a group planning its actions based on any eschatological, millennial, or future theological considerations.

I own a very large collection of the sermons of the Puritans and their successors, and I have read hundreds of these sermons. I cannot recall a single instance in which millennialism was ever raised either as a direct theological consideration or even an incidental reference. I have seen them use the term "millennium" in referencing a chronological or linear timeline of history, but I have never seen that term referenced with any theological action—that is, I have not seen any of their sermons declare or imply that "since we are in the millennium, then we must . . ."

In fact, the Puritan sermons I have studied seem to be similar to those American sermons described two centuries later by Alexis de Tocqueville when he noted that "the American preachers are constantly referring to the earth, and it is only with great difficulty that they can divert their attention from it. To touch their congregations, they always show them how favorable religious opinions are to freedom and public tranquility."[2] That is, they are more focused on the here than the hereafter.

Of course, while I have read many Puritan writings and sermons, I have by no means read all of them, so it might be that Henard and the modern reviewers he cited are describing sources I have not seen. Nevertheless, the overall lack of reference to original sources in this one area may have caused some declarations to be made and conclusions to be reached that I find difficult to sustain historically.

Theocracy and Christian Nation

The terms "theocracy" and "Christian nation," like the phrase "separation of church and state," have in recent years been co-opted by the Secular Left and completely redefined from their original meanings. They have now become pejoratives to be used alongside the common profanity so often launched against those Christians who dare to become active in the civil arena. We should not allow the Left and Secularists to claim ownership over those terms, and Henard has admirably refused to cede this ground. He approvingly reports, "the assumption by numerous historians that the Bible Commonwealths were theocracies still clouds our understanding." Indeed, a "theocracy" is defined as a government in which God is the supreme civil authority, with the government being under His immediate direction and operated by priests who interpret His laws.[3] But since America has a written constitution that gives ultimate direction to the civil authority, and since its leaders are not priests but instead are individuals freely elected by the people, then by what convoluted distortion can America or any of its early colonies be called a theocracy? It is impossible to have a theocracy when the people elect their own leaders under a fixed civil constitution that is their supreme governing authority. Significantly, Christianity in America actually *undermines* theocracy by strengthening rather than weakening free and elective government.

Concerning a "Christian nation," Henard rightfully asserts that "Christianity provided an indelible impression upon the founding of America and its establishing documents. . . . The nation, however, and its documents were profoundly influenced by Christianity. The nation was not just religious; it was Christian." He further notes that "America was founded essentially Christian because of the historical context of her birth."

Such statements encompass the traditional definition of what constitutes a Christian nation, and I think that Henard's characterization of America in these terms is very important.

To relinquish the descriptive of America as a "Christian nation" is to provide critics the shovel by which they can bury four centuries of American history. If we tell the current generation that America is not and never was a Christian nation, then we have repudiated over 300 court decisions to the contrary, hundreds of state and federal laws declaring the opposite, and thousands of pronouncements by early leaders and statesmen. Secularists and Leftists may largely control the universities, the media, and the halls of government, but they should not be given the right to obliterate the memory of tens of thousands of documents that they wished did not exist. I applaud Henard for his unwillingness to renounce four centuries of organic documents and declarations simply to appease a strident group of postmodernists who personally find the characterization of America as a Christian nation to be reprehensible. I hope others will follow his laudable example.

In summary, I thoroughly appreciate Henard's many invaluable contributions and insights in his chapter, especially his obvious reliance on original sources in demonstrating the indispensable contribution of biblical thought in the building of America as an exceptional nation.

Endnotes

[1] Let me offer what I understand to be a generally accepted working definition of some central terms. The word "eschatology" (which came into use in 1844, more than two centuries after the Puritans) refers to one's theological interpretation of: (1) what will happen as the final events of mankind, and (2) when those events will occur. Specifically, eschatology involves a view of when and how the doctrines of the Millennium, Second Coming of Christ, the resurrection of the dead, and the final judgment will be played out; and based on one's views of Revelation 20 concerning the biblical millennium, there are at least three major eschatological views now described as postmillennialism, premillennialism, and amillennialism. Postmillennialism (a term coined in 1851) generally holds that Christ's Second Coming will occur after the millennium ends. Premillennialism holds that the Second Coming of Christ will occur before the biblical millennium—that the millennium will begin when Christ returns. Amillennialism holds that the millennium in Revelations 20 is figurative and not literal—that there will not be a specific designated period with a fixed beginning and end.

[2] A. Tocqueville, *Democracy in America,* vol. 2, trans. H. Reeve (New York: A. S. Barnes & Co., 1851), 134–35.

[3] See, for example, *Random House Dictionary,* 2010, s.v., "theocracy," available online at http://dictionary.reference.com/browse/theocracy, and Noah Webster, *American Dictionary of the English Language* (1828), s.v. "theocracy."

Response to Henard

Jonathan D. Sassi

W illiam Henard's essay argues that while the United States was not founded as a "Christian nation," nevertheless "Christianity provided an indelible impression on the founding of America and its establishing documents." He aims to establish a line of descent from John Calvin's Geneva to the Massachusetts Puritans, especially John Winthrop, and then through Jonathan Edwards to the American Revolution. The common denominator among these individuals and societies was a "religious connectionalism" that linked church and state.

Despite the depths to which Henard plumbs the writings of Calvin, Winthrop, and Edwards, he never ties any of them to the Revolutionary era or the founding of the United States beyond mere assertion. For example, after exploring similarities between Calvin's Geneva and Puritan Massachusetts in their church-state arrangements, Henard concludes that their "connectionalism had not dramatically changed between the sixteenth and seventeenth centuries." He then extrapolates to the eighteenth-century founding of the United States, writing that "One can surmise that the degree of change between the seventeenth and eighteenth centuries, though more rapid than the previous century, was not so great as to alter completely the premise set by Calvin or the Puritans." This hypothesis does not correspond with historical reality. As my chapter demonstrates, enormous social, political, and intellectual changes marked the century between 1660 and 1760. Especially because of the Enlightenment and the ascendance of the principle of religious toleration throughout the Anglo-Atlantic world, it is impossible for one to "surmise" that the premises of Calvin or the Puritans still prevailed by the time of the constitutional convention in 1787.

Henard employs a variety of vague terminology throughout his essay, so it is hard to pin down exactly what link he is trying to establish between Christianity and the American founding. He variously writes of "the Christian paradigm and theology" or "the Judeo-Christian ethic" without unpacking the meaning of those terms. The notion of "connectionalism," to which he often recurs, proves no more precise. Using that term, he lumps Pennsylvania with the other seventeenth-century English colonies. As Henard remarks, "The interesting issue regarding Penn's colony was the fact that religion and government still went hand in hand, as in other colonies." Such a conclusion is simply wrong. Virginia and Massachusetts, the most important English colonies established prior to Pennsylvania, had religious establishments, so Pennsylvania's lack of an established church marked a major departure. Just because Pennsylvania retained a religious test should not lead one to conclude that it was just like everywhere else in keeping church and state connected.

Just prior to his conclusion, Henard makes his best attempt to specify the alleged links between Christianity and the American Revolution, but none of them stand up to scrutiny. Wrapping up a discussion of various points of Jonathan Edwards's theology, Henard posits that the "ability to now personally encounter Christ and interpret Scripture [coupled] with the belief in individual freedom and liberty" makes the coming of the American Revolution somehow understandable. However, he does not elaborate, and I fail to see the connection between Edwards's doctrine of the Trinity and the causes of the Revolution. Henard adds that such theological heirs of Edwards as Joseph Bellamy, Samuel Hopkins, and Isaac Backus supported the Revolution, but, as he noted previously, so did such opponents of Edwards as Jonathan Mayhew and Charles Chauncy, so the link between Edwards and the Revolution remains elusive. Finally, in the same paragraph, Henard claims, "The Revolution did not grow out of a secular call for freedom but from a religious one." If that were the case, however, would not one expect religious themes to predominate in the Declaration of Independence?

Henard continues to reach for connections between Christianity and the Revolution in a long footnote (no. 169) that deals with Harry S. Stout's *The New England Soul*. Henard writes, "The fact that the American pulpit was so intricately involved in the movement of American freedom clearly demonstrates that, by the time of the signing of the Declaration of Independence and the Constitution, Christianity played an indelible role in the nation's founding." I would not deny the role of the "black regiment" of patriot ministers in mobilizing support for the Revolution, but Christianity's role in the Revolution was much more complicated than that. Large numbers of committed Christians either opposed independence or sought to stay neutral in the dispute, so there was no simple transfer of influence to the constitutional convention. Henard goes on to add that "it is a far-fetched idea that, by the time of the writing of the Constitution, America had become purely secular, with only a smattering of religious influence." My chapter certainly does not contend that America had become "purely secular," which would be a preposterous claim for either the late eighteenth or early twenty-first centuries. But the text of the Constitution was intentionally secular, as I argued, in its prohibition of religious tests for office, the preamble's eschewal of a religious invocation, and the First Amendment's further prohibition on Congress's enacting any religious establishment.

Furthermore, Henard misreads the meaning of John Leland's trip to Washington, DC, with the "mammoth cheese." He portrays Leland's visit in January 1802 as an effort to evangelize the capital and sanctify the new nation. Instead, Leland's primary intent was to laud Jefferson's political position and identify the president with the causes of religious freedom and disestablishment in New England. Leland penned the address that he read upon delivering the cheese at the presidential mansion. After proclaiming his townsfolk's "indissoluble" allegiance to the Constitution, Leland observed that "the most prominent" of its "beautiful features" were "The right of free suffrage, to correct abuses—the prohibition of religious tests, to prevent all hierarchy—and the means of amendment which it contains within itself, to remove defects as fast as they are discovered." He added, "we believe the supreme Ruler of the Universe, who raises up men to achieve great events, has raised up a JEFFERSON at this critical day, to defend *Republicanism*, and to baffle the arts of *Aristocracy*."[1] Leland's reference to "Aristocracy" was a jab at Jefferson's Federalist opponents. In short, to the extent that Leland invoked God in his address, he did so in order to highlight the Constitution's prohibition of religious tests and to celebrate the Jeffersonians' electoral success. His goal was the very opposite of furthering the connection between Christianity and government.

I grant that Christians played an important role on the patriot side of the American Revolution. It is surely more than a coincidence that the Calvinists of New England and the Middle Colonies tended to line up behind the Whig banner, but Henard has not cogently explained why that was the case. Moreover, Calvinists were only one group in a religiously diverse coalition of patriots that included theological liberals like Charles Chauncy and Enlightenment rationalists like Benjamin Franklin and Thomas Jefferson. Other, equally committed Christians chose different sides in the struggle. The nation's founding was religiously eclectic and not directly descended from John Calvin and sixteenth-century Geneva. When the Framers came together to create a national government, they made the United States Constitution a deliberately secular document with which people of every religion could live. It hardly bore the "indelible impression" of Christian theology that Henard would have us believe.

Endnote

[1] Leland's address is reprinted in L. H. Butterfield, "Elder John Leland, Jeffersonian Itinerant," *Proceedings of the American Antiquarian Society* 62, no. 2 (1952): 224–25.

Response to Henard

Daryl C. Cornett

William Henard attempts to demonstrate that "Christianity provided an indelible impression on the founding of America and its establishing documents." Although I would not begin to deny the influence of Christianity on the earliest Americans as a whole, I believe Henard's interpretation falters in the same manner that Barton's does, but to a lesser extent. The significant Christian heritage of the American colonies is indisputable, and the continued role of Christian thought on many individuals is easily observed through an abundance of material in the historical record. In regard to the religious identity of America at its founding, the nation was primarily made up of Protestant Christians, among those who were religious. However, Henard does not seek to include the influence of non-biblical/non-Christian ideas also at work during the time of the American Revolution and early republic. It seems because of Henard's desire to accentuate the Christian influence like Barton that he ignores the non-Christian influence, which in turn presents an incomplete historical interpretation.

Henard introduces his treatment with references to recent debates in the public square concerning the proper place of religion. Citing our current president's remarks in 2009, Henard demonstrates with this and other examples the immediate polarization that occurs among politicians and private citizens when assertions are made regarding the place of Christianity in American society.

Henard argues that the United States was founded to be neither secular nor with an established Christian faith. However, he contends that the key Founders and the founding documents were "profoundly influenced by Christianity." He concludes that "the nation was not just religious; it was Christian."

Part of Henard's evidence rests in connecting America's founding to a history of Christian sociopolitical thought. In reference to the fact that John Calvin operated within the assumption that matters of church and state were inseparable in regard to the overarching concern to have a Christian society, Hernard argues, "It is this connectionalism that was passed on to the Puritans and became an essential element in the founding of America, and the First Amendment." The first part of this observation is certainly the historical consensus. The early American Puritans looked to Calvin's Geneva as the model of Christian society. However, it is odd that Henard would claim that it was this connectionalism that was integral to the ideas that became enshrined in the founding of America, and particularly the First Amendment. It would seem more reasonable and accurate to conclude that in the disestablishment of religion at the founding of the United States such connectionalism between church and state was ultimately being rejected. Frankly, the entire section on Calvin as background for the discussion on the development of American government is not particularly helpful. Calvin's views were embodied in the theology and societal vision of the early seventeenth-century Puritans, but had lost considerable ground by the late eighteenth century, over 200 years removed from Calvin himself. By the eve of the American Revolution, New England Puritanism had been seriously infected with Arminianism and Unitarianism, and ideas on government were radically changing as well! Calvin's thoughts on soteriology certainly persisted among many Christians, but the Old World medieval structure of society based on feudalism was giving way to the modern world. These modern ideas may have been nascent in Calvin's world, but were directly appropriated and applied by those (Christian and non-Christian) who read Locke, Rousseau, and Montesquieu.

In addition, the egalitarian spirit that began to supplant the Puritan hierarchical paradigm during the Revolutionary Period was completely antithetical to Calvin's understanding of social order. Biblically, Calvin maintained that citizens had no moral right to rebel against their authorities. A Christian's duty was to obey and suffer as long as necessary until God brought about change. Calvin did allow for resistance and remonstrance to government through magistrates who had been properly placed into their positions of leadership, but never through private citizens taking up arms. According to Calvin's own words, it is inconceivable that he would have approved of the kind of revolution that occurred in the English colonies in the late eighteenth century.[1]

Pointing to the Puritans and other establishment-minded Protestants does not strengthen the idea of the United States being founded on distinctly Christian ideas. There can be no doubt of the heritage and the strong Christian presence at the founding of the country; however, one must be careful not to overstate biblical Christianity's influence on the founding ideals and documents or understate the nonbiblical ideas that impacted the shapers of the new country (i.e., Enlightenment thought). Furthermore, it is anachronistic to speak of the founding of the United States and the Puritans, John Winthrop, Thomas Hooker, Jonathan Edwards and other seventeenth- and early eighteenth-century Puritans as if what they thought and taught came into being with the birth of the United States.

Henard concedes that a span of some 150 years separates the early Puritans from the Declaration of Independence, but he contends that "recognition must be made as to the theological thoughts guiding those who served as the forefathers of the United States." The fact is, again, that Puritanism was in dramatic decline by the Revolution and much of its ideas were in the process of being rejected, most obviously the connectionalism between church and state. Therefore, Puritanism laid a theological foundation in regard to personal salvation and holiness, but its views on social order gave way to something else. The fact is that the Puritan social ideal of a Christian state was ultimately not realized in the birth of the United States. To the contrary, a plan of disestablished religion and a paradigm of individual rights and freedoms were set into motion. Henard concludes, "Though the Massachusetts Bay experiment failed, it set the tone for the direction of the colonies to come." The struggle between personal freedom and established Christianity would continue during the colonial period, but personal freedom won the day at the conclusion of the American Revolution and the drafting of the founding documents.

Henard rightly credits William Penn and Roger Williams with introducing more radical ideas concerning personal liberties over and against coerced religion. He rightly observes that even they, as progressive as they were in their own time, still possessed some establishment biases that surfaced at times. But we should see them, and the minority who thought like them, as the forward-thinking radicals of their day whose voices echoed the loudest into the next generation, finding affinity with ideas of the Enlightenment related to personal liberty.

The section devoted to Jonathan Edwards sheds little light on the discussion of Christianity and American identity. There has been a renaissance of Edwards studies in recent years, but his contribution to America's political ideas is inconsequential. Henard ties Edwards, and rightly so, to the tremendous event of the Great Awakening that preceded the American Revolution. Some historians have attempted to observe a causal connection between the two, most notably Alan Heimert in his 1966 *Religion and the American Mind, from the Great Awakening to the Revolution*. Henard essentially picks up this idea that the emphasis on personal autonomy and freedom characteristic of the Great Awakening, along with Edwards's adherence to the "spiritual sense of Scripture," paved the way for the Revolution. Although there is little doubt of the growing emphasis on personal freedom in both the religious and secular spheres, it is difficult to demonstrate that religious ideas of the Awakening *caused* the Revolution or gave primary shape to its ideals.

In the end Henard's analysis of the role of Christianity in America's background and founding remains out of focus. The interpretation suffers from the lack of acknowledgement of non-religious ideas impacting the minds and actions of the first Americans. In no way does such acknowledgement strip America of its significant Christian heritage. The story of America is not Christian *or* secular, but Christian *and* secular. The real debate ultimately rests on which one at the crucial years of the founding of the country had primary influence on those who led the move for independence. Henard is correct that the Christian faith was important to many who played vital roles in the founding of America and that ultimately the government erected was one that would protect religion from government control and interference. I do not believe he has convincingly demonstrated that conspicuously Christian (biblical) ideas informed the founding documents, even if many of those who gave their consent to them were professing Christians.

Endnote

[1] For a further treatment of Calvinism, including John Calvin's thoughts on revolution, see the author's article, "The American Revolution's Role in the Reshaping of Calvinistic Protestantism," *The Journal of Presbyterian History* 82, no. 4 (Winter, 2004): 244–57.

America Partly Christian

Daryl C. Cornett

An American Identity

The United States of America is complex. It always has been, and it always will be. To pinpoint an American culture that one can define and hold up as some sort of standard is more than merely difficult. American identity is an elusive concept. Whose identity in what time? To search for an "American identity" would seem to imply that there is actually some sort of static identity that has remained consistent throughout our history that can be observed and articulated. American history, like all of history, is dynamic. The reality that we face is the fact that all we have immediately accessible to us is our own experience. The past is not accessible. The more distant the past, it becomes even less accessible and more subject to our own imaginations, speculations, and distortions. What we are left with are interpretations of the past. These interpretations come through popular traditions, stories, myths, and remembrances, and through professional historians who try to piece together the past from the evidence left behind. In the end, however, even the well-studied historian must interpret the evidence, which often reflects the biases and agendas of its source in its own time, and attempt to paint in words the most realistic picture he can. To put it simply: history is an interpretive enterprise at heart, but certainly some interpretations are more convincing and congruent with the evidence than others. All interpretations cannot be equal.

There can be no doubt that the Christian faith, embodied in certain individuals who engaged in religiously motivated activity, has been part of the American melting pot (or if you prefer, salad bowl). But how much has Christianity informed and influenced American culture? What is the relationship between Christianity and American identity? Certainly, it is a complex relationship. But at the heart of the question is a search for identity. We really do want to know who we are as a people. What are our core values? What are the principles on which we stand? Where do these core values and principles come from, if indeed we actually collectively possess them? Behind these and similar questions lurks the reality of influences. These influences are intellectual, economic, political, moral, and religious. What particular combination of influences has given shape to American identity? This is the question we want to attempt to answer as we consider the relationship of the Christian faith to American culture.

Defining "Christian Nation / Country"

Many American evangelicals long to believe that the group of men who successfully led the American Revolution possessed an explicit and guiding Christian worldview. Like every culture that has existed in history, Americans have a long tradition of mythologizing and romanticizing their own past. Conversely, purely humanistic treatments of America's past have completely ignored the impact the Christian faith had on the lives and thoughts of the Founding Fathers of the United States. These more extreme interpretations of the past have produced confusion. Who is telling the truth? The question naturally arises from these competing versions of our history. Was the United States founded as a Christian nation? The question appears simple enough, but a satisfying answer is not, much like trying to pinpoint an inclusive definition of "identity." It is misleading to represent the ideology of the foundation of the United States as strictly Christian. However, it is equally erroneous to deny the obvious influence the Christian faith had on many of the shapers of the country and the role it played in the cultural assumptions of the day.

Much of the existing debate on the religious heritage of the United States is fueled by a lack of defined terms. What does one mean by the phrase *Christian nation*? Does the expression mean a certain minimum percentage of church attendance and membership exists among the population? Can the argument be reduced to mere statistics? Does the meaning relate, not so much to numbers of adherents, but to certain ideologies that crafted the nation's guiding documents and way of life? Is the Christian label justifiably applied simply because those who were religious, even if in a minority, were overwhelmingly some persuasion of Christian? Is a nation rightly thought of as Christian if collectively the people display a minimum level of "Christian" morality? Furthermore, who would set the specifics of this ethical standard? The nuances of many more similar questions appear endless.[1]

One problem in devising a helpful definition of the term *Christian* is caused by the reality of the word's multiple uses. The word is commonly used in at least three general ways: historically, theologically, and morally. Historically, the term identifies a religious movement that began in the first century, centered on the life and message of Jesus of Nazareth. Theologically, the term identifies a set of religious propositions that claim to be the product of God's revelation to mankind, ultimately completed in the life of Jesus Christ. Morally, the term is used to distinguish a certain kind of behavior that is congruent with commonly perceived expectations of the Christian tradition based on this revelation. Therefore, one could claim to *be Christian*, meaning that one is self-aware of being in a continuation of the historical tradition. This use may connote an intimate identification with the faith that gives personal meaning and direction to one's life. However, this use may merely mean one simply is aware of one's given heritage that has been shaped by an obvious Christian context, but to which one has little to no personal attachment. One could hold to *Christian beliefs*, meaning that one is convicted of the truth claims unique to the Christian message. Or, one could *act Christian*, meaning

that one conforms his or her behavior to certain moral expectations prescribed in the Bible, such as honesty, benevolence, or
self-control. This usage is often only mere moralism devoid of
any specific doctrinal commitments. To complicate the matter
further, "Bible-believing" Christians themselves possess vast
differences related to the areas of Christian history, theology,
and morality.

Also, a need persists to define the term *nation*. The etymology of the word as far back as the Latin *natio*, means "birth."
The words *native, nationality,* and *nativity* share the same root
with the word *nation*. Therefore, *nation* most literally refers to
a group of people who share a common birth, or ancestry. Today,
we typically use the word with a broader meaning not bound to
this etymology. Nation has come to be considered interchange-
able with the word *country*, which does not carry the meaning
of belonging by birth. The word *country* comes from the Latin
contra, meaning "against." Therefore, one's country is a place
of residence that defines one's identity and loyalty over and
against other places. Technically, it is more proper to speak of
the United States as a country rather than a nation. Nevertheless, these two words have essentially become synonyms in
modern usage. The reader will notice that I have consciously
chosen to employ the word *country* over the word *nation* in my
discussion. The word *country* better fits the context of early
American history. America from the beginning was an adopted
land for many nationalities.

Abstractly, the word *nation* is used to reference the entity
that is called the United States of America. The word is used in
the collective sense of identity that a people share. This more
abstract use of the word *nation* typically implies group solidar-
ity in heritage, spirit, and attitude. In this sense, being a nation
binds people together with a common identity that encapsu-
lates their personal differences. However, the word is used in
a more concrete manner as well. The term *nation* can be used
to identify an independent people and their governing agencies
that inhabit a specific geographical location. Concretely, the
word is used to reference the governmental infrastructure of the
country. In the United States, people often perceive themselves

individualistically and only think nationally in the matters of the necessities of civil government, the judiciary, and military.

A specific definition of the term *Christian* must be set forth if any discussion on the topic has a chance of being helpful. The term *Christian* is best used to refer to people who have been affected by the religious movement originating from the life and teachings of Jesus Christ, who proclaim a unique message of Jesus Christ as the Son of God, dying and rising to bring redemption from sin and victory over death to those who repent and believe, and whose faith commitments lead them to distinctive religious practices and cause them to embrace certain moral expectations. This is what I mean when I call a person *Christian,* either one I meet today or study as a historical figure. The witness of the historical commitments of people who have called themselves Christians is overwhelmingly congruent with this definition. Obviously, there remains a tremendous amount of room for diversity of thought on many specific topics of doctrine and practice; however, this definition is what I consider the reasonable, irreducible minimum.

When we use the word *Christian* as a modifier for the word *nation*, then we have somewhat altered the meaning of *Christian*. The definition above is an individualistic one. It describes a Christian person. But how does one describe a Christian nation? Again, the word *nation* has two senses—a group heritage to which one belongs by birth or choice, and a country's political organization and the territory it governs. Obviously, there is nothing religious per se about land or government institutions. However, we do properly use the word *nation* with the connotation of a group heritage and the ideological or religious commitments in general of that heritage. Therefore, the historian must carefully consider the interplay between the lives of individual Christians and the societal context within which they have lived. In the end, we must judge the significance of the influence of Christian individuals on the prevailing worldviews, religious beliefs and practices, and morality of the nation as a whole. There always have been individuals committed to belief in Christ and who have practiced and proclaimed that belief. This is the point at which the real debate starts. To what degree can we confidently assert that individual Christians have given shape to their culture throughout the history of the United States?

This essay will attempt to support the following thesis. Although the people who eventually became the United States of America came from a culturally Christian context, the primary shaping ideology of the Revolutionary period was that of the European Enlightenment. The key leaders of the American cause were given more to deistic and Unitarian tendencies in regards to religion and to secular Enlightenment theory in regard to politics. These ideologies were of such strength that even orthodox Christians were swept up into rebellion against their governing authorities and supportive of the secularization of government. The nineteenth century displayed a significant Christianization of the American people up through the Civil War, evidenced by revival and social reform. After the Civil War, steady decline in religious adherence was the impetus for evangelicals to mythologize American history and pine for a return to a golden age of Christian faith and virtue at its founding that never existed.

Prelude to a Country: 1607–1775

From the landing of the first brave colonists until the bold Declaration of Independence, Americans primarily understood themselves as British. They brought with them the English language, culture, religion, and intellectual assumptions. However, from the time the Pilgrims stepped off the *Mayflower* in 1620 until a new government was fully established in 1791, much of the social, economic, intellectual, and religious landscape changed. America was emerging as a country during a time when conceptions regarding politics and social order were undergoing significant changes. New paradigm-shifting ideas were fueling the politics that sparked rebellion. In this section, the intent is to consider the historical context within which the American colonies were emerging.

The first colonists and explorers to land on the shores of the territory that ultimately became the United States of America were conspicuously people from a culturally Christian context. All of these Europeans were not Christian in a qualitative sense, but their cultural identity during these centuries was distinctly part of the broader Christian tradition. They were not Muslims, Hindus, Buddhists, or any other of the world's major religions. Whether they might be described as committed, marginal, or hypocritical Christians, their cultural identity was overwhelmingly Christian. They came from countries where Christianity was the established religion. Some came primarily for the hope of economic gain; some came to establish the ideal Christian society. Many came fleeing the religious persecution and intolerance present in Europe. Regardless of their primary motivation, those who came to America in the seventeenth and eighteenth centuries possessed an indisputable broader Christian identity that surrounded their individuality.

The First English Settlements

Although the history of European influence in the Americas began with the Spanish and French, the English became the foundation for the United States of America.[2] The earliest attempt of colonization by the English in America began with the original 108 settlers planted on Roanoke Island located off the coast of North Carolina in 1585. Although these settlers became discouraged and returned home, another expedition set sail in 1587. However, four years later the settlers of the colony mysteriously vanished.[3]

The first successful band of English settlers founded Jamestown in 1607. Although this group's primary interest, under the direction of the Virginia Company of London, was establishing a colony for economic gain, they were not devoid of a Christian heritage or purpose. The original charter issued by the Virginia Company declared that "the true word, and service of God and Christian faith be preached, planted and used."[4] Intense conflicts with Native Americans and periods of starvation often occupied the primary concerns of these first colonists. However, the early charters of Virginia emphasized the priority of establishing Christian worship in the New World and evangelizing the indigenous people. Further examples of Christian primacy in Virginia include the colony's legislation that required each plantation to provide a place of worship, the colony's provision of lands to be used to support the Anglican ministry, and taxation of individual parishioners to support their local clergyman.

The group of English Separatists that set ashore far north of Jamestown in 1620 and called their settlement Plymouth carried an overtly religious mission. The journey of the Pilgrims to the New World began in Gainsborough, England, just after the turn of the seventeenth century. Here, English Separatists, those who had determined that the Church of England was either seriously corrupted in doctrine and practice or a false church altogether, gathered to worship out of the watchful eye of the state church. Furthermore, they rejected its episcopal government in which the bishops ruled. Instead, Separatists favored a presbyterian or congregational form of church government. Separatists themselves often disagreed with one another on just *how* separate "true believers" should be. Some took a more reforming attitude toward the Church of England and some more abrasively proclaimed it to be apostate. Separatists from the nearby town of Scrooby joined the Gainsborough congregation, and for some time these Christians worshipped together. However, the large group eventually divided into two smaller ones.

John Smyth, former Anglican minister turned Separatist, led one group that remained in Gainsborough. The other group began to gather at Scrooby under the initial leadership of Richard Clyfton. Both groups eventually fled to Amsterdam to escape religious persecution. The Smyth group, under the influence of Mennonite Anabaptists, came to reject the practice of infant baptism as a sign of the covenant between God and the church and adopted believer's baptism. Smyth re-baptized himself and his congregation in 1609. In 1611 a faction of this group followed Thomas Helwys back to England to establish the first Baptist church on English soil.

John Robinson became the pastor of the Scrooby group after its move to Leiden (Leyden), Holland, in 1609. Although he did not accompany the *Mayflower* Pilgrims, he was still their pastor when they departed from England in 1620 and had intentions of joining them; intentions were thwarted, however, by his death. For some time Holland was a safe haven for these English Separatists, but cultural and political issues prompted them to look across the Atlantic to the possibility of forging a new life away from the Old World. Resisting cultural assimilation was becoming increasingly difficult for the English families. Many of the youth were becoming accustomed to worldly compromises and irreligious living in the more liberal culture. In addition, mothers and fathers were finding it difficult to keep the children at home with the family. Some of the young men were leaving to become soldiers or seamen. Politically, what became known as the Thirty Years' War (1618–1648) threatened to end the decade of safety they had enjoyed as refugees in Holland.[5]

Those men and women who stepped off the *Mayflower* defined their venture in purely religious language. In the historic *Mayflower Compact* the colonists committed their allegiance to God and to one another. On November 21, 1620, forty-one men pledged their lives to one another "for the glory of God, and advancement of the Christian faith." Their goal was to establish a society that would have order and civility firmly rooted in the Puritan interpretation and application of the Bible. In his *Of Plymouth Plantation*, William Bradford (1589–1657) described the mind-set of these pioneers in the face of the harsh realities that awaited them. In the following passage Bradford gave the name *Pilgrim* to these English Separatists: "So they left the godly and pleasant city which had been their resting place near twelve years; but they knew they were pilgrims, and looked not much on those things but lifted their eyes to the heavens, their dearest country, and quieted their spirits."[6] Although numerous deaths punctuated the early years, the English Pilgrims persevered to more stable and prosperous times. Only twelve of the first twenty-six men and three of the eighteen married women survived the first winter.[7] Despite their hardship, these enduring Pilgrims began the American national holiday of Thanksgiving, which is celebrated the fourth Thursday in November. In October of 1621 Bradford declared a time of celebration in order to give thanks to God for the harvest. This festive occasion was celebrated with much food and games in the company of Chief Massasoit and his entourage of Native Americans.

The more populous Puritan colony of Massachusetts Bay absorbed the Plymouth colony in 1691. Religiously, it was a virtually seamless transition because the theological lines between

English Separatism and Puritanism were very fine. The one issue that had divided them in England—the validity of separation—seemed a moot point since both groups had physically separated themselves from England in their provincial setting. More than any other force, English Puritanism shaped American culture in the most densely populated and most influential region of the colonies prior to the American Revolution.

Puritanism of the New England Colonies

Puritanism arose as a Protestant movement in England during the reign of Elizabeth I in the latter half of the sixteenth century. Decades earlier, Henry VIII had severed ecclesiastical authority from the Pope in Rome in 1534 and declared the monarch of England to be the head of the church in England. This was the "top-down" manner in which the Protestant Reformation first impacted the Roman Catholic Church on English soil. For many, however, Anglicanism was simply a decapitated Roman Catholicism. Rome no longer had a say in the church's affairs, but the worship and practice of the church remained essentially Catholic. In time, further modifications occurred in doctrine and practice, but the church continued to feel too Catholic for many who wanted the reform in England to go further, as it had in places such as Geneva under the leadership of John Calvin. Eventually, a party of Christians labeled Puritans arose that expressed these concerns. Originally, they desired to bring greater reform to the Anglican Church and "purify" it from its remaining Catholic vestiges. After years of disappointment, many chose a new religious path, concluding that the state church in England was beyond hope, or worse, on a road back toward Roman Catholicism. Many began to perceive that relocation to a provincial setting was a viable option. In the 1630s a large migration of these Protestants made the sea voyage from England to colonial New England. Although economic arrangement with the chartering companies was a necessary ingredient of the overall enterprise, the Puritans understood their endeavor primarily as a holy quest. They viewed their task as establishing a distinctly Christian society that would serve as a model to future generations both in America and in England.

Understanding Puritanism properly demands stepping out of the individualistic and pragmatic mind-set of contemporary American culture. Whereas Americans today stress individuality in matters of religion, the Puritan ideal emphasized the community. At times this emphasis was so pronounced that it led to at least religious coercion and at worst religious persecution. In the Puritan worldview God had always worked and continued to work through covenants with his people. This covenant theology kindled their zeal for doctrinal and moral uniformity. They viewed religious diversity that might lead to heterodoxy as a danger to Christian society. Although Puritans had been the victims of religious discrimination as a dissenting faction in England, this reality did not lead them to abandon an establishment mentality in the New World. The existence of a state church did not trouble the Puritans in England, but rather alleged corruption in that church. One should not interpret the New England Puritans' insistence on religious conformity as hypocrisy, in which the persecuted, once in a more favorable context, became the persecutors. Rather, the Puritans inherited the religious-civil model that extended back into the Middle Ages. This model assumed the supportive role of the civil leaders for the church, primarily to enforce true religion and guard the land from dangerous heretics.

Modern Americans, typically driven by pragmatism in all areas of life, tend to judge any actions, methods, or attitudes by the end result. If something works, then it is good. If something achieves a desired goal, then it becomes acceptable despite any philosophical, theological, or sometimes ethical tensions it may induce. In contrast, New England Puritans evaluated every facet of life by the Bible. It was not only the source for what they believed about God, but also the guide for how they organized and conducted their lives. Although Puritans also emphasized learning in such disciplines as logic and rhetoric, the primacy of the Bible was always assumed. The Word of God, as Puritans most often referred to the Bible, was inspired and without error. They viewed the Bible as God's completed revelation to humanity that one should know and submit to without reservation.

The emphasis on knowing the Bible led Puritan New England to become one of the most literate communities on the globe during the seventeenth century. Puritans introduced the New England Primer into the Boston community in 1690 as the first printed textbook in America. The primer taught children the basics of reading using a rhyming alphabet with biblical content, Bible questions, and the Westminster Shorter Catechism. For one hundred years it served as the introductory text for learning the English language and underscored the prominent role that the Christian faith maintained in the lives of colonial New Englanders.[8] The "Old Deluder Satan Act" of 1647 serves as further evidence of the Puritan wedding of education and the Christian faith. The title of the act came from the legislation's preamble, which stated that Satan was the deluder who desired "to keep men from the knowledge of the Scriptures." This law required that each town of at least fifty families employ a teacher and that a town of one hundred households erect a grammar school.[9] Puritans founded Harvard College in 1636 to train clergy and educate young men to be responsible Christian citizens. Among the goals Harvard desired for its students in the institution's 1646 statutes was the basic desire that "every one shall consider the main end of his life and studies, to know God and Jesus Christ which is eternal life."[10]

The Puritan mind-set was one of hard work and fierce personal piety. When Puritans thought about anything, they considered the religious aspects first. The Christian faith dominated every part of their lives. In addition to the content of their educational textbooks, one can observe how early Puritan settlements methodically reflected the importance of the Christian faith. Their pervasive religious consciousness led them to intentionally locate the meetinghouse in the center of town, symbolizing the centrality of Christianity to the life of the community. The Puritan faith, however, was not a matter of symbol over substance. More than any other single factor, Christianity gave shape to the kind of society they hoped to build in America.

The Puritan ideal was one of simplicity in religious observance and moral purity in daily living. Their theological heritage was that of the Reformed tradition of John Calvin, with its stresses on the utter sinfulness of human nature and the complete sovereignty of God in matters of salvation and the affairs of men. The simple, undecorated buildings for worship were a reaction to what they perceived to be the pretentious, ornate style of Roman Catholicism that had led many down the path of idolatry with its use of icons. And whereas the Mass was the focus of Catholic worship, Puritans refocused their worship on the sermon.

Although Puritans used singing in their worship from the *Bay Psalm Book*, the first book printed in the New World, in 1640, the centrality of the Bible naturally led them to place the preaching and teaching of the Bible at the center of their religious activity. Typically, these sermons stressed the covenant relationship that the people needed to appreciate and keep with God. Historians have separated Puritan sermons into two categories: regular and occasional. The former were the weekly Sunday sermons that stressed the personal covenant God has extended to each sinful individual, and his or her responsibility to this gracious God. The latter were the less frequent sermons that applied the covenant theology to the entire community, emphasizing the importance of continued obedience and moral living of the group.[11] For colonial New Englanders the sermon was the primary source for dissemination of information, both religious and nonreligious. This reality, and the fact that he had a somewhat captive audience, naturally made the clergyman the community's most prominent and influential figure. Mark Noll estimated that the typical New Englander who lived a full life would have listened to around seven thousand two-hour-long sermons.[12]

In the Puritan mind-set, civil and ecclesiastical affairs were inseparable. Some compartmentalization of the sacred and the secular existed, but they did not isolate one realm from the other. Puritans assumed society to be founded on Christian doctrine and practice, and the Christian faith was an inseparable part of true civilization. One could not exist without the other. Collectively, the Puritans perceived their venture in the New World as a holy endeavor to establish a working society that would be governed by Calvinistic Protestantism. They understood their mission in terms of the idea of covenant. Their first governor, John Winthrop, wrote,

> We are entered into covenant with him for this work. . . . For this end, we must be knit together in this work as one man, we must entertain each other in brotherly affection. . . . We shall find that the God of Israel is among us, when ten of us shall be able to resist a thousand of our enemies, when he shall make us a praise and glory, than men shall say of succeeding plantations: the Lord make it like that of New England: for we must consider that we shall be as a city upon a hill, the eyes of all people are upon us.[13]

The thought that life could operate in nonintersecting political and religious spheres was inconceivable. To fulfill this kind of grand religious dream, the coercive arm of the civil magistrate was necessary. For a while this ideal was reality in colonial New England but, in the end, a short-lived one.

In time, dissenting voices arose against the Puritan worldview. Quakers and Baptists challenged the Puritan religious establishment, resulting in fines, imprisonments, public whippings, and a handful of executions. Individuals touting the concept of true religious liberty began to challenge the Puritans' Old World assumption that religious conformity was necessary to preserve orthodoxy. The best example of this struggle in early colonial New England was the dialogue between John Cotton, the beloved Puritan clergyman who served at Boston's Congregational Church for nearly twenty years, and the Puritan turned more radical Separatist, Roger Williams. According to the Puritans' Cambridge Platform of 1648, the civil government and the church functioned in cooperation to ensure the observance of true religion within the community. This statement created by a gathering of Congregational ministers declared that "it is the duty of the magistrate, to take care of matters of religion, and to improve his civil authority for the observing of the duties commanded in the first, as well as for observing the duties commanded in the second table. . . . The end of the magistrate's office, is not only the quiet & peaceable life of the subject, in matters of righteousness & honesty, but also in matters of godliness, yea of all godliness."[14] Four years previously Williams had published a work titled *The Bloudy Tenet of Persecution*. The radical nature of his work in Willliams's own time is difficult for contemporary Americans to appreciate. Although Williams did not win the battle of ideas in his lifetime, his concept of religious liberty did become a distinguishing feature of the new nation about a century later. Whereas Cotton declared with a medieval mind-set that a religious heretic is "not persecuted for cause of conscience, but for sinning against his own conscience," Williams asserted that real liberty should be granted to "the most Paganish, Jewish, Turkish, or Antichristian consciences and worships."[15] At the heart of their debate existed a fundamental disagreement over the definition of conscience. Williams defined religious conscience in the more modern sense—what one chooses to believe freely. In contrast, Cotton understood that true religious conscience rightly informed one's mind, and a person with a rightly informed conscience should not be persecuted.

Williams contended that the civil government could only rightly enforce the second table of the Ten Commandments, which deals with an individual's relationships with others. However, the first table of the commandments (the first four) strictly concerns matters of religious conscience, and the civil magistrate should have no jurisdiction over these. In addition, Williams argued from history. He cited numerous examples of religious persecution in the colonies in an attempt to show how religious coercion inevitably leads to sinful acts of persecution. In the end, other voices echoed and joined Williams's to make certain that Americans would have political assurances of true religious liberty.

The Puritan way of the New England colonies began to wane in the next several generations. The native-born American Puritans did not collectively possess the passion for righteousness that virtually defined the existence of their fathers and grandfathers. Nor had they known firsthand the religious predicaments of the cultural context of England that gave a sense of urgency to the original Puritan cause. In time they softened the religious requirements of the communities, and fewer people were participating in the church, particularly as converted members. By the eve of the American Revolution church membership and religious adherence had dramatically declined. However, Puritan New England was, for a short time, the most thoroughly Christian society America has ever seen.

Religious Diversity Outside New England

Although the Puritan endeavor was the most purely Christian undertaking in the American colonies, those who settled in regions south of Boston bore an overall distinctly Christian identity as well, albeit a less zealous and more diverse one. The middle colonies were home to various Christian groups that allowed more freedom of individual choice in religious matters and practiced more toleration. One author described seventeenth-century colonial America outside Puritan New England as "a mosaic of Christian faiths."[16]

Quakers made their home in Pennsylvania, as did many others such as Lutherans, Moravians, Mennonites, Amish, and various Reformed traditions. William Penn, America's best-known Quaker, secured a charter from the British crown as compensation for debts owed to his father. True to Quaker belief and practice, Penn established a settlement that assured all the colony's residents an environment in which each could follow his or her religious conscience without fear of discrimination or persecution. In 1682 the settlement of Philadelphia, "the city of brotherly love," was founded and the colony flourished under the banner of religious freedom. Likewise, the colony of Delaware, originally part of Pennsylvania, never officially established one particular church and became home to various groups, including Dutch Reformed, Lutherans, and Anglicans.

Because of the reality of religious diversity, particularly in the middle colonies, their charters established no official church. Rhode Island and New Jersey were also home to a variety of brands of Christianity. The early religious diversity that existed in these colonies foreshadowed the religiously pluralistic landscape of the United States. However, this diversity typically did not include the acceptance of clearly non-Christian practices. For example, in Quaker Pennsylvania, laws mandated that any civil officer must affirm the deity of Christ. Laws also forbade practices such as blasphemy and working on Sunday. Despite their more open disposition in matters of religion, these middle colonies in the colonial period still "discriminated against

Catholics and Jews and punished blasphemers who spoke ill of Protestant Christianity."[17]

Baptists began their existence in the New World in Rhode Island under the pioneering work of Roger Williams and John Clarke. Williams and Clarke led the attack on the establishment mentality of New England Puritans, and worked to secure charters for the colony that, like Pennsylvania, would secure freedom from persecution in matters of religious conscience. Clarke, himself imprisoned and fined by New England Puritans, became a strong advocate of religious liberty as exemplified in his work *Ill News from New England* (1652). Clarke, more so than Williams, was a consistent and visible figure for the embryonic American Baptists at this time.

Those loyal to the Church of England predominantly populated the Southern colonies, including Virginia, the Carolinas, and Georgia. George Calvert (Lord Baltimore) chartered Maryland as a haven for Roman Catholics, but in time the Church of England became the established church there as well. In contrast with the settlements of New England, more people in the Southern and middle colonies lived in rural settings. Puritans possessed a greater sense of connectedness because of their emphasis on community and covenant, but they succeeded in realizing a Christian community largely because of individuals' close proximity to one another. Conversely, the geographical distance and relative isolation of the residents of the colonists outside New England made such religious cohesion extremely difficult. For example, in Virginia the average sized parish for a single Anglican minister measured 550 square miles in 1724.[18]

In spite of the less intense and more diverse nature of colonial Christianity outside New England, colonists in these areas still exhibited sufficient evidence to demonstrate the importance of the Christian faith to their culture. This claim does not imply that every individual was personally guided by sincere Christian belief that produced "Christian" behavior. Certainly, Christian influence south of Boston was anemic when compared with Puritan New England. But this difference is only one of degree and not essence. The Southern colonies had clearly established the Church of England. The fact that the middle colonies resisted established religion is proof that the

Christian faith was of primary interest to those who secured such guarantees. Those who led the charge for true religious liberty simply had a different conception of what kind of environment was most conducive to the prosperity of the Christian faith.

In general, three trends characterized the colonies at the beginning of the eighteenth century. Every colony embraced Protestant Christianity and perceived the Bible as central to belief and practice. Further, the colonies desired to ensure that Christianity be favored, even if not officially established in charter. Finally, Christian practice began to wane and people's beliefs were not congruent with certain behaviors, such as in the Southern states' acceptance and defense of slavery.

The Great Awakening

What historians often call the Great Awakening affected the colonies in an unprecedented, corporate manner. Periodic waves of revivalism burned with intensity from place to place during the 1730s and 1740s in New England and as late as the 1760s in the Southern colonies. This spike of spiritual fervor interrupted a trend of overall decline in religious adherence. Religion became the hot topic of conversation and debate and the favored subject for the growing circulation of newspapers. Even if one had remained personally indifferent to the awakening, he certainly would not have been ignorant of it, its impact on the lives of many around him, or the controversies that surrounded it.

Christian groups divided over issues associated with these outbreaks of revival. Congregationalists (Puritans) and Presbyterians separated into pro-revival and anti-revival factions. Those who reacted favorably to the revivals tended to embrace the growing democratic spirit and individualism that were emerging as defining characteristics of American culture. Those who were critical of the revivalism tended to feel more secure with the status quo, frowned on the emotional excess, and were suspicious of the veracity of those who promoted it.

Although the theological center of this revivalism reflected a strong traditional, Calvinistic heritage, the awakening introduced a number of innovations into the religious life of colonial

Americans. The itinerant ministry of the Anglican George Whitefield popularized a new style of preaching that was more appealing to the populace. Instead of reading from a manuscript, he preached extemporaneously. In addition, Whitefield employed an uncommon flare for the dramatic and apparently possessed a rare charisma. In 1738 he arrived for his first of seven preaching tours of the colonies and immediately became a sensation as word spread concerning his ministry. Whitefield did not hesitate to break with tradition and etiquette by gathering large crowds in open fields and on riverbanks. Hundreds would flock to hear him preach, and eyewitnesses reported many conversions to the Christian faith.[19]

Gilbert Tennent was a fiery Presbyterian who was accused of simply being a Whitefield impersonator. Regardless of the validity of the accusation, Tennent shone as a successful evangelist as well during the awakening. Historians remember him primarily for his openly harsh criticism of much of the established clergy in the colonies. In his sermon, "The Danger of an Unconverted Ministry," he cited the failure of many preachers to induce revival and spiritual fervor in their people as proof of their own unregenerate condition. In addition, he admonished those who were not content with their parish minister of "lesser gifts" to seek out another who would supply what is "most good to his precious soul."

Jonathan Edwards, the most notable minister during this period, experienced firsthand spontaneous seasons of revival among his congregation in Northampton, Massachusetts, beginning in 1734.[20] Edwards reported that as people anguished over their sinfulness they often became emotionally broken. People wept bitterly, shouted and shrieked, and even physically collapsed as they heard the messages that emphasized the seriousness of sin and the reality of God's judgment. At other times converts would laugh aloud, clap their hands, shout, and sing. Those like Whitefield, Tennent, and Edwards interpreted these demonstrations as positive signs of true revival. Edwards, primarily known as one of America's great theologians (if not the greatest), was also a strong supporter of and participant in the awakening. In 1741 he published his sermon "The Distinguishing Marks of a Work of the Spirit of God." He defended the validity of revivalism, including its controversial emotionalism. Edwards claimed that God had left sufficient instruction in the Bible to "proceed safely in judging of spirits, and distinguish the true from the false." He claimed that certain items should not be used as evidence for judging an event not to be the work of God, such as an unprecedented level of emotional manifestations. Furthermore, he claimed that such emotional reactions are consistent with a proper apprehension of the gospel message. When sinners truly recognize their condemned state before God, then emotional displays of this distress are appropriate. Likewise, when sinners come into fellowship with God by the receiving of grace, then extraordinary displays of joy are equally appropriate. Edwards even allowed for what modern Americans could only call charismatic-like ecstasy, including visions and "glorious sights." Edwards is most well known for his straightforward sermon "Sinners in the Hands of an Angry God," which paints a vivid picture of the peril of being under the condemnation of God. He defended this sort of preaching in "The Distinguishing Marks." He stated, "Some talk of it as an unreasonable thing to fright persons to heaven; but I think it is a reasonable thing to endeavor to fright persons away from hell, that stand upon the brink of it, and are just ready to fall into it, and are senseless of their danger."[21] Edwards argued that certain positive marks do testify to an authentic work of God. A work can be confidently affirmed as a true work of God when the gospel story is received and believed, sinful behavior is eliminated, the Bible is revered as God's Word, and love is demonstrated among people.

Not all, however, shared Edwards's optimism. The best-known critic of the revivals was the Congregationalist Charles Chauncy. He believed the "enthusiasm" of the awakening to be nothing more than mere emotionalism run amuck. In a letter he described the nature of the preaching style of Tennent as possessing "much noise and little connection." In his criticism of the emotional nature of the revivals, Chauncy wrote, "They observed no stated method, but proceeded as their present thought or fancy led them: And by this means the meeting-house would be filled with what I could not but judge great confusion and disorder." His most poignant criticism, however, struck at the heart of Edwards's argument. He claimed that he had not observed "that men have been made better, if hereby be meant, their being formed to a nearer resemblance to the Divine Being in moral holiness."[22]

Although the Great Awakening appears to have not brought any measurable social improvements, such as movements to abolish slavery or alcohol, or lasting growth to the churches, none can deny that the written record reveals that something happened of religious and social significance. The actual term, *Great Awakening*, was not applied to these eighteenth-century events until the 1840s. Today, historians still debate whether or not the revivalism was truly an awakening that further Christianized the culture. None would doubt that revivalism did take place, but its extent and true impact is debated.[23] The Great Awakening laid a foundation for the revivalism that would come to epitomize Protestant Evangelicalism a century later, including its emphasis on individualism, favor toward emotionalism, the popularization of traveling evangelists, dramatic conversion, and dethroning of traditional religious authorities. Two groups, small at that time, the Methodists and Baptists, became the two largest Christian groups by the middle of the nineteenth century largely because of their embracing and utilization of revivalism. Becoming Christian became much more a matter of personal choice rather than merely a perpetuation of a religious heritage.

An Era of Visionary Christians

This most immediate prelude to United States history—the colonial period—was a time of exploration, settlement, conquest, and religious mission. Among the variety of reasons Europeans began to leave their homelands and come to the North American east coast, the search for religious freedom was foremost for many. The Reformation had tremendously destabilized European society. Tens of thousands had died in "religious" wars, and many more had become the objects of intolerance, persecution, and discrimination by governing authorities because of their dissenting religious views and practices. Because of these realities many began to look optimistically to the New World as an escape from persecution and an opportunity for truer religion. However, these visions of a truer Christian religion did not always agree with one another once planted side-by-side on American soil.

The Puritan quest was essentially to create a Christian society. As noted previously, the first generations of English Puritans that began to populate Boston and its surrounding areas were as religiously motivated as any people that have ever lived in America. They viewed the culture through a biblical lens. In addition, they still maintained a complementary view of church and state. Each one needed the other for support in the combined effort to produce a society that existed for the glory of God. Although the Anglican Church also had its representatives in the colonies, Anglicanism did not tend to match the zeal and tenacious spirit of the Puritans.

Those who emerged as dissenting religious voices in the colonies often were just as enthusiastic for religious devotion as the Puritans. Their vision for Christians, however, possessed some significant differences. Groups of Quakers, Baptists, and Presbyterians often upset the religious status quo of Puritans and Anglicans with their stubborn independency and challenge to some traditional views concerning Christian doctrine and practice. Probably the most significant point of their deviance from the norm was their advocacy for a free church separated from the intrusion of government. According to these Christians, the church and state ought not be thought of as coterminous. The true church is to be separate and come out of the culture.

The so-called Great Awakening sparked a visionary interest as well among many evangelical Christians in the time period. Many heralded the revivals as a "great work of God" and many (including Jonathan Edwards) surmised what they were observing was likely the dawn of the Christian millennium. However, the revival fires soon dwindled and other pressing matters captured people's attentions. Of greater significance, the public concentration on the preacher shifted to the revolutionary statesman, and the impact of Enlightenment thought began to make its ideas felt during the founding years in both the realms of politics and religion, causing the original, bold Christian vision of the earliest English colonists to deteriorate.

Creating a Country: 1775–1783

There has been no more romanticized and memorialized era in American history than the founding period. The high ideals, bravery, and the achievement of the underdogs naturally capture our attention. We have immortalized (for our American moment) the leaders of the Revolution in monuments, paintings, and appellations, and on our money. We tend to think of the Founders with idealized thoughts and speak of them with grandiose language. Often, evangelical Christians add to this idealization a sacrosanct quality which equates the American cause to God's cause. However, this is not an entirely new understanding. Even at the birth of the United States many Christians equated the American cause with God's cause.

Nathan Hatch observed of New England clergy a tendency to view the Revolution as a cosmic struggle. "Sermons during the war stressed repeatedly that American liberty was God's cause, that British tyranny was Antichrist's, and that sin was failure to fight the British."[24] Hatch contends that the clergy transferred the millennial hopes that emerged in the Great Awakening to the political and military struggles after the revivals had burned out, first in the defeat of the despotic, Catholic French and then in the struggle against their own oppressive government. The line between Christianity and nationalism became extremely fine—at times practically imperceptible. The cause for independence became God's sacred cause for the American people.

Rebellious Christians

One of the most vexing questions for critically thinking American Christians concerns the validity of the nation's beginning. When a group of elite men took matters into their own hands and declared their independence from the mother country they also initiated a questionable course of action for Bible-believing Christians. How could a Christian people blatantly rebel against the governing authorities (Romans 13)?

When events began to become extremely tense in 1775, Christians found themselves divided on the issue of separation. Some, swept up in the dissent against the British government, embraced the thought of revolution. These did not sense (or at least admit) that there was a conflict between the teaching of Scripture and seeking independence. Others, firmly tethered to the Scriptures and out of a sense of loyalty, denounced the swelling movement to separate from England.

Two prominent Presbyterian clergymen of the Revolutionary period illustrate this polarization well. John Witherspoon emigrated from Scotland in 1768 to become the president of the College of New Jersey (Princeton). He was a staunch conservative Calvinist who joined the cause for liberty without hesitation. He was elected to the Continental Congress, and he holds the distinction of being the only clergyman who signed the Declaration of Independence. John Zubly was a wealthy planter and pastor in Savannah, Georgia. When the push for independence reached its critical mass, Zubly decided not to throw in his lot with those who were rebelling against their government. Although elected as well to the Continental Congress, Zubly withdrew after he determined that a loyalist position had no welcomed place at the debating table.

These two clergymen are an example of the religious question that Christian men had to resolve concerning the validity of rebellion.[25] Those like Zubly concluded that neither Christian history nor the Bible condoned citizens of a nation picking up weapons and violently rebelling against a divinely appointed and established government. The fact that this government should be acting irresponsibly and somewhat brutish toward its colonial subjects was irrelevant. The overarching, primary principle that steered him toward loyalty was the biblical mandate of submissiveness to government. He simply preached what Scripture clearly stated: "Everyone must submit to the governing authorities, for there is no authority except from God, and those that exist are instituted by God. So then, the one who resists the authority is opposing God's command, and those who oppose it will bring judgment on themselves" (Rom 13:1–2). Zubly was well aware that the colonists had issues with taxation measures levied against them; however, he did not consider burdensome or ill-conceived taxation as a legitimate reason for armed rebellion. He did not turn a blind eye to the blunderings of the English ministry, and he remained a loyal citizen. He rejoiced like other colonists when Parliament repealed the Stamp Act, but he would not allow himself to be swept away by the tidal wave of political dissent. He was sympathetic to the colonists' complaints, but he would not add sin to sin by rebelling. As a Christian he was bound to "pay your obligations to everyone: taxes to those you owe taxes, tolls to those you owe tolls, respect to those you owe respect, and honor to those you owe honor" (Rom 13:7).

Witherspoon rationalized that resistance against tyrannical government was essentially a duty of all citizens, including Christians. He simply ignored such biblical passages that Zubly accentuated. Patriot clergy like Witherspoon rallied colonists to the cause for independence, creating a confluence of political cause and religious devotion. This fact begs the question of appropriateness. Was it "Christian" for people to rebel against their government, asserting their independence, and spilling blood to achieve their goal? Ultimately, the answer must be no, if what we take as our definition of Christian is to be a person who possesses personal faith in Jesus, believes the Bible, and attempts to put its principles and precepts into practice. This is not to say that many of the people involved in it were not Christian, like John Witherspoon. However, it does demonstrate how political ideas and patriotism can take on a spiritual spin, and how Christians and skeptics alike can find common ground on words such as freedom, liberty, and human rights. The noteworthy trio of American Christian historians, Mark Noll, Nathan Hatch, and George Marsden, stated, "The Revolution was not Christian, but it stood for many things compatible with the Christian faith. It was not biblical, though many of its leaders respected Scripture. It did not establish the United States on a Christian foundation, even if it created many commendable precedents."[26]

The Enlightenment Influence

Without discounting religious motivations of Christians during the Revolutionary period, a good historical interpretation must account for the force of social and political ideas emanating from those representatives of the Enlightenment. Although many Christians raised the banner and baptized the cause for independence into their Christian worldview, it was the ideas flowing from the European Enlightenment that had finally moved from mere theory to implementation in the American Revolution.

As Enlightenment thought traversed the Atlantic to the American shore it gradually impacted American culture. It was rarely as radically expressed or overtly anti-Christian as much of its European counterpart; however, its core commitments were essentially the same. Enlightenment thought was above all a confidence in human reason (at least in the intellectual elite). The Enlightenment came on the heels of the period of cultural Renaissance and religious Reformation in Europe in the sixteenth century. Western civilization was in a new era of scientific discovery, technological advance, exploration of the rest of the globe, and rethinking the old ideas that defined government and social arrangements. In the century following the Reformation many Europeans became disillusioned and sometimes even antagonistic toward traditional Christianity. Religious warfare and the advances related to the so-called "Age of Reason" combined to introduce a skepticism now more boldly vocalized.

The moderate form of the Enlightenment that became fashionable among America's educated minority in the eighteenth century was the kind that seemed to promise to be able to hold together faith and reason. The systems of John Newton and John Locke appeared to Christian thinkers as completely congruent with Christian faith, as they did to those men themselves. Typically, Christian philosophers assumed that the teachings of the Christian faith and sound reason would never be contradictory.[27]

Ultimately, the Scottish philosophers emerged as most influential in America. Educators, such as John Witherspoon, introduced their thought in the latter decades of the eighteenth century; this dominated academia through the first half of the nineteenth century. The Scottish version of Enlightenment focused more on practicality and became known as Common Sense Realism. It stressed with confidence that cause and effect were intelligible objects of human reason and that the human senses could be trusted to communicate reality. Thus, humanity's "common senses" were reliable. In addition, all humans possessed a moral sense in regard to issues of virtue. This philosophy seemed to be the weapon of choice for intellectuals to fend off the more skeptical philosophies produced during the Enlightenment. In regard to religion, it most importantly allowed Protestant Christians to incorporate a part of the Enlightenment that was not overtly hostile to the tenets of Christianity. However, even the apparently most congruent forms of the Enlightenment still elevated human reason to a point of equality with divine revelation or above it. Consequently, this rationalism considerably eroded trust in the Bible, even though Christianity would emerge as a stronger cultural influence in the next century. The Enlightenment did not ultimately displace Christianity, but it did alter Christianity. Mark Noll has observed that three streams of ideas converged in the eighteenth century that gave a unique shape to nineteenth-century American culture and Christianity. These were Protestant Christianity, republican political ideas, and common sense moral philosophy.[28]

During the period of the American Revolution, the Enlightenment was at its strongest among the educated elite. The radical political ideas emerging from English and French philosophers became the inspiration for the Founding Fathers. A rejection of hereditary authority and monarchy as arbitrary power and the touting of ideas such as social compact and republicanism were not flowing from the Bible, but from Locke, Rousseau, and Montesquieu. It is not surprising at all to observe that many of the Founding Fathers were men of the Enlightenment, certainly in politics and often in their rationalized version of religion.

An Era of Politicized Christians

The Revolutionary period poses some interesting challenges in regard to American Christian history. This is the founding period of the country that went on to become the greatest world power of the modern era. Still, at the beginning of the twenty-first century, America looms large in the global scene politically, economically, and militarily. However, the beginning was fraught with serious uncertainty about the possibility of military success and disagreement among the colonists over whether separation was either right or wise. This political crisis ultimately forced professing Christians to choose a side. The major issue was whether or not rebellion against England was religiously justifiable. Those who kept their views closely tied to the contents of Scripture found that the cause for independence was nothing more than rebellion, which the Bible clearly condemned. Those Christians who supported physical resistance against the tyranny of Britain generally turned to Enlightenment rhetoric for validation, propped up by poor exegesis and application of the Bible.

With the 1783 Treaty of Paris, the improbable had become reality. The American colonists had fought and won their independence from the greatest military power in the world. Of course, those who had joined the cause reaped the benefits of victory; those who had opposed it lost considerably. During the course of the war John Witherspoon emerged as a leading "Son of Liberty." Today, one still reads books about him as a patriot, politician, and preacher.[29] In Princeton, New Jersey, one can find Witherspoon Street. In contrast, John Zubly suffered imprisonment, the destruction or confiscation of much of his property, and the ignoble label of "Tory."

Forming a Country: 1783–1791

The Founding Fathers

Much historical research and writing has focused on the lives and thoughts of the Founding Fathers of the United States. Biographies abound on American heroes such as Thomas Jefferson, George Washington, Benjamin Franklin, John Adams, and James Madison. The United States remains indebted to such men's courage, vision, and fortitude. The purpose here is to investigate the apparent religious dispositions of those who led the cause for independence in the quest to gain a clearer picture of America's religious heritage.[30]

It is a common teaching that the Founding Fathers were given to a pronounced rationalism in matters of religion informed by the European Enlightenment. The Enlightenment impacted European minds in two general areas: politics and religion.

Politically, the Enlightenment introduced new concepts of society and government. English and French political philosophers were arriving at revolutionary conclusions concerning the best forms of government. Ideas emerged that argued against the historical monarchical forms of government in which authority was an inherited right. Instead, the best government was one in which the people entered into a social compact in which those governed chose the governors. Also, government should consist of various branches of government that would "check and balance" each other. The republican government based on democratic ideals would be the best safeguard against arbitrary power and political tyranny. As common as these thoughts are to Americans today, they were somewhat novel in the eighteenth century. Regardless of their personal religious convictions, the Founding Fathers adopted the political concepts of the Enlightenment.

Religiously, the Enlightenment worked itself out by making religion more natural and universal. Parallel to Newton's natural laws that gave order and predictability to the universe, "enlightened" religion tended to eliminate the supernatural claims of traditional Christianity. Enlightened men regarded biblical accounts of miracles as mere embellishments—the product of superstition, ignorance, and propaganda. Additionally, "enlightened" religion tended to contend that true religion must be by definition universal to all humanity. This concept dismissed any notion of a special revelation given to a particular people at a particular point in history. This naturalization and universalization of the Christian faith led to the emergence of deism, a belief in an impersonal God who has essentially revealed himself universally to all men through nature. The result of this knowledge of deity should lead one to live a moral life. Deists could talk about *acting Christian* because Jesus was a moral man, but they certainly did not believe in the traditional theological tenets of the Christian faith concerning Jesus. In other words, one believed in being *like* Jesus, but not *in* Jesus. Many of the Founding Fathers fit into this religious category. A few prominent examples will demonstrate this reality.

George Washington has been somewhat a religious enigma for historians.[31] On the one hand, he possessed a traditional Christian upbringing within the Anglican Church of Virginia. On the other hand, he displayed a curious reticence about his personal faith that leads one to suspect the level of his commitment to a specifically Christian faith. There is no doubt that he employed the jargon more congruent with deists than traditional Christians. Where he spoke of God or religion incidentally, as statesmen do, in speeches, letters, official statements or orders, he typically chose the enlightened version of God. Biblical titles for God such as Heavenly Father or Lord, and for Jesus such as Savior or Redeemer, do not appear. Instead, Washington demonstrates a clear preference for more generic and depersonalizing titles such as Providence, Heaven, Deity, Supreme Being, Grand Architect, Author of all Good, and Great Ruler of Events.[32]

Washington did attend worship services in the Episcopal Church, although not consistently. What may be most curious, however, is that those around him, including family, friends, and clergy, observed that he conspicuously did not take communion. He never gave an explicit reason for this evasive behavior. Some have suggested that he felt unworthy to receive the elements, possibly heeding the warnings of 1 Corinthians 11. Most likely, Washington found the ritual of the "faithful" partaking of Christ's body and blood offensive to reason and incredulous. Washington, like many other men of his day, affirmed a generic divine providence that governed the affairs of men, but he does not appear to have put a significant emphasis on the dogmas of Christian faith in particular.

The responsible historian must take into account with a figure like Washington the tendency to mythologize. Washington was without doubt the most revered of the Founding Fathers. He was the president who could have been king. He became the symbol of American greatness and virtue. Just as he stood head and shoulders physically above others in a crowd, his personal and political stoic nature engendered almost a religious reverence from others. Early biographies of Washington displayed tendencies to incorporate hearsay as evidence of Washington's supposed Christian piety.[33] Such stories of him conducting communion services before battles, kneeling in prayer in the forest, and the most famous cherry tree incident are, at best, historically weak evidence for Washington's alleged orthodox Christian faith. The better historical evidence paints a picture of Washington as, at best, a marginally committed Anglican who personally held significant skepticism toward the tenets of traditional Christian faith.

Benjamin Franklin was self-educated and the most prominent common man from the Founding Era.[34] However, there was nothing common about the man. His insatiable curiosity and industry led Franklin to distinguish himself among his peers. He was a statesman and diplomat, an inventor and a publisher and writer. The combination of his homespun wit, common sense, and eloquence (not to mention his unpretentious dress) endeared him to many in America, England, and France.

Religiously, Franklin evidenced skepticism toward traditional Christian tenets early in his life. He infrequently attended religious services, although he always made clear his belief in God and the benefit of attending church for encouraging a virtuous society. Like other Founding Fathers (and American politicians in general), Franklin did not major on religious discussion or debate in his extremely public life. When he did speak to religion more directly, he clearly placed himself within the rationalistic and moralistic deism popular in his day. He affirmed the reality of a creator who governed the universe and that the way to render proper reverence to this God was through a moral life that was devoted to doing good for others. Franklin had little to say about Jesus except that he admired his morality and doubted his divinity.

John Adams can appear much more Christian than many of the other Founding Fathers, but in fact he was a Unitarian.[35] New England Unitarianism contended that the original, biblical, and rational form of Christianity was not Trinitarian. Unitarians like Adams recognized the life, teaching, miracles, and redeeming work of Jesus Christ; however, they did not believe in his divinity. Unitarianism was the well-established liberal wing of New England Congregationalism during Adam's lifetime. Unitarians like Adams tended to see themselves as the restorers of "real" Christian faith before the religion of Jesus was turned into a religion about Jesus. The so-called Arian "heretics" from the early fourth century were in fact the true proponents of Christian faith. In addition, Adams rejected the Calvinistic teachings of the total depravity of man and the predestination of people to salvation prior to their existence. However, when Adams was compared with Thomas Jefferson during the election of 1800, supporters often labeled him the clear "Christian" candidate.

Thomas Jefferson has been one of the most cherished of American icons.[36] His enduring legacy is mostly attributed to, but certainly not limited to, his authorship of the Declaration of Independence. Religiously, Jefferson was given to a pronounced rationalism. However, throughout his life, he moved among the Virginian gentry who belonged to the Anglican Church. Like Washington, his cultural inheritance tied him to the institution of the Church of England, even if his own theological and intellectual convictions ran contrary to the official doctrines of the church. He believed that the era in which he lived was in the process of ushering in a more "enlightened" religion, most properly found in Unitarianism. Like Adams, Jefferson was a Unitarian, but with an anti-supernaturalist twist. For Jefferson, traditional Christianity with its belief in a triune God and the supernatural was the product of more ignorant and superstitious cultures of the past and contrary to reason. He believed that he was witnessing the generation that would shake off the burden of institutional Christianity, confidently and naïvely believing that all young men would embrace Unitarianism.

Although Jefferson remained within the circle of his Anglican upbringing and even went to church, one cannot fashion him into a Christian. Even though he respected much of what he believed Jesus taught, he did not believe that Jesus was the Savior, like Adams did. He rejected most of the Bible. He produced a gutted version of the New Testament, which he titled *The Life and Morals of Jesus*.[37] In it he excised all material of a supernatural quality. He reduced Jesus to a benevolent and eloquent moral philosopher who tragically died. Jefferson also founded the first intentionally secularized university in

America. His vision for the University of Virginia was for education finally free from traditional Christian dogma. He had a disdain for the influence that institutional Christianity had on education. At the University of Virginia there was no Christian curriculum and the school had no chaplain. Its faculty was comprised of Deists and Unitarians.

James Madison, our country's fourth president, began his religious journey within the boundaries of orthodox Christianity. Apparently, Madison's mother was a devout Anglican. The infant James received baptism and his upbringing as an Anglican within the established church of Virginia. As a young man his parents chose to send him to the more orthodox College of New Jersey (Princeton) rather than the increasingly liberal William and Mary. While at Princeton Madison gave all the signs of one given to a personal commitment to orthodox Christianity. After graduating he remained an extra year to "read divinity" under the tutelage of President John Witherspoon. Even after he began to pursue a life of statesmanship, he continued to conduct family worship in his home—a mark of orthodoxy.[38] However, as his life moved from a study of theology to a life of politics he became increasingly reticent concerning his personal religious views. Historically, it is difficult to know with certainty where Madison ended up religiously. He does not appear to have been antagonistic toward institutional Christianity, and he did not criticize the Christian faith like Jefferson. Madison was concerned greatly with putting an end to religious persecution and providing constitutionally for freedom for individual religious choice. Whether he leaned more toward a deistic religion in the end or returned to his orthodox roots seems to be consigned mostly to speculation with little strong evidence to support either claim.

Whereas the examples above demonstrate that some of the Founding Fathers were not Christian in their beliefs, the following men give more reliable evidence that they did embrace the cause for independence based on the same political ideologies, but maintained adherence to traditional Christian faith.[39]

Samuel Adams has been referred to as the "last of the Puritans" in the sense that he maintained an orthodox Christian faith although surrounded by deists and Unitarians. He represented Massachusetts in the Continental Congress from 1774 to 1778, being a leading advocate for independence. Unlike so many of his political colleagues, Adams was unquestionably orthodox as a Christian. His rhetoric evidences traditional religious language. He consistently places Jesus at the center of his religious comments, not as merely a moral philosopher, but as Savior and Lord. He led his household with disciplined religious observance, and he regularly attended church and strictly observed the Lord's Day. He often placed great emphasis on the longstanding Puritan notion of covenant. As America unfettered itself from British tyranny, Adams consistently contended that it must devote itself to honoring God to ensure the continued blessing of God.

Elias Boudinot is obscure compared with the more notable Founding Fathers; however, one should rightfully count him among them. He served as president of the Continental Congress, served on various committees, was a signatory of the Treaty of Paris, a representative from New Jersey, and director of the National Mint. As his name hints, Boudinot was of French Huguenot (Reformed Protestant) descent. He was just as involved in the life of the church as he was in politics. He served as president of the General Assembly of the Presbyterian Church, president of the New Jersey Bible Society, and as a founder and first president of the American Bible Society. In addition, he published religious works including *The Age of Revelation: The Age of Reason Shewn to be an Age of Infidelity* (1801), a rebuttal of Thomas Paine's deistic *Age of Reason*. In the dedication to his own daughter he explained:

> I chose to confine myself to the leading and essential facts of the Gospel, which are contradicted, or attempted to be turned into ridicule, by this writer. I have endeavoured to detect his [Paine's] falsehoods and misrepresentations, and to show his extreme ignorance of the divine scriptures, which he makes the subject of his animadversions—not knowing "they are the power of God unto salvation, to every one who believeth."[40]

John Jay may be the best-known Founding Father who appears to have been a Bible-believing Christian. Jay's service

is as impressive as any of the Founders. He served as president of the Continental Congress, and as ambassador to Spain
during the war, and helped negotiate the Treaty of Paris. After
the war he served as secretary of foreign affairs, the first Chief
Justice of the United States, and as the second governor of New
York, and contributed to the Federalist Papers. Like Boudinot,
Jay was an outspoken Christian. He involved himself in the
church and other Christian societies, such as those producing Bibles, and promoting Sunday schools and the abolition of
slavery. He served as the American Bible Society's president
in 1822. In the written evidence, Jay frequently employs overt,
orthodox Christian terminology.

John Adams called John Witherspoon a "leading Son of
Liberty." As mentioned previously, Witherspoon wholeheart-
edly joined the cause for independence while serving as the
president of the College of New Jersey. Witherspoon served in
the first Continental Congress, signed the Declaration of Independence, and served on various committees. Although many
historians have tagged Witherspoon as an enlightened thinker
in regard to his approach to education, he remained a firmly
committed Presbyterian minister. In Scotland he had champi-
oned conservative Christianity against the liberalizing effects
of the Enlightenment. In America he remained consistent in his
loyalty to the tenets of his Reformed heritage. As a statesman
and a preacher, Witherspoon stands out as a clear example of a
Christian founder.

From all of these examples it should be clear to the reader
that our Founding Fathers were just what we would expect—
a mixture of faith and faithlessness in regard to Christianity.
Some give evidence that they may have been genuine believers
in the gospel of Jesus Christ. Others give just as convincing
evidence that they rejected orthodox Christian beliefs and were
given to the deism or Unitarianism produced by the Enlightenment.

In spite of their religious differences, the Founding Fathers
shared a sincere conviction that the American colonies had
reached a watershed moment. Would the colonists bow to the
demands of the British king and Parliament, or would they
defy them and risk losing a military engagement? This chain

of rising tension began with the Stamp Act of 1765, designed to raise revenue for the empire in the American colonies by taxing all legal documents. Colonists immediately remonstrated against this legislation, insisting that it was unconstitutional to impose such a tax on people who were not represented in the body enacting the tax. Although the British Parliament repealed the Stamp Act in March of 1766, it immediately followed the repeal with the Declaratory Act, which stated that Parliament had the right to pass acts legally binding on the colonies in all matters. The 1767 Townshed Acts called for the dissolving of the New York Assembly because of its failure to comply with an earlier law that required the colonies to provide housing for British troops. The accompanying Revenue Act imposed taxes on colonial imports of paper, glass, paint, and tea. England appointed commissioners to the colonies to ensure that the taxes were collected. Skirmishes between colonists and British troops and revenue officials followed these acts of legislation, the Boston Massacre of March 5, 1770, being the most infamous. The 1774 Intolerable Acts (also known as the Coercive Acts) were a series of laws passed as punitive measures against Massachusetts after the colonists had established a pattern of resistance to British policies, most famously, in the Boston Tea Party of December 16, 1773. In September 1774, the First Continental Congress met in Philadelphia as the move toward independence gained speed. Warfare broke out in April 1775, at the Battles of Lexington and Concord. By August of that year George III proclaimed the colonies in an open state of rebellion and declared that now they must either submit to the Crown or triumph in their insurrection. In July 1776, fifty-six Patriot leaders signed Jefferson's Declaration of Independence and the point of no return was finally established.

The Founding Documents

The critical documents produced during the American Revolution and the early years of nation building must be considered in any serious discussion of the role of the Christian faith among the Founding Fathers. One important question should be posed about these documents. Do the foundational political documents of the United States explicitly or implicitly employ Christian ideas or declare Christian commitments?

The Declaration of Independence does not make any explicit references to the Christian faith. It does contain, however, four references to deity. God is invoked in the opening lines, which declare that people have a naturally given right by "Nature's God" to throw off the authority of an oppressive government. Also, the "Creator" bestows "unalienable Rights" on each human, granting each the basic right to "Life, Liberty, and the pursuit of Happiness." After the Declaration lists the colonies' grievances with George III, two more allusions to God appear toward the end of the document. The signers of the Declaration appeal to the "Supreme Judge of the world" to verify the validity of their intentions to separate from England. Lastly, the document closes with these words: "And for the support of this Declaration, with a firm reliance on the protection of Divine Providence, we mutually pledge to each other our Lives, our Fortunes, and our sacred Honor." Although there are significant references to God in this short document, one cannot realistically interpret them as distinctly Christian. A Christian could certainly be comfortable with the language. However, the deist and Unitarian could equally embrace the language with no intellectual tension. Since Jefferson was the primary author of the Declaration, the kind of religious language that it employs should be no surprise.

The Articles of Confederation became America's first formal attempt at setting up guidelines for a national government. The Founding Fathers first drafted the Articles in the late summer of 1776; however, they were not completely ratified by all thirteen colonies until March 1781. There is little of religious interest in the Articles. The thirteen articles are essentially pragmatic, dealing with the goal of mutual loyalty, issues of representation, taxes, boundary issues between states, regulating money, and so forth. The Congress arrived at these articles during the distraction and interruptions of the war, all the while negotiating the tension between the need for a national government and the desire for state sovereignty. The inadequacy of the document prompted the push for a better and more enduring document after victory had been secured over

Britain. In the conclusion of the Articles of Confederation rests the single reference to deity styled the "Great Governor of the World." Again, this ambiguous reference to God can politically work to the religious tastes of Christians and deists alike.

The Constitution, adopted as the guiding document for our federal government in 1787, makes no references to the divine other than the cursory "in the Year of our Lord" at its conclusion. The fact that the Constitution is silent in regard to the Christian religion is significant in itself. Unlike the Mayflower Compact there is no religious agenda in the Constitution. There is not a hint of desire in bringing glory to God or to advance Christianity in the society. The absence of such language, even as empty cultural formality, is highly conspicuous, and one should interpret it as a deliberate and strategic omission.[41]

Three Critical Issues: Federalism, Slavery, and Religion

Americans had won the war for their independence from Great Britain. However, they now had to find a way to bring thirteen independent former colonies together to make a unified country. The roadblocks to such unification were numerous. Immediately, competing visions for the nation began to emerge, and an acrimonious spirit often resulted between the parties committed to differing political ideologies. Leaders hotly debated how best to place a hedge of protection around the people's liberties and provide a governmental scheme that could provide for the common good—one that would have the most promise to provide the greatest context for societal stability and economic prosperity. As the discussion crystallized, the debate centered on the advantages and disadvantages of two different arrangements—the first being a paradigm that emphasized a strong federal government, the second being one that stressed a confederation of states with significant independence from the federal government.

The overarching concern during the late 1780s was about power. In whom should the new American government invest significant political power? The debate over the benefits and threats of a centralized government was intense. Federalists such as John Adams, Alexander Hamilton, and James Madison thought the best chance of success for the new country was a government that provided strength through unity. The only way such unity could be achieved was through a strong national government. Republicans like Jefferson feared the investment of power into a centralized government. The best chance for a just and free society that kept the human tendency to abuse power in check was in a confederation of sovereign states that voluntarily cooperated while maintaining a high degree of self-determination. In the decades following the Revolutionary War, bitter political fighting took place as the grand experiment of America took flight. In the end the Federalist vision prevailed, but not without much acrimony and ultimately a civil war.

One of the apparently glaring contradictions of the Revolutionary era is the fact that white slaveholding elites mounted a rebellion against the mother country, claiming that they would not be made slaves to British tyranny, while they held black Africans in bondage. This has been a consistent point of criticism aimed at the Founding Fathers. If the United States of America was in the process of being born a Christian country, then how could such a moral blind spot persist?

The institution of slavery at the time of the Revolution was as old as human history itself. Slavery had traversed the ages and was common all around the globe. The Bible itself attests to the fact that slavery was part of the social makeup of the ancient world. The Atlantic slave trade, however, introduced an unprecedented era in the transportation and selling of human beings for slave labor. The major colonizing nations of the time, namely England, France, Spain, and Portugal, all participated in removing Africans from the African west coast and shipping them to the New World. From French Canada to Spanish South America, settlers utilized African slave labor for the developing New World economy. During the eighteenth and nineteenth centuries, slave traders took millions of Africans to the New World. European investors in the mass production of products such as sugar, tobacco, coffee, and rice quickly came to depend on African slaves for huge profit margins. As planters produced these commodities in greater, less expensive quantities, the demands back in Europe for them increased, which in turn created more demand, which reinforced the need for slave labor.[42]

Compared with the Caribbean and South America the number of Africans imported to the British colonies of North America was significantly smaller, with most of it occurring before the American Revolution. The presence of black slaves throughout the colonies by the time of the Revolution was an accepted societal norm. However, as the crisis with the mother country spilled over into war, questions concerning slavery began to be posed by blacks and whites alike.

In the early years of desperation during the war the American government commissioned some black slaves to fight for the cause of independence, many earning their freedom through such service. Ideological questions soon surfaced among some who wondered about the propriety of claiming "natural rights" and "liberty" for oneself and denying it to another, simply based on ethnicity. It is well known that some key leaders, such as Thomas Jefferson and George Washington, owned slaves. How could these supposedly "Enlightened Christian" men condone such blatant hypocrisy? Most likely the answer lies in acknowledging the deeply seated racism that the typical white person of European descent had toward the black person of sub-Sahara Africa. Conceptualizing and treating Africans like beasts of burden had become a conditioned disposition for white Americans. The enslavement of millions of Africans in the New World helped to create the racism (viewing Africans as inferior), which in turn worked to justify holding them as slaves. The longer that slavery continued in the New World, the stronger the racism grew among whites. One can reasonably conclude that the reality of slavery caused the racism that would continue to persist long after the abolition of slavery.

As the Framers of the new country set about their work, the issue of slavery was unavoidable. By this time the leaders of the Southern colonies, particularly in South Carolina and Georgia, were against the emancipation of black slaves. Although the physical battle for independence had been won, the newborn country was anything but secure. As legislatures from these "united" states met to draw up the regulations by which the governors would govern, it was obvious that the slavery issue posed a great threat to the unity they needed. It seems clear that the consensus among the founding leaders was that the ideology of the Revolution would inevitably lead to the emancipation of black slaves. However, the consensus also was reached that the time for the application of "liberty" for all had not quite arrived. Therefore, the Constitution drafted and adopted in Philadelphia in 1787 provided the guarantee that the future Congress would not have the power to prohibit the importation of slaves until after 1807.[43]

This compromise over the great contradiction of slavery only delayed the inevitable controversy. In the meantime, while the infantile nation began to learn to walk, the American South became heavily dependent on slave labor and the reinforcing, coterminous racism deepened. Many of the Founding Fathers naïvely believed that slavery would die a natural death as "enlightened" men created an increasingly better society. Those who believed that the high-sounding words of the Declaration of Independence would eventually persuade all decent people to manumit their slaves greatly underestimated some ugly products of human depravity, including greed, racism, cruelty, and fear. In actuality, slavery was more strongly woven into the fabric of the American South in 1807 than it was in 1787.

The question of religion was also significant. Framers of the new government eventually settled on a new paradigm for the relationship between government and religion, specifically Christianity. Their immediate model was one they had inherited from the Reformation, particularly that of the Reformed tradition. From the earliest English Separatists and Puritans to the Anglicans, most Englishmen conceived that the government existed to promote and protect true religion. Only the more radically minded Anabaptists and Baptists dared to challenge this societal assumption. During the sixteenth and seventeenth centuries these groups of "free church" minded people were in the minority and lacked political power. However, by the time Americans secured independence from England, much had changed that ultimately altered how people began to think about the relationship between government and religion.

By the end of the Reformation, one of the consequences was becoming clearly evident—Christendom was irreparably fractured. The snowball effect of the early, successful dissent against Rome had resulted in many anti-Catholic groups that

had serious differences with each other. The American colonial experience had evidenced this new reality. Both Puritans
and Anglicans had unsuccessfully attempted to encourage and
enforce religious uniformity. However, the reality of a multi-
faceted religious landscape was inescapable. If a new nation
with Christian religious assumptions were to establish a state
church, then which one would it be? How could the government
establish one faith tradition (Congregationalism, Presbyterianism, Anglicanism) without unleashing a torrent of religious
dissent from the others and from the growing number of minority sects (Quakers, Baptists, Moravians)? Emerging from both
pragmatic and ideological arguments from Christians and non-
Christians, legislators reached a final answer to this vexing
problem over religion. Deists had long been accusing institutional Christianity of being an arbitrary power that had helped
inflict human suffering. Many minority Christians, such as
Quakers and Baptists, agreed from their experience. Prior to
the war, New England Congregationalism had been in serious
decline with the "enlightened" Unitarianism on the rise. During
the war the Anglican Church had suffered because of its attachment to the hierarchy of the Church of England. Therefore, circumstances had considerably weakened both of the established
forms of Christianity in the colonial period. They simply had no
real ability to stand against the inertia of the shifting thought
concerning the relationship of government and religion.

In the end, the First Amendment to the Constitution put
the immediate debate to rest. The federal government declared
that it would not establish any particular form of religion. Furthermore, the government would not intrude into the personal
religious lives of its citizens; it would guarantee all citizens the
right to observe or not observe religion according to their own
consciences. In other words, the government would no longer
see itself in a supporting role for religion. Religion would be a
personal and voluntary choice without interference or coercion
from the new federal government.

This new arrangement led to the common expression today
of "separation of church and state." The idea of a "wall of separation" is not stated in the Constitution or the First Amendment; however, the sentiment is present. The radical Roger

Williams wrote in the middle of the seventeenth century that a wall should exist between the two.[44] The disestablishment of religion is one of the most significant moments in American history. Today, we still find ourselves debating vigorously at times how to apply the idea to specific situations. The debate becomes particularly intense when religious activity intersects the domain of the public tax dollar.

An Era of Adjusting Christians

In these crucial beginning years of the history of the United States many challenges confronted American Christianity. The two significantly paradigm-shifting challenges were the rationalistic attacks of the Enlightenment on traditional, Bible-believing Christianity, and the official and intentional disestablishment of the church by the federal government. These realities brought a time of adjustment as Christians faced the fact that religion would truly be a voluntary commitment. The disentanglement of church and state took some time. Religious tests for public offices still existed in some places into the 1830s. However, the country made the transition, and the separation of church and state introduced a societal experiment that continues today.

Can the Christian historian credibly assert that the building blocks of the United States rest on biblical Christianity? Without denying the influence of the Christian tradition on English culture or the fact that individual Christians were involved, the answer to the question is no. The preponderance of evidence suggests strongly that the primary ideas that compelled the colonists to rebel against England and to establish their own nation germinated from the soil of the Enlightenment, not the Bible. The deist's worldview retained a place for the acknowledgment of divine providence, but jettisoned traditional Christian theological propositions concerning the person and work of Jesus. A significant number of the most influential men of the Founding Era were of this deistic / Unitarian mindset. Furthermore, the documents they produced to charter and guide the new country were obviously de-Christianized in comparison with earlier colonial documents, such as the Mayflower Compact or the charter of Harvard. Politically, the Founders intentionally secularized the state while the Christian religion and morality still guided many cultural assumptions. Individualism was the grand winner of the revolutionary period. In regard to religion, the individual could now choose with impunity to adhere to any variety of Christian faith or none at all.

It is hard to understate the significant intellectual shift that took place in the area of religion in Western society in America with the adoption of the First Amendment. People of faith (including ministers) had to adjust to the new voluntarism on which the church depended. This was especially felt monetarily as governments, federal, state, and local, gradually weaned American ministers off the public tax dollar. Jefferson likely thought that the passing of the First Amendment would help release people from the oppressive dogma of traditional Christianity in addition to providing for basic liberties. However, in the decades after its passage the United States experienced a tremendous surge of Christian activity in both revivalism and reform.

Defining a Country: 1791–1865

The first half of the nineteenth century was the greatest Christianizing period in the history of the United States. The young nation entered into a period of rapid growth and expansion. Further successful conflicts with the British, Mexicans, and Native Americans boosted national confidence as America continued to fulfill its "manifest destiny." However, this time was also filled with serious problems. As slavery was gradually disestablished in Northern states, it became more ensconced in the South, creating a spirit of acrimony between Northern "progressives" and Southern "conservatives." Industrialization of the North had created new problems. Industrialists wasted no time in exploiting poor whites, many newly arrived immigrants, and children in the mass production of goods in factories. Although the American West during this time has been somewhat romanticized, in reality it tended to be a brutal, lawless place characterized by alcohol abuse, cattle rustling, prostitution, and vigilantism. The U.S. birth rate at the turn of the century was approximately 50 births per 1,000 people, and around

40 percent of Americans lived in places that had been unsettled in 1760. Within a single lifetime (ca. 1775–1849), Americans settled parts of the West stretching from the Appalachians to the Pacific.[45] As the nation rapidly grew and expanded so did its problems. However, through all these tremendous growth pains, the United States had defined itself in various ways by the closing decades of the eighteenth century.

Christian Awakening and Social Change

At the turn of the century, different areas of the country began to experience religious revival. This revivalism eventually earned the label Second Great Awakening because of its pervasiveness and longevity. Studies have demonstrated that during the Revolutionary period traditional Christian adherence was declining.[46] The religious intolerance of the Reformation period and Enlightenment thought had eroded many peoples' trust in revealed religion. However, the first half of the nineteenth century witnessed an undeniable reversal to the so-called Age of Reason.

At the turn of the new century news of fantastic revivals began to spread. In the beginning these revivals occurred on the Western frontier, the first well-known one happening at Cane Ridge, Kentucky, in 1801. The camp meeting, as it became known, soon became a staple feature of the frontier. As the adventurous, common people moved west—those who had more to gain by going than staying in the East—so did the down-to-earth Methodist and Baptist preachers. By the middle of the nineteenth century Methodists and Baptists made up the two largest bodies of faith in the United States. Revivalism, however, occurred in other areas of the country besides the western fringes. New York state experienced phenomenal revival in the early nineteenth century. The most prominent revivalist to emerge from this area at this time was Charles Finney, a former Presbyterian, technically a Congregationalist, but in reality possessing a nondenominational spirit. Finney brought the revivalism of the frontier camp meeting to the urban setting. Historians commonly dub him the father of modern revivalism because his "new measures" launched and popularized a whole new evangelical mentality within American Christianity that

continues today. Revival was not new in itself, but the revivalism of Jonathan Edwards and George Whitefield hardly resem-
bled the revivalism of Finney. Whereas Edwards and other
eighteenth-century Calvinists understood revival to be the
supernatural, sovereign work of God, Finney defined revival as
natural. It was an event that could always be produced by the
proper means.[47]

The first half of the nineteenth century witnessed a surge
in Christian adherence. This evangelical renewal and growth
took place in the minority movements that had only been
embryonic during the Revolutionary period. Groups such as the
Methodists and Baptists fit within the orthodox boundaries of
Christianity, and they inculcated the new egalitarian and individualistic spirit unleashed by the Revolution combined with
an unmatched zeal among their clergy. In addition, these ministers did not have to jump through rigorous hoops of education
and ordination like ministers from the older, mainline denominations. These groups did not necessarily consider education
unimportant, but on the frontier a simple Holy Spirit "calling"
to preach would suffice. The preacher's legitimacy as a true
minister of the gospel would be evident in his ability to preach
with passion, uphold a moral lifestyle, and win souls. There can
be no doubt that the common man's preacher, willing to go to
where the people were going, reaped a bountiful harvest.

Temperance and Abolition

A hallmark of the nineteenth century was in the crusades
against what many viewed as societal evils. These moral crusades dovetailed naturally with the upsurge in Christian adherence that also characterized the time period. The two most
prominent reform efforts of this time addressed the consumption of alcohol and the owning of slaves. In both cases Christianity served as the moral compass that helped invigorate the
movements. Although there were certainly those activists who
did not root their moral dissent in their commitment to the
Christian faith, the vast majority of support for the movements
as a whole did come from "church people." The public outcry
against alcohol began to increase with the popularization of
distilled liquors. Christians had not typically been opposed to

alcoholic beverages such as beer or wine, but the destructive force of "hard liquors" was becoming evident to all. Methodist John Wesley and the Quakers were condemning the practice of distilling toward the end of the eighteenth century. The Founding Father and medical doctor Benjamin Rush published a work in 1785 titled, "Inquiry into the Effects of Ardent Spirits Upon the Human Body and Mind."

As people of faith increasingly condemned the production and consumption of distilled alcohol, the new Untied States government attempted to control the industry and raise federal revenue through taxes and license fees levied on its producers. These policies sparked the so-called Whiskey Rebellion of 1793 in Pennsylvania, which was in reality a protest against taxation. In 1802 Congress repealed such taxes, which gave President Thomas Jefferson reason to rejoice, believing the targeted taxation antithetical to a democratic and free society.

At first the temperance movement in the United States targeted distilled alcohol. Temperance leaders first created associations in 1808 in New York and in 1813 in Massachusetts, with wide support and promotion from the pulpit. In time many were advocating teetotalism and legislation to outlaw the production and sale of all kinds of alcohol. By the eve of the Civil War, without government restrictions of any kind, the liquor industry boomed. But as the alcohol flowed in greater, cheaper, and less restricted quantities, so did the vitriol of the activists determined to see the Devil's brew outlawed. Preachers and women led the march of reform as the country's conscience and industrialists and politicians addressed the pragmatic aspects. No one disputed that alcoholism was tied to social ills such as poverty, domestic abuse, poor worker production, and crime. Evangelist Charles Finney delivered a sermon in 1843 titled "God Under Obligation to Do Right." He observed that once the public began to see clearly the evil effects of alcohol, the moral imperative became clear and the sordid history of American alcohol abuse would serve as a national reminder of her past foolishness.

Under a moral government, I suppose it was impossible for God to bring about the temperance reformation, until the nature and tendencies of the use of alcohol could in some way be known. But when its nature was developed, its tendencies perceived, and its history written in the blood of millions of souls, there were then sufficient materials on hand, with which to assail it and crowd it back—shall I say to hell from whence it came? The monster intemperance, came up upon the length and breadth of the land, clad in a mantle of light. He found his way into every habitation, and smiled, and dealt out excitement, and deceived the nations. Alcohol was every where regarded as a friend. Its presence was deemed indispensable to health and happiness. It was prescribed by the physician almost as a catholicon. It was taken even by the clergy as an auxiliary in the discharge of their holy functions. All classes of persons supposed themselves to be blessed by it. And until it had destroyed its millions, so deep were its deceptive influences, that men could not be awakened to regard it as an enemy. But now its mask is off. It is known. Its history is written in blood, and who does not know that for the use of future generations this history is an indispensable safeguard?[48]

Christians in churches began to swear off the use of any kind of alcohol, including the varieties of lower alcohol content such as beer and wine. In some groups teetotalism became an indelible part of being Christian. Among Baptists the so-called Brown Church Covenant made abstinence from alcohol an expectation for church membership, including the commitment of its members "to abstain from the sale and use of intoxicating drinks as a beverage." This covenant began finding acceptance in Baptist churches in the 1830s, and was greatly popularized when James Pendleton added it to his widely used church manual. This confession is still in use in smaller, rural, traditional Baptist churches today. Beginning in the 1840s some states began to issue their own prohibition statutes; however, the laws were not ultimately successful. Enforcement was difficult and the legislatures that passed them ultimately repealed the laws or state supreme courts ruled them unconstitutional.

The Civil War interrupted the momentum of the Temperance Movement. Nevertheless, prohibitionists renewed and strengthened their efforts after the war. During the war the federal government placed new taxes on liquor and beer, which continued to increase and peaked in 1868 at $2 per gallon. The consequence of such stiff taxation was rampant violation of revenue laws and decreased federal revenue from the sale of alcohol. In 1869 Congress reduced the tax to 50 cents per gallon and federal revenues soared as producers stopped evading the tax.

Although politicians were greatly concerned with how the liquor industry could be controlled and exploited for federal revenue, many Americans were simply tired of the destructive force of alcohol. The cause that originally called for temperance in drinking escalated into an effort to prohibit fully the production and sale of all alcoholic beverages. In the 1870s women entered the fight against alcohol in force. They founded new organizations that rapidly grew. The Women's Christian Temperance Union (founded 1874), headed by Frances E. Willard, was committed to a program of moral persuasion and education to raise a public conscience over the evils of alcohol. Individuals like Carrie Nation worked outside any organization with a more direct approach. In 1890 she became weary of the liquor scene in her home state of Kansas. On her own (sometimes joined by other women), Nation would enter a saloon, sing, quote Scripture, pray, and then proceed to smash bottles of booze with her hatchet.

The issue of alcohol produced the short-lived Prohibition Party, which ran presidential candidates. However, with the political pressure exerted by the Anti-Saloon League (founded 1895), the idea of a national prohibition against alcohol began to look more like a real possibility. The combination of Christian activists and political lobbying eventually led to Congress's adoption of the Eighteenth Amendment prohibiting "the manufacture, sale, or transportation of intoxicating liquors." This law went into effect in January 1920 and remained the law of the land until the Twenty-first Amendment repealed it in 1933.[49]

Abolitionists were no less impassioned for their cause, and the issue was even more controversial for the nation. Like the alcohol issue, slavery had moral, economic, and political facets. The American people had always possessed diverse opinions about the ethical dimensions of slavery from its introduction to the colonies in the early seventeenth century. From 1777 to 1804 all the states north of Maryland abolished slavery on their own, which was the outcome the Founding Fathers had hoped for and expected. However, during that same time the Southern states had become more dependent economically on slave labor and more accustomed to and accepting of the social arrangement of master and slave. The sectional division may have adopted a Jeffersonian "live and let live" attitude, but several controversial realities forced the debate and ultimately the conflict. As the nation expanded westward, debate ensued concerning whether slavery would be permitted in these new territories. The Compromise of 1850 abated the fracturing of the union, but while this approach tried to satisfy such morally and politically polarized sides, it ultimately failed to maintain unity. The implementation of the federal Fugitive Slave Act (part of the 1850 compromise), which required runaway slaves be returned to their masters, only served to fuel the abolitionist cause in the North and create a more active and efficient Underground Railroad for fleeing slaves. The national temper was on edge concerning slavery. Harriet Beecher Stowe's *Uncle Tom's Cabin* (1852) helped stir an emotional and sympathetic response that strengthened the abolitionist cause. From 1854 to 1859, anti-slavery and pro-slavery factions spilled blood for control of the Kansas Territory. John Brown, a militant abolitionist who had participated in the "civil war" in Kansas, led the 1859 attack on Harpers Ferry, Virginia, bringing sensational attention to the slavery debate. His unsuccessful raid on a federal armory, which ended with his capture and execution, nevertheless was inspiring to many who appreciated his passion (even if not his approach) for the emancipation of slaves and foreshadowed the violence to come. In 1857 the U.S. Supreme Court handed down the infamous Dred Scott decision. The case was essentially an extension of the ongoing debate about how to deal with the slavery issue in the newer American territories that were becoming states. Scott's master had taken him into the free state of Illinois and the free Wisconsin Territory for a significant time. Therefore, Scott sued for his freedom, reasoning that he was now technically a free man since he had resided in free territories. In the end, the Supreme Court ruled that

Scott was his master's property and not entitled to the same privileges as a U. S. citizen. Furthermore, the court ruled that past restrictions on slavery in the Western territories by Congress were unconstitutional and that the popular sovereignty of the people in each state should decide the fate of slavery in its own territory. This decision also fueled the abolitionists and strengthened the new Republican Party, determined to stop the spread of slavery.

In the midst of the political rancor, Christian voices arose to decry the evils of slavery in America. In the eighteenth century Quakers had sternly denounced slavery as an unchristian practice. The moral argument for the emancipation of slaves in America derived from a commitment by many to the Christian faith, from which they surmised slavery was wrong. Although some professing Christians in the South did use the Bible to sanction slavery, the louder conspicuously Christian voice railed against it. Charles Finney added to his revivalism not only temperance, but abolitionism as well. The Grimké sisters, Angelina and Sarah, left their home in South Carolina after being awakened to the sin of slaveholding. Forsaking home and family, they appealed to Southern Christian women to see the suffering of slaves. They went on to become popular abolitionist speakers in the North. Theodore Dwight Weld (who married Angelina Grimké), a ministerial student at Oberlin (Finney's college), became a key Christian spokesman for the American Anti-Slavery Society. His work included recruiting and training people for the cause as well as writing. In 1837 he published the pamphlet, "The Bible Against Slavery." Although not all abolitionists were Christian, there is no doubt that many of the key abolitionist leaders and much of the abolitionist constituency were evangelical Christians.

It should come as no surprise that Abraham Lincoln emerged as the most theological president (at least in his rhetoric) in United States history. The time that he occupied the highest office in the land coincided with the strongest currents of Christian revivalism and reform in the country's history. Prior to his presidential campaign, Lincoln gave his "House Divided" speech in 1858. The occasion was his nomination as a candidate in Illinois for the U. S. Senate; therefore, it primarily contains criticism for his opponent. However, it is the ominous opening words of the speech that appear prophetic. Lincoln begins by declaring that the national agitation over slavery was worsening. He said, "In my opinion, it will not cease, until a crisis shall have been reached, and passed." Invoking the words of Jesus, he continued, "A house divided against itself cannot stand. I believe this government cannot endure, permanently half slave and half free. I do not expect the Union to be dissolved—I do not expect the house to fall—but I do expect it will cease to be divided. It will become all one thing or all the other." Three years later these sober words proved to be sadly insightful.

Theologically Americanized Christianity

As the young United States embarked on her childhood years in the nineteenth century, change was not limited to economics, population, geographic expansion, and reform issues. One area of life receiving a tremendous ideological overhaul was Christian theology. The democratic spirit of the nineteenth century not only infused political ideas, but exerted itself in force onto Christian interpretation and application of the Scriptures. One might say that many now viewed the Bible through the lens of democracy. The Revolution had so fused together the cause of political liberty, religious liberty, and God's righteous cause for independence that this confluence of ideas was inevitable.[50]

The result of the democratization of the populace was the demise of Calvinism's claim to be the orthodox Protestant interpretation of Scripture. During the seventeenth and eighteenth centuries the vast majority of Anglicans, Congregationalists, Presbyterians, and Baptists were committed to a Calvinistic interpretation of the Christian faith. A minority had existed that expressed anti-Calvinistic views since the Reformation period; however, they were overwhelmingly perceived as heterodox. In the colonial period, American Christians tended to assume a Calvinistic understanding of the gospel. Jonathan Edwards had stated that the fear of Arminianism (anti-Calvinistic theology) was part of the impetus for the revivalism his congregation experienced in 1735.

However, during the Revolution, some Calvinists began to compromise the view that a sovereign God had divinely established the social order and government by his unquestionable will. Many chose not to submit to the governing authorities, and rationalized away the typical Calvinist disposition. In addition, the Enlightenment had expressed itself not only in attacks on traditional Christianity in general, but on Calvinism in particular. Once the high-sounding rhetoric of liberty and freedom captured American minds and hearts, and that rhetoric became reality through a successful rebellion, it was a short time before many overlaid these political ideas onto their biblical interpretation. The result was a rational impasse. For many people the Calvinistic depiction of God seemed like divine tyranny, depriving men of their natural liberties and pursuit of happiness. The God of the Calvinists was a despot, arbitrarily deciding who would inherit eternal life and who would be damned. Certainly, some simply rejected this perception by opting to reject traditional Christianity altogether. Many others, however, chose to recast their understanding of God with a theology more congruent with individual freedom and confidence in human ability. The once-feared and despised Arminian position now found fertile ground to take root. American democracy had turned the fallow theological ground, and American individualism had watered the seed of anti-Calvinistic thought. In a short time a crop of Arminianized preachers and churchgoers became the new majority theology. True Calvinists did not vanish, but they gradually became the new minority among Protestants.

The Civil War: The Defining Moment

One can perceive that Americans still debate causes of the Civil War. Many Southerners today still are likely to refer to the event as "The War of Northern Aggression" or "The Second War for Independence." Those who use such terminology point to the issues of states' rights and federal aggression as the chief causes of the conflict. However, many Americans have come to accept that the war was essentially caused by the deep divide over slavery. The American Civil War was no different from any conflict in that many of the combatants did not agree on what critical issue they were fighting about, and both sides believed their cause was just. Both political and moral ideologies running parallel fueled the conflict.

Politically, the debate partly settled on what constituted fair or unfair taxation by the federal government. In addition, the debate concerning the proper jurisdiction of the federal government in states was foremost. In actuality, these two issues collided. The passionate debate over federalism, beginning with the contentious presidential election between Jefferson and Adams in 1800, had only intensified.[51] The Civil War was a climactic conflict that finally settled this longstanding debate with federalism emerging victorious. Lincoln preserved the union at the cost of the Confederate states' sovereignty.

In addition to political ideas, the issue of slavery was an indelible part of why the war ultimately happened. As mentioned, slavery was a divisive issue for decades before shots were fired on Fort Sumter. Whereas the agrarian-based Southern economy had come to depend on slaves, the industrial North had not. Slavery was neither considered right by every person who lived in the South, nor did all Southerners own slaves. However, the culture at large had become accustomed to the social arrangement, and no great movement indigenous to the South attempted to put it to an end. Abolitionists in the North, many of them evangelical Christians, had come to view slavery as a systemic evil of the South. Once the war commenced it was easy for many to interpret the conflict as a crusade "to set men free."

Ironically, the Civil War occurred at a time when Christianity was possibly exerting the most influence it ever had in America. Reform movements, such as abolitionism, had primarily emerged from Christian activists. The question of who used whom politically in the slavery debate is irrelevant. The fact is that evangelical Christians by the time of the Civil War had come to exert a considerable influence on American culture at large.

An Era of Reforming Christians

From the turn of the nineteenth century through the Civil War the United States defined itself. Political leaders made crucial decisions about westward expansion, and with the blood and sweat of the people tamed wilderness and forged a country.

As European rivals gradually withdrew from North America, the United States solidified its ownership and control over an area many times larger than the original thirteen states.

Keeping such a vast territory united was a monumental task in the nineteenth century. Modern Americans, who are accustomed to interstate travel by land, jet plane by air, instant mobile communication, and e-mail, have a difficult time appreciating the fact that travel from the settled East Coast to places like Tennessee or Kentucky in the early 1800s took weeks by river, horse, cart, or foot (or a combination). This travel was difficult and dangerous. Communication was slow and interests tended to be overwhelmingly local. The fact that regional interests, political differences, economic realities, and moral crusades ultimately coalesced to precipitate a war between the states was hardly startling to those who lived in 1861, albeit regrettable.

Christians once again found themselves in a religious subculture deeply divided along moral lines. In the Revolutionary period, the consuming Christian question concerned the validity of rebellion. During the Civil War the preoccupying question concerned the moral acceptability of slavery. The two primary moral crusades of the time period were temperance and abolition. However, as tension between the states reached its bloody crescendo, the moral issue of slavery moved to the forefront. Of course, there was not unanimity among Christians on the issue.[52] Some Christians, primarily those defending the Southern way of life, argued that slavery was not incongruent with the Bible and Christian culture. They pointed out that the Bible neither condemned slavery, nor did it mandate the manumission of slaves. On the contrary, certain parts of Scripture seemed to condone the relationship between master and slave. One's Christian duty was to be the right *kind* of master or slave.[53] Abolitionist Christians reasoned that the Bible only recognized the reality that slavery existed in the ancient world, but that it did not explicitly condone the practice. Furthermore, they argued that slavery was incompatible with the higher ideals of the Christian faith. Christ's teachings of love for God and neighbor could not coexist with slavery. A nation that sought to honor God and grant true liberty to its citizens could no longer tolerate this "peculiar institution."[54]

The American experiment that the Founding Fathers launched in the eighteenth century found its general direction in the nineteenth century. The deep divide on political and moral issues climaxed with a civil war that greatly settled in which direction the country would move to govern itself. The aftermath of the war posed new and challenging problems, but it settled the question of federalization. During this time Christianity enjoyed its most influential time on the broader American culture. It was an era of growth in Christian adherence and activity and of the application of Christian faith to public morality and politics. Finally, it was a time when Christianity emerged with a uniquely democratic twist poised to encounter the challenges of the next century.

Fine-tuning a Country: 1865–Present

The post-Civil War era of the United States has been a time of exponential change in such areas as politics, technologies, education, industry, economics, public values, and religion. The nineteenth-century Antebellum period and the crisis of the Civil War set the course of a much stronger guiding federalism. The following years witnessed a country struggling to recover from its war wounds, rebuild a decimated South, assimilate former slaves as free Americans, reform its labor system, and possess and tame the West.

The face of American life drastically changed as communication and travel became easier and more reliable, practically all the land was taken away from Native Americans, and the country abandoned its isolationism and became a global power after its participation in two world wars. Among many Protestant Christians, the late nineteenth and early twentieth centuries were battles against Roman Catholic immigration, Darwinism, and German higher criticism of the Bible.[55] Each of these posed an apparent threat to the norm—Protestant America. The great political threat of the twentieth century emerged as communism. The 1940s and 1950s produced a surge in civil religion as a response to the perceived anti-Christian and totalitarian agenda of the communists. This surge included the insertion of the phrase "under God" into the Pledge of Allegiance.

The latter part of the twentieth century witnessed the ascendancy of the computer age and space travel, while the consequences of slavery were still being felt in the social unrest caused by segregation and the civil rights movement. Religious diversity and the liberalization of American culture dramatically increased, while politicians and activists hotly debated issues related to church and state and morality. The disillusionment of the Vietnam War era led to decades of rebellion, frustration, and heavy experimentation and popularization of recreational drugs and sexually promiscuous lifestyles. In the 1960s, the Supreme Court began to apply the Fourth and Fourteenth Amendments particularly to the previously private issue of birth control, culminating in its application to the abortion issue.[56] The Reagan era of the 1980s ushered in a new surge in political and moral conservative reaction to much of the negative impact of America's liberal social drift. Part of this conservative resurgence was a new emphasis on the so-called Christian nature of America. This was the time when religiously conservative Christians began aggressively to lay claim to American identity. Part of the strategy of the crusade against intellectual and moral liberalism was to convince people that America had been founded a Christian nation, the country had corporately backslid, and a course of renewal was needed in the church house and the statehouse.[57]

The New Church and State Paradigm

In the midst of all the colossal changes of the late nineteenth and twentieth centuries, the discussion of what role Christianity would play in public life intensified. As the country entered into its so-called Progressive Era after the Civil War, the often-presumed place Protestant Christianity held in American public life began to be increasingly challenged.[58] As Catholic and Jewish populations grew, debates over the propriety of the promotion of Protestant Christianity in public schools intensified. In Western civilization the close tie between education and the church is a historical reality. However, in the United States, as the implications and applications of a disestablished religion began to play out, Christians began to observe that separation in reality meant secularization.

The original Jeffersonian interpretation of the First Amendment as a "wall of separation" has become the political mantra for those who desired to see no government endorsement of Christianity. It took some time, however, for this interpretation to become the common application. Many local and state leaders correctly observed for quite some time that the federal constitution only limited Congress from establishing religion. Therefore, a local community could promote religion in the public arena with impunity as long as the vast majority of citizens took no offense. In the nineteenth century Protestant Christianity was essentially a publicly endorsed religion because the population was overwhelmingly Protestant, and those who were not Christian tended to accept the status quo place of religion in society. The Supreme Court of the United States was relatively quiet on the subject of church and state throughout the nineteenth century, but the twentieth century witnessed a surge in cases related to the constitutionality of civil religion.[59] Essentially, the Supreme Court has indeed emerged as the supreme arbitrator on the debate between secularists and traditionalists.[60] Increasingly, the interpretations of the Constitution have been used to place parameters on local laws, typically ruling certain local legislation and statutes "unconstitutional." Many times these rulings are based on an interpretation of the "spirit" of the Constitution because of the Constitution's lack of specificity on many issues. The Constitution has proved to be an insufficient document in at least two fairly obvious ways. First, the Constitution has grown over time with the addition of amendments, now holding at twenty-seven, demonstrating that periodic adjustments and additions are needed. Second, it has naturally been more distanced by time from its origination, therefore having to be applied and reapplied to all of the social, cultural, political, and religious changes since then, which have been significant. Over time, by necessity a small group of judges have applied the limited vision and articulation of the Founding Fathers to matters of religion and ethics, often disagreeing strongly with one another. Whether or not placing the ultimate interpretive power of the Constitution in the hands of nine people is wise is an entirely different discussion.

This societal experiment that began with the disestablishment of religion has now taken shape with an established new paradigm of the proper relationship between church and state. Since the age of Emperor Constantine in the early fourth century, the Christian faith had been part and parcel to Western civilization. The creation of the United States of America occurred at a time when the cultural assumption that religion must be supported by the state was beginning to weaken because of the Enlightenment. When the new United States federal government launched disestablished, voluntary religion, no one really could have known what to expect. Now, more than two centuries later the paradigm shift is complete. American society has secularized the public square and privatized religion. Of course there are still leftover entanglements where civil religion intersects the public sector. For example, prayer in Congress, religious mottos on money, and the existence of military chaplaincy all testify to the Christian presence and influence that has always been present in the United States. These items and others like them are cultural holdovers that persist because of strong tradition and emotional sentimentality, but are somewhat inconsistent with the federally enforced secularization of most public spaces.

An Era of Reclaiming Christians

Since the Civil War, American Christianity has lost much of its place in the public square. The foundation laid by the Founding Fathers in the Constitution has now had time for a structure to be placed on it. It should not be surprising that this structure has emerged to be a secular one. The Founders intentionally disestablished religion in the interests of protecting citizens from coercive religion, and steered clear of overtly Christian language in the documents that we still look to for guidance; however, most of them in their own time could not have anticipated the erosion of the public sway of Protestant Christianity.

As this secularization began to take firm hold of the country's persona, two opposing reactions began to crystallize. As secularists repeated the phrase "separation of church and state" over and over, removing Christian instruction and recognition in the public arenas, an intellectual and moral liberal drift occurred. The individual freedom that hallmarks American culture became increasingly used to justify bolder public articulation of the irreligious, whereas before, the influence of Protestant Christianity on the public square served as a reminder of moral ideals, even if individuals or the true social realities, like segregation, contradicted them. Consequently, the moral legacy of the latter twentieth century has been one of more open anti-Christian behavior and ideologies. There is no doubt to a Christian or non-Christian who has "eyes to see" that popular attitudes and dispositions have changed in the United States. Public voices no longer extol the traditional family as the ideal. The high levels of divorce and cohabitation are unprecedented. The pervasiveness of pornography, like a virus infecting the country, has become epidemic, particularly with its exploitation of an unregulated Internet. Activist homosexuals are positioning themselves to be the next civil rights movement, attempting to place themselves into mainstream America. The entertainment industry, including movies, television, music, and video games, has been on a consistent slide into increasingly gratuitous images of violence, vulgarity, and sex.

However, while this moral slide and liberal drift occurred, many reacted to it with a more vocal Christian message and activism. Christians in America, especially since the 1980s, have made their voice louder in many ways. In spite of the obvious immorality that often depicts American culture, there is more Christian activity than ever. Secularists have effectively pushed the Christian faith out of the public space, but it has blossomed in other ways. One should consider the number of active Christian congregations in the United States compared with other countries, the number of private schools, colleges, and universities committed to education with a Christian worldview, the various parachurch organizations that pursue an evangelistic or benevolent mission, the growing trend in homeschooling for the purpose of including some religious training, and the burgeoning Christian music and publishing industries. These are just some examples of how Christianity today still shows signs of vibrancy in the United States. Since the Reagan era the religious right or "values voters" have made a tremendous impact in national elections. Many Christians have determined to reclaim America for God. However, Christians must understand the biblical strategy for reclaiming, the political realities we choose to live with, and the historical record that we must treat with integrity.

Conclusion

The biblical strategy for Christianization is not through the temporal government. History is full of examples of the horrific outcomes of state-defined, -mandated, and -enforced Christianity. When Christians begin to desire the government to establish religion, even in what may seem the most benign ways, they are asking government to turn down a road that only ends in discrimination at best and persecution at worst. To turn a country's collective heart back to God, Christian people should worry less about a symbolic monument of the Ten Commandments being removed from a courthouse, and be concerned more with their own family and church families actually putting them into practice in their lives. Christian individuals need to understand that real Christianization occurs when people authentically respond to the proclamation of the gospel, leading to changed spiritual conditions and reformed behaviors. Biblically, the light of the gospel is to shine from the church house and homes rather than the statehouse. At one time the statehouse reflected that light, and it may do so again one day; however, Christians must understand it may be easier to get politicians to pander to their values than to do the real work of sharing the gospel, offering food to the hungry, defending the helpless, and seeing America change one soul at a time.

Christians must also understand that we have chosen to live in a free society in the United States. A free society is by nature a more permissive society. In other words, behaviors are divided into the areas of private and public. Things private are considered matters of personal choice that supposedly do not infringe on the basic rights of others; therefore, a secularized law system does not prohibit these behaviors. Government tends to consider many individualist behaviors as private affairs, including sexual orientation, patronage of pornography, greed, anti-Christian activism, and, since 1973, abortion. In contrast, government considers behaviors such as theft, murder, abuse, and fraud public affairs because the consequences affect others, and the laws of the land prescribe punishment for offenders. Sometimes the public and private converge, as with child pornography or abortion. On the one hand, government allows the private use of pornography to be legal. On the other hand, the government condemns child pornography as criminal because this kind of pornography has moved into the public arena of abuse. On the one hand, a woman now has a constitutionally protected right to an abortion based on principles of personal rights to privacy. On the other hand, since 2003 partial-birth abortion has been banned as a public practice because a more mature fetus begs the question of the recognition of the unborn's humanity and, therefore, the humaneness of the act. This federal ban was upheld by the Supreme Court in 2007 in *Gonzales v. Carhart* with a 5–4 ruling.

The fact is our sense of morality comes from either a religious or secular foundation, and the secular worldview is more liberal and permissive. The government is secular; therefore, it does not attempt to impose morality guided by any particular religion, although it does recognize certain limits to personal behavior. Christians must understand that the best strategy for influencing a democratic, secular, liberal government is by activism. Politically, this means lobbying. If Christians feel strongly enough about an issue such as abortion, then they must lobby, petition, remonstrate, and mobilize themselves to effect change. They must support and get candidates elected who share their concern. This is what Baptists did during the constitutional period to make sure the federal government would ensure real religious liberty for all Americans. This is what individuals such as Martin Luther King Jr., Rosa Parks, Ralph Abernathy, and Medgar Evers did in the case of fighting racial segregation and discrimination. It was their leadership with the force of many men and women, black and white, that awakened the moral conscience of a country.

Lastly, it is of little use to mythologize the past. The United States of America has been a grand experiment in the realms of politics and religion. What the Founding Fathers chartered was an innovation in Western society. The historical reality is that the ideas of the Enlightenment primarily guided those in the Founding Era, supplemented by the rhetoric of civil religion that reflected the dominance of Protestant Christianity. As the country matured, Christians were an indelible part of the moral reform and social progression that took place through the Civil War and into the early twentieth century. The nineteenth century was America's significant period of true Christianization. The early twentieth century received the effects of the previous century, and conspicuously reflected it through the 1950s. Since then, America has experienced significant secularization of the public domain and moral liberalization. Some conservative reaction and resurgence has occurred since the 1980s, but not enough to place the Christian faith back on the pedestal from which secularization knocked it.

A Christian whose strategy is to fight for public Christian values should focus on being Christian himself in his church and family and involve himself in effective Christian activism. An ineffective way for a Christian to fight for public Christian values is to mythologize the past so that one's opponents legitimately find him incredulous. A desire to see America be more Christian does not depend on America having been more Christian in its past. Being disingenuous with history and cursing the darkness cannot bring true awakening. A biblical worldview, reinforced by a good awareness of history, teaches us that only the transforming light of the gospel of Christ can affect authentic change in enough individuals so that the broader culture may reflect it, although always imperfectly.

Endnotes

[1] For example, see a recent work, C. Smith, *Christian America? What Evangelicals Really Want* (Berkeley: University of California Press, 2000).

[2] The story of Christian presence in America begins prior to Jamestown or the Plymouth Pilgrims. Long before the United States became a sovereign country by the hands of English rebels, the Spanish and French were exploring and exploiting parts of North and South America. Christopher Columbus's ships sailed under the flag of Roman Catholic Spain on four voyages from 1492 through 1504. The early French explorers also came with the scepter of Roman Catholicism. Although one finds evidence of the early presence of Roman Catholics, particularly in Florida, Texas, New Mexico, Arizona, and California, the

legacy of the founding of the United States belongs to English Protestants. However, the Catholic stamp remains fixed in the names of cities, such as St. Augustine, Sante Fe, San Francisco, and many others. Spanish missions still stand in California that were founded during the same time that American Patriots were separating from the mother country on the eastern seaboard. In contrast with the conquering spirit of the Spanish, French explorers took a much milder approach, focusing more on establishing trading posts and settlements. The evidence of early French Catholic presence in North America remains in the religious character of certain cities in the United States, such as Louisville, Kentucky, and New Orleans, Louisiana. Particularly obvious is the French Catholic heritage of Quebec, Canada. Like the Spanish, the French in time fell to the growing hegemony of the new nation born from the British colonies.

[3] E. Gaustad and L. Schmidt, *The Religious History of America*, rev. ed. (New York: HarperCollins, 2002), 36.

[4] As appears in W. W. Sweet, *Religion in Colonial America* (New York: Charles Scribner's Sons, 1942), 29.

[5] See D. O. Beale, *The Mayflower Pilgrims: Roots of Puritan, Presbyterian, Congregationalist, and Baptist Heritage* (Greenville, SC: Ambassador-Emerald International, 2000). Beale's work is a concise and lucid account of the formation of the Pilgrims and their journey to colonial New England.

[6] W. Bradford, *Of Plymouth Plantation, 1620–1647*, ed. S. E. Morison (New York: Alfred A. Knopf, 1989), 47.

[7] Gaustad and Schmidt, *Religious History*, 52.

[8] For example, the primer reads: (A) In Adam's Fall We sinned all. (B) Heaven to find, The Bible Mind. (C) Christ crucify'd For sinners dy'd. (D) The Deluge drown'd The Earth around. (E) Elijah hid by Ravens fed. (F) The judgment made Felix afraid. This memory device helped children learn the alphabet and indoctrinate them to the Christian faith simultaneously.

[9] A. Carden, *Puritan Christianity in America: Religion and Life in Seventeenth-Century Massachusetts* (Grand Rapids: Baker, 1990), 186.

[10] As appears in R. Hofstadter and W. Smith, eds., *American Higher Education: A Documentary History*, vol. 1 (Chicago: University of Chicago, 1961), 8.

[11] For an excellent treatment of the Puritan use of the sermon see H. S. Stout, *The New England Soul: Preaching and Religious Culture in Colonial New England* (New York: Oxford University Press, 1986).

[12] M. Noll, *A History of Christianity in the United States and Canada* (Grand Rapids: Eerdmans, 1992), 47.

[13] J. Withrop, "A Modell of Christian Charity," in *Issues in American Christianity: Primary Sources with Introductions*, ed. K. J. Hardman (Grand Rapids: Baker, 1993), 21–22. The spelling and rules of capitalization from this source have been modernized in the citation here.

[14] W. Walker, *The Creeds and Platforms of Congregationalism* (Boston: Pilgrim Press, 1960), 236.

[15] For a good treatment of the particulars of this debate, see part I of R. Ferm, ed., *Issues in American Protestantism: A Documentary History from the Puritans to the Present* (Gloucester, MA: Peter Smith, 1969). For a fuller treatment of Roger Williams's ideas see E. S. Morgan, *Roger Williams: The Church and the State,* rev. ed. (New York: W. W. Norton, 1997), and E. S. Gaustad, *Liberty of Conscience: Roger Williams in America* (Grand Rapids: Eerdmans), 1991.

[16] Noll, *A History of Christianity in the United States and Canada*, 62.

[17] J. Butler, *Becoming American: The Revolution before 1776* (Cambridge, MA: Harvard University Press, 2000), 189. See chapter five, "Things Spiritual," for a good treatment of the early religious diversity of colonial America. Butler

also gives attention to religious issues concerning women, Native Americans, and African slaves during this time period. For a more thorough examination of the religious diversity that existed in America from its beginning, see also his early work *Awash in a Sea of Faith: Christianizing the American People* (Cambridge, MA: Harvard, 1990).

[18] Ibid., 63. The Church of England also suffered from other disadvantages in the American colonies, such as having no American bishop to give cohesion to the church.

[19] See H. S. Stout, *The Divine Dramatist: George Whitefield and the Rise of Modern Evangelicalism* (Grand Rapids: Eerdmans, 1991).

[20] See G. M. Marsden, *Jonathan Edwards: A Life* (New Haven: Yale University Press, 2003).

[21] J. Edwards, "The Distinguishing Marks of the Work of the Spirit of God," in *Jonathan Edwards on Revival* (Edinburgh: Banner of Truth, 1999), 108.

[22] R. Ferm, *Issues in American Protestantism*, 89, 93.

[23] For revisionist interpretations, see J. Butler, "Enthusiasm Described and Decried: The Great Awakening as Interpretive Fiction," *Journal of American History* 69 (September 1982): 306–9, and F. Lambert, *Inventing the Great Awakening* (Princeton: Princeton University Press, 1999).

[24] N. O. Hatch, *The Sacred Cause of Liberty: Republican Thought and the Millennium in Revolutionary New England* (New Haven, CT: Yale University Press, 1977), 22.

[25] For a fuller treatment of the comparison of Witherspoon and Zubly see D. Cornett, "The American Revolution's Role in the Reshaping of Calvinistic Protestantism," *Journal of Presbyterian History* 82 no. 4 (Winter 2004): 244–57.

[26] M. A. Noll, N. O. Hatch, G. M. Marsden, *The Search for Christian America*, (Colorado Springs: Helmers & Howard, 1989), 100.

[27] Still the definitive work in this area is H. F. May, *The Enlightenment in America* (New York: Oxford University Press, 1976). See also M. A. Noll, *Princeton and the Republic, 1768–1822: The Search for A Christian Enlightenment in the Era of Samuel Stanhope Smith* (Princeton: Princeton University Press, 1989).

[28] For the most erudite work on this topic, see M. A. Noll, *America's God: From Jonathan Edwards to Abraham Lincoln* (New York: Oxford, 2002).

[29] See L. H. Butterfield, *John Witherspoon Comes to America* (Princeton: Princeton University Press, 1953); M. L. Lemmon Stohlman, *John Witherspoon: Parson, Politician, Patriot* (Philadelphia: Westminster, 1976); M. Rose, *John Witherspoon: An American Leader* (Washington DC: Family Research Council, 1999); L. G. Tait, *The Piety of John Witherspoon: Pew, Pulpit, and Public Forum* (Louisville: Geneva, 2001); J. H. Morrison, *John Witherspoon and the Founding of the American Republic* (Notre Dame, IN: Notre Dame Press, 2005).

[30] See E. S. Gaustad, *Faith of Our Fathers: Religion and the New Nation* (San Francisco: Harper & Row, 1987); D. L. Holmes, *The Faiths of the Founding Fathers* (New York: Oxford University Press, 2006); G. S. Wood, *Revolutionary Characters: What Made the Founders Different* (New York: Penguin, 2006).

[31] See J. J. Ellis, *His Excellency: George Washington* (New York: Alfred A. Knopf, 2004).

[32] Holmes, *The Faiths of the Founding Fathers*, 65.

[33] M. L. Weems, *The Life of George Washington* (Philadelphia: Joseph Allen, 1800), and Edward C. McGuire, *The Religious Opinions and Character of Washington* (New York: Harper and Brothers, 1836).

[34] See W. Isaacson, *Benjamin Franklin: An American Life* (New York: Simon & Schuster, 2003).

[35] See D. McCullough, *John Adams* (New York: Simon & Schuster, 2001).

³⁶ See J. J. Ellis, *American Sphinx* (New York: Alfred A. Knopf, 1997); E. S. Gaustad, *Sworn on the Altar of God: A Religious Biography of Thomas Jefferson* (Grand Rapids: Eerdmans, 1996).

³⁷ In Jefferson's short introduction to his Bible he clearly explains his views toward orthodox Christian belief. "I have made a wee-little book from the Gospels which I call the Philosophy of Jesus. It is a paradigmatic of his doctrines, made by cutting the texts out of the book and arranging them on the pages of a blank book, in a certain order of time or subject. A more beautiful or precious morsel of ethics I have never seen. It is a document in proof that I am a real Christian, that is to say, a disciple of the doctrines of Jesus, very different from the Platonists, who call me infidel and themselves Christians and preachers of the Gospel, while they draw all their characteristic dogmas from what its author never said nor saw. They have compounded from the heathen mysteries a system beyond the comprehension of man, of which the great reformer of the vicious ethics and deism of the Jews, were he to return on earth, would not recognize one feature." M. Harrison and S. Gilbert, eds., *Thomas Jefferson in His Own Words* (New York: Excellent Books, 1993).

³⁸ Holmes, *The Faiths of the Founding Fathers*, 93.

³⁹ See Holmes, *The Faiths of Our Founding Fathers*, chapter 13.

⁴⁰ E. Boudinot, *The Age of Revelation: The Age of Reason Shewn to Be an Age of Infidelity* (Philadelphia: Asbury Dickins, 1801).

⁴¹ J. Eidsmoe, *Christianity and the Constitution: The Faith of Our Founding Fathers* (Grand Rapids: Baker, 1987). This work is a prime example of an attempt to Christianize the Constitution on mere inference. He identifies fifteen principles built into the framework of the Constitution that are "either derived from, or at least compatible with, Christianity and the Bible" (72–73). The key here is what can be interpreted to be implicitly compatible with Christian tenets versus what is not explicitly Christian in the Constitution. None of the fifteen principles listed are explicitly Christian, although compatible. This begs the question: If the Founders drafted the Constitution as a Christian document, then why conceal the fact by excluding clear Christian language? There may have been religious/cultural assumptions at play, as in any time with any group of people, but the fact that overt Christian language is omitted is more telling of the motivations of the Founders and their overall religious dispositions than any points of congruence the Constitution may have with the Christian faith.

⁴² For an excellent and thorough treatment of the history of slavery with particular emphasis on the relationship between the Atlantic slave trade and the development of the New World see D. B. Davis, *Inhuman Bondage: The Rise and Fall of Slavery in the New World* (New York: Oxford University Press, 2006). The benchmark work focused on American slavery particularly remains A. J. Rabateau, *Slave Religion: The Invisible Institution in the Antebellum South* (New York: Oxford University Press, 1978).

⁴³ See Constitution of the United States of America, Article I, Section 9. The section does grant the right for Congress to tax slaves up to ten dollars per person.

⁴⁴ R. Williams, *The Bloudy Tenet of Persecution* (n.p., 1644).

⁴⁵ S. J. Keillor, *This Rebellious House: American History and the Truth of Christianity* (Downers Grove: InterVarsity, 1996), 105. See chapters 5 and 6 for his treatment of the nineteenth century.

⁴⁶ See M. Noll, "The Revolution, the Enlightenment, and Christian Higher Education in the Early Republic," in *Making Education Christian: A History and Mission of Evangelical Colleges in America*, eds. J. A. Carpenter and K. W. Shipps (Grand Rapids: Eerdmans, 1987). Noll states that between 1748 and

1806 the number of Princeton graduates entering the ministry declined from 47 percent to 13 percent. William C. Ringenberg records that at "Dartmouth in 1798, only one member of the class of 1799 publicly professed the Christian faith; at Yale in 1796, only the senior class could claim more than one such believer." See W. C. Ringenberg, *The Christian College: A History of Protestant Higher Education in America* (Grand Rapids: Eerdmans, 1984). Jon Butler contends that the documents produced in the founding of the United States are symptomatic of the overall religious decline that had been taking place. He writes, "The religious world invoked in the Declaration was a Deist's world, at best; at worst, the Declaration was simply indifferent to religious concerns and issues." See *Awash in a Sea of Faith*. The authors of *The Search for Christian America* describe the Revolutionary period as "marked by declining concern for church, weakness in evangelism, and general spiritual lassitude." Sydney Ahlstrom penned in *A Religious History of the American People* (New Haven, CT: Yale University Press, 1972) that "The revolutionary era was a period of decline for American Christianity as a whole. The churches reached a lower ebb of vitality during the two decades after the end of hostilities than at any other time in the country's religious history." In *The Churching of America 1776–1990* (New Brunswick, NJ: Rutgers University Press, 1992).

[47] See C. E. Hambrick-Stowe, *Charles G. Finney and the Spirit of American Evangelicalism* (Grand Rapids: Eerdmans, 1996).

[48] Charles Finney, "God Under Obligation to do Right," available online at http://www.gospeltruth.net/1842OE/420914_god_obligation.htm (accessed July 26, 2007).

[49] For good overviews of the Temperance Movement see the article "History of Alcohol Prohibition" posted by the National Commission on Marihuana and Drug Abuse at http://www.druglibrary.org/Schaffer/LIBRARY/studies/nc/nc2a.htm (accessed December 16, 2010).

[50] For a thorough treatment of this subject, see N. O. Hatch, *The Democratization of American Christianity* (New Haven, CT: Yale University Press, 1989).

[51] See J. Ferling, *Adams vs. Jefferson: The Tumultuous Election of 1800* (New York: Oxford, 2004).

[52] See M. Noll, *The Civil War as a Theological Crisis* (Chapel Hill, NC: University of North Carolina, 2006). Noll expounds on the great theological and hermeneutical divide between North and South that preceded the war. Christian leaders wrestled to an impasse over what the Bible said or did not say about slavery in the American context.

[53] For example, R. Furman, "Exposition of the Views of Baptists Relative to the Coloured Population of the United States" (1822), University of North Carolina, Documenting the American South, available online at http://docsouth.unc.edu/index.html.

[54] See http://antislavery.eserver.org/religious for primary source documents.

[55] For a concise treatment of the history of Roman Catholics in the United States, see J. T. Fisher, *Communion of Immigrants: A History of Catholics in America* (New York: Oxford University Press, 2000).

[56] The Fourth Amendment and the Fourteenth Amendment were judged to imply a citizen's basic "right to privacy," which became the hinge argument on which decisions handed down by the court on cases dealing with birth control and abortion turned. The Fourth Amendment, part of the original 1791 Bill of Rights, states, "The right of the people to be secure in their persons, houses, papers, and effects, against unreasonable searches and seizures, shall not be violated, and no warrants shall issue, but upon probable cause, supported by oath or affirmation, and particularly describing the place to be searched, and the persons or things to be seized." The relevant section of the Fourteenth

Amendment, ratified in 1868, states, "No state shall make or enforce any law which shall abridge the privileges or immunities of citizens of the United States; nor shall any state deprive any person of life, liberty, or property, without due process of law; nor deny to any person within its jurisdiction the equal protection of the laws."

[57] One can find numerous examples of this interpretation, especially since the Bicentennial. Writing in 1979, John Woodbridge, Mark Noll, and Nathan Hatch observed, "During 1976, evangelical publishers turned out an array of titles along these [civil religion] lines: *America: God Shed His Grace on Thee, One Nation Under God,* and *Faith, Stars and Stripes.* Churches sponsored celebrations under banners '200 Years Lord of Our Nation' and 'Let Christ's Freedom Ring.' A host of evangelical magazines, many of which had little else in common, fell in step to extol America's Christian heritage, the biblical origins of American government, and the spiritual insights of the founding fathers." See J. D. Woodbridge, M. A. Noll, and N. O. Hatch, *The Gospel in America: Themes in the Stories of American Evangelicals* (Grand Rapids: Zondervan, 1979), 209.

Prominent leaders who emerged in force from the late 1970s such as Jerry Falwell and James Kennedy reacted to the morally soft rhetoric of Jimmy Carter, even though the latter's claims of being "born again" had elevated the hopes of many Christians. The debate on abortion and the Equal Rights Amendment sparked a war of words over "family values," and the Christian right mobilized to reclaim America for God at the conclusion of the liberal and culturally unsettling 1960s and 1970s. For a good journalistic survey of the prominent figures and issues, see W. Martin, *With God on Our Side: The Rise of the Religious Right in America* (New York: Broadway Books, 1996).

An example of the claim of the religious and moral decline of America with a call to "reclaim America" is P. Marshall and D. Manuel, *The Light and the Glory: Did God have a Plan for America?* (Grand Rapids: Revell, 1977). The authors conclude, "The opening pages of this book mentioned some social indicators of the lifting of God's grace—the rapidly decaying morality, the disintegrating American family, the acceptance of rebellion and violent crime as the norm for modern life. But recent natural phenomena also seem to bear witness to it. There have been earthquakes, and droughts and floods; there have been untimely frosts, a slight but significant drop in the average mean temperature, and freak weather conditions which have lately seen hurricanes in California, and more snow in northern Florida than on Cape Cod, and the worst winter in the east in our history. . . . it would seem that God's Controversy with America has begun in earnest. . . . So we modern Christians must humble ourselves and renew the horizontal as well as the vertical aspect of our covenant with God. If we do this, He will hear, and forgive our sins, and heal our land" (355–58).

[58] The Progressive Era was from the 1890s through the 1920s. It was marked by activism that led to prohibition of alcohol, women's suffrage, and significant labor and election reforms. Theodore Roosevelt and Woodrow Wilson were important Progressive presidents.

[59] See E. S. Gaustad, *Proclaim Liberty throughout the Land: A History of Church and State in America* (New York: Oxford University Press, 2003).

[60] I use the label "traditionalist" to refer to those who desire to see the older symbols of civil religion in the public spaces, such as schools—those who think that somehow these public spaces should retain the Judeo-Christian heritage as symbols of America's overall identity as a "Christian nation."

Response to Cornett

David Barton

L et me begin by extending my sincere thanks to Daryl Cornett for undertaking and overseeing this project. Hopefully, the final work as he has envisioned it will prove useful now and for generations to come. I am grateful for the honor he extended me of being included within the purview of this endeavor.

There is much to applaud in his essay. He did an especially excellent job in his exposition of the Second Great Awakening and tracing its religious influences throughout the nineteenth century. I was also thrilled to see him properly recognize that America had more than just five Founding Fathers.

Few of today's writers seem to know that there were actually more than two hundred Founding Fathers, including the fifty-six signers of the Declaration, the fifty-five at the Constitutional Convention, and the ninety who framed the Bill of Rights. Indisputably, some had more influence than others, but the fact that they are unknown today does not mean that they were unimportant—a truth repeatedly demonstrated by previous generations.[1] Cornett's contribution is certainly a laudable return to that former practice.

While I have many areas of strong accord with Cornett, I do have some differences. Most of these stem from statements wherein I believe that his analysis rests more on the allegations of modern historians than on original documents.

Jefferson's Secular University

Concerning Thomas Jefferson and his University of Virginia, Cornett repeats the oft-recirculated modern assertions that "Jefferson also founded the first intentionally secularized university in America. . . . He had a disdain for the influence that institutional Christianity had on education. At the University of Virginia there was no Christian curriculum and the school had no chaplain." These charges are readily disproved by numbers of original documents, including early newspaper ads run by Jefferson's university to recruit its students. For example, in the Washington, DC, newspaper, *The Globe,* the Rev. Mr. Tuston—the chaplain of the university (a position Cornett said did not exist)—discussed religious life at the school. He noted that "the privilege of erecting Theological Seminaries on the [grounds] belonging to the university was cheerfully extended to every Christian denomination within the limits of the State" and that the university's "chaplains [are] appointed annually and successively from the four prominent denominations in Virginia [Episcopalian, Presbyterian, Baptist, and Methodist]." He pointed out that the university had "a Sabbath School" and that "the monthly concert for prayer is regularly observed in the pavilion which I occupy." He further extolled that "[i]t has been my pleasure on each returning Sabbath to hold up before my enlightened audience the cross of Jesus—all stained with the blood of Him that hung upon it—as the only hope of the perishing."[2]

Modern critics apparently have not consulted such original documents, or even Jefferson's own writings about the school, for Jefferson succinctly stated that he had personally arranged the university curriculum so that religious study would be an inseparable part of the study of law and political science.[3] He also specifically designated space in the university's Rotunda for chapel services[4] and declared that students were expected to attend weekly divine services.[5] He further announced his expectation that students would actively participate in the various religious schools which—as Chaplain Tuston noted above—Jefferson had invited to locate adjacent to and upon the university property.[6] The university also extended preferential financial treatment to students pursuing religious careers, suspending payment of tuition for "ministers of the Gospel and young men preparing for the ministry."[7]

I believe that Cornett's incorrect claim stems from his acceptance of the assertions of modern historians rather than from investigating original documents for himself.

The "Enlightenment"

Cornett credits the European Enlightenment with producing much of the thought behind the American Revolution. It is indisputable that a number of Enlightenment writers were indeed relied on during the American founding, but a fact frequently overlooked today is that many Enlightenment writers were *not* secularists.

Enlightenment writers can be divided into two distinct groups: those with an overtly Christian viewpoint (such as Baron Puffendorf, Hugo Grotius, Richard Hooker, and William Blackstone), and those with an overtly secular viewpoint (such as Voltaire, Denis Diderot, David Hume, Claude Adrien Helvetius, Jean-Jacques Rousseau, Sir Nicholas Malby, and Guillaume Thomas François Raynal). Significantly, it is from the former and not the latter group that American political ideas were primarily drawn.

This fact is proven by the extensive work of political scientists who documented that the four most-frequently invoked Enlightenment writers during the Founding Era were Charles Montesquieu, William Blackstone, John Locke, and David Hume.[8] Of the four, only Hume is from the secular Enlightenment camp. But if the Founders chose to quote primarily from philosophers with a religious and not a secular perspective, then why cite Hume? After all, unlike the other three, Hume had openly declared, "I expected, in entering on my literary course, that all the Christians . . . should be my enemies."[9]

Strikingly, the Framers regularly invoked Hume in order to rebut rather than endorse his political theories. For example, John Adams rejected him as an "atheist, deist, and libertine";[10] James Madison considered him a "bungling lawgiver"[11] with many of his theories being "manifestly erroneous";[12] John Quincy Adams denounced Hume as "the Atheist Jacobite";[13] and Thomas Jefferson found him "endeavoring to mislead by either the suppression of a truth or by giving it a false coloring."[14] Jefferson even lamented the early influence that Hume had once had on him: "I remember well the enthusiasm with which I devoured it [Hume's work] when young, and the length of time, the research and reflection which were necessary to eradicate the poison it had instilled into my mind."[15]

Hume was also roundly criticized by Framers such as John Witherspoon, Benjamin Rush, Patrick Henry, and others.[16] Such a vehement reaction against a secular philosopher does not support the thesis that the Founders relied on such writers for their ideas. Furthermore, historians have also documented that, "There is not a right asserted in the Declaration of Independence which had not been discussed by the New England clergy before 1763."[17]

Therefore, to attribute the Framers' thinking solely to the writings of the secular Enlightenment is to reject the extensive work of modern researchers as well as the work of earlier historians.

The American Revolution as an Act of Rebellion

Cornett claims that the American Revolution occurred because "deistic and Unitarian tendencies in regard to religion . . . were of such strength that even orthodox Christians were swept up into rebellion against their governing authorities." He further asserts, "Those Christians who supported physical resistance against the tyranny of Britain generally turned to Enlightenment rhetoric for validation, propped up by poor exegesis and application of the Bible." That charge may reflect Cornett's personal interpretation of history based on his own theological views of passages such as Romans 13, but his charges do not accurately reflect the historical theological (and not Enlightenment) debates over that issue.

The theological examination of resistance to governing authorities had been a subject of inquiry during the Reformation (two centuries before the Revolution), including by Frenchman John Calvin, German Martin Luther, and Swiss Reformation leader Huldreich Zwingli. Numerous other theologians also addressed the issue in that period.[18] Those theological discussions continued in England during the brutal reign of Henry VIII (1491–1547), the repressive abuses of James I (1566–1625), and the ruthless rule of the Tudor monarchs, including that of Bloody Mary (1516–58). Those Reformation writings actually underpinned the military action that resulted in the Glorious Revolution of 1688 in which England made its first attempts to separate state from church and provide representative government.

It is not surprising that such theological discussions should have occurred during the Reformation, for autocratic leaders threatened by biblical teachings attempted to suppress the spread of those teachings through bloody purges, brutal tortures, and barbaric persecutions. Remember that French leaders killed 110,000 Reformation followers and that Henry VIII (as well as Edward VI, Mary, Elizabeth I, James I, and subsequent monarchs) also utilized public executions, burning at the stake, mutilation, hanging, and disemboweling against Reformation followers.

So when autocratic tyranny began to increase in America preceding the Revolution, those ancient theological debates were renewed. The Quakers and some Anglicans adopted the position set forth by Cornett, but the Presbyterians, Lutherans, Baptists, Congregationalists, and most other denominations adopted the viewpoint set forth by Luther, Calvin, and other Reformers. They further relied on the scriptural analysis set forth in other early important theological works, including the 1556 *Short Treatise of Politic Power and of the True Obedience which Subjects Owe to Kings and Other Civil Governors* by Bishop John Poynet, and the 1579 *Vindiciae Contra Tyrannos* (*A Defense of Liberty against Tyrants*), published in response to the horrific St. Bartholomew's Day Massacre. Significantly, John Adams recommended both of these theological works to readers who wanted to understand the thinking that led to American government.[19] Another early influential theological work was the 1644 *Lex Rex* by Scottish theologian Samuel Rutherford, written to show that the law is king rather than vice versa.

Relying on such theological writings, most Christian denominations during the Founding Era held that, according to the tenor of numerous Scriptures, they were forbidden to overthrow the institution of government and live in anarchy but that they were not required to submit blindly to every law and policy. (The scriptural model for this position was repeatedly validated when God Himself raised up leaders such as Gideon, Ehud, Jepthah, Samson, and Deborah to throw off tyrannical governments—leaders subsequently praised in Heb 11:32 for those acts of faith.) Therefore, a crucial determination in the colonists' biblical exegesis was whether opposition to authority was simply to resist the general institution of government, or whether it was instead to resist tyrannical leaders who had themselves rebelled against God. That the Founders held the latter view is evidenced by the fact that the first national motto proposed for America in August 1776 was "Rebellion to tyrants is obedience to God"[20]—a summation of the 1750 sermon[21] by the Rev. Dr. Jonathan Mayhew, a principal figure in the Great Awakening.

Cornett's claim that the Founders "generally turned to Enlightenment rhetoric for validation, propped up by poor exegesis and application of the Bible" merely reflects the side he has taken in that theological debate—the same as if he had been a Quaker arguing against a Presbyterian, or an Anglican against a Congregationalist. However, just because he may disagree with the theology of Calvin, Luther, Mornay, Rutherford, and other theologians does not mean that from a historical viewpoint the Americans' approach was "propped up by poor exegesis and application of the Bible," or that the Founders "generally turned to Enlightenment rhetoric for validation." It simply means that he disagrees with their theological interpretation.

Let me emphasize in the strongest terms that my presentation of areas of disagreement with Cornett is in no way to be construed as a rejection of his work or scholarship, nor is it intended to show areas of bitter dispute; neither is the case. To the contrary, I greatly respect and appreciate his work while holding some points of divergence; the danger of this short review is that it might appear otherwise.

Endnotes

[1] See, for example, J. Sparks, *The Library of American Biography* (New York: Harper & Brothers, 1834–65); J. Sparks, *The Library of American Biography: Second Series* (Boston: Charles C. Little & James Brown, 1844–65), sixty volumes; H. C. Lodge, J. T. Morse, Jr., J. K. Hosmer, and many more authors, *American Statesmen* (Boston: Houghton, Mifflin & Co., 1883–1922), forty-eight volumes; J. S. C. Abbott, W. Gammell, W. O. Stoddard, and many more authors, *Makers of American History* (New York: The University Society, 1905), twenty volumes; etc.

[2] *The Globe* (September 8, 1837), 2; advertisement for the University of Virginia, printing a copy of a letter from the Rev. Mr. Tuston, the chaplain of

the University of Virginia, to Richard Duffield, Esq. (originally printed in the *Charlestown Free Press*). *The Globe* was published in Washington DC.

³ Thomas Jefferson to Judge Augustus B. Woodward, March 24, 1824, in T. Jefferson, *The Writings of Thomas Jefferson*, vol. XVI, ed. A. Lipscomb (Washington, DC: The Thomas Jefferson Memorial Association, 1904), 19.

⁴ "A Meeting of the Visitors of the University of Virginia on Monday the 4th of October, 1824," in T. Jefferson, *The Writings of Thomas Jefferson*, vol. XIX, ed. A. Lipscomb (Washington, DC: The Thomas Jefferson Memorial Association, 1904), 449–50.

⁵ Ibid,, 449.

⁶ Ibid,, 449–50.

⁷ *The Globe* (August 2, 1843), 2; University of Virginia advertisement.

⁸ D. S. Lutz, *The Origins of American Constitutionalism* (Baton Rouge, LA: Louisiana State University Press, 1988), 143.

⁹ David Hume to Benjamin Franklin, February 7, 1772, in B. Franklin, *The Works of Benjamin Franklin*, vol. V, ed. J. Bigelow (New York: G. P. Putnam's Sons, 1904), 325–26.

¹⁰ Diary entry, June 23, 1779, in J. Adams, *Diary and Autobiography of John Adams*, vol. II, ed. L. H. Butterfield (Cambridge, MA: Belknap Press, 1962), 391.

¹¹ James Madison to N. P. Trist, February 1830, in J. Madison, *The Letters and Other Writings of James Madison*, vol. IV (New York: R. Worthington, 1884), 58.

¹² J. Madison, "Essay on Money," in ibid., 464.

¹³ J. Q. Adams, *An Oration Addressed to the Citizens of the Town of Quincy, on the Fourth of July, 1831* (Boston: Richardson, Lord & Holbrook, 1831), 15.

¹⁴ Thomas Jefferson to John Norvell, June 11, 1807, in T. Jefferson, *Memoir, Correspondence, and Miscellanies, From the Papers of Thomas Jefferson*, vol. IV, ed. T. J. Randolph (Boston: Gray and Bowen, 1830), 80.

¹⁵ Thomas Jefferson to Col. William Duane, August 12, 1810, in T. Jefferson, *The Writings of Thomas Jefferson*, vol. XII, ed. A. A. Lipscomb (Washington, DC: the Thomas Jefferson Memorial Association, 1904), 405.

¹⁶ J. Witherspoon, "The Absolute Necessity of Salvation through Christ" (January 2, 1758), in J. Witherspoon, *The Works of John Witherspoon*, vol. V (Edinburgh: J. Ogle, 1815), 242; Benjamin Rush to James Kidd, May 1794, in B. Rush, *Letters of Benjamin Rush*, vol. II, ed. L. H. Butterfield (Princeton, NJ: Princeton University Press, 1951), 748; G. Morgan, *Patrick Henry* (Philadelphia: J. B. Lippincott Company, 1929), 366. See also W. Meade, *Old Churches, Ministers, and Families of Virginia*, vol. II (Philadelphia: J. B. Lippincott Company, 1857), 12, wherein Henry applauded Dr. Richard Watson's attack on Hume, which described Hume as being "revengeful, disgustingly vain, and an advocate of adultery and self-murder [suicide]."

¹⁷ A. M. Baldwin, *The New England Clergy and the American Revolution* (New York: Frederick Ungar, 1958), 170.

¹⁸ J. Calvin, *Institutes of the Christian Religion*, trans. H. Beveridge (Edinburgh: Calvin Translation Society, 1845), Book 4, Chapter 20, available online at http://www.ccel.org/ccel/calvin/institutes.html; M. Luther, *Temporal Authority: To What Extent Should it be Obeyed?* (1523); *Americanized Encyclopaedia Britannica* (Chicago: Belford-Clarke Co., 1890), s.v. "Huldreich Zwingli"; J. Harty, *The Catholic Encyclopedia* (New York: Robert Appleton Company, 1912), s.v. "Tyrannicide," available online at http://www.newadvent.org/cathen/15108a.htm. See also Rev. J. C. Rager, "Catholic Sources and the Declaration of Independence," *The Catholic Mind* XXVIII, no. 13 (July 8, 1930), available online at http://www.catholiceducation.org/articles/politics/pg0003.html.

[19] J. Adams, *A Defense of the Constitutions of Government of the United States of America*, vol. III (Philadelphia: William Young, 1797), 211.

[20] John Adams to Abigail Adams, August 14, 1776, in J. Adams, *Letters of John Adams, Addressed to His Wife*, vol. I, ed. C. F. Adams (Boston: Charles C. Little and James Brown, 1841), 152.

[21] J. Mayhew, *A Discourse Concerning the Unlimited Submission and Non-Resistance to the Higher Powers* (Boston: D. Fowle, 1750), 37–38.

Response to Cornett

Jonathan D. Sassi

Daryl Cornett clearly articulates the argument that "the primary shaping ideology of the Revolutionary period was that of the European Enlightenment." His essay traces an overarching historical trajectory of waxing and waning Christian influence over approximately four centuries. He begins with the seventeenth-century founding of the English North American colonies, which he depicts as deeply Christian in their aims and culture. The eighteenth century, however, witnessed the triumph of the Enlightenment, which blazed with such power that during the American Revolution religion exerted comparatively little influence. Evangelical Protestantism then enjoyed a recrudescence during the antebellum period, which was followed by Christianity's long retreat from cultural prominence during the latter part of the nineteenth century and throughout the twentieth.

There is much in Cornett's chapter with which I am in agreement. First and foremost, he and I concur that present-day American Christians are ill served by mythologizing about a "Christian nation" of yesteryear and that "Christians must understand . . . the historical record that we must treat with integrity." I can also only nod in agreement when I read that Cornett concedes most of my chapter's argument for the religiously eclectic and secular character of America's Founding Era. For example, he writes that the Framers of the United

States Constitution "intentionally secularized the state," and he depicts the eighteenth century as a time of growing religious diversity.

However, I question his schema of a Puritan seventeenth century followed by an Enlightened eighteenth and evangelical nineteenth century. This declension thesis of early American religious history—most famously associated with the work of Perry Miller—long held sway but has been called into serious question in two important books, Patricia Bonomi's *Under the Cope of Heaven* and Jon Butler's *Awash in a Sea of Faith*. Both challenge the notion that the Christian foundations of the colonies were very deeply laid in the seventeenth century; rather, they argue that it was during the first half of the *eighteenth* century that religious denominations firmly took hold and prospered in the British colonies. In this interpretation, New England is seen as an anomaly for its early success in establishing its Congregational Way compared with the tenuous Christian beginnings in most of the other early colonial regions.[1] Likewise, Cornett's depiction of a solidly evangelical nineteenth century needs greater complexity. Certainly evangelicalism strongly flavored the culture of the nineteenth-century United States, but the antebellum era too was a highly eclectic period that witnessed the rise of Adventism, Mormonism, and Spiritualism to name just three manifestations of a diverse religious ferment.[2] Most important for the purposes of this volume, Cornett overstates the Enlightenment's impact on the Revolutionary era. Ironically, in order to support my argument for the "religiously eclectic" nature of the Founding Era, I have to buttress the Christian credentials of both the patriot clergy and some of the Founding Fathers.

Cornett judges the American Revolution to have been unjustified from a biblical point of view. He indicts the patriot clergy for "poor exegesis and application of the Bible." However, clerical supporters of the Revolution, such as John Witherspoon, spoke from a "just" war tradition that reached as far back in Christian history as Augustine of Hippo. Witherspoon also reflected the English historical experience of the previous century when the "divine right" of the Stuart kings had been repudiated and replaced with the doctrine that resistance to tyrants was legitimate.[3] As he preached in a fast-day sermon in May 1776, "If your cause is just—you may look with confidence to the Lord and intreat him to plead it as his own. You are all my witnesses, that this is the first time of my introducing any political subject into the pulpit. At this season, however, it is not only lawful but necessary, and I willingly embrace the opportunity of declaring my opinion without any hesitation, that the cause in which America is now in arms, is the cause of justice, of liberty, and of human nature." Reading Witherspoon's sermon today, one can hardly conclude that he tossed his Bible or theology to the wind. He urged his auditors to "an attention to the public interest of religion, or in other words, zeal for the glory of God and the good of others," and concluded with a prayer that "God grant that in America true religion and civil liberty may be inseparable, and that the unjust attempts to destroy the one, may in the issue tend to the support and establishment of both."[4] In short, for someone like Witherspoon, Enlightenment philosophy cannot entirely explain his political stance; instead, he powerfully synthesized Enlightenment principles with the Reformed tradition. One reason that the Revolution was so divisive was precisely because each side—patriot, loyalist, and neutral—could justify its position with an appeal to scriptural proofs.

Cornett also portrays the religion of the major Founding Fathers—Franklin, Washington, Adams, and Jefferson—to have been deism, but they cannot all be lumped together under one umbrella. Benjamin Franklin may best be characterized as a deist, but not George Washington. It is an exaggeration to dismiss his faith as merely "marginal." The most thorough recent examination of his religious beliefs makes a compelling case that he was a devoted, if laconic, churchman, who expressed his faith in ways that were typical of the eighteenth-century Virginia upper class.[5] Although also a Virginian of a similar social background, Jefferson should not be placed in the same religious pigeonhole as Washington. Jefferson's intellectual journey really did make him "a sect by myself" as he phrased things, unlike Washington who was a much more conventional Anglican. And while Jefferson's beliefs can be characterized theologically as Unitarian, he also should not be put in the same boat as John Adams, whose Unitarianism was of the locally grown, Harvard variety. In the end, this mix of Founders' beliefs supports my argument for the Founding Era's religious eclecticism. As Cornett also writes, there was "a mixture of faith and faithlessness in regard to Christianity" among the Founding Fathers.

The final third of Cornett's essay is essentially a sweeping postscript that brings his story forward to the present day, and as such most of it is beyond the purview of my essay. However, his depiction of the abolitionists calls for comment. "Although some professing Christians in the South did use the Bible to sanction slavery," he writes, "the louder conspicuously Christian voice railed against it." While abolitionists like William Lloyd Garrison—who announced his antislavery crusade in the opening issue of his newspaper, *The Liberator*, by writing, "I WILL BE HEARD"—probably did have louder voices, their position was not necessarily more "conspicuously Christian" than their opponents'.[6] Southern Christians by and large had made their peace with slavery during the early republic. Some, like the Reverend Charles Colcock Jones, a Georgia planter and missionary, sought to evangelize the slaves and Christianize the peculiar institution, while others, such as James Henley Thornwell of South Carolina's Columbia Theological Seminary, could state matter-of-factly that "the relation betwixt the slave and his master is not inconsistent with the word of God."[7] In the North meanwhile, many conspicuous Christians hardly "railed against" slavery. Many of the North's most prominent evangelicals were adherents not of abolitionism but of colonization, the supposedly more moderate solution to the slavery issue whereby emancipated slaves would be sent from the United States to an overseas colony such as Liberia. To take just one example, the New Jersey Whig politician and college president Theodore Frelinghuysen had a distinguished career of service within the antebellum era's "benevolent empire" of evangelical reform organizations. At various times, Frelinghuysen was president of the American Board of Commissioners for Foreign Missions, president of the American Bible Society, vice president of the American Sunday School Union, and a leader of the Congressional Temperance Society among other offices. In addition to these evangelistic and moral reform societies,

Frelinghuysen also lent his support to the American Colonization Society, which he served for many years as a vice president.
His case was not unusual. Established Northern evangelicals
patronized colonization societies for much of the antebellum
period and viewed abolitionists as dangerous radicals.[8] Cornett is correct to credit evangelical Protestantism with fueling
abolitionism, but evangelicalism could just as easily be enlisted
in support of a range of other positions in the slavery debate.
Twenty-first-century Christians who wish to confront history
with "integrity" have to admit as much.

Endnotes

[1] P. U. Bonomi, *Under the Cope of Heaven: Religion, Society, and Politics in
Colonial America* (New York: Oxford University Press, 1986); J. Butler, *Awash
in a Sea of Faith: Christianizing the American People* (Cambridge, MA: Harvard
University Press, 1990).

[2] Butler, *Awash in a Sea of Faith*, 242–55; M. A. Noll, *A History of Christianity in the United States and Canada* (Grand Rapids: Eerdmans, 1992), 191–99.

[3] M. B. Endy, Jr., "Just War, Holy War, and Millennialism in Revolutionary
America," *William and Mary Quarterly* 42, no. 1 (1985): 3–25; Bonomi, *Under
the Cope of Heaven*, 189–216.

[4] J. Witherspoon, "The Dominion of Providence over the Passions of Men"
(Princeton, NJ, 1776), in *Political Sermons of the American Founding Era,
1730–1805*, ed. E. Sandoz (Indianapolis: Liberty Press, 1991), 529–58, quotes
on 549, 553, and 558.

[5] M. V. Thompson, *"In the Hands of a Good Providence": Religion in the Life
of George Washington* (Charlottesville: University of Virginia Press, 2008).

[6] W. L. Garrison, "To the Public," January 1, 1831, in *William Lloyd Garrison
and the Fight against Slavery: Selections from* The Liberator, ed. W. E. Cain
(Boston: Bedford/St. Martin's, 1995), 72.

[7] C. L. Heyrman, *Southern Cross: The Beginnings of the Bible Belt* (New
York: Knopf, 1997), E. Clarke, *Dwelling Place: A Plantation Epic* (New Haven,
CT: Yale University Press, 2005); Thornwell quoted in M. A. Noll, *America's
God: From Jonathan Edwards to Abraham Lincoln* (New York: Oxford Univer-
sity Press, 2002), 393.

[8] T. W. Chambers, *Memoir of the Life and Character of the Late Hon. Theo.
Frelinghuysen, LL.D.* (New York, 1863), 213–51; H. Davis, *Leonard Bacon: New
England Reformer and Antislavery Moderate* (Baton Rouge, LA: Louisiana
State University Press, 1998).

Response to Cornett

William D. Henard

D aryl Cornett takes the approach that America's founding came primarily through the influence of the Enlightenment, moving away from the perspective that Christianity
played a more prominent role in America's beginnings. Though
I personally disagree with this conclusion, I appreciate Cornett's approach. He begins his analysis by defining the words
Christian and *nation*, opting to utilize the term *country* instead
of *nation*. I find his logic interesting, agreeing that America was
not by nature or in origin Christian by any sense. Those whom
we would call *Native Americans* obviously were not Christian
until evangelized by the Europeans. Therefore, it might do all of
us well to more accurately refer to ourselves as a *country* rather
than a *nation*. America, when compared with other nations,
finds itself much more a blending of many cultures than that of
just predominantly one. Yet that fact does not diminish, in my
opinion, the greater role that Christianity played in America's
founding, much more than what Cornett sees. Where I would
agree with Cornett, and what is significantly emphasized in all
of these essays, comes from the concept of historical interpretation. While some in today's world should be classified as historical revisionists, that category does not describe the authors in
this book. One does immediately discover, however, how each
writer interprets history differently.

As Cornett moves through his recollection of history, he correctly identifies the important role that Puritanism and English Separatists played in the development of American culture.
No doubt exists, in my mind, that these men and women came
to establish a Christian society. While they came under the aus-
pices of economic gain, as supported through their investors in
England, they also sought to evangelize the New World. Cornett also sees some impact of the Great Awakening, although
I believe that he does not see it as playing as significant a role
as I do. Where I see a disconnect comes in Cornett's transition from the years of Great Awakening to the influence of the

English Enlightenment. I believe he discounts the continued role that Christianity played in America's move toward revolution and democracy, even to the point of some contradiction. For example, he reminds his readers that the Enlightenment played a significant role in America's founding. The next section, however, he returns to the importance of the Christian clergy and theology by referencing Nathan Hatch:

> the clergy transferred the millennial hopes that emerged in the Great Awakening to the political and military struggles after the revivals had burned out, first in the defeat of the despotic, Catholic French and then in the struggle against their own oppressive government. The line between Christianity and nationalism became extremely fine—at times practically imperceptible. The cause for independence became God's sacred cause for the American people.

I believe that a part of his mistake lies in his understanding of the term *Christian*. Cornett asserts:

> Was it "Christian" for people to rebel against their government, asserting their independence, and spilling blood to achieve their goal? Ultimately, the answer must be no, if what we take as our definition of Christian to be a person who possesses personal faith in Jesus, believes the Bible, and attempts to put its principles and precepts into practice.

The issue at hand is not primarily *Christian* but that of hermeneutics. Cornett correctly says that the direction these revolutionaries took did not mean that they were not Christian. It also does not mean, however, that it was not biblical, at least in their perspective. Cornett places his concept of Christianity as norm, rather than seeing his position as interpretive, as one must do with the colonial clergy who supported the Revolution. Whether I agree with them or not is a matter of actually biblical interpretation, not Christian interpretation, even if my interpretation is incorrect. The revolutionaries might have been wrong in believing in the Christian cause for war, but it was not unchristian, in my opinion. While Cornett correctly defines *Christian*, he mistakenly applies it. This fact may be the reason that he sees a greater influence of the Enlightenment than perhaps really took place.

Cornett applies this Enlightenment perspective in his interpretation of the Founding Fathers. It is interesting to note that both Cornett and Barton quote the same individuals yet arrive at two totally different conclusions with regard to the significance of Christianity in their lives and decisions. Cornett sees them as primarily influenced as deists, while Barton holds to a stronger Christian impact. Obviously, interpretation of writings plays the key role in this matter, since no one is able to personally interview the Founders themselves. One can understand Cornett's leaning toward Enlightenment, as he believes that deism played a much more important role. That conclusion, though, is a purely hypothetical one.

In my chapter, I quoted from George McKenna, who stated:

> Even Jefferson wasn't much of a Deist, if by Deism we mean the notion that God is a celestial watchmaker who wound up the universe one day and then let it run by its own laws. In his Second Inaugural address Jefferson professed the need for "the favor of that Being in whose hands we are, who led our fathers, as Israel of old, from their native land and planted them in a country flowing with all the necessities and comforts of life, who has covered our infancy with his providence and our riper years with his wisdom and power." Jefferson's God, at least, the one he publicly professed, was not a detached watchmaker but a God who actively intervenes in history. Franklin, another supposed Deist, recalled that he had toyed with it in his youth but ultimately rejected it because it was not "useful"—it seemed to lack any moral compass. In his later years he expressed very emphatically his belief in an interventionist God. "The longer I live," he said at the Constitutional Convention of 1787, "the more convincing proofs I see of this truth—that God governs the affairs of men. And if a sparrow cannot fall to the ground without his notice, is it probable that an empire cannot rise without his aid?" . . . The men who led the American Revolution and drafted the Constitution may

not have been punctilious about specific tenets of Christian orthodoxy, but virtually to a man they were convinced that God had a hand in the "new order of the ages" called America and hoped that they were doing it according to his will.[1]

Thus, readers will attempt to interpret history and perhaps can find in their own conclusions what they believe the person was trying to say. The danger all of us face as historians and interpreters is that we will begin with our own conclusions and then seek to find historical statements that will defend our position. We tend to become more eisegetes rather than exegetes.

What I believe is the same mistaken interpretation occurred with Jonathan Edwards. Some interpreters of Edwards have tried to connect Edwards' with John Locke, believing that Locke and the Enlightenment directly shaped Edwards's theology. George Marsden commented with regard to this thought:

> Jonathan's exhilarating reading of Locke, Newton, and a host of other modern thinkers convinced him that he stood at a pivotal point in New England's history.
>
> . . . By the time of the electrifying ecstasies of his conversion experience in the spring of his first graduate year, he was also enthralled by a sense of a special calling. He felt called to use the new learning in defense of God's eternal word.
>
> His attitude toward Locke provides the best example. Locke opened up exciting new ways of looking at things, especially regarding the relation between ideas and reality. Locke was crucial in setting Edwards' philosophical agenda and shaping some of his categories. Yet Edwards was no Lockean in any strict sense. When, as a tutor at Yale a few years later, he recorded his views of Locke in his notebooks, it was to refute him or go far beyond him. As others have observed, Edwards was "a miser who critically appraised his treasure."[2]

I believe that this assessment easily conveys perfectly legitimate reasons for drawing a completely opposite conclusion from the one described by Cornett.

I would follow this same pattern of logic in responding to Cornett's reference to the founding documents, particularly in that they did not make any specific reference to Christianity. A review of both Calvin's *Two Kingdoms* and Roger Williams's *Two Tables* demonstrates an understanding of the distinction between the role of government and that of the church. As I explained in my chapter, I believe that the philosophical development with regard to the role of religion and government originated with Calvin and his contemporaries. While this perspective moderated, I do not believe that the Founders had moved so significantly away from these ideas that they would reach the point of becoming more secular or enlightened in their interpretation than they would be Christian. Even Barton offers this same distinctiveness, expressing a difference between theological dogma and social and practical application.

While Cornett offers some compelling reasons for an Enlightenment influence on American government, I do not believe his conclusions to be without flaw. Though I would disagree with those who might still want to call America a Christian nation, I do believe that recognizing the direct influence of Christianity on the founding of America, both politically and spiritually, to be the correct assessment.

Endnotes

[1] G. McKenna, *The Puritan Origins of American Patriotism* (New Haven, CT: Yale University Press, 2007), 46.

[2] G. Marsden, *Jonathan Edwards: A Life* (New Haven, CT: Yale University Press, 2003), 63–64.

Name Index

348

Steiner, B. C. *78*
Stein, S. J. *226–27, 242–43*
Stiles, E. *35, 76, 118, 133, 146*
Stoddard, S. *219–20, 222, 224, 239, 241*
Stoddard, W. O. *331*
Stohlman, M. L. *322*
Story, J. *51, 69, 82, 150, 154*
Stout, H. S. *108, 143–44, 225, 232, 240, 243, 250, 321–22*
Sweeney, D. A. *223, 242*
Sweet, W. W. *71, 243, 321*
Swift, Z. *52, 82*

Tait, L. G. *322*
Taylor, Z. *44*
Thomas, E. *85*
Thompson, M. V. *337*
Thorpe, F. N. *69–70, 77*
Toon, P. *238*
Torbet, R. G. *240*
Trenchard, J. *121*
Trist, N. P. *332*
Truman, H. S. *45, 80, 168*
Trumbull, J. *46, 81, 146*
Tweed, T. A. *77*
Tyler, J. *44, 80*
Tyndale, W. *6*

Vanderkemp, F. A. *76*
Vandrunen, D. *238*
van 't Spijker, W. *237*
Van Tyne, C. H. *71–72*
Veazey, C. W. *74*
Voltaire *328*
von Schwenkfeld, K. *6*

Walker, W. *321*
Wallace, M. *143*
Ward, J. *68, 74*
Ward, N. *10*
Ward, W. R. *114, 143*
Washington, B. T. *57, 84*
Washington, G. *40, 44, 47, 51, 71, 76–77, 79, 90–91, 103, 123, 131, 133–35, 146–47,*

150, 154, 160, 167, 232, 285, 287–89, 297, 335
Washington, M. *74*
Waters, T. F. *70*
Webster, D. *11, 31, 41, 70–71, 75, 78*
Webster, N. *14–15, 29, 32, 34, 56, 71–72, 75–76, 83, 86, 248*
Weems, M. L. *322*
Wellman, S. *237, 245*
Wells, W. V. *75, 78*
Wesley, J. *114, 119–20, 144, 304*
Westen, J. *165, 236*
White, C. E. *239*
Whitefield, G. *12, 114, 221, 276, 303*
White, T. *240*
Wigger, J. H. *147–48*
Willard, E. *57, 84*
Willard, F. E. *306*
Willard, J. *13*
Willard, S. *12*
Williams, C. *46, 81*
Williams, J. *219*
Williams, R. *10, 16, 22, 98–99, 106, 158, 195, 207, 210–18, 234, 240–41, 255, 271–72, 274, 300, 321, 323, 342*
Williams, W. *241*
Wilson, B. *86*
Wilson, J. *51, 63, 65, 82, 86, 150*
Wilson, W. *44, 80, 168, 325*
Winthrop, J. *105, 108, 142–43, 191–93, 196, 199–201, 211, 246, 249, 255, 270*
Winthrop, R. *31, 76*
Wise, J. *5, 12, 16, 69–70, 72*
Wishart, G. *7*
Witherspoon, J. *41, 57, 66, 76, 78, 84, 86, 89, 120, 144, 159, 188, 281–83, 285, 290, 292, 322, 328, 332, 334–35, 337*
Withrop, J. *321*
Wood, B. *143*

Subject Index

Scripture Index